"Much has been written about the events of June 6, 1944, but this new book by Jared Frederick gives us a refreshing glimpse into what happened on that 'Longest Day.' In *Dispatches of D-Day,* Frederick has culled over 150 period newspapers and magazines to bring us unique insight of the most pivotal battle of World War II as seen through the eyes of those on the fighting front, their families, and the news media. The result is a well-woven story that is rich in detail and engrossing to read."

— Larry Alexander, best-selling author of *Biggest Brother: The Life of Major Dick Winters, the Man Who Led the Band of Brothers*

"Frederick has mined a vast archive of newspaper coverage of the Normandy invasion to craft a fresh and vivid account of this momentous event. Hundreds of American journalists in Europe chronicled the invasion, and thousands more reported on the home front. Instead of focusing on the reminiscences of aged veterans written long after the fighting, Frederick draws from period accounts to capture the voices of young soldiers and war-weary civilians telling their remarkable stories as they unfold. *Dispatches of D-Day* brings us the war as it is happening, before the ink is even dry."

— Rick Beyer, *New York Times* best-selling author of *The Ghost Army of World War II*

"Jared Frederick reintroduces long-lost stories of personal heroics, anguish, and innovation from June 1944 in this excellent amalgamation of eyewitness accounts. The book reveals the sharp journalistic insights and hometown candor that's made the invasion one of the most compelling news stories in all of history. Readers will not only gain new appreciation of battlefield struggles, they'll see how Americans of the 1940s thought and expressed their emotions. *Dispatches of D-Day* serves as a fitting tribute to the Second World War's 75th anniversary."

— Marcus Brotherton, *New York Times* best-selling author of *We Who Are Alive & Remain, A Company of Heroes,* and *Shifty's War*

"Newswriting has often been called 'the first rough draft of history.' In *Dispatches of D-Day*, Jared Frederick pores over this rough draft—recorded on the battlefield and in American towns—and finds forgotten stories of heroism, loss, and humor. This book sees the war through the eyes of a soldier reading *Stars and Stripes*, of his worried family scanning their local paper for reports. It is a welcome point of view."

— Ryan C. Brown, journalist and author of
Pittsburgh and the Great Steel Strike of 1919

"Historians have laboriously picked at the bones of Operation Overlord for the last 75 years. This is where today's understanding of the D-Day landings comes from. However, Jared Frederick has put all of this to one side and adopted a completely fresh approach. Using a huge array of sources and press archives, he has analyzed the censored and nuanced news reports of those heady days. In doing so, he has performed a very valuable service. Now for the first time we read of the invasion as it was seen and understood at the time. *Dispatches of D-Day* is a unique and very refreshing read. It is an important and timely addition to the history of the Normandy campaign."

— Dr. Peter Caddick-Adams, author of
Sand and Steel: The D-Day Invasions and the Liberation of France

"With absorbing detail and nonstop energy, Jared Frederick has penned an eloquent page-turner that will quickly become a must-read for any student of history. An engaging combat narrative and fascinating reflection of life on the home front, *Dispatches of D-Day* is most importantly a timely meditation on the roles of the press in a free society. Included in these pages are vivid testimonies of the invasion, written in the moment and now salvaged from the archives. These are stories that have not seen the light of day in 75 years and reveal the otherworldly sense of immediacy and excitement felt by Americans during that momentous campaign. Frederick captures the essence of the D-Day experience in this stirring examination of a country at war."

— R. C. George, author of *Lightning Sky: A U. S. Fighter Pilot
Captured During World War II and His Father's Quest to Find Him*

"The invasion of Normandy initiated the final allied march to victory in Europe in World War II. The extensive military planning and execution has been analyzed in depth. But how did the home front hear about and receive news of the events in Normandy? In his latest work, Jared Frederick has taken the important task of disseminating the official and unofficial news and its impact on the American public. *Dispatches of D-Day* combines all of these stories into a fine narrative that not only reveals what we know about the invasion of Normandy but what we did not know, or fully understand, about America in June 1944."

– John Heiser, noted military historian
Gettysburg, Pennsylvania

"Jared Frederick's *Dispatches of D-Day* is a unique, well-written, and exceedingly well-researched contribution to the extant literature about that pivotal day in June 1944. Comprehending that history was current events to those who lived through it, he has captured better than any previous author how the American and British public and U. S. military personnel actually *felt* about D-Day. Frederick also highlights that the independence of the modern press corps was reinforced by its reportage of the momentous event. This is a book about an historical episode seventy-five years ago, but it is written in a way that truly makes the people of the past live again by using their own words. In so doing, Frederick has succeeded where many historians fail. Anyone with a serious interest in America's involvement in WWII will find his work fascinating and essential."

– Dr. Christian B. Keller, Professor of History,
U. S. Army War College, author of *The Great Partnership*

"It is now more important than ever to understand the invasion in its fullest possible historical, social, and cultural context. Reaching that objective requires dedication and shrewd effort due to the fact that the subject is crowded by nostalgia, mythology and, therefore, distortion. This is why Jared Frederick's *Dispatches of D-Day* comes at a good time and fills a much needed gap in the historical scholarship. The book also calls on a very well selected bibliography of secondary sources—which is an aspect of this book's contribution to scholarship that cannot be understated. Frederick has done us all a great service by merging these

sources into a single volume that will well serve anyone with an interest in the cross channel attack that brought war to Normandy."
– Martin K. A. Morgan, author of *The Americans on Day: A Photographic History of the Normandy Invasion*

"Long before 'fake news,' hundreds of dedicated, eager, and often courageous newspaper reporters went into the Army camps, on board the Navy ships, and onto the landing beaches, in order to witness and chronicle the making of history. Here is the story of the Allied invasion of Normandy—D-Day, as it is popularly known—as experienced and reported by scores of correspondents from more than a hundred American newspapers in big cities and small towns alike, each of whom sought to provide the readers back home with the first draft of history. The result is an intensely personal account from a hundred viewpoints that collectively provides a truly unique portrayal of what happened at D-Day."
– Dr. Craig L. Symonds, author of *Operation Neptune: The D-Day Landings and the Allied Invasion of Europe*

"In an age when the value of journalism has come into question, Jared Frederick offers timely and intricately researched context on the pivotal day of the 20th Century—D-Day—to suggest there's no replacement for eyewitness accounts when putting history into perspective. From soldiers on the beach to students back home, from trained correspondents to civilians caught in the crossfire, *Dispatches of D-Day* reminds us that the written word—delivered in magazines, newspapers, and letters—is integral to our understanding of events that have shaped our world. Much has been written of this historic day, but Frederick breaks new ground with nuggets of insight that add richness to our understanding of this singular event and reinforcement for the values of journalism."
– Bob Welch, author of
American Nightingale and *Easy Company Soldier*

DISPATCHES of D-DAY

A PEOPLE'S HISTORY of THE NORMANDY INVASION

JARED FREDERICK

Jared Frederick

VALOR PUBLISHERS
Centennial, Colorado

Valor Publishers, an imprint of WordServe Press
A division of WordServe Literary
7500 E. Arapahoe Rd. Suite 285
Centennial, CO 80112
admin@wordserveliterary.com
303.471.6675

Cover Design: Jared Frederick
Interior Book Design: Greg Johnson

Front Cover Image:
Soldiers of the 4th Infantry Division's 8th Regiment stand alongside members of the 70th Tank Battalion and flightless glider men of the 101st Airborne's 327th Infantry Regiment as *LCT 8* veers toward Utah Beach on D-Day. (Official U. S. Navy Photograph, National Archives, 80-G-59422.)

Back Cover Image:
New Yorkers gaze at the news ticker in Times Square as invasion briefs pour in. (Office of War Information Collection, Library of Congress, LC-USW3- 054017-C.)

Ordering Information:
Quantity sales: Special discounts are available on quantity purchases by corporations, associations, and others. For details, contact the "Special Sales Department" at the address or phone number above.

Jared Frederick, September 30, 1987
First Edition: April 2019
ISBN: 978-1-941555-41-5

"Our countries fight best when our people are best informed."
– Gen. Dwight D. Eisenhower, 1944

"Real war is never like paper war,
nor do accounts of it read much the way it looks."
– Ernest Hemingway, 1944

Dedicated to the members of the free press.
The work goes on.

Read free supplemental material on the author's website at
www.jaredfrederick.com

Receive updates, photos, and historical content by following
the author on Facebook at "Historian Jared Frederick"

TABLE OF CONTENTS

ABBREVIATIONS

88s: 88-mm Flak guns
AAF: Army Air Forces
AEF: Allied Expeditionary Force
AP: Associated Press
ARC: American Red Cross
AWOL: Absent Without Leave
B-17: Boeing B-17 Flying Fortress (four engine heavy bomber aircraft)
B-24: Consolidated B-24 Liberator (four engine heavy bomber)
B-26: Martin B-26 Marauder (two engine medium bomber)
BBC: British Broadcasting Corporation
BWRS: British War Relief Society
C-47: Douglas C-47 Skytrain (Allied transport aircraft)
CBS: Columbia Broadcasting System
CIO: Congress of Industrial Organizations
CO: Commanding Officer
CP: Command Post
D+1: One day after D-Day, and so on.
DNB: Deutsches Nachrichtenbüro (Nazi "German News Office")
DUKW: General Motors nomenclature: D (Design) indicates the model year, 1942; U refers to utility (amphibious); K symbolizes all-wheel drive; and W stands for dual-tandem rear axles. These vehicles were known colloquially as "Ducks."
ETO: European Theater of Operations
FDR: Franklin D. Roosevelt
FEPC: Fair Employment Practice Committee
G-1: Personnel staff
G-2: Intelligence staff
G-3: Operations staff
G-4: Logistical staff
GI: General Issue (nickname describing an American soldier)
HMS: His Majesty's Ship (British)
HQ: Headquarters
INS: International News Service
LCI: Landing Craft Infantry
LCM: Landing Craft Medium
LCVP: Landing Craft Vehicle Personnel
LST: Landing Ship Tank
MG: Machine Gun
MG-42: Maschinengewehr 42 (German "Machine Gun 42")

MP: Military Police
NAACP: National Association for the Advancement of Colored People
NBC: National Broadcasting Company
Non-com (or NCO): Non-Commissioned Officer
OCS: Officer Candidate School
OSS: Office of Strategic Services
OWI: Office of War Information
P-38: Lockheed P-38 Lightning (two engine fighter); also the name ascribed to a GI can opener
PIR: Parachute Infantry Regiment
PR: Public Relations
PT: Physical Training
PW (or POW): Prisoner of War
PX: Post Exchange (general store)
RAF: Royal Air Force (British)
ROTC: Reserve Officer Training Corps
SHAEF: Supreme Headquarters Allied Expeditionary Force
S&S: Stars and Stripes
SOE: Special Operations Executive
SS: Schutzstaffel (Nazi "Protection Squadron," fanatic paramilitary loyalists)
TNT: trinitrotoluene
UP: United Press
UPI: United Press International
USS: United States Ship
WAC: Women's Army Corps
Warco: War Correspondent
WAVES: Women Accepted for Volunteer Emergency Service (Naval)
XO: Executive Officer

WWII U. S. Army Ranks and Abbreviations
(Listed lowest to highest)

Enlisted Men:
Pvt. – Private
Pfc. – Private First Class

Non-Commissioned Officers (NCOs):
T/5 – Technician Fifth Grade (corporal)*
Cpl. – Corporal
T/4 – Technician Fourth Grade (sergeant)
Sgt. – Sergeant

T/3 – Technician Third Grade (sergeant)
S/Sgt. – Staff Sergeant
T/Sgt. – Technical Sergeant
1st Sgt. – First Sergeant
M/Sgt. – Master Sergeant
*Technician ranks were usually designated as trade skill positions. Such personnel were not typically tasked with leading troops, but the necessities of combat could dictate otherwise.

Warrant Officers:
FO – Flight Officer (Air Forces)
WO – Warrant Officer
CWO – Chief Warrant Officer

Company-Grade Officers:
2nd Lt. – Second Lieutenant
1st Lt. – First Lieutenant
Capt. – Captain

Field-Grade Officers:
Maj. – Major
Lt. Col. – Lieutenant Colonel
Col. – Colonel

General Officers:
Brig. Gen. – Brigadier General
Maj. Gen. – Major General
Lt. Gen. – Lieutenant General
Gen. – General
General of the Army

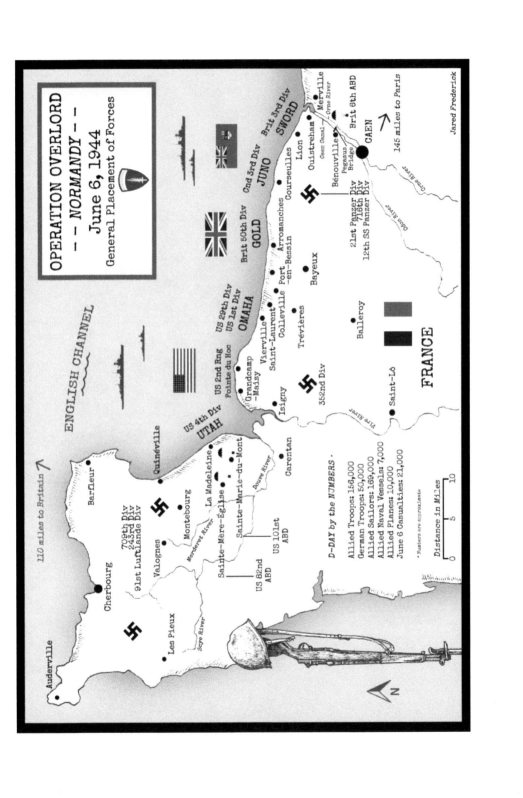

OPERATION OVERLORD
-- NORMANDY --
June 6, 1944
General Placement of Forces

ENGLISH CHANNEL

110 miles to Britain

Auderville

Cherbourg

Barfleur

709th Div
243rd Div
91st Luftlande Div

Montebourg

Valognes

Les Pieux

Quinéville

Sainte-Mère-Église

La Madeleine

Sainte-Marie-du-Mont

UTAH
US 4th Div

US 82nd ABD

US 101st ABD

Scye River
Merderet River
Douve River

Carentan

US 2nd Rng
Pointe du Hoc

Grandcamp
-Maisy

Isigny

OMAHA
US 29th Div
US 1st Div

Vierville
Saint-Laurent
Colleville

352nd Div

Saint-Lô

Vire River

Trévières

Balleroy

Bayeux

Port
en-Bessin

Arromanches

GOLD
Brit 50th Div

JUNO
Cnd 3rd Div

Courseulles

Lion

Ouistreham

SWORD
Brit 3rd Div

Caen Canal
Pegasus
Bridge
Bénouville

Merville
Orne River
Brit 6th ABD

CAEN

Odon River

Orne River

145 miles to Paris

21st Panzer Div
716th Div
12th SS Panzer Div

FRANCE

D-DAY by the NUMBERS.

Allied Troops: 156,000
German Troops: 50,000
Allied Sailors: 169,000
Allied Naval Vessels: 7,000
Allied Planes: 10,000
June 6 Casualties: 21,000

* Numbers are approximate

Distance in Miles

0   5   10

N

Jared Frederick

PROLOGUE

Dependence

The city was asleep. The vibrant neon storefronts illuminated the soaked streets of Austin's Congress Avenue. Groggy students at the University of Texas dozed on their textbooks while cramming for approaching exams. The intermittent clap of thunder over the nearby mountains roused them from their scholarly slumber. Dormitory study sessions remained active as lounge radios murmured in the background. Graceful late-night tunes "wavered, sputtered, and crackled with storm static." Only five more hours of study until the breakfast halls opened. It was 2:30 a.m. on Tuesday, June 6, 1944.

Suddenly, a strained voice from New York cut the choppy melodies and declared, "We now take you to London." From a communications building on the other side of the Atlantic, an Army officer with a slight southern drawl delivered much-anticipated news with calm deliberation. "Under the command of General Eisenhower, allied naval forces supported by strong air forces began landing allied armies this morning on the northern coast of France."

"That was it," wrote Horace Busby of the student newspaper. "D-Day, H-Hour had arrived."

In near-synchronized fashion, lamps clicked on in dormitories across the Forty Acres. "Roommates were rolled out of bed, lights snapped on as fast as word could be screamed down hallways, telephones began to ring, and a rain-drenched Austin came to life," observed Busby. Households were awakened by impassioned, anonymous bellows of "the invasion is here, the invasion is here." The dim glow of console radios warmly brightened living rooms as families convened with uneasy revelry. A flock of 750 congregated for a prayer service at the Baptist Church. The young ladies of the Scottish Rite Dormitory were awakened by church bells at 4:40. Several wept for their brothers and boyfriends. Not for another hour did the naval ROTC cadets in nearby Andrew Dormitory receive word when a limber newsboy darted from his jalopy exclaiming, "Invasion on. . . . We're killing them all." The front-page layout had been set for two months in anticipation of this moment. Within seconds, the cadets were madly spinning the dials on every radio within reach. All soon grew somber.

The soft light of morning revealed empty breakfast tables at the Chuck Wagon cafeteria in the ornate student union. One unknowing woman sat at the island counter and ordered food before she noticed the headlines and screamed, "My brother, my brother!" In lecture halls, oblivious faculty members initially dismissed student exclamations of the invasion as distasteful pranks to adjourn class. After hearing the preliminary excitement, many students deflated with an air of dejection. "[Y]ou feel sick and weak inside but there's no point in breaking down, I guess," stated one girl. Other female students despondently re-read months-old correspondence from their significant others in uniform. They pondered what the future may bring.

Tenseness gripped the entire city that evening. Local radio stations replaced late night jazz with martial tunes of a patriotic flavor. Cocktail parties evolved into "listening parties." Cafés and corner drugstores sold thermoses of black coffee for night owls awaiting coveted updates. Others simply wandered the wet streets of the Texas capital, contemplating what all of it would mean. "D-Day, H-Hour had arrived and passed, and four years of waiting continued," Busby concluded. "Berlin was many lives away."[1]

Sixty-nine years later I, too, deliberated the meanings of D-Day while pacing in the rain. I accompanied a group of college students to the battlefields of France, where our odyssey was often as agitating as it was edifying. The March trip was marked by one of the worst snowstorms in decades, with over a foot of snow and wind gusts up to 100 miles per hour. Prime Minister Jean-Marc Ayrault declared a national state of emergency and deployed the military to futilely clear roads with backhoes. In transit from Calais to Caen, we became stranded in the port city of Le Havre, seeking refuge in a shady waterman's hotel with equally suspicious sailors wishing to carouse. When the roads finally cleared, the truer adventure lay ahead. The typically green pastures of Normandy closer resembled the wintry aura of the Ardennes. Over the next week, our enthusiastic caravan circuitously crisscrossed the snowy landscape, paying tribute at landmarks with iconic names.

Our final day in France was fittingly spent at the Normandy American Cemetery and Memorial at Colleville-sur-Mer, overlooking Omaha Beach. The usually pristine burial ground was slightly out of sorts. Scores of the cemetery's majestic trees had toppled and were completely uprooted by the recent storm. Red and white caution tape flapped in the heavy breeze as we mutely walked the grounds. The unfortunate destruction of landscaping failed to detract from the evocative scenery. One cannot help but be moved by the 9,388 white crosses and stars dotting the garden of stone. Fifteen minutes away, more than double that number rest in the La Cambe German war cemetery. The undergrads, who delivered impassioned presentations at the graves of soldiers from their hometowns, were transfixed by the imagery of human loss.

With the student remarks complete, all were invited to roam the cemetery before we boarded our purple coach bus to Paris. The well-manicured grass resembled thin velvety carpet akin to a putting green. The snow had dissipated but the rains grew steadier as temperatures rose. Many sought shelter at the visitor center to dry. I found myself walking unaccompanied up the paved path recognizable from the opening scene of *Saving Private Ryan*. I gazed outward on the English Channel and envisioned the vast Allied armada that once circled miles offshore on a similarly dismal morning. The relentless sea winds soaked my jacket as I contemplated the horrific struggle that transpired on the now placid sands below.

I hiked the grounds further and recognized I was now truly alone, with no other single person in sight. Solitarily I stood, with only the men buried beneath my muddied boots as company. The only sounds were the gentle wisps of rain and the American flag briskly clanking against its pole. It was twenty years to the day that my grandfather, Utah Beach veteran Thomas W. Nycum, Jr., had passed away. Yet I realized he lived nearly a half-century longer than the men under these headstones. The epiphany was surreal if not spiritual.

The experience was further heightened upon my discovery of the grave of 2nd Lt. Robert P. Spatig, a Pennsylvanian in the 4th Infantry Division's 22nd Regiment. The fact that the twenty-five-year-old officer was from my home state and served in my grandfather's division was not what immediately caught my eye. A franc, two pennies, and a quarter—all stamped in the 1940s—rested atop Spatig's cross. According to a tradition among veterans, the coins were ostensibly left by a comrade who was with the lieutenant when he was killed on June 23, 1944. The simple tokens served as powerfully tangible reminders that the Second World War was not long ago. Many of its stories remain unwritten. From countless sons and daughters of deceased veterans I have heard the lament, "He never talked about it."

These notions were reinforced weeks later when a student entrusted me with yellowed newspapers he recovered from a dumpster. An elderly neighbor who lived during the war years had passed away and her children were cleaning house. The wartime periodicals were of no use to the family, despite the obvious meaning they held to the original owner. As my students and friends often do, the pupil salvaged the frayed newspapers because he knew I appreciated "old stuff like this." Scanning the pages, I was mesmerized not only by the level of detail but also the personal nature of stories shared—reports of individual heroics, transcribed letters from overseas, slices of home front life, and revealing advertisements. Like many primary sources, the pages were time capsules of a bygone era. My curiosity peaked.

What originated as inquisitiveness morphed into a consuming quest. I initially endeavored to gather original newspaper sources for experiential classroom activities regarding the Normandy invasion. Over 300,000 transcribed words later, I realized I had amassed a tale worthy of sharing beyond the confines of the lecture hall. Ultimately, this book arose from a seemingly simple inquiry: What was the D-Day experience for Americans of 1944? Newspapers of the period offer readers all the tools to answer that question. Unlike many oral histories and memoirs of decades later, periodicals from the war years offer a sense of telling immediacy. Their words drop us in the middle of an incomplete chapter. The temporary removal of hindsight allows us to walk in their shoes, even if only for a moment. While no firsthand accounts of momentous events such as D-Day are all-knowing or flawless, those published perspectives are undeniably fresher and not as shrouded by the fog of war. In most instances, I endeavored to keep their original commentary intact.

Dispatches of D-Day is not intended to be a comprehensive history of the Normandy invasion—far from it. Rarely did I analyze the strategic decisions of corps commanders, outline the sweeping movements of divisions, or explain the intricacies of counteroffensives. Such is not my aim. If anything, the book is a snapshot of the American psyche at a crossroads moment.

While prominent figures such as Dwight Eisenhower and famed correspondent Ernie Pyle loom largely in this narrative, much of the story is carried by persons relatively unknown to the historical record—individuals whose war experiences have not been thoroughly outlined since 1944. Entwined with the syndicated reports of established journalists, wartime reflections found in hometown newspapers offer a rich mosaic of a nation preparing for, executing, and reacting to one of the largest military operations in history. This is a story of how people *felt*, subjectively and viscerally, about the war at home and abroad. The narrative is a reflection of how journalists and combatants conveyed the struggles of a people through words and imagery. Such human accounts were the palpable connective tissue between the civilian and military worlds. Accordingly, the tale I present is organic in nature, bottom-up rather than top-down.

As is the case with the historical record of any military engagement, deciphering fact from fiction can be a daunting task—even when the source material is fresh from the era. Alfred Baer, who scaled the cliffs of Pointe du Hoc with the 2nd Ranger Battalion, astutely noted, "What actually took place on that small portion of the Cherbourg Peninsula can never adequately be told. At best, it can merely be hinted at, and can never be completely understood by anyone who was not himself present on the Pointe that bloody morning." I empathize with his view. [2]

Undeniably, some of the eyewitness accounts featured in this book could be considered suspect. Misremembering details, particularly regarding the chaos of combat, is human nature. Even so, these stories comprised the raw reports that molded readers' perspectives of D-Day. In this context, even equivocal yarns became part of the invasion's early historical memory and should not be flatly ignored. The book is not merely about an event but also feelings and perceptions.

I cannot claim to compete with the mastery of authors such as Cornelius Ryan, Max Hastings, Antony Beevor, or Rick Atkinson—all of whom have chronicled the many facets of Operations Neptune and Overlord with sharp precision and enduring impact. I do, however, seek to place a few stones atop this solid academic foundation. In conveying together the civilian and military elements of D-Day, I aspired to reveal the all-consuming nature of the Second World War on American society. The implications of invasion were far-reaching, whether one was a child participating in scrap drives, a mother welding in a Detroit factory, or an infantryman advancing up the beach. The war was universal in scope—from Main Street to the frontline.

Fittingly, these human connections underscored D-Day as perhaps the most substantial news story of the 20th century. While the much-covered tales of Charles Lindbergh's transatlantic flight, the Kennedy assassination, and Apollo 11 deserve recognition as pivot points in journalistic reporting, none of them carried the intimately personal weight in terms of community impact as did D-Day. Normandy's invaders hailed from every village and city across the nation.

Nobody could escape the ramifications of June 6, 1944. In this regard I recognize D-Day not purely as an historical event but as a collective emotional experience—one which continues to pronounce lasting lessons about war and life.

In wake of the conflict's sometimes-troubling realizations, notions of maintaining and supporting a free press grew increasingly paramount in the United States. Beyond preserving moral superiority over their totalitarian enemies who stifled free speech, Americans passionately demanded promptness and transparency from their press and government. D-Day emerged as the symbolic crucible in which the democratic tradition of free expression could long endure. History reveals that democratic society has always placed limitations on civil liberties in wartime. Military exigencies often demand secrecy and the dissemination of half-truths. Eisenhower and federal entities such as the Office of Censorship struggled to safeguard classified information while also protecting the First Amendment. Compromise was the key to success.

According to author Michael Sweeney, "Complete lack of censorship would have helped the enemy. Complete government control would have been intolerable in a nation that had been born during revolution in which the press played an active role and that had cemented freedom of expression." Reporters therefore successfully self-regulated their own words—offering enough truth to be honest but not so much truth as to be seditious. For instance, the five beach code names of Omaha, Utah, Gold, Juno, and Sword largely did not appear in period accounts due to security measures. While the *New York Times* pled that wartime information not be "arbitrarily suppressed," editors nonetheless drew a line in the sand. "Where there is a choice that might affect the safety of our crews there can be no doubt that it is better to publish too little than too much," the paper assured readers. Through this complicated terrain, the free press nonetheless remained the exemplar of democracy— the protector against deceptions both foreign and domestic. Citizens depended on journalists to ensure civil protections just as they expected soldiers to shield them from the Axis.[3]

"The story of how people reacted to the news of the invasion presented one of the biggest news stories of all time," reported Iowa's *Ottumwa Daily Courier* on July 26, 1944. A booklet published by the American Newspaper Publishers Association, entitled *When D-Day Came,* revealed "a nation united in prayer; shows people avidly devouring newspapers for detailed reports from the front; and reproduces headlines, stories, pictures, and maps of the invasion." The bureau assiduously reiterated what so many readers had long proclaimed. "The dependence of the people on their newspapers," the booklet stated, "has probably never been so dramatically demonstrated. Never has the newspaper's indispensability as the source of full information been more apparent. Radio broadcasts seemed merely to sharpen people's appetites for the more complete information in their newspapers. They wanted all the news they could get."

Customers flocked to newsstands, tossing nickels for the latest editions. Other eager readers congregated at newspaper offices to obtain copies even before paper boys set out on morning bicycle routes. "Editions were quickly exhausted. Circulations soared," added the association, "with the available newsprint supply the only limiting factor." In D-Day's immediate wake, newspaper editors and advertisers exhibited a manner of patriotic unselfishness, placing paramount stories above profits. This form of "public-spiritedness" marked a new flexibility and timeliness among periodicals. The chapters that follow strive to interpret the meaningful roles of the media in wartime, balanced with the accounts it presented to an ever-anxious public.[4]

Newspapers of my own era are replete with articles delving into governmental accountability, public information, political propaganda, totalitarianism, racial unrest, military operations, and perceptions of the press. These contemporary topics endlessly highlight the ongoing historical importance of the Second World War in our modern world. On personal levels, the momentous clashes in Normandy fostered profound meaning for readers on both sides of the Atlantic. The campaign's dramatic human experiences carried as much weight as the strategic consequences themselves. Additionally, the invasion incited demands for domestic betterment. At home and abroad, the Axis and Allies alike recognized what hung in the balance.

Stars and Stripes, the official U. S. Army newspaper, stockpiled 300 tons of paper to report the impending campaign. Typically printed on four pages due to rationing, the periodical was humble in size but impressive in scope. It was the dutiful mouthpiece of GI Joe. The soldier's favorite rag opined that March, "The most fateful spring of the war is here."[5]

The sooty brick and cobblestone streets of London practically quivered under the anticipation of the moment. The ominous wails of screeching air raid sirens and German bombs heightened the lingering fervor of the masses. The city smelled of smoke and scorched life. Yet the resolve of the beset residents failed to waver. Even as members of the Allied armies sought reprieve with besieged civilians in crowded gin joints, little else but drifting thoughts of the approaching assault on the mainland crossed their minds. They waited.

The gloom of winter was past, and amid a new spring full of potential and promise Allied military strategists were "sowing the seeds of total German defeat." The grim harvest of war was soon to follow. Few people on the planet could ascertain exactly when or where the colossal undertaking would yield its momentous results. As the European wintertide slowly thawed, an army of liberation was soon to emerge from the gray mist of the English Channel—and the entire world awaited its desperate gamble.[6]

Every pocket of civilization daily scanned newspapers and tuned radios for coveted hints of Western Europe's liberation. Civilization seemed to hinge on it. Newspapers would trumpet its arrival with bold, black and red lettering adorning wide front pages. The global population psychologically participated—and access to dispatches was the lifeblood of those stirring emotions.[7]

Much like the combatants who waged the war, American reporters from all walks of life molded interpretations of the conflict's potential outcomes. The correspondents of World War II served as barometers for truth and compasses of morality to a society desperate for news and thirsty for consolation. The staccato clicks of reporter typewriters echoed throughout the smoke-filled press rooms of London as forces amassed for the big jump. Few of the writers doubted the power of the sword but all exhibited the might of the pen. Despite their many limitations and challenges, correspondents served as the apostles of international discourse during the world's darkest hours.

Stars and Stripes, in conjunction with an extensive press corps, did all within its power to nurture military confidence. Established during the Great War, the soldier newspaper was resurrected in 1942 as an independent entity of the Army. Its writers religiously dodged big brass attempting to curtail editorial independence. The paper blossomed with new editions and offices anytime the American military domain expanded. With each passing month, *Stars and Stripes* grew bolder in its soldierly commentary and griping. Believing such freedom of expression detrimental to an army's professional bearing, the likes of Douglas MacArthur and George Patton judged the flexibility of military newspapers with rankled disdain.[8]

However, periodicals heralded innovation and deconstructed the myths of Nazi superiority. "Hitler once yelled that his New Order in Europe would last a thousand years. He guessed wrong," the newspaper ridiculed. Editorials featured within the publication further proclaimed the war as a struggle for a vast future—a righteous expedition to secure the safety of generations yet born.

This patriotic vigor was tempered by the sinister realities of combat. Hanson W. Baldwin of the *New York Times* wrote on June 4, "The invasion as seen from England does not hold the prospects of an easy victory. The struggle is bound to be hard and rigorous; the Germans have been preparing for it as well." The outcome may "hang by a thread. The odds are not heavily weighted in our favor, yet we have reasonable chances for success, or the invasion of Western Europe would not be undertaken." Baldwin's forthright power of assessment earned him a Pulitzer Prize in 1943 following the Battle of Guadalcanal.[9]

Inoculations of truth served as antidotes to the perils of fascism. Liberty could not endure without the power of fact. *Stars and Stripes* assured readers that the quest to self-educate "will in itself make you a better-informed soldier, a better educated American. And in the days ahead, when it becomes your job to help decide issues on which the future all depends, your knowledge of the big picture will make you a better citizen, and in a small way that will help make this a better world."[10]

Servicemen publications such as *Yank* simultaneously offered space for enlisted men's observations, inquiries, and quibbles. Seaman William C. Rand bluntly wrote, "My bitch is about that outrageous beribboned, becollared, bebuttoned insult to a full-grown man—the Navy uniform. . . . I'm mildly proud of my branch of the service, but I'm intensely angered by the pajamas I have to wear to work." Few could have imagined such belligerence being propagated in the dutiful literature of the Wehrmacht.[11]

Pulitzer Prize-winner Otto Tolischus offered a foreboding prognostication of Germany's curtailment of rights in his 1940 book *They Wanted War*, an in-depth examination of Hitler's meteoric rise of oppression. The freedom of the press was a sacred heritage in America but was considered a peculiar doctrine in militarized Europe. Liberty "is beside the point in a land that spurns it—a land which had rejected Western liberalistic civilization, and which sought to build a new world on entirely different foundations," wrote Tolischus. In that new world, all manners of criticism were outlawed and he who "flayed the foe most and cheered his own cause loudest" emerged triumphant. The so-called Lap-Dog Press of the Third Reich was born of the fiery ambition to coerce public sentiment by inciting division and spewing misinformation.[12]

America's embracing of free speech did not prevent all manners of constraint. Federal agencies such as the United States Office of War Information (OWI) disseminated propaganda and incomplete truths on a widespread basis. In many instances, however, the press dutifully conformed to security measures. Like other spheres of civic life, duty was predicated upon sacrifice. The shortcomings of the United States were diminished by the press in the name of the greater good. Although they naturally lacked hindsight and objectivity, reporters did not believe themselves the conveyors of propaganda because their truth was delivered with moral imperative. President Franklin Roosevelt's press secretary, Stephen Early, was astounded by this trend in the weeks following Pearl Harbor. "It is an amazing fact to me to see the press and radio asking *for* rather than standing solidly *against* such a thing as censorship," he declared. [13]

Reporters and editorialists distinguished between voluntary restriction and forced censorship—thereby deviating from rigid enemy protocols. Those under the umbrella of Allied protection demanded broad-mindedness. Noted French journalist and historian Geneviève Tabouis cast ripples with her outspoken Parisian newspaper *L'œuvre* as the brutal tides of fascism swept through Italy, Spain, and Germany in the 1930s. Forced to flee France prior to its 1940 capitulation, she pursued her work with religious zeal in New York City—demanding that solid journalism not be compromised by insecurity.

Seven weeks prior to the Normandy invasion, the Associated Press (AP) penned a revealing portrait of Madame Tabouis: "Europe's most famous woman journalist believes so strongly in freedom of the press that she wants a freedom-of-the-press-tribunal made a part of the postwar organization for peace. She also would like to see a freedom of the press clause incorporated in the peace treaty as foremost newsmen and politicians have advocated." Only through the obliteration of totalitarian censorship could notions of democracy globally flourish. [14]

On June 3, the *Denton Record Chronicle* argued the press only had itself to blame if it was overtaken by larger political or economic interests. "We are not likely to have lasting security against war until the channels of news are cleared of the pollution that many of them still carry," the paper contended. "[M]onopoly has given way to a relatively free exchange of international news—only to have the hard-won freedom taken away by stifling censorships of a new war." Reporters desired accessibility of information for public benefit. The deeds of the Fourth Estate became the legitimate interest of the free world. [15]

Editorialists of Abilene, Texas pulled no punches in their demands for candor. "Freedom of the press is the first of the freedoms, without which none of the others is possible," the writers argued. "Hitler went after the press first, after the pulpit second, after education third. These are the instruments of Truth, and the totalitarian concept could not live in an atmosphere of truth." Through deceit, lies, and murder, the squashing of valued institutions led to "the prostitution of all those healthy normal instincts inherent in our civilization. And you can bet your bottom dollar that when freedom of the press ceases to be, the other freedoms follow as a matter of course." Americans took this vexing outlook to heart as the dominoes of Europe and Asia collapsed. [16]

In that time, the principles of Roosevelt's "Four Freedoms" became sacrosanct. Freedom of speech, freedom to worship, freedom from want, and freedom from fear were heralded as ideological blueprints for a robust future. By correlating American privileges to the desired rights of oppressed peoples in foreign lands, Roosevelt set a foundation for an interconnected global society. While FDR did not always abide by his own standards, his perception of freedom remained a pillar of the country's framework. According to constitutional scholar Linda Eads, citizens "traditionally balanced their nation's broad security needs against an individual's right to express his or her opinions." The balance was a delicate one. D-Day was thus to be a cornerstone of the campaign to perpetuate the inherent rights of American life. [17]

Horrifically, the only manner in which American virtues could endure was through the expenditure of the nation's youth. In the months leading to D-Day, newspapers offered daily testimony of the mental and physical preparation of GIs. The *Evening Independent* of Ohio, for instance, frequently published slice of life articles regarding local sons. One such brief noted, "Carefully trained, rough and ready for battle, soldiers of an infantry unit in England are anxiously awaiting D-Day to put their training into practice and fight their way to Berlin. Among the battle-ready soldiers in this unit is Cpl. John J. Klett, age 28." Hardly the stuff of notable headlines, humble features as such offered peace of mind to beset civilians and sprinkled community context in the broader news of the war. [18]

Future Pulitzer-winner Don Whitehead of the Associated Press reflected on the transition from home front to battlefront in a May 19 piece. "The fateful day is drawing nearer when thousands of American youths—some hardened by months of training, some in actual combat—will storm the shores of Europe in the supreme test of the infantryman in World War II," he guaranteed. Having witnessed the trials of the battle for Anzio, Whitehead possessed no illusions of the forthcoming strife.

"The hopes of millions of enslaved people rest with GI Joe," Whitehead continued. "He's the guy who will carry the greatest burden of battle,

12

take the hardest blows of the enemy, and endure the greatest hardships." Those preparing to storm French shores were just common guys, Whitehead insisted. Only years earlier, they bicycled their paper routes, ordered ice cream sodas at corner drug stores, or played tackle on high school football teams. They lived in a different world now—a world of painful deprivation. The average Joe-turned-GI Joe now had placed on his shoulders an honorable burden. On the distant coast, he would soon face a tested foe seasoned by four years of battle. "That's a big job for GI Joe, a tough, bloody job," Whitehead added. "But he's the man who can do it. He did it in North Africa, in Sicily, and on the beaches of Salerno where the 88-mm guns were waiting. It's the long road home—and that's really where he wants to be."[19]

Pierre J. Huss, the intrepid correspondent who personally interviewed Hitler in the 1930s, also conveyed unique insider perspective. D-Day, he surmised, would "explode into full fury the all-out war in its 20th century conception. The shock of that impact is expected to be of unprecedented violence, fostering the hope that a quick knockout can be scored." Huss excelled in keeping his readers grounded in reality. Not all reports out of London could be cheerily optimistic. Drudgery and slaughter were inevitable—and Americans needed to brace themselves for that harsh reckoning.[20]

Despite foreboding attitudes, citizens attempted to remain resolute during these days of duress. Their pep was all too often exhibited in small and intimate write-ups featured in homespun newspapers. Pennsylvania's *Lebanon Daily News* ran a seemingly trivial report entitled "Family Hero" on the front page. "A cablegram from England ended Mrs. Charles Morrison's several-weeks search for a missing ration book," it said. "Her son, Master Sgt. Walter G. Morrison, wired, 'Found your number four ration book in pocket. Will return by mail.'"[21]

The miniscule acknowledgement of a warm gesture is not as meaningless as it seems. As one wartime advertisement proclaimed, "Morale is a lot of little things." It is the "little things that help lift the spirits, keep up courage. Little things that are part and parcel of our American way of life." Beer. Cigarettes. Life Savers candy. A courteous overseas greeting. These were the "little things" that molded Americans' perceptions of their war and themselves. The wholesome nature of Sgt. Morrison's act provided the idealistic comfort citizens desired of their servicemen—a vision akin to scenes rendered by Norman Rockwell.[22]

As teams of correspondents braved the Atlantic to report the looming contest, many shared the attitudes of their best-known colleague. Ernie Pyle—bald, scrawny, and eternally discerning—felt the same as when he embarked to war-torn Britain in November 1940. He said, "I will be scared. I know I will feel small and in the way among a people who are doing a job of life and death." Despite his misgivings, a voice within him beckoned, "Go."[23]

Less than four years later, Pyle found himself in the muddy trenches of Normandy's dense hedgerow country. Incoming German shells shaved the thick vegetation above him, pattering his weathered steel helmet with splinters and foliage. Pyle's ears rang like "a high-tone bell" as the rounds plowed into the dark earth. Burning debris and thick, brown French soil poured on the shaken reporter. An anxious American soldier jumped into Pyle's foxhole.

"Are you a war correspondent?" the GI asked.

Pyle replied in the affirmative.

"I want to shake your hand." The rifleman reached around a small bush and the two clenched their dirty palms. The soldier said no more. He did not have to.[24]

PART I: THE COUNTDOWN

No easy hope or lies
Shall bring us to our goal,
But iron sacrifice
Of body, will, and soul.

– Rudyard Kipling

CHAPTER 1

Of Beer and Bombs

The crowded mess hall was perfumed with the aroma of flapjack batter and hot bread. The sizzle of the industrial griddle could be tauntingly heard from the nearby company street. The heat emanating from the formidable Army kitchen stoves afforded the little warmth to be found in the wood frame and tarpaper structure. Cooks prepared to pour scoopfuls of syrupy peaches from hefty drums. Nearly as loud as the clang of pots and pans was the line of grumbling stomachs awaiting morning sustenance. Hurry up and wait, the famished GIs bickered. Standing in line twenty minutes for grub and having five minutes to eat it seemed their daily sunrise ritual. The food itself was not wholly objectionable, only the haste in which it was expected to be consumed. Recovering from heavy doses of physical training, the greenhorns gulped cupful's of steaming black coffee—the soldier's universal antidote for fatigue. Eyelids drooped even as the men filed in their tiresome breakfast queue. The fare would be greatly needed. More calisthenics were the order of the day. Amid the bustle, Bill Manning of Troy, New York spotted his old high school football coach strutting past the chow line. "I was going to run up and say hello, but someone called me and that's the last opportunity I got to see him," Manning wrote to his family. And off to PT he went. [25]

The island of Great Britain had become a fortress unto itself. Between late 1943 and mid-1944, hundreds of thousands of Allied troops piled into the dingily quaint ports and villages of England, retracing their father's footsteps of a quarter century earlier. The island nation was to be the base for invasion. "Britain may look a little shop-worn and grimy to you," forewarned a serviceman's guidebook. "The British people are anxious to have you know that you are not seeing their country at its best. There's been a war on since 1939. Tile houses haven't been painted because factories are not making paint—they're making planes." The

Yanks did not mind. There was plenty of distraction to be found, both noble and mischievous. [26]

Buzzing about England's "hive of activity," Yanks confessed a growing admiration of Britain's "splendid defiance" and "coolness under stress." Allan Morrison, the only African American staffer of *Stars and Stripes*, applauded the unflappable Brits. One GI interviewee remarked, "The folks back in America more than 3,000 miles from where the fighting will take place, are sweating out the opening of the Second Front. These [British] people go about their daily business as though nothing were in the wind. When D-Day comes, I'll wager most of these people hardly bat an eyelash."

Between the World Wars, the coastal resorts of the United Kingdom sprawled with springtime guests. "Visitors from all over England lolled on the benches facing out to the water or sunned themselves on the balconies. These were stenographers and professionals, factory workers and industrialists, relaxing by the sea. Today many such hotels are occupied by the services, British and American." On the terraces and ledges where newlyweds once gazed now sat young men training for war. Mingling among the masses, Morrison wrote, "One plays 'Shoo, Shoo, Baby' on an accordion that has battered its way across one continent and an ocean and may yet give out with 'St. Louis Blues' on the Wilhelmstrasse." On the British piers and boardwalks where lovers once strolled, the areas were littered with signs declaring, "Civilians are forbidden to loiter or talk to soldiers." [27]

As Bill Manning's brief encounter demonstrated, searches for family and friends in the invasion shuffle developed as a favorite soldierly pastime. Discoveries of siblings and old acquaintances offered a taste of home in this foreign land. Brotherly rendezvous offered moments of much-desired levity. Writing to his parents in Fredericksburg, Texas, S/Sgt. Bruce Jordan was ecstatic upon locating his lieutenant brother, Eldred. "[H]is hair even still sticks up," Bruce ribbed, "and not much worse for the wear! The cuss is homesick, but he looks fine—even if he is an officer!" Similar joy was expressed by artilleryman Jim Carroll, who uncovered his twenty-two-year-old brother, Joe, amidst a gaggle of infantrymen. Jim's homeward letter chronicling the chance meeting exemplified the contrasting worldviews of veterans and fresh enlistees:

17

Dear Mother, Dad, and All,

I said in my last letter that when I wrote to you again, I would have something more interesting to write. Well, I finally got around to see Joe, but I had a hard time finding his barracks, where he is located, which is about 75 miles from where I am stationed. I was sure glad to see him. He looks good, but has lost a little weight and seems a little nervous, but this is not to be wondered at after coming through the Sicily campaign. He said he had three close calls there. I told him that his being nervous was probably due to smoking too much. Joe didn't like it because he had to go through all the training over here that he went through at Camp Hood, Texas. I told him it was all in the days work, and that we are not over here for pleasure.

He had a small German gun, and an Italian watch and a few other odds and ends, but someone stole them from his bag. I took him a couple cartons of cigarettes, some candy and gum. He got the day off and we sure had a fine visit. A soldier from Reynoldsville, who accompanied me on the trip, recognized Joe as soon as he saw him. He said he used to skate with Joe. We had a 48-hour pass and had to hurry back, but we felt that we were well paid for making the long trip. Joe is to get a furlough soon and is going to pay me a visit. I am feeling fine, and hope the folks at home are too. Tell all the neighbors I said hello. Write soon.

> *Your son,*
> *Jim*[28]

Notions of love and family were no more apparent than in the sudden surge of British war brides. Among the newlyweds was Jacqueline Leigh Mallory, daughter of the Allied invasion air forces commander, Air Chief Marshal Sir Trafford Leigh Mallory. The young lady grew smitten with Flight Officer William Doherty of Hammondsport, New York and was speedily engaged to the dashing twenty-seven-year-old airman. The presence of Allied generals at their wedding made for a notable article of interest for reporters.

In wider terms, the American Red Cross (ARC) estimated anywhere between 40,000 to 60,000 British women married American service members. So great was the number of marriages in London and so drastic were the wartime shortages of silk that the women of Kennebec, Maine initiated a charitable campaign to donate wedding dresses overseas. The spike in matrimonies became a goldmine of propaganda. What better way to promote the Allied pact than with the sacred vows of marriage? [29]

While the war birthed many families, it separated even more. In Salt Lake City, Arline Parton penned a bittersweet note to her husband, Joseph, informing him of the birth of their son. "I'm certainly glad it's a boy," the father enthusiastically responded. The local newspaper reported the newborn "has already decided to be a bombardier on a Flying Fortress as is his dad . . . but his mother claims that all he does right now is to sleep and eat the whole day long." Dad hoped the war would not last as long as the article surmised. [30]

Transatlantic correspondence materialized in many forms. Phyllis Jane Conrad of Circleville, Ohio had maintained a written relationship with a London pen pal since 1935. From 3,000 miles away, Conrad learned of continuous English sufferings. In March 1944, Conrad was so moved by one letter that she submitted it to the *Circleville Herald* for publication. The Conrads frequently mailed food, clothing, dresses, and Betty Crocker dehydrated soup packets. The recipient expressed her gratitude in a heartfelt response, part of which read, "It means a lot to me, Phil, because we've had a reduction on clothing coupon allowance. . . . Honestly, Phil, it's awfully hard to make do. For baby, it's terrible." She movingly concluded, "I do value our friendship and look on you as my dearest friend, as the sister I never had. I pray our friendship will last all our lives." [31]

The devastation unleashed upon Britons did not go unnoticed by American personnel. Cpl. Oral Morrison remarked to his parents that Americans "didn't know what war is compared with the people of England." Likewise, Ensign Billie Neel of the USS *LST* (Landing Ship Tank) *517* wrote to family with shock and conviction. "One day I was ashore and went through a certain city of fairly large size," he vaguely conveyed. "It was bombed terribly bad. Entire blocks had been leveled to the ground by bombs. A huge cathedral that once had been famous and beautiful was in complete ruins." Neel entered the formerly regal church, listened to an impassioned sermon, and felt as if God spoke to him. "A people like this who have suffered can no doubt feel a need for God more than those who have never been faced with the stern realities of this war." Neel's resolve was reflected in the attitudes of countless sailors, soldiers, and airmen who established intimate bonds with their British neighbors. Through individual experiences, GIs discerned their war not as a political feud but as a humanitarian enterprise. D-Day had the potential to alleviate the sufferings of the beleaguered Brits.[32]

The ensign was not alone in his sudden disposition toward religion. According to J. W. Collins in his popular column entitled "1st Sergeant's Call," roughly 40% of Americans in the European Theater of Operations (ETO) regularly attend religious services. Chaplain Curtin Tierman was pleased by the sudden uptick of spiritual fervor. "This number is considerably higher than among soldiers in the states," declared one reporter. "In the last few months there has been an increase in the church attendance. Colonel Tierman says that the air raids and expectations of taking part in the invasion have made ETO soldiers aware of the seriousness of war." Catholic, Jewish, and Protestant chaplains, or "Holy Joes" as they were referred, were not spared overtime duties.[33]

While soldiers sought theological consolation, a crisis of a different manner swiftly unraveled. A substantial housing crunch left many GIs on leave temporarily homeless. Soldiers slept in train stations, on park benches, and in guttery stoops. As *Stars and Stripes* attested, "Hundreds of American soldiers arriving in London on pass and furlough are failing almost every night to get beds at ARC clubs and are being forced to sleep on chairs, floors, and in large air raid shelters because many units are overstepping their London quotas." The popular Army cartoon strip "Private Breger" offered a humorous visualization of this conundrum. The sketch depicted a soldier penning a letter by candlelight in a cavernous hallway completely filled with shelter half tents. The caption read, "Dear Folks: You'll be proud to hear I'm living in a real old twelfth century castle."[34]

Acclaimed war correspondent Ernie Pyle offered his own jocular interpretation of England's crowdedness in a May 11 piece. "If the Army fails to get ashore on D-Day," he wrote, "I think there are enough American correspondents here to force through a beachhead on their own. There are gray men who covered the last war, and men from the Pacific, and there are little girls and big girls and pretty girls, and diplomatic correspondents and magazine contributors and editors and cubs and novelists. If *Dog News* doesn't get a man over here pretty quickly to cover the dog angle of the invasion, I personally will never buy another copy."[35]

Pyle rose as the ultimate embodiment of the World War II reporter. His balance of wit, sincerity, technical detail, strategic assessment, and warm personal portraits made him a household name. From Africa to Anzio, his writings gained him affection among the troops, who sometimes referred to him as a best friend of the "dogface." Employed by the mighty Scripps-Howard media empire, his widely-distributed columns appeared six times per week. Having travelled 150,000 miles in his journeys, his prior investigative odysseys lured him to Alaskan gold mining camps and Memphis trash dumps. His lively reports exhibited a zestful punch many correspondents lacked. Followed by thirteen million loyal readers, scores recognized him as "Mr. America."[36]

Correspondent Ernie Pyle ascended as perhaps the most celebrated reporter of World War II. His endearing descriptions of GI life won him international acclaim. Despite his prior experiences in the combat zone, Pyle feared D-Day's frightful possibilities. (1)

Novelist John Steinbeck, himself a war correspondent, summarized Pyle's skills most vividly. "There are really two wars and they haven't much to do with each other," he remarked. "There is the war of maps and logistics, of campaigns, of ballistics, armies, divisions and regiments—and that is General [George] Marshall's war." At the same time, "there is the war of the homesick, weary, funny, violent, common men who wash their socks in their helmets, complain about the food, whistle at the Arab girls, or any girls for that matter, and bring themselves through as dirty a business as the world has ever seen and do it with humor and dignity and courage—and that is Ernie Pyle's war."[37]

The tiny Indianan was astounded by the volume of press assembled to cover the invasion. "At last report there were around 300 correspondents here," he marveled. "They say transmission facilities are being set up to carry a maximum of half a million words a day back to America. While in London we correspondents can wear either uniforms or civilian clothes." Since the reporters had no ration coupons to buy suits, uniforms were the singular style.

Although short on wardrobe, Pyle earned luxurious London accommodations thanks to his noteworthy credentials. He once might have felt guilty for indulging in such pleasure, but he had invested enough time in foxholes and filth to be pampered for once. "I don't feel the least bit ashamed anymore," he rationalized. The reporter grew accustomed to hot baths, room service, and weekly mail deliveries in his plush quarters. AP reporter Hal Boyle, whose own stellar work was overshadowed by Pyle's, often joked of his colleague, "There goes that social-climbing columnist."[38]

Posh hotel suites aside, reporters were enticed by the gravity of anticipated happenings. "Obviously no correspondent knows when the invasion will be or where," Pyle claimed. "I imagine you could count on your fingers all the Army officers in England who know." Correspondents constantly stood at the ready, their packs always prepared. "Only a few will go in on the initial invasion or in the early stages. Some of the eager ones have tried to pull strings to get front seats in the invasion armada," Pyle continued. "Others with better judgment have just kept quiet and let matters take their course."[39]

Shortly after his arrival in London, Pyle was awarded the Pulitzer Prize for his compelling accounts of the American infantryman. One soldier stationed at Anzio even called the forty-three-year-old newsman "the best reporter in the whole damn world" and wondered "how a dried-up little guy like that gets around so much." The introspective Pyle enjoyed a distinct camaraderie with his fellow correspondents as they prepared for their monumental assignment.

James Long of the Associated Press was among those 300 reporters jammed into the press offices of the Supreme Headquarters Allied Expeditionary Force (SHAEF). From a nearby room, Eisenhower's communiqués were issued twice daily. Long, like Pyle, was awed by the talent pounding away at the typewriters. "The greatest news reporting staff ever assembled to record a single explosive page in world history is ready to cover the invasion of Europe—the biggest news story since the deluge." Correspondents from Russia, China, France, America, Britain, and Canada were devising every conceivable angle of covering the imminent flood into Europe. [40]

While those in the SHAEF press office created puns about deluges and surges, an April drought, which meteorologists claimed was Britain's worst in three decades, brought acute conditions to thousands of square miles. Even this isolated calamity had the potential to unhinge certain elements of the Allied war machine. For nearly five years, the British had confronted every shortage imaginable. By contrast, the AP observed, "Chops, stews, steaks and roasts were served on American dinner tables during the last three months at a higher rate than any year since 1908—and will drop only slightly during April, May and June." Given the proposed window for invasion, the springtime unavailability of meats for U. S. consumers stands as no coincidence. [41]

Even with the prior availability of food products on the home front, American citizens were encouraged to be self-reliant, thrifty, and agricultural. The *Circleville Herald* declared in late May, "More and better victory gardens are needed." Because fewer Allied ships were being sunk in the Atlantic, there was a temporary surplus of goods. However, it "will soon be gone," the paper dimly foretold. "Victory Gardens are not toys to be disregarded when tired of them. They are an important and much needed part of fighting the war." [42]

In New York City, Mayor Fiorello La Guardia pled for residential co-operation with the Department of Sanitation's collecting of salvaged materials. He asked residents to separate paper and cans from household trash to assist with the mammoth wartime recycling effort. "With D-Day approaching," wrote the *New York Times*, "the need for salvaged paper to manufacture packaging material for war supplies and equipment was said to be acute. It was pointed out that every five pounds of paper saved could make seventy-three cartons for K field rations." Meanwhile, the Eagle Pencil Company sought to collect twenty tons of waste paper by having its 1,000 employees scrounge the streets. From scrap drives, to war bond campaigns, to Victory Gardens, the American war effort was expansive in scope. [43]

Military priorities were even more pronounced in Great Britain. In the five months prior to invasion, English households produced twelve million landing reserve cartons consisting of 170 million components including rations, first aid supplies, and survival kits—freeing factory workers to lend 1.5 million man-hours to other wartime duties. Stateside newspapermen hoisted Britain's dedication as a source of inspiration. "Is it too much to ask," begged California's *Oakland Tribune*, "that we set cartons and waste paper aside and deliver them to the nearest firehouse or welfare agency?" [44]

Regardless of domestic shortages, GIs enjoyed a perpetual tide of care packages and home front delights. Lions Clubs across America initiated a "Smokes for Soldiers" campaign resulting in the shipment of thousands of Lucky Strikes and Chesterfields while other parcels satisfied the sweet tooth. Sgt. Richard Whiting of Bedford, Pennsylvania penned in one letter, "I received a box of assorted nuts, peanuts, cigarettes and fudge from my 'best girlfriend.'" He shared the peanuts with buddies but concealed the fudge. Whiting also explored London in-depth. The Chartered Insurance Institute of Great Britain offered Americans complimentary maps and travel literature. Whiting strolled into the grand hall of the institution and was greeted by a receptionist offering a tour. The man was amazed that Whiting's first question was not the typical GI inquiry of "Where can I get a dame?" [45]

Young Andy Rooney of future *60 Minutes* fame offered waggish insight on carnal impulses. The flyboys he wrote about "had been hauling regularly" and thus "had to take care of their physical needs." GI pleasure-seekers practically stampeded from train cars and buses in pursuit of romantic merrymaking. Such Yanks, known as "Piccadilly Commandoes," were not particular in their sexual selections. Likewise, prostitutes did not lack patrons or distracted targets of pickpocketing. The "good time girls" offered thorough "wall jobs" for eight bucks a pop, said Rooney. Such was the degree of promiscuity that couples need not even find a discreet locale for intimacy. A Yank simply wrapped his mate in his wool overcoat and committed the deed while leaning against the nearest lamppost. [46]

Surprisingly, the Medical Department revealed the Army's venereal disease rate dropped dramatically in this time. Eye-popping sex education classes were instituted in the Army and Navy to avert the diminishing of invasion manpower. Prevention measures notwithstanding, GIs fathered over 24,000 Anglo-American babies out of wedlock despite the widespread availability of prophylactics. One condom package inscribed with the phrase "Le Transparent" showcased the French flag as a rousing suggestion of European liberation. [47]

Shady transactions pervaded all corners of the big city. *Stars and Stripes*—ever the loyal agent of the soldier—complained of London's many hucksters and flim-flam men: "Details of a lucrative racket whereby gullible American soldiers are being fleeced by a few London taxi drivers acting as 'guides' were revealed by *The Sunday Dispatch* yesterday." Some sixty cabmen earned as much as £40 per week by offering carloads of GIs half-hearted excursions. Sgt. Victor Palousek was slow to anger on such matters, sympathizing with the Brits who generally made "very little money, about thirty cents a day." He added in a homebound letter, "The girls don't have any lipstick, perfumes, or other cosmetics but just the same are nice looking. The British soldiers are pretty friendly—but don't like it when other boys take their gals away from them." Palousek acknowledged he would have felt much the same way had the roles been reversed. [48]

On the topic of transportation, the United Press's rising star, Walter Cronkite, faced unexpected language barriers that hindered travel. Departing his UP office on London's Fleet Street, he frequently hitched a taxi to Jack's Club, a popular watering hole for celebrities and war correspondents.

"Fourteen Orange Street," Cronkite told his cabby.

"Beg pardon, governor?" was invariably the confused reply.

Cronkite learned to elaborate. "Orange Street . . . between Leicester Square and the Haymarket."

"Ew, governor, *Orange* Street," the driver replied. Off to Jack's they drove. [49]

Dialect confusion was not a dilemma singular to London. British soldiers who sojourned to America on a goodwill tour encountered similar predicaments. The Tommies' conversations were not without moments of irony, as *Stars and Stripes* attested: "M/Sgt. Simon Sagle of the ETO received a letter from his little niece who is attending grade school in Philadelphia. She writes, 'Yesterday two British soldiers visited our classroom—they could not speak very good English.'"[50]

James "Scooty" Reston, however, was not lost in translation. The slick, Scottish *New York Times* reporter commenced his work at the London bureau the same day World War II began. He now wildly anticipated the reversal of Nazi aggression. "The American invasion of Britain is proceeding at an incredible rate," he wrote. "The army of the republic moves silently; its arrival and departure are carefully and correctly blotted out, but the rise of its strength and influence in this is unmistakable." Never before in history had "so many men been moved across the Atlantic as in the last six months."

Beyond reporting the daunting logistics of war, Reston offered additional color commentary on the war's romantic elements. "American soldiers in this expeditionary force are much more accustomed to the companionship of women than British men of the same age." Consequently, "the British girl in her teens tends to be shy where the American girl is self-assured." Notwithstanding the audaciousness of many lustful Yanks, the reporter concluded that "the British people who remember our last AEF are constantly remarking that this is the best-behaved American army they've seen." Apparently, GI Joe was of a tamer breed than his Doughboy father.[51]

Demonstrations of adequate behavior aside, the natural temptations of a testosterone-filled fighting force composed of youngsters wishing to "get lucky" before "kicking the bucket" were uncontrollably apparent. As the "GI Philosophy" section in *Stars and Stripes* aptly attested, "A rude and vulgar man is one who stares at a girl's figure when she's doing her best to display it." The British adage that American troops were in fact, "Overpaid, oversexed, and over here" was far more than a clever quip.[52]

Ernest Hemingway basked in the lively indulgences of London. The WWI veteran and provocative author of *For Whom the Bell Tolls*, Hemingway had an insatiable fixation for the enlivening dangers of the battlefield and the barroom. At the outset of World War II, he jury-rigged his fishing vessel to cavalierly hunt German U-boats in the Caribbean.

Navigating through the male-dominated worlds of journalism and military bureau-
cracy, female correspondents proved their mettle on bases and battlefronts alike. Shown
left to right are: Ruth Cowan (Associated Press), Sonia Tomara (*New York Herald Tribune*), Rosette Hargrove (Newspaper Enterprise Association), Betty Knox (*London Evening Standard*), Iris Carpenter (*Boston Globe*), and Erika Mann (*Liberty* magazine). (2)

He met future wife and fellow reporter, Martha Gellhorn, at a cocktail
party. The couple's 1940 wedding (his third) was bookended by their
dual coverage of the Spanish Civil War and the Second Sino-Japanese
War. Their legendarily tumultuous marriage would not survive a third
war.

As both wrote for *Collier's Weekly,* Gellhorn sought autonomy and the
desire to rise above her husband's shadow. Incensed by her ambitions
of self-reliance, Hemingway caustically challenged her, "Are you a war
correspondent, or wife in my bed?" Thenceforth, he constantly attempted to block her journalistic forays to the front. Dogmatic military
bureaucrats aided him. Gellhorn would have none of it. "It is necessary
that I report on this war," she avowed. It was her right to record the

events she deemed noteworthy. Nobody was going to deprive her of the privilege, and she was not to be outdone.

When Hemingway arrived in London on May 17, he immediately darted to the pub of the fashionable Dorchester Hotel. Perpetually in need of female accompaniment, he soon became enamored with Mary Welsh of *Time* magazine, who incidentally was already married to Australian war reporter Noel Monks. In no time, Hemingway informed her, "I don't know you, Mary. But I want to marry you." The proposition later became reality—wife number four.

In the meantime, Hemingway's pre-invasion antics ran afoul. As one biographer claims, "His odd combination of benignity, gaiety, and boorishness did not make him universally popular during these early weeks in London." Some colleagues believed he was playing a character while others simply regarded him as a childish alcoholic. Hemingway's joie de vivre was spoiled by a horrific automobile accident. While in a drunken stupor following a binge party, Hemingway entered a car with photographer Robert Capa and was subsequently hurled through the windshield. Gellhorn grudgingly visited his bedside and, at that moment, both knew their fiery marriage was over. The two would go on to report D-Day in their own ways. Both were about to live and write history— separately.[53]

Hemingway was not the only military man enchanted by high life along the Thames. Cpl. Tom Wilcox of Wellsboro, Pennsylvania brightly described London as the cosmopolitan capital of free Europe. "It is an odd turn of fortune's wheel that the same Lad who sipped sodas at the Palace, clambered over the old cannon on the Green, and has engraved in his heart on every bumpy red brick on Main Street, should find a warm comradeship here with Czech, Polish, Dutch, Norwegian, French, and British soldiers," he confessed. The looming invasion was truly a global affair. England certainly had not been fighting alone these past four years.

Wilcox found the level of destruction in the ancient city disconcerting. "After being here a while," he said, "it becomes a perfectly natural thing to saunter past blocks of razed buildings, shattered walls, and crumbling cellars." Wilcox hated to admit that an air raid "was a spectacular thing to see." The "barrage thrown up at the intruders unintentionally presents a master display of brilliant lights, dazzling multicolored flares, white flashes of rocket guns, and the resounding cr-r-r-umps of

Ack-Ack rumbling and rising to meet the invader." Though temporarily exhilarating, the "incendiary threats" posed by Germany otherwise deprived Wilcox of his sleep. Many GIs experienced their first bombardments that March during some of the worst raids since the Blitz. Hundreds of Yanks "helped British firemen and air raid patrol workers to extinguish incendiaries, fight fires, and assist injured persons from buildings," noted *Stars and Stripes*. The wholesale eradication of entire neighborhoods inflamed the ire of Americans.[54]

Impromptu actions of bravery during enemy air raids became commonplace. Pfc. Earl Hedrick of Arista, West Virginia was a steward at a 9th Air Force station and did not expect to be exulted as a hero. However, he rose to the occasion when his London holiday was disrupted by incessant German bombing. "Hedrick saw incendiaries fall and went to the fire. Hearing a child's cries, he forced his way into the building, found her cowering in a burning room, picked her up, and reached the street seconds before the walls and ceiling collapsed." Hedrick was no mere administrator.[55]

Through widespread humanitarian efforts, sympathetic Americans funded innumerable forms of philanthropy. One campaign raised $28 million in cash and supplies for the purchasing of civilian ambulances, hostels, hospitals, underground shelters, and food. The British War Relief Society (BWRS) acted as a charitable conduit for the noteworthy mission. Among its projects was the construction of two dozen nurseries for the "bomb-shocked" children of the region. In a heartrending account, one nursery attendant offered tragic testimony of her pitiful patients. "They are all under five, but they look like old men and women," she admitted. "Their skin is yellow and wrinkled. They have bags under their eyes, and they suffer continuously from hysteria and nervous panic. The prevailing symptoms are continuous crying, complete lack of interest in living, distaste for food, and in extreme cases, actual blindness."

Even with the continuation of Lend-Lease, former BWRS president Winthrop Aldrich chanted a resounding emotional appeal for the preservation of civilian aid. Lend-Lease was "a war measure intended to further the war activities of the various nations; it is in no sense a measure for civilian relief," he cautioned. Contextualizing British appreciation of American support, Aldrich said of the beneficiaries, "Some of these people, meeting me, tried to express their thanks. But they couldn't find the necessary words. Instead of speaking they broke down and cried," he kindly recalled. "The people of Britain will not forget that when so many of their homes were reduced to mere piles of bricks, and when their wives and children were crippled and maimed and bomb-shocked, American help was forthcoming. To receive assistance from a friend when in need is to establish the true value of friendship." This continuous assistance marked a "rebirth of faith not only in friendship but in the ultimate ideal of the brotherhood of man," Aldrich tearfully concluded. [56]

In one of her thousands of newspaper columns, First Lady Eleanor Roosevelt reciprocated the emotion following her visit to Great Britain. She remarked, "If it were only the spirit of the people of this country, which one feels everywhere here, I should feel grateful for having experienced it." Mrs. Roosevelt added, "I think that my faith in the goodness and strength of human beings has been greatly enhanced, and that is something for which I am deeply grateful." [57]

The meager monthly salaries of $50-$96 for U. S. enlisted men and non-commissioned officers did not dissuade gamely fundraising for European brethren. As early as September 1942, *Stars and Stripes* announced, "It will be the goal of this publication, with your help, to raise a fund sufficiently large to help support 500 orphans for a period of five years. This will provide each child with 20 pounds per year." By March 1944, the paper surpassed its original goal and embarked upon the effort of raising £100,000. Certain American units were presented the opportunity to sponsor and "adopt" individual British orphans who subsequently became unit mascots. GIs heartily embraced the title of honorary "uncles." On the eve of the invasion, the pious deeds bespoke a sense of unanimity even more than it demonstrated paternalistic pity. Americans increasingly thought of British youth as their own. [58]

For these reasons and more, British children generally adored their American guests. Lt. John Van Arsdale of the Air Forces placed a notice in the *Norwich Evening News* in search of golf balls. He received this reply: "Dear American officer, I am Peter Turner, age 9. Will you like me to swap my four golf balls for two packets of candy or chewing gum? Please write or phone. I get home from school about 4:30. Sorry I haven't got more. If you fly a B-17 or B-24, you can have them for nothing!" Lt. Van Arsdale readily accepted the generous offer. So ravenous were English youth for Wrigley's that "Got any gum, chum?" became their unofficial mantra. An American would dare not walk down a street without a pack in his pocket for fear of being mauled by sugar-craved urchins.[59]

Regrettably, tensions lingered behind the harmonious veneer. The contributions of black troops in England were practically imperceptible in the pages of newspapers. Typically confined to auxiliary duties as cooks, stewards, clerks, and drivers, African Americans could occasionally rise as segregated engineers, tankers, or artillerists. White officers who commanded black troops often outgrew their former prejudices, but conservative parameters consistently limited the upward mobility of their men. One white corporal responded to an interview on racial issues with the *London Sunday Dispatch*, noting, "In the first place it is not as bad as most outsiders seem to believe. The fact is that we are not opposed to the Negro 'getting ahead in the world' if he goes about it in the right way. We do object, however, to negro men sexing with white women." GIs stationed in Britain felt "forced to accept race equality" in a society devoid of Jim Crow. The corporal concluded that "the white GIs just can't stand to see [a] nice looking white girl necking with a big black negro. We're not fighting for that kind of 'democracy.' We could have it without fighting if we wanted it."[60]

When Barbadian sergeant Arthur Walrond of the Royal Air Force (RAF) was attacked by an American soldier for dancing with a white woman, the former journalist penned an impassioned plea to the British government. "I have never been trained to think in terms of nations or races and I had hoped that four years of war would have at least taught the world this lesson," he complained. "But the long-standing underlying prejudice for colored people despite their value, ability or achievement still remains to rear its ugly head and leaves a most distasteful gap to be bridged." Walrond never saw the justice he demanded. He was killed in a mission over Germany only hours after he cited his grievances.[61]

While the segregated Tuskegee Airmen soared to excellence in the Mediterranean, African Americans were blocked from combat duties in the 8th Air Force based in England. Despite bigotry in the ranks, amicable associations among African American personnel with the British populace prevailed. One black officer confessed to a reporter, "The English people had made our lives worth living." Yet these civil interactions, too, were often curtailed by superiors. The military exerted segregation in villages and pubs on designated days to preempt racial clashes. The unjust circumstances prompted one soldier to remark after the war, "we black troops went overseas to fight the Germans, but we had to fight the Yanks first."[62]

The uncomfortable truth that many within the Greatest Generation aired racist tendencies defies the moral mandate they themselves ascribed to the liberation of Western Europe. Their willingness to free the oppressed of France while turning a blind eye to the plight of their own citizens remains a tragic irony. Further intolerance was exhibited in a June 1944 poll in which a quarter of participants thought Jews were America's greatest threat. While the underpinnings of American society were heralded as the last best hope for free civilization, existing notions of justice nonetheless outlined extraordinary limitations.[63]

African American troops repetitively spurned inaccurate racial assumptions and excelled beyond the expectations of even progressive superiors. *Stars and Stripes* offered one glowing review of a unit's achievements exactly two months prior to D-Day. "A Negro engineer battalion completed a huge camp for GIs in the ETO 5,000 hours ahead of schedule," the paper noted. Especially "commended for his share in the achievement was Sgt. Carl Leonard Spells of Philadelphia. Spells coordinated the work of carpenters, plumbers, bricklayers, electricians, and concrete mixers into an effort that lopped over 200 days off the original estimate." In a more symbolic sense, these crews paved a road toward the equality they so deserved.[64]

To build upon these accomplishments the *Pittsburgh Courier*, the African American newspaper of Steel City, launched the "Double V" initiative representing *Victory at Home, Victory Abroad*. The theme was proposed by James G. Thompson, a cafeteria employee at a Kansas air plant, who wrote, "Should I sacrifice my life to live half American?" A *Courier* staffer claimed, "[T]his country is worth defending; things will be different for the next generation; colored Americans will come into their own, and America will become the true democracy it was designed to be," but not without sacrifice and stalwart persistence.[65]

Where racial strains percolated America's ranks, cultural divides between Limeys and Yanks dissipated. The word "we" was applied to Brits and Americans in a collective rather than singular definition, boasted writer Richard Wilbur. In preparation for the mutual task of liberating France, soldiers of the two nations conducted exchange visits to their respective camps. "What they have learned of each other has been healthily enlightening." The interactions nurtured empathy and congeniality. "Because of the British soldier's extreme politeness, you would think he was a sissy, but he is far from that, for he is a tough and rugged soldier," observed a Signal Corps sergeant.

"There is nothing strange or freakish about the British soldier," an infantryman agreed. "He responds to friendship, has a good sense of humor, and is very cooperative. The only difference is his accent and his way of saying things. Overlook his accent . . . and you'll discover a fine, lasting friend and the best fighting companion you'll ever want next to you in battle."

The Lend-Lease Personnel Exchange System facilitating the visits was composed of American and British officers who wished to strengthen the bonds of alliance. Small sections of ten soldiers at a time were hence swapped to and fro. Amid the dialogue, cordial discrepancies were inevitably recognized. "Differences in discipline, attitude, pay, food, freedom, medal awards, ranks, and sanitation were acknowledged and talked over. Americans envied some British characteristics; British envied some American characteristics." When the visitations concluded, "many of the British soldiers gave us names and addresses of their families in England and wanted us to spend any future leaves with them," one GI claimed. "It was a swell experience—in fact I'd call it smashing." Stereotypes of Americans soldiers were quickly deflated. Brits who previously "considered all Yanks movie stars, millionaires or gangsters" now thought differently. [66]

Tom Wilcox was taken aback by Hollywood's influence on the British mindset. "I don't believe you have any idea how profoundly the American movies are influencing British thought," he observed. "It is really hard to find an English movie or hear anything but American swing songs. If you said you lived near Chicago, women fainted in terror and men expected you to pull a Tommy-gun from your vest pocket." Preconceptions of Americans being cowboys or gangsters were "fairly well erased now. We are surprised to find that the English don't all wear stiff collars and monocles and that people are pretty much the same underneath the surface of customs and tradition." [67]

The surprise was reciprocal. "As I always thought that the Americans were all blow and brag, I received a pleasant shock." The GI outlook on life, observed a British sergeant, "seems much more frank and self-assured than the average British man's, and they are all convinced that America is God's country." The Brits were impressed by the Yanks' cheap cigarettes, tidy barracks, modern vehicles, and bottomless water supply. GI chow was deemed unenviable, however. One Brit referred to Yankee victuals as "rich, sickly food." A lance corporal astutely noted, "Rather mixed way of cooking food. Lots of varieties, no doubt because of the various nationalities in the U. S. Army." With the exception of canned fruit, American grub was thought too spicy and sugary in contrast to English culinary preferences.

Discussion of tastes transcended food and style. Europe's alcoholic beverages received mixed reviews among GIs who considered themselves connoisseurs of intoxicating spirits. M/Sgt. Gilbert Amis wrote to his parents in Harlingen, Texas of his lukewarm reaction. "The drinks here are all served un-iced," he complained. "Beer has numerous classifications. Guinness Stout is a beer supposedly good for nursing mothers and invalids but is partaken of by anyone married or over 40. It looks like cough syrup and tastes like you know what. It has a very bitter taste."

However, Ike's press officer identified pubs as venues to strengthen international camaraderie. "A lot of real friendships and a lot of real understanding is developed over a glass of beer," he assured. The pub was described to Americans as "the poor man's club" where it was best not to obnoxiously intrude. The ale served there, although not as potent as peacetime brew, could "still make a man's tongue wag at both ends."[68]

Alcohol was not the only means of escape. Correspondence and care packages created tangible links to family and often presented lucrative home front luxuries. The precious spare moments homesick soldiers had were often occupied with letter-writing. Other reprieves consisted of rereading crinkled letters skimmed over twenty times before. The boys sniffed envelopes to rekindle the nostalgic smells of homesteads and loved ones. The scent of mom's perfume or pop's pipe tobacco elicited warm memories of a distant, prior life. Military personnel treasured and prodigiously catalogued their letters as if the sheets were invaluable, ancient scrolls. Service members exhibited commitments to penmanship at astounding rates. "Cpl. John C. Albanese takes over the letter-writing championship," exclaimed *Stars and Stripes*. "Anybody who writes 455 V-Mails in one month and 1,130 in three months on his own time deserves it. By contrast, Sgt. Edward P. Hopkins of Flint, Michigan received 117 letters in two days."[69]

Within their correspondence, many disclosed grave doubts of the future. S/Sgt. Wandell Riddle expressed pessimism to the *Whitewright Sun* when he demanded, "Please send me the price of a five-year subscription, as I expect to be absent for quite some time." The paper responded, "If the war lasts that long, there won't be any paper left to print *The Sun* on, so we are not accepting any five-year subscriptions."[70]

The Nazis attempted to capitalize off such anxieties expressed in print. As American writer Wade Werner scrawled from Lisbon, "In an apparent attempt to bolster German morale on the eve of the Allied invasion of Western Europe, Nazi propagandists are filling German newspapers with dispatches picturing both Britain and the United States as suffering from hysterical tension bordering on panic." The various dispatches asserted "that people in England are turning to religion, mysticism, spiritualism, or quack fortune tellers for comfort." Little could pacify the anticipation of "the costliest and most deadly gamble in all history," the German propagandists claimed. At the same time, Werner contended that the Nazis themselves were "honeycombed with defeatism" as they converted swank resorts into makeshift training centers for Germany's increasingly childlike ranks.[71]

To ensure GIs fully comprehended the villainy of their foe, *Stars and Stripes* designed a two-page spread in its May 18 edition. The feature included numerous entries from Hitler's manifesto *Mein Kampf*, the anti-Semitic rant that catapulted the Fuhrer to power. One highlighted excerpt shouted, "Everything we admire on this earth today—science and art, technology and inventions—is only the creative product of a few peoples and originally perhaps of one race. On this race depends the existence of all culture." Undeterred by America's own racial standoffs and unsavory eugenics history, notions of a "master race" predicated on the obliteration of civilizations appalled American soldiers. Even a year prior to their discovery of Hitler's death camps, GIs bore grim expectations of Germany's abhorrent ambitions. They only prayed their intervention would not arrive too late.[72]

CHAPTER 2

"A Mechanical Niagara"

Over the flak-filled skies of Hamburg and Schweinfurt, the invasion of Europe was already on. As a result of relentless Allied bombing, once-illustrious centers of German industry and culture increasingly resembled glowing heaps of red ash. In March 1944, Army Air Forces chief Henry "Hap" Arnold pressed the point to inquiring reporters. "We are invading, and not at some remote beachhead. We are hitting the enemy where he lives. He knows if he cannot stop us, he's licked." The increased tempo of aerial assaults was no sideshow of impending amphibious operations. An architect of strategic bombing, the silver-haired Arnold took flying lessons from the Wright Brothers and once soared as a movie stunt pilot. Now, he facilitated some of the most destructive fury ever witnessed in warfare. "This plan is simply to destroy Germany's ability to make war," he asserted. "The missions we send out are not to be confused with what used to be called air raids. A great mission of today is a planned battle."[73]

In the months prior to D-Day, the U. S. Army Air Forces and the Royal Air Force unleashed a perpetual stream of death from the shrapnel-laden clouds of Germany. Swarming deep into the Third Reich, thousands of heavy bombers announced the true opening of the Second Front. It was only the beginning. DeWitt Mackenzie of the Associated Press religiously offered analysis of this crucial air war. Educated at Syracuse University, "Mack" later witnessed the carnage of the First World War and was nearly killed in the process. Featured globally in some 800 newspapers by the 1940s, he transmitted the war in relatable terms. In describing Allied bombing, he said, "One of Hitler's tough problems is to guess when the full fury of the storm will break."[74]

Mackenzie questioned the willpower of Nazi endurance in the face of such incomprehensible firepower. That February, the Allies unleashed some 100,000 tons of explosives on Germany. Pillars of smoke swirled

The invasion of Europe commenced months before June 6. As early as March 1944, Army Air Forces chief Henry "Hap" Arnold contended, "We are invading, and not at some remote beachhead. We are hitting the enemy where he lives." With a supreme numerical advantage over the Luftwaffe, Allied airmen continued aerial bombings on D-Day and beyond. Here, American B-26 Marauders swarm through bursts of flak over Normandy. (3)

miles above Gothic church spires as stunned civilians rummaged through blackened rubble in search of loved ones—and the insufferable weight of air offensives had yet to reach maximum intensity. "I believe we yet are able to see a display of Allied aerial striking power which will stagger the world," predicted Mackenzie. "What's going on now is fairly mild compared with what is still to come, especially on D-Day."[75]

That belief seemed difficult to accept for the airmen who actually flew missions. "The flak was terrific," exclaimed S/Sgt. Mayer Brudner of Brooklyn after one particularly grueling foray. "We must have had it for two hours of the nine-hour flight. Berlin must have flak guns in every street, every house, every apartment." Casualty rates hovered around a staggering twenty-five percent for many missions. Beyond flak and enemy fighters, survivors withstood eight- or ten-hour roundtrips in the subzero temperatures of uncompressed fuselages. They scraped frost from the same bulky flight suits sometimes soaked by their own urine. Their misery produced compelling, if not shocking, results. "The Allies have total air supremacy," lamented a German Panzer officer. The sensation of standing powerless against American and British planes elicited a paralyzing vulnerability. The demoralization was especially notable given the totalitarian quest to project constant strength. Affirming national resolve proved increasingly futile in the face of strategic bombing. [76]

The gargantuan invasion efforts required not only meticulously-skilled pilots but a vast entourage of clerks, mechanics, cops, cooks, and paper pushers. Because of airmen's harrowing duties, those on ground crews invariably strove to ease the hardships of comrades. For instance, the technical prowess of Sgt. John Foster of Altoona, Pennsylvania proved invaluable in the assembling of portable mess halls to feed hungry mechanics on runway repair lines. Foster constructed his "Spam Wagon" with a discarded truck chassis, salvaged sheet metal, and rusty water tanks to keep chow heated. War was indeed the mother of invention. [77]

Army bakers toiled on an even larger spectrum to ensure fresh bread for the boys. "When the invasion armies push into Western Europe, rolling with them—or not far behind them—will be mobile outfits equipped to 'punch' huge bathes of dough and remove endless trays of gray-brown bread from field ovens." Working on a quick-paced twenty-four-hour schedule, bakers could fire their ovens in bivouac or combat conditions. Daily production for a single bakery unit could peak at 15,000 loaves— enough to nourish 60,000 soldiers. Baker Joseph P. Franklin of New Orleans once loved preparing and devouring fresh bread, but the monotony of doing so on an industrialized scale substantially diminished the joys of his vocation. Handling 5,000 loaves of bread each shift, he agonized, "In the last six months I've smelled enough bread to last me for 60 years." The impression of an army marching on its stomach was no less true for Eisenhower than it was for Napoleon. [78]

Seasickness proved less curable than hunger. In anticipation of D-Day, *Stars and Stripes* offered friendly recommendations for averting the dreaded "Sea-Heaves" and chunder: Avoid liquid or greasy food for it all has "a tendency to get uneasy and slosh about a bit." Take "on large snootfuls" of fresh air at short intervals. "And for gawdsake lay off that stogy. If you have any gum, chum, that will be the time to slap it in your kisser. This keeps you swallowing, and few of us are built to accommodate two-way traffic at once. Don't watch the sea. It suggests things to your stomach." The worst element of seasickness was the dry heaves—the sensation of having to upchuck when one's stomach was empty. Despite warnings, thousands of armada passengers would grow dreadfully ill during their journeys. [79]

While *Stars and Stripes* made vain overtures to keep fire buckets and toilets free of puke on sea-bound vessels, the newspaper prudently prepared soldiers for other forms of anguish. In the article unbelievably entitled "'Bullets Don't Hurt,' Wounded Say," staff writer Ralph Harwood offered rationale to place anxious pre-invasion minds at ease. "Piecing together the individual stories," he wrote, "it becomes clear that men who have been actually wounded themselves know that it isn't as bad as they thought it would be and that they realize how vitally important it is for wounded men to keep still, bandage their wounds quickly, and then lie quietly waiting for the aid man to arrive." While the advice was solid, few accepted that a Mauser round or shell fragment would be as painless as Harwood optimistically inferred. [80]

Ernie Pyle knew better. He endlessly witnessed men bleed out in the rugged hills of Italy. His emotionally-charged article, "The Death of Captain Waskow," testified to an evil truth of war that few French invaders had yet experienced. Pyle possessed no misconception of what awaited the men. How could "any survivor of war . . . ever be cruel to anything, ever again?" he pondered. [81]

Notwithstanding what the future may have portended, Pyle marveled at the ingenuity and scale of America's vast naval fleet prior to his departure from Italy to England. One vessel that especially caught his fancy was the LST, a boat he referred to as "the outstanding ship of our amphibious forces." The vessel was "a great big thing, big as an ocean freighter. The engines and crew's quarters are all on the back end. All the rest of the ship is just a big empty warehouse sort of thing, much like a long, rectangular garage." Every piece of cargo was covered in rubber to protect it from the seas.

Resembling the jaws of a beached whale, the cavernous mouth of the LST opened to send forth clusters of vehicles ashore. As many as twenty Sherman Tanks could roll out from the ship's belly directly onto a beach or dock. The vessels—along with the versatile landing craft known as the Higgins Boat—would be vital to operational success. As British Prime Minister Winston Churchill suggested to U. S. Army Chief of Staff George Marshall that January, "the destinies of two great empires . . . seemed to be tied up in some god-damned things called LSTs."[82]

The amphibious nature of Operations Neptune and Overlord required a shatterproof trust between land, naval, and air forces. In no time, ground troops and navy personnel harmonized in their training endeavors and extracurricular activities. In March, an Army-Navy team initiated construction of a giant supply depot in England that included 11,000 feet of roadway. In building the lanes, the crews also cemented bonds of camaraderie. "The Navy provides plenty of entertainment on the post," one article noted. Their commander stated "that requests from his Army men for passes to town have dropped about 50 percent since they've been stationed there. Two Army engineers are now members of the Navy football team." So much for the timeless Army-Navy rivalry, he suggested.[83]

Unsurprisingly, the logistical diversification of the invasion sparked minor crises of identity. Soldier journalist G. K. Hodenfield was swift to cite this paradox. "The Old Army was never like this," he exclaimed. "In the Old Army no self-respecting soldier would be found dead in a uniform with 'U. S. Navy' neatly stenciled on the back. In the Old Army no self-respecting topkick, assuming there is such an animal, would yell, 'Ahoy there, mate, tell the skipper to send two of his deckhands ashore.'" Then again, this was *not* the Old Army. The distinctive enterprise informally known as "The Army's Navy" was a harbor craft company thoroughly equipped with tugs, motor towing launches, cranes, and barges. The same week as Hodenfield's rant, the House Naval Committee authorized another $1.8 billion for the construction of landing craft since the Navy had just surpassed its previous $32.6 billion appropriation.[84]

Invasion resources were often ferried across the Atlantic by the intrepid members of the Merchant Marine, unsung heroes of the war despite their perilous journeys into U-Boat-infested waters. One out of every twenty-five Merchant Mariners perished in the war—the highest casualty proportion of any American service during the conflict. In England, *Stars and Stripes* writer Allan Morrison remarked, "where piers and quays jut out for miles and ships of the United Nations merchant navies move in and out with their cargoes for waging war, the port units

Army Deuce-and-a-half trucks slowly back into the open bow of a Landing Ship Tank (LST) as a gaggle of sailors, correspondents, and 1st Division men stand by. *LST 134* (in the background) later evacuated wounded from Omaha Beach and eventually served at Okinawa. *LST 134* crewmember Edward Reilly recalled of the invasion, "It was a 'go' come hell or high water." (4)

are recognized as very important agencies."

Lt. George Vaux of the aptly-named Watertown, South Dakota was one of many officers scrambling around the figurative ant farms of English ports. "When the men handle military equipment, they realize more forcefully that their work is of great importance to the preparations for the Second Front," said Vaux. While dockworkers did not confront the hazards of their contemporaries on the high seas, they risked life and limb, nonetheless. "Broken arms, smashed fingers and legs, and numerous other injuries speak for the hazardous nature of the work. Often a steel cable snaps and the broken strand swings wickedly down, smashing anything in its path." One gang member was even pinned against a vehicle when a two-ton sugar pouch nabbed him. Port workers literally "sweat out the invasion." [85]

The mountains of material grew as a stupendous feat of managerial corralling. As historian Craig Symonds noted, "American equipment and supplies soon began filling up some twenty million square feet of warehouse space and then overflowed into another forty-three million square feet of open storage." The docking ships were filled to the brim "with supplies of every kind, from beans to bullets." Over 1,000 camps and 100 air bases bustled with the sounds of preparation. One could not be but impressed by the colossal undertaking. [86]

Weaponry of every manner was stockpiled. Endless rows of M-1 Garands and Thompsons glimmered with factory finish. On the home front, civilians contemplated additional styles of armaments to support the campaign. An Ohio worker, "with an eye to D-Day, suggested having 1,000 pounds of bees dropped behind the Nazi lines before the allies landed." His theory was that the swarm would "outfight" the Wehrmacht. "The more they swat the bees, the madder they get, so while the Nazis are fighting the bees, our boys could blow them off the earth," the would-be strategist explained. Nothing came of his peculiar proposition for "Bee-Day." [87]

Merchant ships comprised only a fraction of the nearly incomprehensible number of vessels converged. Writer John Moroso was stunned by the overwhelming assemblage of boats and materiel. "The greatest armada of ships in world history, from warships and merchant ships to fishing boats, is gathered in Britain for the invasion of Western Europe." Never before had "so many landlubbers been placed in command of ships, lives, and supplies. That is, landlubbers prior to brief intensive

preparation for the role they will have to play on D-Day." Moroso identified one of the lubbers as the "husky, lively Captain John A. Potts, a
comparative youngster of 35 who has amazed the British with his
speed." Originally from Los Angeles, Potts relocated to Brooklyn and
found employment with the Bull Steamship Line. He was strikingly
qualified for the high-pressure tasks of wartime wharfs. "In one area,
where the British railroad controls the docks, cargoes piled up and shipping became stagnant. Potts borrowed 150 army trucks and relieved the
congestion." The railroads pitched a fit, but the docks remained clear. [88]

With cunning alacrity, GIs seamlessly applied skills from former vo-
cations to their new professions. One United Press International correspondent was particularly intrigued by three men working "off in a pasture, under some trees" in "a sort of overgrown packing case, half as big
as a boxcar, with a door built into one side." A captain emerged from
the rickety entranceway and jovially said, "We're expecting a general to
come look us over this afternoon and I thought we ought to try to get
the place in a little better shape."

What manner of work was conducted in this glorified glider crate? Inside, the reporter discovered the home of the Army's lone soil-test labor-
atory. The ramshackle facility was staffed by two captains and a corporal whose experimentations would provide engineers valuable data
for constructing reliable roads and runways. The officers gave "sure-fire
directions as to how to eliminate mud, without paving, in areas where
supplies are unloaded from trains. They stay busy, sampling soil from
all over the United Kingdom." [89]

Soil experts played a curiously exclusive role in D-Day preparations.
Correspondent W. W. Chaplin reported days following the invasion that
elite squads of scientists previously journeyed to France under cover of
darkness to determine how much weight the sands of Normandy could
bear. They inched along on their stomachs, collecting samples for study.
Under unsuspecting Nazi noses, they "learned where tanks, bulldozers,
and big guns could be put ashore without bogging down." [90]

According to the April 1945 edition of *Golfdom* magazine, one pedolo-
gist-turned-scout was "selected to make the dangerous trip to Normandy" in advance of the invasion. "He was shown how to make a rapid
survey, how to take the soil samples, and how to distinguish areas suitable for vehicles." During the failed Dieppe Raid into France on August
19, 1942, Allied vehicles became stranded in the pebble beach, serving

as one of several ingredients for ultimate disaster. Nearly two years later, to say the Allies needed to be on firm ground was no pun.[91]

Behind every engineer, dock manager, dentist, lab technician, and mechanic was a bureaucrat—a "desk jockey" who generally knew what the hell he was doing. He could differentiate between Class D, E, F, and N forms for a soldier's pay. He insisted the boys complete their $10,000 life insurance policies. He served as the observant bridge between untested officers and milk-fed enlisted men. His weapons of choice were the Eagle Sunbeam, the Dixon Federal No. 2, and "the heavily armored Eversharp." He contended with nobody's bullshit, regardless of rank. Sgt. J. W. Collins referred to him as a true "unsung hero in this war." Every orderly room had a pencil pushin' sergeant with "his .40 caliber pencil doing a job that is tough" and vastly underappreciated.

Collins insisted the duty was "no picnic." The non-com daily navigated his way through an agonizing labyrinth of technical and logistical minutiae. "Each time the Allies advance on to the next post," Collins wrote, "the clerks go right along with the troops and set up an office. The orderly room men, operations, intelligence, and operational clerks are always on that advance echelon helping to build up a new base." Collins posed various hypothetical questions to his readers: Did you ever try typing eight copies of a memorandum in a heavy wind? Did you pay the men on the last day of each month? Did officers receive their per diem? If one could not relate to these scenarios, they had no room to judge the deskbound sergeant. In his world, the "battle of the typewriter is going on in all its fury, for the paperwork of the army does not cease when the army gets into the field . . . it increases."[92]

The shuffling mounds of mail and administrative tripe waited for no man. Cpl. George McConnell of North Adams, Massachusetts recognized this while sorting mail at an 8th Air Force station "somewhere in England." He oversaw the daily transfer of 7,000 pounds of letters.[93]

The exchange of correspondence was divinely important to the mental well-being of garrisoned troops. Beyond personal letters, GIs enthusiastically sought additional reading materials. Books became ubiquitous in the ETO, particularly the portable Armed Services Editions that could handily fit within a jacket pocket or helmet liner. In the estimation of writer Molly Guptill Manning, "Every soldier and sailor abided by a strict policy of swapping and exchanging books, no matter how worn. The print could be smudged, the pages ripped or falling out, and still a book would continue to make the rounds." One sailor dared to claim, "To heave one in the garbage is tantamount to striking your grandmother."[94]

The GI's fondness for reading was reflected in the establishment of makeshift libraries throughout the British Isles. Librarian Charles E. Barret of Muskegon, Michigan converted a former stable into perhaps the largest service library in Europe. The reading area "is white, clean, and comfortably furnished with big chairs and almost 2,000 books. The range of reading material covers mysteries to technical publications." So popular was the library that Barret did not have a single vacation day for half a year. In addition to a multitude of donated materials, the federal government supplied personnel worldwide with some 120 million books. As one poster proclaimed, "Books are weapons in the war of ideas." As they likewise demonstrated with their avid reading of newspapers, GIs heralded literacy as a moral quality of the democracy they intended to preserve.[95]

While reading served as a timely diversion for service members, literacy also made apparent the glum reckonings of air warfare over Europe. For instance, March 1944 newspapers chronicled the tragedy of a B-17 gunner who perished on his first mission due to asphyxiation. The crewman became wedged in the plane's doors he attempted to manually close. Because none of his comrades could abandon their posts, the sergeant morbidly hung from the bomb bay for the duration of the flight. Among the hundreds of airmen returning from that same Berlin operation was Sgt. Tommy J. Bryant, who barely survived his eighteenth mission. "The raid was nearly as bad as I had expected," he exclaimed. "The target was burning when we left. It was hit plenty hard."[96]

The success of daylight precision bombing did not come without consequence. On March 22, Mary Colburn of Carthage, Texas received bittersweet words from her son, Finis. "God bless you and keep you until we meet again," he wrote. Appallingly, Mrs. Colburn received a telegram six days prior indicating her son was killed in the skies over Germany while flying with the 379th Bomber Group. The chilling message from the grave offered a final farewell but rattled the emotionally dejected mother to the core. "It was a telegram that tore the hearts of his devoted parents and submerged a community into silent sorrow," the *Carthage Panola Watchman* confessed. "We are aware of the fact that life walks hand in hand with death," the periodical continued. "Yet, we are never prepared to give up a man like Finis Colburn." Although he was no longer in the land of the living, the memory of Finis lived on, the *Watchman* assured. The canonization of war fatalities coalesced as a tragically repetitive pattern in the obituary sections of American newspapers.[97]

Episodes of horror were often coupled with salutes of gratitude. During one precarious mission, twenty-year-old sergeant Forrest Vosler of Livonia, New York was mauled by German shrapnel. His injuries did not prevent him from saving comrades after their battered bomber crashed into the Channel. Though his legs were shredded by bits of flak and bleeding profusely, Vosler managed to repair the plane's radio while holding a wounded crewmate above the icy waters. Before the aircraft plummeted into the sea, the sergeant offered to bail out to lighten the plane's load. Vosler lost his right eye as a result of the incident. Reading of Vosler's incredible tale and believing him to be completely blind, University of California student Pauline Venard selflessly offered him one of her own eyes to restore partial sight. The airman considered the proposal "the acme of heroism." Although he thought Venard a braver soul, Vosler was awarded the Medal of Honor exactly three months after D-Day.[98]

The lethal routines of air warfare inflicted tolls psychological as well as physical. Capt. Robert W. Spence, a Fortress pilot and veteran of air campaigns over Africa and Italy, remarked, "We fly in weather that would ground the ducks back home. Flak hit and bent the steel buckle of my parachute above my chest like a mule kicked me, leaving me unharmed. My oxygen system failed over the target. Flak blasted my bomb bay while I had bombs aboard but missed the bombs somehow. Sometimes we go so far over Germany that we are nearer Russia than England." Even if one was spared from flak, fewer were spared mental anguish.[99]

Regardless of the enemy's withering air strength, fierce opposition is what "Hap" Arnold expected all long. "The Luftwaffe," he said, "will have to scrape the bottom of the barrel, and they won't get much after that but splinters in their fingers. Our barrel, though we may have to dig deep in it, still has much left." The war of attrition proceeded at a staggering pace.[100]

Given the dire circumstances, Lt. Gen. Jimmy Doolittle often encouraged levity on his air bases. A Medal of Honor recipient and hero of the famed Tokyo Raid of April 1942, Doolittle was a master of fighter tactics and comprehensive air strategy. Appointed commander of the 8th Air Force in January 1944, his task of softening the German war machine was a daunting one. Nonetheless, Ernie Pyle loved Doolittle's contagious sense of humor and talents as a storyteller. "He is bold and completely fearless. Along with that he has a great technical mind and a highly perfected education in engineering," wrote Pyle.

"In addition to his professional skill he is one of the most engaging humans you ever ran across." The bald 5'6" general fiendishly reveled in spreading false rumors about himself. He claimed his old nickname was "Curly" and mockingly threw back his head as if brushing locks from his eyes. Doolittle jokingly claimed he was once six feet tall, but his constant anxiety prompted physical shrinkage. "He is the only man I've ever known who can tell stories all evening long and never tell one you've heard before," Pyle marveled. "He can tell them in any dialect, from Swedish to Chinese."

Above all else, Doolittle enjoyed poking fun at his own shortcomings. Following one particularly harsh mission, the general inspected a badly damaged Flying Fortress. Noticing the tail gun turret was shot away, Doolittle turned to the gunner and asked, "Were you in there when it happened?"

The gunner sheepishly replied, "Yes, sir."

As Doolittle turned away, the irked gunner bellowed to a comrade, "Where in the hell did he think I was, out buying a ham sandwich?"

A fearful officer hushed, "My God, man, don't you know who that was?"

"Sure, I know," the tail-gunner growled, "and I don't give a damn. That was a stupid question."

Doolittle overhead the rebuff but did not care. It *was* a stupid question. He often recounted the story with humorous humility. As Pyle knew all too well, "the heartbreaks and tragedies of war sometimes push all your gaiety down into the depths. But if a man can keep a sense of the ridiculous about himself, he is all right. Jimmy Doolittle can."

Another day at headquarters, Lt. Gen. Doolittle noticed a Capt. Doolittle on a roster. The surname was not a typical one and the general made a mental note to look up the officer. Several days later the general's phone rang, and the caller stated, "This is Captain Doolittle."

"Oh yes," replied the general. "I had noticed your name and I meant to call you up sometime."

"I'd like to come in and see you," the captain said.

"Why yes, do that," said the general. "I'm pretty busy these days, but I'll switch you to my aide and he'll make an appointment for you. Glad you called, captain. I'll look forward to seeing you."

"But Dad, this is me. Don't you recognize me? I've got a package for you from Mom," exclaimed junior, a B-26 pilot with the 9th Air Force.

The general screeched, "Well why in hell didn't you say so in the first place!" [101]

Few servicemen had opportunities to personally connect with family in such ways while overseas. Accordingly, airmen aspired to one ambition over any other: survive all their missions and earn one-way tickets stateside. The year prior, the flak-scarred B-17 *Memphis Belle* became one of the first bombers to complete a tour of duty. Thanks to the venerated William Wyler wartime documentary on the crew, the members of the famous bomber arose as war bond-selling celebrities. The Fortress's old crew chief, M/Sgt. Joseph Giambrone of Norristown, Pennsylvania, returned to his former English base on May 12 for the Technicolor premiere of the film. Giambrone "got a special cheer when a shot of him painting the 25th bomb on the ship's nose flashed on the screen." The airmen hoped to reach their own 25th missions someday. Until that moment, there were many more flights to chart and many more cities to bomb. [102]

CHAPTER 3

Scuttlebutt

"What the hell is *D-Day?*" The phrase was everywhere—in headlines, advertisements, and even on prayer cards. Despite the omnipresence of the ambiguous military jargon, few newspaper readers had comprehension of its formal meaning. Indeed, all were aware that the expression portended invasion, but what did that "D" represent? One inquisitive housewife columnist from Chicago sought a legitimate answer. Her husband did not have one. "I'd already asked everyone else I knew," she wrote. "I'd even decided maybe it was sort of a Bronx perversion as in 'Dis is de day.'" To her satisfaction, a fuller definition appeared shortly thereafter in *Time*. Likewise, the *Abilene Reporter* conveyed a similar explanation of invasion vocabulary:

> *The Army has designated the letter 'D' as a symbol for the unannounced day on which the invasion will begin officially. The symbol is taken from the first letter of the word 'day.' In addition, the exact hour on which the blow will be struck is known in the Army as 'H' hour. The symbol is taken from the first letter of the word 'hour.' Only a select few know the day and the hour. To the rest of the world, for the moment, it is only known that on 'H' hour of 'D' day the invasion will begin.* [103]

Readers remained unconvinced. Weeks later in Wichita, the local paper attempted to resolve the issue. "People have been trying to make 'D' stand for doom, destruction, and death. You may as well quit the guessing game, for D-Day and H-Hour have no significance." Yet, the periodical received so many inquiries about D-Day terminology that *Wichita Daily Times* staff writer Frank Collay penned a letter to the Secretary of War for official verification. Readers thereafter learned the phrases were first used during the Battle of Saint-Mihiel in 1918. Secretary

Henry Stimson further clarified, "These terms are used to designate the day and hour of the start of an operation when the day and hour have not yet been determined, or when secrecy is essential." Therefore, unquestionable military logic suggested D-Day merely meant "Day-Day." Many readers were undoubtedly disappointed by the lack of poetic creativity. [104]

Uncertainties regarding invasion lingo were no less apparent in Britain's innumerable military camps. A May 11 United Press brief from New York indicated, "Mrs. Arthur J. Bowler was shocked and not a little alarmed when a V-Mail letter arrived from her corporal husband in England, saying 'Your letter was the first time I ever heard the expression 'D-Day.'" [105]

The theme of D-Day permeated all realms of American life and was often applied to issues completely unrelated to operational scenarios. Citizens adopted the phrase when discussing stateside events both trivial and substantial. Maj. Carl Schwab of Atlanta visited public schools throughout May 1944 to discuss preventative measures against mosquito breeding. His educational program delivered to 2,000 elementary students was entitled "D-Day." Meanwhile, one Texas newspaper proclaimed, "It's D-Day in Your Garden. Don't let insects strafe your Victory Garden!" In northern Illinois, the opening of fishing season spelled "D-Day" for the survival of the black bass. One newspaperman offered grim prognostication for lackluster students at the end of their academic year. "To Junior, who hasn't had an A or B this semester, it's D-Day when teacher issues the report cards," he warned. On the evening of June 5, ladies of Bonham, Texas hosted a "D-Day Dance" for aviation students from nearby Jones Field. The date of the festive social was unwittingly timely. [106]

In a graduation sermon, one preacher incorporated a D-Day motif in his parting homily to pupils. The reverend declared there were many "D's" the graduates must practice in life. They had to dare, deny, and dream. "D-Day could mean Draft day for a lot of the graduates, he said. It is really Dismissal Day for the graduates so that they may face other D-Days of life which are sure to follow. The other D-Days pertain not only to the invasion of enemy countries but for successful invasions into business and professional life." In Maine, the *Daily Kennebec Journal* stimulated similar civic engagement on the second anniversary of the Women's Army Corps. "This is D-Day and H-Hour for women," it said.

"The terminology is military. . . . Literally, it refers to combat. For women, it refers to duty." Their reward would be measured intangibly through patriotic idealism and the gratitude of faithful brothers and husbands, the *Journal* assured. *D-Day* served as a symbolic rite of passage.[107]

According to newspapers, "personal" D-Days arrived in many forms. The moment came early for boy hero Clifford Wherley. On May 23, the youth from Elmwood, Illinois turned seventeen and became legally eligible to serve in the armed services. However, Wherley already possessed ample military experience. Bypassing the suspicions of recruiters, he had enlisted at age fourteen. In the ensuing years, the juvenile airman flew three missions with his childhood hero, Jimmy Doolittle. He participated in "air attacks on Palermo, Pantelleria, Tunis, Gabes, Sfax, Sardinia, and Kasserine Pass and is credited with shooting down one enemy plane, plus the probable destruction of fifteen others," reported the *Altoona Mirror*. His parents promised to maintain his secret, but the mother divulged his underage status after reading horrifying reports of air warfare. Wherley was immediately shipped home. On his seventeenth birthday, however, he reenlisted with the Air Corps Reserve and aspired to become an air cadet. In the eyes of the press, Wherley's tale was emblematic of a youthful generation whose personal D-Days would give rise to a bright future.[108]

Similarly poignant, Rabbi Israel Goldstein of Temple B'nai Jeshurun in New York City declared that teenagers receiving Jewish confirmation were "experiencing a spiritual D-Day in their young lives." The prospects of a postwar world were promising, he contended in his sermon published by the *New York Times*. Moral pleas in light of the Holocaust were urgently evocative. "The debacle of the international gangsters is at hand. Our own United States will come out of this war strong and free," he promised. However, could greater racial and religious security arise from the ashes? "Will the American people have the wisdom to recognize that anti-Semitism is a front for anti-democracy?" Not all of America's enemies were to be found exclusively overseas.[109]

Invariably, D-Day was also employed as a descriptive of calamitous happenings. According to Utah's *Ogden Standard Examiner* on April 25, "Heavy rains in five states of the Mississippi watershed resulted in thousands of acres of farmland to be inundated and forced many towns in the Mississippi flats to be evacuated." The disaster was referred to in several newspapers as "Mississippi D-Day." In illustrating events positive and negative, the phrase was utterly inescapable in the lexicon of wartime language. Its cultural prominence was supremely undeniable.[110]

Mixed signals and hearsay of invasion developments were simultaneously a source of agitation among readers. Susceptibility to enemy propaganda remained a considerable concern. War Information Director Elmer Davis petitioned citizens to remain vigilantly considerate of D-Day's perilous implications. He beseeched them to ignore Axis reports of Second Front operations and assured that invasion news would originate from London and *only* London. "I hope the American people remember that [Nazi propagandist] Joe Goebbels is in business for his own health—and not for theirs," the OWI chief announced in an interview. "When it's really in the works, you can be sure the Allied command in London will announce it shortly after it begins."[111]

Shockingly, word was announced in London earlier than Eisenhower anticipated. At a swank cocktail party at Claridge's Hotel, Maj. Gen. Henry Miller of the 9th Air Force avowed to a group of socialites, "On my honor the invasion will take place before June 15." The possibly intoxicated general was discreetly reported to higher powers. Ike was incensed and immediately demoted Miller to lieutenant colonel, shipping him stateside under a cloud of disgrace. "The Supreme command allowed this information to be cabled abroad today after holding it up several weeks for security reasons," reported the Associated Press on June 7. Miller graduated with Eisenhower from West Point in 1915 as a member of the esteemed "Class the Stars Fell On." Regardless, the supreme commander would not tolerate babblers who willingly jeopardized his men. Even breaches of minor scope had the potential to wreak unspeakable havoc. Eisenhower made a public example of Miller to serve as a warning against would-be tipsters.[112]

All the while, Secretary of War Stimson shared Elmer Davis's fears of widespread misinformation. As the *Lowell Sun* attested, the secretary issued a warning against false invasion reports originating from the German propaganda bureau. Such subterfuge could inflict emotional chaos on the home front and hamper the war effort. There was perhaps one saving grace: "If, as Secretary Stimson expects, the Germans attempt to build up a false invasion, the only people that may be duped by it will be those living in the Reich who have no means of exposing the material put out by the Goebbels mill of lies."[113]

Erroneous reports were bound to emerge from the overbearing tension. On June 3, a "false announcement of Allied landings in France turned the 48 states upside down" and "created a hoax rivaling Orson Welles's Martian invasion," commented *Stars and Stripes*. Millions tuned into the radio flash declaring, "Eisenhower's headquarters announced Allied landings in France." The report was quickly withdrawn. The bulletin was accidentally transmitted to the United States from the AP's London Bureau by a staffer practicing her teleprinting. The premature alarm "gave the U. S. two minutes to cheer, pray, and otherwise mark the long-awaited opening of the Second Front." Sirens precipitately announced the invasion as far away as Buenos Aires. Radio reports echoed as distant as Santiago and Moscow. Joan Ellis, the young lady responsible for the honest but dire mishap, fainted when recognizing the magnitude of her grievous error. The girl begged America for forgiveness. The *Mayfield Messenger* of Kentucky responded, "Tell the British girl who flashed the invasion Saturday that we all love her and that she scooped up the world." The *Portland Oregonian* simply stated, "To Joan Ellis, to err is human."[114]

The following day, Mollie Panter-Downes of the *New Yorker* wrote of London's boiling anticipation. "In the curious hush of the moment—a hush that is not merely figurative, since Londoners haven't been awakened by sirens for a month—it seems as though everyone is existing merely from one ordinary day to the next, waiting for the great, extraordinary one."[115]

Many Americans naturally expected Ernie Pyle to have the inside scoop on the invasion's proposed date. As he departed from Naples to London, GIs joked with him, "Well, that's the tip-off. When you leave for England, the invasion must be about ready." Pyle was flattered by such assumptions but assured them, "I don't know a bit more about the invasion than you do." The reporter rationalized that he merely awaited warmer English weather until he sojourned northward. "These old bones ain't what they used to be—they never were, as far as I can remember."

Notwithstanding the physical tolls of combat, the Italian campaigns pressed a heavy psychological weight on Pyle. He prayed there was purpose behind all the misery he witnessed. "There is little solace for those who have suffered, and none at all for those who have died," he argued. "If by having only a small army in Italy we have been able to build up more powerful forces in England, and if by sacrificing a few thousand lives here this winter, we can save half a million lives in Europe this summer." The lethal arithmetic tormented Pyle either way.[116]

Journalist Walter Lippman—a champion of free speech, a co-author of Woodrow Wilson's Fourteen Points, and originator of the word stereotype—noticed similar strain on American soldiers. GIs were weary of the blind adoration heaved upon them from a far-removed home front. They felt unworthy of distinction. The mood of the American public was, in Lippman's view, becoming "nervously sentimental and hero-worshipful." Civilians "palpitate with schemes for injecting noble thoughts of violent hatreds into the Army," he complained. Soldiers repelled the sentiments and met the contempt with apathy.

GIs were consumed with their own fears and obligations. Few appreciated the incessant badgering of civilians to launch the invasion. The "civilian can understand military morale if he will imagine how he would feel if suddenly someone tapped him on the shoulder and said: Come, my friend, you will now perform an operation for appendicitis." D-Day could not be hastily executed, and combatants prepared for the mission in their own ways. They were "no longer bewildered civilians filled with anxiety and stage-fright about a task they do not understand and to which they feel inadequate. They feel their own power." A civilian could never fully comprehend that undeniable truth.[117]

Correspondent John Moroso witnessed a different manner of preparation on the camouflaged shores of England as nurses, doctors, and medics scrambled in an immersive D-Day dress rehearsal. The teams ensured "the best possible care of our sick and wounded," he wrote. Generals, admirals, and lesser officers observed with binoculars as "jeeps carrying Red Cross flags rushed from inland places to the shore, where men sprang from foxholes to carry stretchers to waiting boats." He expressed pride in their work—even if it was only practice. To Moroso's surprise, though, antipathy toward anxious civilians was voiced here as well. "Military people, particularly the navy men," he said, "are a bit tired of folks back home—principally those in high places—who issue statements about when the war in Europe will end. Over here they feel that nobody knows and guessing among the politicians and military men in Washington stirs up grumbling among those who will have to fight the war to the end." The servicemen knew the enemy was weakened, but the invasion would still be "a pretty rough party." Their war was not an assortment of timetables but a desperate game of survival. [118]

Most invasion participants could do little more than wait and train. Even these elements posed lethal prospects. As reported on the front page of Oregon's *Eugene Guard* on March 22, "Twenty-nine American soldiers were killed and eight injured, at least one seriously, when explosives were set off accidentally in training activities somewhere in England." No other details of the tragedy were provided, and the incident was largely buried in American newspapers. Indications of military malpractice were generally veiled if not fully concealed by official censors. In the eyes of the War Department, little good could derive from such disclosure. [119]

Censorship of the March mishap paled in comparison to another calamity the following month. The AP reported on April 28, "Nazi invasion speculation hit a feverish tempo today as Berlin dispatches said that German bombers attacked masses of invasion vessels in undisclosed harbors of Western England last night and continental commentators began naming definite invasion dates." A "vast outpouring of speculation came from Nazi and neutral microphones, some contradictory and some nonsense." The report of an aerial attack on invasion ports and vessels originated from the Swedish newspaper *Piteå-Tidningen*, which had a correspondent in Berlin. A German communiqué also stated, "that Nazi motor torpedo boats attacked a destroyer-escorted British convoy on the English south coast this morning, torpedoing a destroyer and sinking three of the convoyed vessels." [120]

For once, the German broadcasts were not outright falsehoods. In fact, the truth was even worse. Exercise Tiger was an amphibious training operation located near a slice of the British coast known as Slapton Sands—an area chosen for its geographical similarities to Normandy's shores. Eisenhower insisted that live ammunition be used in the exercise to accustom GIs to combat conditions. A friendly fire fiasco ensued on April 27, with scores of soldiers mowed down by their own men. The following morning, problems were exacerbated when nine German E-boats slipped past British escorts and preyed upon unsuspecting LSTs. Pandemonium erupted. Two LSTs sunk within minutes after torpedoes ripped through their hulls. Two more were significantly damaged—one by friendly fire. Survivors screamed, "We're gonna die!" as they clung to debris in the bleak Channel waters.

A "series of mistakes and misunderstandings" was the root of the melee, an official investigation concluded. The findings were too little, too late for some 750 Allied personnel killed in the affray. Untold numbers of corpses washed ashore the bright beaches of Slapton Sands in the following weeks. A horrified Eisenhower immediately authorized a cover up. The dead were secretly buried in a cemetery outside London while the details of their fates were kept from their families for decades. More men perished while training for the Utah Beach landings than were actually killed on June 6. Nobody read of any of it in the headlines of 1944.

American admiral Don P. Moon held himself accountable for the disaster. "Moon really broke down," one of his officers admitted. The overworked admiral oversaw the subsequent Utah landings but suffered from acute depression. Two months after the invasion, Moon sat on his cabin sofa, placed a Colt pistol to his head, and pulled the trigger. The suicide note nearby read, "My mind is gone. . . . I am sick, *so* sick." Surprisingly, Moon's tragic end ran unfiltered in the papers. As was reported in *Colorado's Greeley Daily Tribune*, "Moon had taken his own life as a result of combat fatigue." He was the final victim of Slapton Sands. [121]

As officers discovered, the war was a momentous process of trial and error. Naval commander Beverly M. Coleman, a former Washington lawyer, served as a control officer for amphibious forces. On D-Day, he planned to stand offshore in a small warship and direct waves of landing barges toward the beach. "We learn a little more in every operation and expect to go on learning," he told a reporter. "This is a new way to fight a war, and there are some things we have to pick up as we go along. One thing is certain, though. We know every invasion will have its own problems, a few hard nuts to crack." His mind constantly speculated about invasion day, its terrain, and the passengers he would shepherd to the shoreline. Above all else, Coleman was concerned about the weather. [122]

Lt. Jim Gray was thoroughly disgusted. Catching flak was one challenge, but English flight conditions were another. "I'd just like to fly in a little Texas weather for a change," the airman griped to Ernie Pyle.

"It's dark and cloudy and rainy most of the time, and it changes like lightning," the reporter concurred. The pilots "said that sometimes they would start to take off and the other end of the runway would close in before they got there. How those mighty air fleets ever operated at all is a modern miracle." The *New York Times* agreed, noting, "Weather has been one of the great handicaps with which Allied fliers have had to contend." Their missions continued but many of them dropped bombs blindly into soupy clouds below. [123]

All seemed discomforting and dreary. Thick fog and brisk bouts of rain, mixed with high oceanic winds, doused infantrymen maneuvering along the British coast. As one sergeant in the Big Red One grumbled, "If hell is any worse than this, I don't want to go there." Lt. Roy Lee Jones, a stout athlete from West Texas State, complained that England had only two seasons—bad and worse. Sgt. J. W. Collins offered an equally blunt assessment: "Annual Weather Report—Spring came to London on a Sunday this year—and left the same day." [124]

Mother Nature is an unsung combatant of war. Regardless of the conflict, memories of weather and temperature are often the most vivid among campaign-tested veterans, even decades after the fact. While foggy weather at Dunkirk spared thousands of Allied troops in 1940, poor weather typically deterred offensives—and atmospheric conditions could yield misery and hardship. Initial Allied landings in North Africa were hampered by taxing waves. In Sicily, strong currents shuffled landing craft far off course. A 33-knot wind churned the waters, instigating widespread seasickness in the ranks. In the opinion of writer John Ross, "The weather could be an enemy more potent than any defense the Germans might mount." Accordingly, some 500 weather stations dotted the British Isles to gauge meteorological developments. [125]

Spring weather swayed a seesaw of uncertainty. An April drought in southern England prompted restrictions on water and dairy products. The Associated Press soon after headlined, "Weather Ideal for Invasion in Western Europe." Lack of rain meant less mud, more airfields, and fewer French rivers to ford. "The big allied worry is that bad weather may break on D-Day." Strong winds would generate monstrous waves in the Channel and debilitate paratrooper and glider incursions. "A storm is certain to cost the lives of thousands of soldiers trying to land on the beaches. One day of bad weather would more than offset months of good weather, if it came at the wrong time." A particularly apprehensive meteorologist noted, "Any army would be damned unlucky if it got bogged down after mid-May."[126]

By that time, the worst fears of Allied planners materialized. The *Somerset Daily American* reported on May 18, "Bad weather and the massing of allied bombers for renewed blows spared Europe its usual avalanche of bombs for the fourth straight day today." Torrents of rain and formations of low-hanging clouds likewise grounded Nazi defenders. "For those wondering about the dangers of such a weather lull coinciding with D-Day, it is safe to predict that only the worst weather will be allowed to interfere with air operations during the invasion." The grounding of Allied planes would not necessarily preclude amphibious landings, but it was a contingency plan few invasion architects wished to pursue.[127]

Weather was arguably the most critical component of the invasion, opined Frederick Graham of the *New York Times*. "The most brilliantly conceived and thoughtfully worked out plans may fail utterly if the weather conditions on D-Day, and several days thereafter, should prove unfavorable," Graham reported from foggy London. However, not all news was cause for despair. The "Allies are in better position to anticipate the weather and make more reasonably accurate forecasts than the Germans, because weather travels from west to east." The Allies operated stronger weather data machines, he assured. Mack Mackenzie presented more prudent optimism. "While the zero hour can't be guaranteed weeks in advance," he wrote, "what can be fairly well guaranteed is that things will follow a certain course after the zero hour has been reached." Ike possessed mountains of military intelligence but not even a four-star general could dictate weather.[128]

An army of meteorologists compiled data for months in advance. According to reporter Bascom Timmons, long range forecasts were created for a slew of hypothetical D-Days. "This reconnaissance," Timmons observed, "carried on jointly by the American and British weather centers, operated far out into the Atlantic some 900 miles, two and three times daily." But under what conditions would the invasion occur? One accurate prognostication appeared in the *Brownsville Herald* on May 25. The columnist declared, "The weather will be freakish on D-Day, cool and wet." The predictor was a sombrero-sporting cartoon character simply named "Don Pedro."[129]

In early April, Eisenhower chose the stately Southwick House near Portsmouth as his advanced headquarters. The mansion was populated with a herd of logisticians and typists. A gigantic map of France adorned a tall parlor wall. The space became mission control for invasion. Here, Ike's meteorologists informed him of the small window of opportunity to trigger the assaults. Only the spans of June 5-7 and June 19-21 combined the optimal conditions for low tides, moonlight, and dawn. Delays beyond those dates may have prolonged the invasion until 1945—an alternative deemed madly inconceivable. The guessing games ensued, and Ike religiously referred to a team of meteorologists including Group Capt. James Martin Stagg, a Scottish geophysicist and Polar explorer-turned-weatherman. His work later prompted the *Washington Post* to call his D-Day projection the most important weather forecast in history. Until that forecast, Ike chain smoked and secretly agonized. As he later recalled, the "consequences that would ensue were almost too terrifying to contemplate." [130]

Planners scrutinized North American weather to predict future Channel conditions, but challenges persisted. As *New York Times* scientific columnist Waldemar Kaempffert recognized, "In a fog the Channel is usually smooth and ideal for an easy crossing. But what of the planes above that must see and protect landing parties and parachuters who bail inland? What is wanted is a combination of reasonably smooth water and good visibility." Eisenhower hardly had either. One meteorologist later disclosed to the press that if the June 6 plan had not been carried out as executed, the "initial heavy landings would have been caught in a gale and almost certainly would have faced destruction." Eisenhower's scientists bristled at the prospect. [131]

Beyond weather woes, restlessness infused overcrowded England. Severe cuts in railroad passenger service left thousands stranded throughout the country. Travel timetables were placed on "a virtual day-to-day basis," with troop and supply trains receiving top priority. As many as fifty trains were cancelled at some stops without prior warning. "We are in the hands of the authorities," explained officials at one London station. The overlapping appearance of German air scouts over Britain "added to the sense of invasion immanency." British hatred of the Nazis intensified further when learning of forty-seven RAF officers executed during the so-called Great Escape from Stalag Luft III in Poland. *The*

Daily Dispatch referred to the incident as "mass murder" and called on Parliament to initiate inquests.

Nazi radio estimated as many as 3.5 million troops were poised in southern England for "a thrust against the continent." The German newspaper *Berliner Börsen-Zeitung* freely acknowledged Allied strength but rebutted with mention of Germany's swift armored forces on standby. "The Allies hardly will be able to out-tank us immediately after the landing," the paper boasted. To offset such narratives, American field commanders were issued twenty-four-page booklets "urging their full cooperation with war correspondents in sending an accurate report of the fighting speedily back home to counteract Nazi propaganda."[132]

An atmosphere of "tense expectancy pervaded bustling London" as the "great all-out battle in Europe" approached. However, as Howard Kingsbury Smith of the International News Service observed, "The attitude of the British people is one of calm, serious, restraint. They are fully conscious that one of the most epochal chapters in the history of the universe is about to be written in blood."

Known as one of "Edward Murrow's Boys," Smith belonged to a tight clique of CBS journalists. Years earlier, he interviewed Hitler and high-ranking members of the Third Reich. Smith's eloquent 1942 book, *Last Train from Berlin*, offered harrowing accounts of Nazi oppression. He coincidentally received his visa to depart Germany on December 7, 1941. Smith embraced the opportunity to return to Europe and witness Germany's capitulation. "The most impressive thing," he wrote in May 1944, "is the tremendous hum of great aerial armadas bound day and night for the continent to soften up Hitler's European fortress. Listening to the steady, awesome roar of thousands of American and British planes, one realizes they are sounding the death knell of Nazi Germany."[133]

While countless Englanders tackled pre-invasion measures in stride, others keenly worried for their adopted American sons. On June 3, British-born Barbara Wace of the Associated Press offered compelling portraits of matronly Britons bidding farewell to their symbolic offspring. "In the little towns of Britain where American troops are waiting for D-Day," she remarked, "some GIs have found something a lot more like home than Nissen huts and canvas tents." When H-Hour arrived many an English housekeeper would be anxious about "her" American boy.

Mrs. Hughes, the short but lively wife of a linotype operator, wailed, "My Jack's such a help—I don't know what I'd do without him."

A white-haired Mrs. Facey, also a British hostess, added, "My Fred doesn't help—but goodness, it's nice to have a boy around the house again. Nobody could be nicer than my Fred." The war already claimed Facey's true son.

English families were initially apprehensive of the friendly invaders. "To tell you the truth, we were terrified," admitted Hughes. "The idea of a strange man arriving to live in the house—and you hear such stories. And they didn't give you any chance to say no." The hosts quickly overcame their early misgivings.

Hughes's neighbor, the eighty-seven-year-old Mrs. Hancock, felt reinvigorated by the presence of American soldiers, offering her renewed purpose in life. Pvt. Jerry La Guardia of the Bronx essentially found himself a caretaker in the Hancock household. He did not mind, often reading to the elderly woman who graciously welcomed him into her home. "She used to say she couldn't think why she wasn't allowed to die," Hughes remarked of Hancock. "She was no use to the war. But when she got Jerry, she felt quite different. It's made all the difference to her."

Mrs. Facey chuckled, "I'll miss Fred too—and poor old Dick. That's his twin brother. When he gets locked out of his billet for being late, he comes around here, and I never know if I'll find one or two in the morning when I take in their tea."

For each Yankee guest, British home owners received fourteen cents per room, seven cents for heat, and two cents for hot water. Service members were fed at their own messes, but many sought the delights of the English kitchen instead. The arrangement "took a bit of getting used to," claimed one husband. "The British man's home is his castle, you know, and we're used to privacy. But you just can't help liking these boys—I'll certainly miss my four when they go. We had four more before, and they were shifted, but they often come back when they've a day off." The housing arrangement was "the best thing in the army," affirmed Sgt. Wilton L. Willis of Cairo, Georgia. The accommodations offered a true touch of home. [134]

The comfort found in English dwellings did not suggest the Yanks were always at ease. Liberation fever resounded throughout Europe. According to Tom Wolf, the potency of "Factual Propaganda" fostered

"German Jitters." The chief challenge remaining for journalists was the ability to convey updates "to news-hungry citizens" of occupied nations. In Wolf's opinion, the Allies were "exceedingly obliging on this score." In addition to monthly magazines dropped into Europe, four-page specials chronicled Russian successes and the annihilation of the Luftwaffe. The implication: "Your day of liberation is coming." Angst intensified as the Allies simultaneously approached Rome that spring. DeWitt Mackenzie assuaged readers by noting, "You can't just set D-Day like an alarm clock." One week prior to the invasion, Mack added, "We have no cause to fret—as a lot of good folks are doing—for Allied luck is running strong. Let Der Fuehrer do the stewing."[135]

Joseph Stalin also intensely waited on the invasion sidelines as Russian war fatalities neared twenty million. The opening of the Second Front would be a source of immense relief upon the beleaguered peoples of the Soviet Union. Gayle Talbot reported that March, "London disclosed that Russian navy and army officers witnessed and participated in recent American pre-invasion exercises somewhere on the English coast. The Allies have long desired that the Soviets gain a better appreciation of the difficulties attached to amphibious operations." Soviet observers in communication with Stalin watched with great interest and impatient concern as the long-awaited mobilization uncoiled. If the grand strategy unfolded as planned, Allied commitments in France would inexorably disrupt the operations of the Wehrmacht and alleviate pressure on the bloodbath of the Eastern Front. Stalin resolutely believed that applying political pressure on the West would induce the drive across the Channel.[136]

But where? *New York Times* correspondent Hanson Baldwin further pondered potential invasion sites. The Nazis were defending nearly 4,000 miles of coast from the North Cape to the Pyrenees. Would landings take place in Denmark, the Netherlands, Belgium, or perhaps France itself? Each region boasted advantages and disadvantages, but none would be easy. "No one can tell until D-Day where the blow will fall," wrote Baldwin. Until the strike was evident, the Germans had few options but to man coastal positions stretching from Norway to the Spanish frontier. Russia did not care where the invasion would occur, but when.[137]

In a hearty statement sent to President Roosevelt and subsequently released to the press, Stalin declared, "I am strongly convinced that the

time is near when the successful struggle of the armed forces of the Soviet Union, together with the armies of the United States and Great
Britain on the basis of the agreements reached at Moscow and Teheran,
will lead to the final defeat of our common enemy, Hitlerite Germany."
It was at the conference of the Big Three in Iran six months prior to D-
Day that the nations "agreed on the timing and scope of the Anglo-
American blow at Germany's western flanks." As one American writer
observed, "The impression here is that the Russians are counting on
final victory in Europe this year." Stalin's Minister of Foreign Affairs,
Vyacheslav Molotov, echoed the sentiments of his Communist chieftain.
"[N]ow the time has come when the armed forces of the Allies are preparing for decisive joint operations against our common enemy." He
dramatically underscored, "[T]he enemy soon will feel the strength of
the joint blows." Invasion promised to even the balance.[138]

Many politically-inclined Americans retained a pre-existing skepti-
cism of the Reds. Few cared to have the Russians dictate where, when,
or how American troops should invade Europe. Republican congress-
woman Jessie Sumner of Illinois voiced her apprehension on the floor
of the House of Representatives. She demanded the opening of the
Western Front be delayed "until assurances are given that Russia will
renounce all claims to absorbed lands and U. S. military authorities
agree that the invasion is necessary and feasible." She considered full
concentration on the Pacific and the possibility of consolidating operations under Gen. Douglas MacArthur. Russians shuddered at the
thought.[139]

Sumner's assessments were emblematic of broader domestic views.
Grayson Jordan of Gillespie County, Texas plainly wrote his local newspaper, "You see, very frankly, I distrust the Russians. I don't like their
government and I don't like their revolutionary ideas. Before I go any
further, I must say this. I do admire their spirit and their heroic stand
against the Nazi war machine. But because they fight well in defense
of their own soil is no reason to believe that they are angels." While the
Russians were on "our side of the fence," that by no means dictated that
America "should bow to their every wish and fall in love with them.
When you aid a maiden in distress you do not necessarily fall for her."
Grayson mistrusted Russia's intentions and despised its conquering at-
titude. Concentrate on Japan, he argued.[140]

Grayson's hopes never developed, although his wariness of Russia likely deepened. Debate over aborting invasion plans subsided as mountains of men and materiel further accumulated in Britain. In America, invasion talk was "on all U. S. lips," reported C. V. R. Thompson of the *London Daily Express.* Frequently writing with humor, Thompson previously wrote *I Lost My English Accent,* a comedic account of his adventures in 1930s America. The Brit applied a similar liveliness in describing invasion vigilance. "Somewhere in that vast slab of building known as New York's Radio City," he wrote, "a man sits day and night beside a button. One touch on that button and all kinds of things will happen. Comedian Bob Hope will be cut off in the midst of a thousand-dollar wisecrack, crooner Frank Sinatra will be stopped in the midst of a two-thousand-dollar blue note, or Senator Whooziz will be interrupted in the midst of a fine piece of election oratory." For just a moment, America's premier radio station would go silent. An excited voice, "trying desperately to be calm," would then say something akin to this: "It has just been announced that American and British troops have landed on Fortress Europe."

At face value, Americans awaited the moment "with unruffled calm." But it was a deceptive calm, Thompson presumed. It "is not really calm at all. I think every American realizes that with the flick of that button the war is suddenly going to be brought much closer than 3,000 miles, much closer than it was even when the Japanese attacked Pearl Harbor." Thompson was right. Since America's entry into the war, the size of the Army alone sprouted from 1.6 million to nearly eight million members. Many of the enlistees and draftees would soon find themselves in the hedgerows of France. "Americans at home are thinking that for many of them the war is about to begin, and they are ready." [141]

Celebrated Australian writer and London's *Daily Express* war correspondent Alan Moorehead was a seasoned veteran of the North African Campaign and later authored a thoroughly scrutinizing biography of Bernard Montgomery. Moorehead detected an ongoing strain of anxiousness in the ranks. "Everybody felt it," he noted. "Over all the camp, over a hundred other such camps, over all the Army at that moment there was this same dead weight, this same oppressive feeling that the delay might continue indefinitely, growing more and more unbearable as the days went by. The invasion was already like an over-rehearsed play." [142]

In blunter, private terms, Pyle irritably diagnosed his own case of cabin fever: "If I hear another fucking GI say 'fucking' once more, I'll cut my fucking throat." [143]

The Allies sat indolent, temporarily restraining their own might, contended DeWitt Mackenzie. The men were in their prime and restlessly ready to trounce. The array of battle was "so well set that they could strike at will," he contended. "There's an atmosphere of vast power held in leash, pending the arrival of that mysterious moment which the favored few of the Allied high command have chosen." The secret was perhaps the greatest in history. [144]

For the corps of reporters, invasion puzzlement failed to dampen the energy. The spirited Robert Capa, the Hungarian-born photographer for *Life* magazine, once said, "For a war correspondent to miss an invasion is like refusing a date with Lana Turner after completing a five-year stretch in Sing Sing." One would be mad to miss the opportunity. [145]

CHAPTER 4

"Invasionitis"

An army of shadows prepared its retribution. Its prowess was not measured by training or weaponry but willpower, the agility to deceive and survive. In occupied France, stalwart members of the resistance amassed intelligence and materiel for the long-awaited day of salvation. For four insecure years the cobblestone streets of Paris and docks of Cherbourg echoed with the ominous click of the jackboots. The people, one vivacious and inviting, were subjected to endless intimidation and internment by Hitler's sinister legions. The Vichy puppet government betrayed its citizens in the name of expediency and a toxic thirst for power. Pre-existing currents of class warfare and political upheaval accentuated the divisions and violent score settling. The citizenry became "magnificent pawns" in the hands of authoritarian despots. [146]

But not all were helpless. Middle-aged art historian Agnés Humbert was determined to fight. Her ideals were as colorfully impassioned as the artistry imparted to her by mentor Maurice Denis. She grew incensed by the contempt Nazi occupiers exhibited to French hostages; their arrogant smiles gleamed as brightly as their spotless boots and buckles. When she saw them absconding with fine Parisian cloth and shoes for shipment to Germany, she declared, "We simply have to stop them." [147]

From this deeply-rooted resentment, the resistance was born. For those dangerously involved in the underground, D-Day would serve as the ultimate vindication of their sufferings. French playwright, novelist, and resistance advocate Claude Aveline wrote of his anticipation for invasion nine months before it occurred. The "sea is gradually preparing for the storm," he said. "It must succeed! There must be no quarter for those who have none! No piece of rotten wood must remain afloat, no buoys, no wreck! France must be relentless! Only then will her resurrection not only lead her to victory but also establish her in peacetime."[148]

Americans were galvanized by the level of fortitude. The *New York Times* heaped endless praise on the courageous exploits of the freedom fighters. "How does it feel to be a French patriot in France?" the paper posed that April. "What must be his thoughts, his longings, his expectations as he sees the invasion storm-cloud looming in the west? The world can make a close guess. The world is not ignorant of what goes on inside France." In that dangerous universe, the Atlantic Wall was no wall against truth. The resistance fighter endured the perils of the Gestapo, traitorous neighbors, suspicious friends, and covert actions in the name of preserving truth. He was a "soldier in an army without uniforms and poorly armed," added the *Times*. Yet the sheer determination of those without guns was a weapon of searing power. "Such thoughts must be in his mind on the eve of D-Day." The burden of waiting would soon cease.[149]

Journalists such as A. J. Liebling of the *New Yorker* made similarly impassioned testimonials of the underground's daring feats. The resistance published insurgent periodicals with a readership of at least 50,000. The first papers appeared as early as autumn of 1940. The readers faced imprisonment or death if apprehended by the occupiers. A lover of all things Parisian, Liebling was immeasurably pained to learn of France's tribulations under fascist rule. He felt morally compelled to assist the resistance in any way conceivable. In turn, he sought to interview any resister, refugee, or immigrant willing to tell their tale. The people would not—*could not*—be silenced. Sharing such anecdotes in his subversive newspaper, *Combat*, Albert Camus hoped "to inspire a new truth and a new France."[150]

While French writers were prolific during occupation, many of their manifestos often failed to appear in U. S. headlines. Secrecy and communication obstacles frequently obliged stateside newspapers to depict French allies as faceless friends in the dark. Analysis was left to expatriates and Allied correspondents previously stationed in France. The vague illusions generated a mysterious aura enveloping the resistance. The deeds of the underground were all too often left to the imagination of Hollywood and radio. Naturally, the Nazi rulers disseminated less flattering hype of the guerillas.

Via a broadcast to Europe's conquered, Robert Sherwood of the OWI predicted an end to the enemy's disinformation. "In this great historic year of 1944, the Allied radio will bring you tremendous news," he announced. "And the day is not far distant when your own radio stations will be free to tell you the truth instead of the tremendous lies of the Nazi collaborationists and quislings." BBC announcements piercing the airwaves over bootleg radios kindled tremendous excitement among the oppressed. Despite Nazi-imposed limitations, Europeans devised creative means of camouflaging radios in tin cans, buckets, cupboards, ovens, beds, and barns. Through news reports, codes, and discreet messages, the radio was a catalyst of French empowerment. [151]

Romanticized portrayals of the resistance in the films *Casablanca*, *The Cross of Lorraine*, and *Uncertain Glory* spurred passionate sympathy for the French but commonly failed to exhibit complex political and social dynamics. Additionally, the Free French relationship with the United States proved problematic given that America openly recognized and negotiated with the Vichy government in North Africa and elsewhere. Freedom fighters thought these acts a betrayal of the national liberation effort. [152]

Challenges persisted with vigorous debates over France's political destiny. Wes Gallagher, the future president of the AP, was well-versed on the fraught tensions between Britain, Free France, and the United States. Constantly stressing objectivity in reporting, he later said, "We are not a vehicle to serve the 'national interest' as defined by politicians, but to publish the truth as we see it." In a straightforward report, Gallagher commented, "Only Washington approval of a proposal submitted by Gen. Charles de Gaulle for governing occupied parts of France was lacking today in the framework of political organization for the invasion of Western Europe. Plans have been approved for military government in the Netherlands, Norway, and Belgium." The proposal was purportedly sanctioned by Eisenhower but awaited Roosevelt's final authorization." [153]

Diplomatic delays revealed underlying contentions behind closed doors. Roosevelt feared de Gaulle possessed dictatorial aspirations and was hesitant to recognize him as the head of a provisional government. Concerned with the endangerment of French autonomy after liberation, de Gaulle flouted Allied leadership while corralling the rival factions of his nation. When de Gaulle met with Eisenhower, Ike produced a pre-view copy of the latter's planned address to French citizenry on D-Day. The proclamation made no mention of the provisional government and ordered the resistance to follow Allied commands until a new political framework could be established. Ike and de Gaulle maintained a cordial association but held reservations about each other's motives. [154]

An impression of heightened political peril hung over the Allied part-nership as the diplomatic crisis failed to improve that spring. "Now, as the invasion hour approaches," wrote *The Times* of London on June 3, "the need for a solid agreement on civil administration becomes daily more urgent." New York's *Herald Tribune* offered a more candid assess-ment and blamed FDR's "offended pride and mere prejudice" toward de Gaulle. [155]

The press espoused the narrative of inner distrust. While Eisenhower conveyed his misgivings of the French to George Marshall, the presi-dent privately countered, "I still think Eisenhower does not quite get the point. He evidently believes the fool newspaper stories that I am anti-de Gaulle, even the kind of story that I hate him, etc. All this, of course, is utter nonsense. I am perfectly willing to have de Gaulle made President or Emperor or King or anything else so long as the action comes in an untrammeled and unforced way from the French people themselves." Regardless of private admissions of openness, the Franco-American alliance seemed stonewalled. [156]

At the grassroots level, a "heterogeneous group of civil affairs special-ists" with G-5 prepared to roll out the red tape for reestablishing trust-worthy government in France. Gene Currivan of the *New York Times* wrote, "The broad plan is to remove all office-holders who are confirmed Nazis, but to retain where possible those in civil service who are invol-untary members of the Nazi party and will cooperate with the new mil-itary government." In the meantime, the officers educated themselves in French politics and polished their language skills. [157]

Like civil affairs facilitators, correspondents served compelling roles in bridging gaps and reestablishing lines of communication. DeWitt Mackenzie was one who commiserated with the Free French and openly despised Vichy leader Pierre Laval—whose fascist tendencies placed him in front of a firing squad the following year. Laval's violent militia known as La Milice française garnered widespread disdain by embracing Gestapo tactics in abducting dissidents and Jews bound for exploitation and extermination. Mackenzie remarked of the collaborator, "Laval isn't a nice person. The first time I looked him in the eye I immediately decided that if I ever got in a poker game with him, I should tote a gun. However, he's crafty and he's smart. When he forecasts civil war in France, he isn't thumping an empty tub."

Laval's association with the Nazis was an unforgivable offense. Mackenzie rightfully predicted the quisling was fearful of invasion. This trepidation was made evident via a broadcast intercepted by America's Blue Network. Laval supposedly announced, "Massed formations of Anglo-American parachutists will be dropped over France. They will seek the cooperation of French partisans, and civil war will break out in France. For months I have worried about the possibility of a landing." And for good reason, Mackenzie jabbed.[158]

International News Service reporter Ralph B. Jordan, also known as "RBJ" or "Jock," was a buoyant journalist and former publicist for Metro-Goldwyn-Mayer. He rubbed shoulders with the most iconic screen legends of the age. Jordan was paid well and comfortably supported his family, but the money did not buy him fulfillment. Weary of the Louella Parsons brand of tabloid journalism, Jock sought eventual reprieve from movie-making spin control. Studio PR offices scrupulously regulated their labels and shielded their stars. Jordan grew jaded by the self-indulging system. As his biographer noted, "RBJ preferred uncovering the real thing, rather than manufacturing something to be fed to the Hollywood press corps. The advent of World War II gave him the opportunity to return to his first love [of reporting] with a vengeance."[159]

"Jock" deftly utilized his investigative skills and keen observation while reporting the enigmatic movements of the resistance. He wrote on May 17, "As the Allied invasion of the continent looms in Europe, a fairly clear picture of the important assistance expected from the French underground has been pieced together from Fighting French sources in New York and discloses that a nightmare of sabotage and even battle has been prepared for the Germans on D-Day and thereafter." The curtain was soon to rise. The INS zealously protected its confidential sources associated with the movement. According to those informants, the onslaught against occupying forces would unleash in phases: Strikes were to commence on transportation facilities. All forms of public utilities and travel were expected to grind to a halt. The para-lyzing of buses, trolleys, and power plants would wreak chaos behind the lines. Railroad sabotage—already underway—would intensify. Ration supplies would be set ablaze under cover of darkness to pull German provisions from other fronts. The same could be surmised of man-power needed to replace French strikers. Some five million members of French labor unions were to cease their work at H-Hour.

Finally, there was the Maquis. The subversive army of outlaws, "composed of thousands of young Frenchmen who have been hiding and training and working in the mountainous and wooded regions of France, will spring into action with more sabotage and battle," wrote RBJ. "They will cut the railroads and highways in their areas during the invasion and fight whenever the odds are not too great. But their greatest value will be as guerillas picking off small groups of the enemy and being as much a nuisance as possible."

"Maquis" was a phrase said to be of Corsican origin that described "the thick undergrowth typical of large parts of the island." Partisan units frequently operated within the deep recesses of French woodlands and mountains, forming into nimble squads of ten to twenty. "They are of all classes and political parties and are required to promise absolute obedience to their leaders." The outfits were often supported by the Jed-burghs—specially trained operatives of America's Office of Strategic Services (OSS) and Britain's Special Operations Executive (SOE), which supplied and coordinated mass acts of sabotage. The SOE dropped some 10,000 tons of supplies into occupied France prior to the invasion.

Allegiance to the Maquis promised constant peril. "About 75,000 Maquis have been killed or executed as a result of their past fights," Jordan concluded. "Their numbers are presently estimated at 200,000, but they are poorly equipped and only partly trained, as they work most of their days helping farmers near their hideouts and only drill and go into action occasionally." The home guardsmen demonstrated unyielding spirit and an undying eagerness to rid the fascists from their soil. Jock's report served as a stirring substantiation of the underground to American readers. The *San Antonio Light* assured subscribers that the Maquis "Await D-Day Too." Their wait was four years in the making. [160]

Bitter resentments intensified within those four strenuous years. "People who are hungry know how to hate and kill," rationalized UP staffer John Parris, who maintained confidential contacts in Belgium, France, and Norway. Parris followed the exploits of "the silent armies of the blackened-out countries" with heightening anticipation. He savored the potential of the war's "crowning story." Parris's communication with the resistance might as well "have been lifted from a Hollywood movie scenario," mused the United Press. At 2 a.m. one morning, Parris's London telephone unexpectedly rattled. A deep voice on the line uttered, "It's a seven-pound boy." The code phrase alerted Parris to the arrival of a secret message from Belgium. Devising foxy techniques of intelligence gathering allowed him to compile hidden tales originating from "dark, hidden places of the European fortress." The Belgian memorandum indicated that "special execution squads" were "waiting to strike down German officers and traitors." The air was electric with the irresistibly dangerous desire to resist.

A separate communiqué from a guerilla leader exclaimed, "Tell your American newspaper friends that we are ready. France will live again, but it will be a new France. . . . Children will dance on the streets." Parris predicted the invading Allies would "be met with cooperative revolutions wherever they land." Allied psychologists, writers, and foreign language experts printed 125 million leaflets to be dropped into France—all of them offering warnings, safety suggestions, and political appeals. In the interim, underground leaders impatiently awaited D-Day to exact vengeance. [161]

The Associated Press wrote on May 24, the "Allies adopted a firm military approach" in summoning French patriots for the dawn of liberation. The government-controlled BBC informed the underground of its quickly-approaching missions. "It is no longer a question of voluntary service. It now is an order to you," the broadcast demanded. "You are to keep out of German hands and hold yourselves in readiness for the day of action. That is the duty of every Frenchman." That same day, invasion echoes literally reverberated through the Strait of Dover as British guns thundered away at a German convoy attempting to chug through the Channel. Nazi artillery on the French Coast answered in kind with sporadic firing from Calais, Cap Griz Nez, and Boulogne. For the next half hour, British salvos illuminated the coastline.

An intriguing Paris broadcast by Vichy essayist Robert de Beauplan offered context of the national mood. The pundit declared American and

British bombing had mauled France's railroads while sabotage debilitated the country's hydroelectric systems. Furthermore, "the temper of the population, especially that of Paris, is rising. . . . Frenchmen are blaming the Germans for all this misery." Allied analysts pondered how and why such a message was broadcast. Was the statement yet another ploy to lure the invaders into false serenity? The eyes and ears of the French resistance were all the more important during this vital stage. "Let nothing escape you," Eisenhower informed the underground. "Pool your knowledge. Take the utmost care not to give information to anyone but known patriots. Be patient, above all, and hide your actions until the word is given."[162]

The patriots impeccably succeeded. An October 1943 issue of *Life* magazine remarked, "Practically all the Allied war plans for the invasion of Europe are based on information about the conquered territories supplied by underground intelligence systems. Most of the information would never have reached London if the exiled governments were not there." For instance, a painter from Caen bicycled down the French coast and rendered images resulting in a fifty-five-foot map of fixed German positions. Desperation stimulated unparalleled creativity in the ranks of the Maquis. Allied access to accurate intelligence was imperative—even if that information was brought to pass with a paintbrush. Elsewhere, intelligence gatherers collected vintage seaside postcards to gain even the slightest insights of French coastal topography.[163]

As the former United Press bureau manager in Paris, Ralph Heinzen shared his intimate perspectives of the French mentality. Heinzen was arrested by the Vichy the same day U. S. forces landed in French North Africa. Like reporter Taylor Henry, he was interned by the Germans and eventually repatriated to America via a diplomatic exchange. Less than twenty-four hours before the Normandy invasion, he wrote, "The French underground is a hard reality, a clandestine force which has been biting at the German back for four years. Its present mobilized strength is 320,000 well-armed militants and a million or more reservists at the disposal of the Allied high command."

Heinzen recalled the dreary days of 1941 before the United States entered the fray. "I saw the underground in its first offensive—the slaying of German soldiers and officers on the blacked-out streets of occupied Paris." The resistance was born "as a guerilla force whose chief role was to take a steady toll of German lives in revenge. Its first killing was the midnight stabbing of a German soldier in the darkened exit of the Porte Dauphine subway station. Today it is virtually a corps of sabotage engineers," Heinzen approved. "Some fought the German, Italian, and Spanish fascists in Spain six years ago. The underground is a political melting pot but its whole policy is pure nationalism."

On D-Day the underground was expected to materially diminish all German operations. "Its role will be to cut communication, dynamite bridges and viaducts, open dams, destroy power lines and railroads, ambush the enemy, report his concentrations and movements, and spy on his secret preparations. Its execution squads will corner and kill a long list of blacklisted traitors to France." The teams of assassins were composed of disaffected army officers but also "patriots from all walks of life, all creeds, and all political beliefs, whose only crime was to hate Germany." For this crime, countless scores were added to the Gestapo's directories of death. Thousands more renounced the Hitler-Laval pact by averting forced labor and military conscription. Laval previously planned to remit 260,000 conscripts out of the 400,000 Frenchmen who came of age each year. The populace had contrary aims.

Heinzen recognized five primary pockets of resistance throughout France: Paris, Lyons, Toulouse, Grenoble, and Valenciennes. In an alpine refuge along the French border of Italy, the underground staved off numerous attacks by the Milice and Germans. The Frenchmen raided isolated farms and villages while also receiving sustenance from British transport planes. Nightly coded broadcasts kept the underground appraised of the flight schedules.

At the end of 1943, Laval published a summary of terrorist activities that served as an "unexpected tribute" to the effectiveness of the uprisings. The menu of conspiracies included 9,000 bombings between October and December; 900 assassinations of generals, priests, and attorneys; 640 incidents of railroad sabotage; and 4,400 acts of arson targeted at French harvests. Other incendiary feats included 65,000 gallons of gasoline blown up, the incineration of train stations, the obliteration of iron works, the stealing of armored cars, and the rescue of a Canadian bomber crew near Montluçon "under the very noses of the Germans." The efforts only intensified in 1944.

Sadly, the rebellious campaign was not "without its toll of patriot blood." In that same season 21,000 "terrorists" were arrested, and multitudes met untimely fates. As Heinzen was repatriated from a concentration camp in April 1944, he read in a Bordeaux newspaper that seven trials were held in France the previous day. French and German authorities tried 167 suspects and sentenced all but twenty-five to death. The executions took place within two hours of the verdicts. The trials commenced every day, month after month, with ghastly efficiency.[164]

Reporter Taylor Henry was equally incensed by fascist atrocities. He relished the thought of French partisans stirring mayhem behind the lines like an uncontrollable wildfire. As Henry traveled through France following his release from German captivity, he saw "trainloads of German equipment already loaded on flat cars ready to roll towards the invasion coast. It will be the job of the French partisans to see that none or only a fraction of this equipment reaches its destination." The French were worthy of the task. "Their plans are already well laid," he wrote. "They have charts of the possible movement of all German troops and supplies and are ready to strike at a moment's notice to blow up bridges, rip up rails, cut telephone lines, attack radio communications centers, and throw extemporized barricades across the roads over which the German divisions must roll." Little would be spared.

The underground readied to guide paratroopers when Allied airborne units were "flung behind the German lines." With prepared shelter and "an intimate knowledge of roads and rivers and secret hideaways," the freedom fighters were an immeasurable asset. Unfortunately for the staggering abundance of mis-dropped parachutists, not enough guides would be found. Even so, there "will be no question of their attempting to form a junction with the Allied invasion troops," promised Henry. The merging of the diverse fighting forces was a fully intended consequence of Overlord.[165]

Louis Marin, the seventy-three-year-old anti-Vichy politician who had fled France in disguise, simplified the situation to reporters from his London hotel that April. There were only two classes of people in occupied France, he contended—collaborationists and anti-collaborationists. The former had seen its day. As Marin predicted, the day of deliverance was near. The *Piqua Daily Call* of Ohio expressed the nail-biting anticipation by sharing the "D-Day slogan" of the resistance. "Choose your Hun: there won't be enough to go around."[166]

* * *

The skies of June 5, 1944 were morose. The heavens opened with torrential rains as high winds and thick clouds impeded visibility. Planes were grounded on the many sodden airfields of England while their crews squinted upward from Nissen huts. As the rain pattered their tin roofs, the bomber boys intensely scanned the far horizon, searching for any break in the foul weather. They smoked, played cards, gazed at lewd pinups, and paged the latest edition of *Yank*. On the Channel, invaders competed with the uneasy sways of a heavy sea. Swales powerful enough to swamp smaller vessels mercilessly pounded British and American boats. The elongated LSTs shimmied and vibrated with each crash of the waves. Warnings of the dreaded "Sea-Heaves" became a sickening reality for thousands of landlubbers now hurling vomit. The fetid odor of regurgitated chow emanated from every passageway. One Navy corpsman shoved cotton balls from sick bay up his nostrils.

Nauseous soldiers sought distraction; gambling emerged as a prevailing form of escapism. Even this pastime, reported Kenneth Dixon, revealed lively invasion overtones. "Soldiers have put thousands of dollars in pools and each one is picking a particular date—either by individual choice or by lots. Additional thousands have been put up in personal bets as to whether the invasion will or won't come by a certain date," Dixon wrote. Incidentally, many bets were already paid off by early June. The rumor machine was operating at maximum capacity, offering wisecracking GIs opportunities to share witless humor.

One soldier fiendishly asked, what will they do if we cannot sail across the Channel?

The question was greeted with impassive shrugs.

"Why, they are going to drain it, of course."

The ongoing pains of seafaring presented the men little concept of the big picture. As far as many could gather, their journey was another toilsome training exercise. As one sailor reflected, "We loaded and unloaded various troops and equipment time after time. . . . We were never sure if each practice might be the real thing."[167]

The forbidding conditions of the Channel compelled many to predict a delayed invasion, including Erwin Rommel. The German field marshal departed his headquarters after weeks of inspecting and strengthening the undermanned Atlantic Wall. Few mustered the pluck to challenge

Hitler's assertion that the invasion could not occur anywhere but the Pas-de-Calais. Months earlier, Rommel introspectively roved the beaches and confided in staff member Hellmuth Lang. "The war will be won or lost on the beaches," predicted Rommel. "We'll have only one chance to stop the enemy, and that's while he's in the water . . . struggling to get ashore." The first twenty-four hours of the invasion would be the crucial moment in determining the fate of Western Europe. For "the Allies, as well as Germany, it will be the longest day," the field marshal concluded. The sudden interlude of leaden weather, however, offered Rommel the flexibility to depart France, organize military matters elsewhere, and attend his wife Lucie's fiftieth birthday celebration on the fateful date of June 6. [168]

Back in London, the typewriters maintained their constant percussion. Beyond the ink-smeared Platen rollers, news of the invasion was to be relayed through a revolutionary wireless circuit connecting London to the international community. The UP's transatlantic-leased circuit spanned the ocean from England to a receiving station in Valhalla, New York, where telegraphic signals instantly transcribed messages onto a teletype machine. Six months of invasion coverage preparations enabled the United Press to impart flashes from London to New York "and on to Chicago, Kansas City, Atlanta, and Los Angeles in less than two minutes," wrote correspondent Virgil Pinkley. The UP man was inordinately well-traveled for his day. A former editor of the University of Southern California's *Daily Trojan*, he later journeyed to Europe on a cattle boat seeking new vocational opportunities. Landing a position with the London office in 1929, he subsequently covered Mussolini's 1935 invasion of Ethiopia and the 1936 Berlin Olympics. During World War II, Pinkley navigated 175,000 miles across forty-three countries. He planned to see the war through to its end. [169]

Pinkley described his thirty-seven fellow UP correspondents as "physically toughened and highly trained" reporters who would "participate in virtually every initial operation." They circled camps, airdromes, and ports in the months prior to gain fuller context. "United Press war correspondents will storm ashore with the first assault troops, cover air activities, and go to battle stations on ships shelling the coast and pouring men and supplies into beachheads," he advertised. Lauded UP reporters covering the air war included Douglas Werner, Robert Richards, Collie Small, Henry Tosti Russell, Dudley Ann Harmon, and Walter

Cronkite, who was "considered one of the leading Anglo-American aviation experts."[170]

Cronkite, the future television anchor later known as the "the most trusted man in America," was only twenty-seven years of age. Already sporting his suave mustache, he distinguished himself in the annals of wartime reporting as the "youthful dean of American air-war writers in London." In the months leading to D-Day, Cronkite participated in a North Atlantic U-boat hunt, which he later derided as "the most miserable 24 hours I ever spent." He joined B-26 bombing runs on military installations in France and industrial targets in Wilhelmshaven, Germany. Venturing where few reporters had flown before, Cronkite wrote after one mission, "An hour and a half ago I was over France with 1,000 other young Americans. . . . Censorship forbids describing what I saw down there during my flight, the first war correspondent over the forbidding strip of coast about which secrecy and rumor have cast a fascinating air of mystery. Neutral sources have insisted that the installations are long range rocket gun emplacements—an assertion which tight-lipped military authorities have neither confirmed nor denied." His cryptic analysis exemplified the press's delicate balance between security and transparency.

Cronkite's published wartime letters to his wife, Betsy, offer fascinating contrast between the reporter's public observations and personal emotions. He reflected upon his own anxieties while dining in a London bar that May. Engaged in typical scuttlebutt with colleagues, he soon after wrote home, "I was standing there chatting . . . when Mrs. Gaston, wife of the owner, lit the gas heater in the fireplace. It went PUFF as gas heaters have a way of doing. I jumped a foot and threw my beer half way across the room. That amused everybody—U. S. war correspondent with invasion jitters."[171]

Like most soldiers or airmen, Cronkite grew dangerously attached to the men with whom he served. As Pyle knew all too well, this fidelity was psychologically precarious. Friends were bound to die. Cronkite's article entitled "Nine Crying Boys and a Flying Fort" testified to the bittersweet kinship reporters shared with combatants. One B-17 returned to base following a mission during which only a single bullet struck the plane. The fragment pierced the windshield and the heart of the beloved twenty-six-year-old captain. The reporter watched as the bloodied corpse was gently lowered from the cockpit. The crew wept hysterically. Cronkite cried too. [172]

Growing madly weary of writing the "bombing beat," Cronkite learned German with the intention of garnering post-invasion exclusives. Although he was assured a bureau chief position following the invasion, Cronkite was still flustered. Like untold thousands of GIs, he desperately missed his wife. He even tried to temporarily relocate Betsy to London because, "I want you to see with me and everything I do I want you to do with me," he wrote her. As their fourth wedding anniversary neared, Cronkite expressed anger at Germany for his absence at home. "Two whole years out of our lives," he fumed. "It makes this war with Hitler a pretty personal matter. I want to take out on him and all those responsible the months that we have missed and the hundreds of days we never shall be able to regain." [173]

As Cronkite seethed over lost time and love, Don Whitehead considered the uncertainties of the near future. At 9:30 a.m. on May 29, Whitehead received a phone call from Lt. Jack Redding, formerly of the *Chicago Herald American.* Following some casual discussion, Redding hinted, "I'd like you to come over in an hour, and it would be a good idea to bring a musette bag. You might go out of town for a day or two." Such were the words the reporter had long awaited.

Whitehead and a small herd of colleagues were whisked to a hotel room by guards and ordered to make no phone calls, no notes, or leave without appointed escorts. Each journalist received a SHAEF overseas visa which read, "No correspondent may quit the overseas theater during the validity of this overseas visa without the express permission of the supreme commander." The troupe was soon after dashed out of London to an undisclosed location in the country. "Only Lieutenant Sam Brightman, former Washington correspondent for the *Louisville Courier Journal,* knew where we were going," Whitehead recorded.

At a hidden camp, Capt. Robert Hughes—the field censor of that sector—read "the stringent rules of censorship" by which the correspondents were to abide. The men were split up, sent by jeeps on back roads to avoid towns, and were embedded with units preparing to board ships. Maj. Owen B. Murphy of Lexington, Kentucky was relieved to see the reporters on the move. "I've been throwing another extra sock in my bag each time I heard the rumor we were leaving," he exclaimed. "Now that you boys have shown up, I guess it's official this time." Accompanied by

John Thompson of the *Chicago Tribune*, Whitehead received the "warm-est welcome" by a general. "Regard yourselves as members of this unit," the commander announced. "You have complete freedom of movement and I want you to get all the information you can. We are ready to help you all in any way possible. The people at home won't know what is happening unless you are given information and I want them to know."

The general then smiled. "You both know how to take care of your-selves and won't forget to duck," he warned. "But if an unlucky shell should get you, we'll do all we can. If you're wounded, we'll take care of you. If you're killed, we'll bury you. Meantime, we'll feed you." Visions of a theoretical last supper entered the reporters' thoughts.[174]

The duo was subsequently dispatched to the Coast Guard transport vessel USS *Samuel Chase* and passed time playing poker with the ever-lively Robert Capa. The three correspondents were offered prophetic in-sight by Col. George Taylor of the 1st Infantry Division. "The first six hours will be the toughest," he promised. "This is the period during which we will be the weakest. But we've got to open the door. . . . Hell, we might as well face it. We're playing with lives in this game." Lips otherwise kept invasion secrets locked—even after ships set sail. Lt. Gen. Omar Bradley huddled with three journalists aboard the USS *Augusta* and quickly backpedaled when he inadvertently referenced plans to "swim 64 tanks ashore." Even with only hours to go, the amphibious "Donald Duck" tank remained a closely-guarded secret.[175]

John Hall, a British newspaperman, later took pride in not heedlessly spilling invasion beans. For weeks prior to embarkation, he nightly heard the roads ring with the commotion of tanks, trucks, and men com-muting toward the coast. "We could hear them all the time, but when daylight came it was difficult to find them," wrote Hall. Vehicles and trailers were nestled deep in British woodlots and beneath roadside hedges. "Men crowded out of sight into hotels, private houses, and even ships. They slept on floors and even on counters." Hall thought the whole process a grand exercise in wartime wizardry; entire armies van-ished in the night.[176]

The magnitude of the operation astonished Whitehead. "It was as though man for centuries had lived, begotten offspring, and labored to-ward this moment which would shape the world's history for all time to come." Whitehead pondered how much blood would soon stain Nor-mandy's sands. He questioned how many "homesick youths bobbing around us in assault craft would get beyond the beach." Even though the Big Red One would be among the few battle-tested American units to hit the shores, Whitehead expressed heartache for its many inexperienced foot soldiers. All the training in the world could not psychologically prepare them for the forthcoming task. [177]

While Whitehead nervously swayed toward the soon-to-be-infamous Omaha Beach, momentous news hit the presses—not from Normandy, but Italy. The BBC reported the fall of Rome. After nearly a year of combat across Sicily and southern Italy, the ancient city had finally capitulated. Reports indicated, "The people of Rome have crowded onto the streets to welcome the victorious Allied troops. The first American soldiers, members of the 5th Army, reached the centre of Rome late last night after encountering dogged resistance from German forces on the outskirts of the city." Under the command of Lt. Gen. Mark Clark, GIs marched into the first of the three Axis capitals. In a stateside broadcast, FDR exclaimed, "One up, two to go." The president's enthusiasm was quietly tempered. Unlike most of the world, he was aware of the near-simultaneous events unfolding 1,000 miles to the northwest of Caput Mundi.

DeWitt Mackenzie, however, felt as if a great weight had been lifted. "Ejection of the Nazi vandals from the Eternal City will be accepted the world over as a guarantee of Allied ability to demolish Hitler's fortress Europe—truly a propitious introduction to the D-Day which will mark the final assault," he observed. "That seems to me to be the outstanding aspect of this grand achievement by the arms of civilization. The moral effect will be tremendous." The act would serve as an overwhelming rebuttal to Der Fuehrer's diatribe of that week: "The year of invasion will bring Germany's enemies an annihilating defeat at the most decisive moment," boasted Hitler. Mackenzie welcomed the challenge. [178]

Romans meanwhile slung wildflowers and liberally passed red wine to ruffled American liberators. Pope Pius XII delivered a speech from St. Peter's balcony, declaring, "In recent days we trembled for the fate of the city. Today we rejoiced because, thanks to the joint goodwill of both sides, Rome has been saved from the horrors of war." At his first Allied press conference, the pope was greeted by strident photographers who shouted, "Hold it, Pope—we gotcha in focus." British general Sir Harold Alexander was openly pleased with his own campaign, calling the endeavor "daring, unconventional, and brilliant."

Flaunting white neckerchiefs and their ubiquitous unit emblem, infantrymen of the Big Red One enjoy a moment of levity on a French-bound vessel. Eisenhower thought of the division as his Praetorian Guard. "You've got what it takes to finish the job," he assured them. The African American soldier at right may have belonged to an accompanying barrage balloon battalion. (5)

The German press claimed its troops had been withdrawn solely to prevent the destruction of the historic metropolis. "The struggle in Italy will be continued with unshakable determination with the aim of breaking the enemy attacks and to forge final victory for Germany and her allies," assured the Nazis. The grim forewarning fell deafly upon the ears of jubilant Allied combatants. Indeed, ghastly onslaughts to the north had yet to exact their toll. In netting the shiny prize of Rome, Mark Clark permitted much of the enemy force to flee and fight another day. The capture of the Italian capital proved a greater contribution to the propaganda war than the shooting war—a similar claim made by some in the wake of Paris's eventual liberation. Publicity mattered. [179]

"A big question which must already be in many minds is whether the capture of Rome completes another section of the Allied jigsaw puzzle," wondered Mackenzie. "It's possible, of course, that there may be several subsidiary offensives before D-Day itself arrives." Fortunately for Mackenzie's nerves, this was not to be the case. Yet even at this eleventh hour, training and transportation continued in England. The *Lincoln Nebraska State Journal* reported on June 5 that "the convoys still moved eastward." Troop and supply levels increased daily to the extent that "the British Isles were in danger of sinking beneath their weight. Thus, the invasion was prepared; thus the time ultimately came to H-Hour of D-Day for the invasion on which hangs the hopes of enslaved Europe." The mental preparation proved timely. [180]

Likeminded Americans braced for invasion with poetry and prayer. Soulful words of comfort, no matter how trite or concise, were welcomed by the troubled masses. The following verse by Daniel J. O'Connor appeared in Ohio's *Sandusky Register Star News* the day prior to invasion. The words imparted the major themes of America's collective D-Day discourse:

D-DAY
The day of invasion will darken the skies
When daybreak is garbed in a frightful disguise
As thousands of ships bearing destiny's men
Strike swiftly for justice and freedom again.
The mightiest blow, time has ever conceived
Will fall, as positions are firmly achieved

And many will perish when D-Day arrives
That peace, in the future, may nourish our lives

The sea and the skyways will bristle with power
And bombs will explode in a deafening shower . . .
A beachhead . . . another . . . then weapons of war
Will slide the ramps as they're hurried ashore.

As D-Day approaches, our duty is clear:
Speak little, when strangers are hovering near
A word that you drop may seem harmless, indeed
And yet be the key that our enemies need.
Make duty your by-word and live for the day
When life is resumed the American way
Give all that you can to the effort supreme
And D-Day will herald . . . America's dream.[181]

Fear. Sacrifice. Death. Duty. Freedom. These abstract tenets served as the intangible elements that universally bound together a desperate nation. The inevitable carnage served purpose, citizens assured themselves. D-Day represented all they were and all they aspired to be. The fate of their descendants depended upon the outcome. The trivial guessing games and estimations were soon to end as a million Allied youth formed themselves for the butchery of the beaches and beyond. The struggle was not theirs alone. The seeds of D-Day's success were planted on the home front, and it would be there where the invasion's tolls would be felt hardest. Multitudes of American families gathered around their dinner tables that Monday evening, unaware of how profoundly the coming day would alter their lives.

The momentous decision to initiate the operation did not come lightly. On his frequent strolls around the regal SHAEF headquarters at Southwick House, Eisenhower puffed cigarettes to clear his overburdened mind. During one sojourn, Ike encountered NBC correspondent Merrill "Red" Mueller. Red belonged to a correspondent quartet including Robert Barr of the BBC, Stanley Birch of Reuters, and Ned Roberts of the AP. The four men incessantly stalked Ike and, most of the time, Eisenhower did not mind. The same could not be said for the tenacious chief of staff, Walter Bedell Smith, who insisted reporters be quarantined.

But as Barr recalled, Ike's "Christlike wisdom" intervened. Eisenhower artfully chided Bedell Smith, "I've made all four of them staff officers. And if they tell what they know, then they'll be shot. Now what else can happen to *you*?" This undying support of press accessibility forever endeared the reporters to the general.[182]

"Let's take a walk, Red," Ike requested of Mueller that June morning. With head drooped and hands in pockets, Eisenhower was silent as they nimbly paced the estate's gravel pathways. "Ike seemed completely preoccupied with his own thoughts, completely immersed in all his problems," Mueller recalled. The reporter wished to pose questions, but the general's thoughts were elsewhere.

Ike retired to his austere "circus wagon" trailer and appeared to be "bowed down with worry . . . as though each of the four stars on either shoulder weighed a ton." The three colored phones in the commander's caravan respectively connected to Washington, Southwick House, and Churchill. According to the *New York Times*'s Raymond Daniell, SHAEF resembled a massive "thinking machine" of military capacity, but only Eisenhower could unleash its vast power. Mueller sensed the isolated heaviness of command as incomprehensible. "I think at times I get a bit homesick," Ike lamented to George Marshall weeks earlier.[183]

Mother Nature did not ease Eisenhower's predicament. The invasion was originally scheduled for June 5. However, a low-pressure system swept in north of Scotland, wreaking havoc on the seas and skies. Eisenhower postponed the operation and awaited further meteorological insight from Group Captain James Stagg. If the weather did not soon clear, the tides and moon would not be suitable for another two weeks— perhaps even July. Conditions had potential for improvement, but the generals desired more scientific assurance.[184]

At 4:15 on the morning on the fifth, rain still dribbled down the immense windows of the manor. The elegant staff room was gripped with tension as officers convened. Black coffee and tea were served in heavy doses. The sleepless Stagg stood before the Allied command with the most important forecast of his life. "Well, I'll give you some good news," he began. "Gentlemen, no substantial change has taken place since last time, but as I see it, the little that has changed is in the direction of optimism."

The answer was suitable enough for Eisenhower.

"Let's go."

The air in the room cleared as officers scrambled in all directions to initiate the complex invasion process. Stagg remarked that the generals and their subordinates seemed like "new men" in the wake of his analysis. The momentous order had finally been delivered. The transformation "was a marvel to behold," said the Scottish weatherman. Eleven years later, when Ike was invited to speak at Penn State's commencement by his university president brother, rain threatened to compromise the ceremonies. When presented alternatives, Eisenhower indifferently uttered, "You decide. I haven't worried about the weather since June 6, 1944." [185]

Ports, bases, camps, hospitals, offices, and press rooms awoke with a flurry of unprecedented activity. "It's on!" exclaimed officers among themselves. Australian reporter Alan Moorehead shared Stagg's sentiments. "That evening the soldiers were told the plan and what they had to do," he wrote. "The change was electric. The suspense was snapped. A wave of relief succeeded it. Now that the future was known and prescribed, everything would be easier." Moorehead knew their destination was France. When he tendered £10 to the paymaster for a currency exchange, he was handed francs. Other troops received coins stamped from recycled cartridge shells, which the *Philadelphia Inquirer* acknowledged as "peculiarly appropriate." [186]

Charles A. Smith of the International News Service in London remarked earlier that day, "Generalissimo Ike Eisenhower's first communiqué announcing that troops of the allied nations have landed on the continent of Europe cannot come too soon for the people of Britain." The declaration "will release tremendous pent-up emotion. But here it's an emotion that's been repressed for an unhealthy length of time." A case of "invasionitis" firmly gripped the populace. The nation was "a whispering gallery" where the "smallest crumb" or "flimsiest straw" of military information was eagerly devoured. This angst was not to be confused with depression, defeatism, or doubt, Smith assured. Rather, commoners were "pathetically anxious" with excitement. [187]

Eisenhower's decision was the first measure in alleviating the paranoia—but only the first. Although appearing calm and confident, Ike was deeply unsettled by the events he set into motion. He escaped the intensity of headquarters with an unscheduled visit to paratroopers of Company E of the 502nd Parachute Infantry Regiment (PIR) in the 101st Airborne. Eisenhower encountered the soldiers as they donned their

100-plus pounds of gear and blackened their faces for the night jump. An entourage of reporters and cameramen followed, resulting in one of the best-known D-Day photographs. The image was widely reproduced in American newspapers, although censors scratched out the "Screaming Eagle" patches on every uniform to conceal unit identity.

The casual visit was no publicity stunt. Eisenhower was informed by Air Chief Marshal Sir Trafford Leigh-Mallory that perhaps eight out of every ten paratroopers would not survive the invasion. Ike desired to see their faces in person and wish them well. He talked football, fishing, and ranching with the boys. The commander struck a conversation with a fellow Kansan named Sherman J. Olyer. The young man was initially so frozen with emotion that he could not remember his own name. Eisenhower asked the private from Wellington if he was frightened.

The answer was yes.

Eisenhower consoled Olyer with grandfatherly wisdom. "Well, you'd be a damn fool not to be. But the trick is to keep moving. . . . You lose your concentration, you'll be a casualty. The idea, the perfect idea, is to keep moving." The advice was sound. Olyer lived until 1999.[188]

Concealing his immeasurable strain, Ike feared for them. He subscribed to his own advice and carried on. When Eisenhower formally announced the invasion to his trusted SHAEF reporters, staffer Harry Butcher was mesmerized by the general's poise. "As usual," said Butcher, "he held them on the edge of their chairs. The nonchalance with which he announced that we were attacking in the morning and the feigned nonchalance with which the reporters absorbed it was a study in suppressed emotion that would interest any psychologist."[189]

After the news conference, Ike drafted a letter outlining the possibility of failure. Inadvertently dating his admission of responsibility *July* 5, he warily wrote, "Our landings in the Cherbourg-Havre area have failed to gain a satisfactory foothold and I have withdrawn the troops. My decision to attack at this time and place was based upon the best information available. The troops, the air and the Navy did all that bravery and devotion to duty could do. If any blame or fault attaches to the attempt it is mine alone." Although the statement would be rendered unnecessary, Eisenhower's self-accountability was one of many traits that earned him endearment. Equally significant, Ike genuinely cared for his men—and they knew it.[190]

Only hours prior to D-Day's airborne operations, Gen. Dwight D. Eisenhower conversed with members of Company E, 502nd Parachute Infantry Regiment, at the 101st Airborne Division's post in Greenham Common, England. Although the general appears stern, he largely discussed fishing, football, and farming. Sporting the #23 tag is 1st Lt. Wallace C. Strobel, who turned twenty-two the day this photo was taken. (6)

Moorehead empathized with Ike's predicament. The operation's scale seemed unfathomable. "It was absurd to try and rationalize the thing that had to happen. . . . It was not fear that oppressed you, but loneliness. A sense of implacable helplessness. You were without identity, a number projected in unrelated space among a million other numbers." The cheerless thoughts prompted twenty men in Moorehead's assigned unit to desert only days before the invasion.[191]

Don Whitehead recognized a similar loneliness in Eisenhower. The general was beset by a glorious burden, the solitude of command. "The leader of the long-awaited invasion will be playing with gigantic stakes

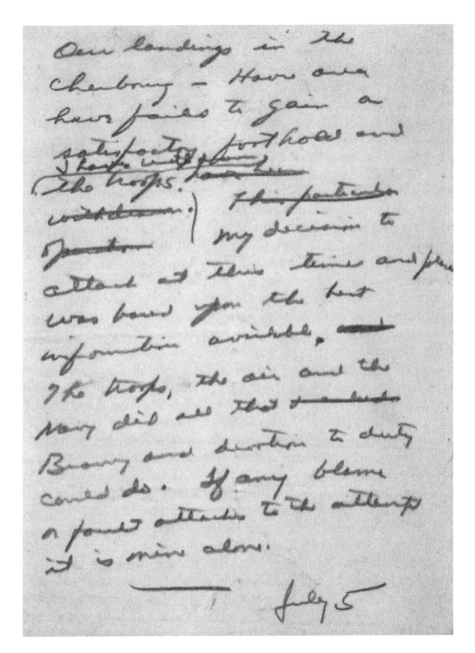

Planning for the possibility of failure in France, Eisenhower scribbled an honest confession of guilt on June 5—one that fortunately would not be needed. Under the strain of the moment, Ike misdated his statement *July* 5. (7)

when his legions sail against the enemy. No other American general ever was called upon to risk so much in manpower, in ships and guns, and materials produced by the hands of American labor." What would result, no one could know.

New Zealand Prime Minister Peter Fraser declared weeks earlier at a London press conference, "I cannot say whether the impending attack on Germany is to be a success. We all hope and believe it will be. If it is not, we will have to set our teeth and go into it again." The repercussions of failure seemed boundless. "But the gamble will be made," Don Whitehead agreed. It must. "All odds have been assessed in months of careful study, planning, and preparation. All the risks have been calculated, even to the carrying heights of the tides." Ike meticulously scrutinized the odds, and now was the time to roll the dice. One year earlier in North Africa, the Allies liberated a continent from Nazi tyranny. Today, Whitehead concluded, "they are preparing to free another."[192]

"To put one's self in the place of the war leaders is to feel the crushing responsibility they bear as they give the signal for invasion," agreed Anne O'Hare McCormick of the *New York Times*. "Never has the fate of so many depended on the judgment of so few." Yet to mentally place one's self in the conditions of the tormented French farmer was to understand what the great venture meant and why it had to be undertaken. Robert Cooper of London's *The Times* likewise recognized the magnitude of the gamble. "Four years ago, almost to the day," he wrote, "the tide of war had flooded from the east into the French Channel ports before swirling back on Paris and far beyond. Now the tide has turned, and in this suspended moment in history the first mighty wave is gathered before it crashes down on the enemy's beaches."[193]

The armada of roaring planes departed in astounding numbers. Murrow said it all sounded "like a giant factory in the sky." That evening, Red Mueller stood next to Eisenhower as glider tow-planes lifted from the runways of rural Newbury. Mueller turned to Ike in the hope of posing a few questions but immediately paused. He noticed tears filling Eisenhower's eyes. "The strain is telling on him," Harry Butcher noticed. "He looks older now than at any time since I have been with him." Aide Kay Summersby recalled, "He was as nervous as I had seen him and extremely depressed."

Dusk fell and the hum of C-47 engines faded in the remote distance. Ike briefly adjourned to an airborne headquarters at a nearby manor.

Having circled countless camps that day, the general was famished. He sat in solitary contemplation, indulging in an ample serving of dough-nuts and coffee. A crackling fire in the darkly paneled parlor offered faint illumination. Eisenhower was even deprived the companionship of his Scottie dog, Telek, who was quarantined in accordance with Eng-land's rabies control law. The general was truly alone.[194]

Over a thousand miles away, Lt. Gen. Mark Clark was displeased by the concurrence of Roman and French liberation. "The sons of bitches," he groaned about SHAEF. "They didn't even let us have the newspaper headlines for the fall of Rome for one day." Robert J. Kinchen, an 85th Division infantryman in Clark's army, offered a more poignant sign of relief. When told by Sgt. James O'Neill of *Yank* that the Second Front had at last opened, Kinchen replied, "I didn't believe it, but I am taking your word for it. I'm damned glad it finally came. For a long while, es-pecially when we were at Anzio, we never thought they'd start it." Hope-fully, fortunes would be brighter in Normandy.[195]

In the dining room of Rome's Albergo Città, the new headquarters of the British press corps, Godfrey Talbot of the BBC wailed to his col-leagues, "Boys, we're on the back page now. They've landed in Nor-mandy."[196]

Vague reports of invasion soon splashed across newspapers. Numer-ous American periodicals even proclaimed D-Day on the front pages of June 5 evening editions. The sheets—stamped with maps, sweeping analysis, and technical details, also incorporated humble traces of hometown candor similar to that printed in the *Huntingdon Daily News*: "God save our splendid men, send them safe home again." For many a youthful GI, the prayer would go unheard.[197]

91

PART II: THE ASSAULT

Sombre the night is.
And though we have our
lives, we know
What sinister threat lurks
there.

– Isaac Rosenberg

CHAPTER 5

"Well, This Is It"

He was awakened by the sudden rattling of his bed stand. Loose pocket change subtly jingled atop the dark wood. The drone intensely grew as the entire household shuddered with a wave of vibration. British columnist John Hall roused himself from a deep slumber and groggily shuffled to the nearest window. Gazing skyward into the dark blue of the pre-dawn, he gasped. He later recorded on that morning of June 6, "Since four a.m. the ground has been trembling to the roar of aircraft as heavy troop-carriers, gliders, bombers, and fighters sped across the Channel." In the faint light of the full moon behind clouds, Hall caught glimpses of silhouetted formations pressing southward. The incessant drumming of plane engines was followed by an otherworldly stillness— a soundless interlude Hall would never forget. There was "not a shot, not a bomb, not a siren, not even the rumble of a tank. As daylight broadened, everyday life restarted just as if this was any other day." To the contrary, this day was certainly no ordinary one. [198]

Among those soaring toward Fortress Europe was Pvt. Faye W. Thabet of Point Pleasant, West Virginia. He was older than most; at thirty-two years of age Thabet was a veteran of the African, Sicilian, and Italian Campaigns. Standing 5'9" his build was common for a GI. A first aid man in an 82nd Airborne glider battalion, he had enjoyed spring in a country estate he thought to be haunted. He reveled in the splendor of English gardens. In a recent letter to his folks in Appalachia, he described his profession in layman's terms. "[W]hen a man is wounded I run or crawl to him. . . . I said to my buddy, 'we have a job to do, we got to do it.'"

His convictions did not spare him from the cyclone of violence. Determined to rescue others, the Mountaineer was ultimately unable to save himself. His hometown congregation affixed a white star on their Service Flag in his honor. The local newspaper warned that he would not be the last fatality. The "Hitlerites are going to battle until the last glimmer of hope is dead," wrote the *Athens Messenger*. "That is going to mean terrible fighting, and probably heavy casualties." Thabet's name would ultimately be inscribed on a death muster including fifty-six other local sons. [199]

Days and weeks before news of loved ones appeared in headlines, reporters filled the void with sweeping summaries and autobiographical accounts of invasion. Mandated to withhold initial stories chronicling D-Day mobilization, many writers were thereby granted time to craft the most significant articles of their careers. In that time, Don Whitehead described his herd of fellow reporters as "an annoying and mysterious band of roving gypsies." Two days prior to the scheduled assaults, Hanson Baldwin and his cadre of warcos were summoned by vague yet revealing orders to Room 60 of London's Admiralty. The pewter light made for a bleak morning. Rain trickled down the dirty window panes of the great hall. Soggy cloth rags covered missing sections recently blown out by bombs. Custodians had been sweeping the shattered bits of glass. Nearly fifty American war reporters, radio commentators, and photographers convened. Their steel helmets and field bags piled the corridor downstairs. Sharpened pencils were at the ready.

At 8:30 a young American lieutenant rose at the front of the room. "Gentlemen," he announced, "for those of you who were not here last week I might as well introduce myself. I am the staff press liaison officer of the United States Allied Naval Command Expeditionary Forces. My name is Smith. The Chief of Staff has okayed a certain amount of briefing for you here this morning. I think possibly you will all want to take notes on this. Oh, by the way," he smiled, "this is not a dry run."

The reporters loosened, exhaling a deep, collective breath. Few were surprised but all were enlivened. Ten days earlier, the correspondents had gathered in a similar manner, were briefed, sent on a two-day train journey, and then detained at a naval port—all as an exercise. Round two was no drill. "Today it was the real thing," Baldwin excitedly wrote, "and they knew it instinctively." The newsmen immediately embarked in two predetermined groups by bus and rail to separate ports. "The rain did not seem an auspicious beginning for the greatest operation of its kind in military history," Baldwin continued. "But, with the fickleness of the English climate, in an hour or so out of London the sun was shining on neat hedgerows and patchwork fields."

Reaching port, the writers and their military agents were funneled into a heavily guarded Nissen hut for additional orientation. From that point until H-Hour, no reporter was permitted to dispatch any notes or articles. Both the men and their words were quarantined until further notice. As reporter scuttlebutt ensued, Rear Admiral Alan G. Kirk, senior American naval commander, soon entered the crowded space. Flickering off his damp coat and cap, Kirk exchanged pleasantries with each correspondent. Poised commandingly at the head of the room, the admiral unveiled the first operations chart on the wall and declared, "Gentlemen, we are going into France." One could have heard a pin drop, Baldwin remarked. For months he and his colleagues speculated over the invasion's exact time and location, but here now were the finer details craved by reporters for so long. The journalists sat wide-eyed as one of the most secretive undertakings in human existence was outlined piece by piece.

Kirk concluded his conference with an air of realistic optimism. "I don't want to make this sound gloomy," he said, "but I just want to tell you this is tough; that we have a lot of problems and plans to handle those problems. I think we are going to handle them exactly, perhaps, when we plan, but we are going to handle them." At this hour, apprehensive consolation was as best as could be expected. Ushered to a nearby shack for an "all-American" meal, the correspondents were served rationed delicacies not tasted in months. One reporter wisecracked to a lieutenant, "Don't you think after that we ought to be able to pick the menu for this last meal?" Following the sumptuous dinner, the correspondents broke off in parties of twos and fours to their designated cruisers and LSTs. For once, they did not talk. They hardly whispered. Someone not "in the know" might have overheard them. There were only "occasional low whistles of amazement as they pondered what they had heard." The sloshing beat of boots through puddles marked their upbeat cadence to the ships.[200]

Until H-Hour, officers were compelled to remain voiceless. When a large wall map of Normandy was unveiled to Air Forces pilots and navigators the commander cautioned, "Anyone who divulges any of the information given at this briefing will be shot."[201]

Correspondent Mary Welsh (soon to become Ernest Hemingway's fourth and final wife) was awakened by the telephone around 4 a.m.

"Take the curlers out of your hair and get going," a military liaison proclaimed. "I had no curlers, but I got going," Welsh later wrote. Marjorie Avery of the *Detroit Free Press* was dreaming of riding a freight train in Australia "when violent knocking at the door announced a phone call," she recalled. "It was SHAEF with a message to proceed at once to a designated place. Ten minutes later, with my eyes half shut, I was on the street."[202]

An endless current of words and images soon transmitted across the seas and into periodicals circling the globe. The *New York Times* was astounded by the unrivaled volume of information. From June 6-11, more than 2.5 million words composed by over 300 correspondents chronicled invasion happenings. The gush of text multiplied from 400,000 on D-Day to 800,000 on June 9. Over 100 photos were filed daily over the wire service. Not since the transatlantic flight of Charles Lindbergh had such an effusion of news crisscrossed the ocean. Office newsmen and technicians dwelled at their desks for days. In the SHAEF press room, hungry correspondents shared strawberry shortcake as their sole invasion day meal.[203]

The staffers of *Stars and Stripes* likewise pounded away on their typewriters with renewed zeal. The scene was nothing short of bedlam, wrote Robert Moora. The paper "had literally a thousand times more material on the assault than it had space for." Reporter work consisted of boiling down the invasion's most sensational and important storylines into a digestible narrative. As the managing editor, Moora "took the prerogative of writing the lead story, the account of the landings."[204]

Composing a confident send-off for the June 7 edition, the paper remarked, "Dressed in full battle regalia and armed with the most effective death-dealing weapons ever devised, American combat troops, their long training period over at last, quietly slipped out of British ports early yesterday morning bound for the beaches of France." Each GI was a walking arsenal. Every deck was overflowing with infantrymen adorned with lifebelts, gas masks, assault vets, ammo pouches, eighty rounds of M-1 ammo, TNT pole charges, grenades, entrenching tools, wire cutters, bandages, eight days of provisions, cigarettes, and 200 francs—the equivalent of four American dollars. Like reporters, the Yanks were detained prior to embarkation. Over 1,000 guards were posted on the perimeters of marshalling areas with orders to shoot anybody attempting departure. Not even Army cooks were permitted inside the wire. Food was prepared elsewhere, trucked in, and handed to distributors through barbed wire enclosures.[205]

With their cross-channel odysseys under way, many a GI recorded episodes of juvenile playfulness and carousing. Cpl. Victor M. Wingate's homeward letter was published in Maryland's *Frederick News* and offers compelling insights of combatants preparing for war. "On the ship there was the customary activity of American troops in passage. A couple of blond huskies, about twenty years of age, wrestled across the bunks. A dozen poker games were in progress simultaneously and, of course, the inevitable galloping dominoes game (or Harlem Polo as it is called in some circles) drew a large crowd." A lengthy queue for cookies and candy at the ship's PX underscored a childlike sweet tooth among "the men." Handfuls of GIs stretched across their bunks, browsing old French textbooks and quietly repeating phrases. By midnight, however, hardly a book, candy box, or eyelid was open. A few night owls continued their hushed poker game in the corner. Wingate slept soundly until his dreams of home were interrupted by the ship's loudspeaker blaring forth, "Wake up, turn out, wake up, turn out." The voice proclaimed they all would soon be in "the land of Napoleon, Joan of Arc, and Lafayette. Vive L'Amerique." The long wait was over.[206]

Ernie Pyle was among the scores of passengers pondering his own future and the outcome of the war. Of the twenty-eight correspondents in his assault group, well over half were combat veterans. So-called "old-timers" such as Clark Lee, Tex O'Reilly, Bill Stoneman, Jack Thompson, and the prolific Don Whitehead gravitated together. "We conjectured on when we would get the final call, conjectured on what assignments we would draw, for few of us knew what unit we would go with," wrote Pyle. "And in more pensive moments we also conjectured on our chances of coming through alive." Whitehead and Lee appeared jittery. They had little illusion of the task ahead. "And frankly," Pyle confessed, "I was the worst of the lot." He endured periods of depression and suffered from nightmares. "All the time fear lay blackly deep down upon your consciousness," he admitted. "It bore down on your heart like an all-consuming weight. People would talk to you and you wouldn't hear what they were saying."[207]

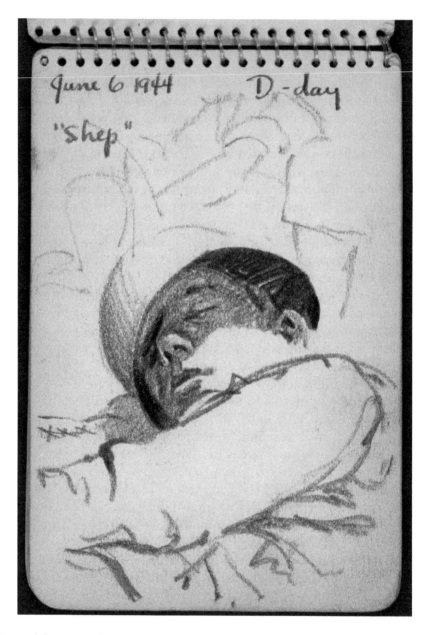

Artist and future modernist architect Victor Lundy vividly captured the character of his comrades through dozens of pencil sketches in his wartime diary. Among the subjects was his buddy, Shep, who managed to catch a few winks on June 6. The "war experience just hypnotizes young men," Lundy remembered. (8)

On another ship, a sergeant collected non-essential items from the men, lightening their loads for the dire undertaking. He thought it a pity to deprive his soldiers of their overcoats at this cold, last minute. The sergeant turned and discouragingly uttered to a reporter, "Maybe this *is* the last minute."[208]

Battlefield fears or not, invasion participants comprehended a profound sense of historical—if not spiritual—gravity associated with the occasion. After flying a D-Day mission, Capt. Leonard Wilkening wrote from his English base, "the King of England has just started to talk and perhaps you are listening to him. This day will be remembered in history, I'm sure."[209]

Few soldier accounts of D-Day appeared in newspapers the same week as the invasion. Most families and hometown papers would not receive individual testimonies of the assault until late June or early July. Loved ones grasped at straws during interminable weeks of gnawing uncertainty. In the interim, reporters painted the invasion panoramic with strikingly broad brushes. They spoke of equipment and materiel, the scale of operations, the tonnage of bombs, and ordnance expended. They illustrated maps of Western Europe while reprinting canned radio broadcasts and public assurances. Early reports often unveiled the vast drama without introducing any of its cast members to audiences.

The June 7 issue of *Stars and Stripes* (which featured the capture of Rome on the front page) exhibited generic language repeated and reiterated countless times in the global press: "Allied armies, supported by more than 4,000 ships and 11,000 warplanes, stormed the northern coast of France in the dark hours of yesterday morning to open the decisive battle for the liberation of Europe, and by nightfall had smashed their way ten miles inland to Caen, between the vital ports of Cherbourg and Le Havre." German and Vichy radio stations simultaneously recounted intense episodes of street combat as Allied troops slinked into French villages.

Along the eighty-mile-wide front, Allied troops "landed on French soil from the choppy waters of the English Channel and from the storm-studded skies," *Stripes* continued. Over 600 naval guns thundered at Hitler's emplacements. Churchill announced the invasion to a rapturous Parliament. "So far, the commanders who are engaged report that everything is proceeding according to plan," he declared. "And what a plan!" After conferring with Eisenhower, Churchill called upon King George, declaring that "many dangers and difficulties which appeared at this time last night to be extremely formidable are behind us. The passage of the sea has been made with far less loss than we apprehended." A SHAEF spokesman said early hurdles were "no cause for pessimism." The foul weather, which postponed the invasion for twenty-four hours, ruffled the Channel and caused considerable nail-biting. "But the landings were made," an officer concluded, "although some of the troops undoubtedly were seasick."[210]

Early blanket spin control statements failed to accurately interpret D-Day and its many human elements. In contrast to bloated press releases, journalist James Long encapsulated the landings in a manner that few official statements could. Long quoted a naval officer who described D-Day as "one of the greatest cases of mass seasickness in the history of the world."[211]

Military news outlets sought perhaps to relieve doubt above all else. In describing D-Day's finale, *Stars and Stripes* claimed the "beachhead was so secure, a Ninth Air Force pilot reported after a flight, that American soldiers were visible standing alongside roads, leaning on their rifles and awaiting chow." Maj. Roy "He Never Sleeps" Craft, a former San Francisco newsman and assistant to Maj. Gen. Charles H. Corlett, greeted the guarantees with a grain of salt. He confessed, "In our own case we have, by careful propaganda, elaborate understatements, half-truths, and a few deliberate whoppers convinced our wives (if not the neighbors) that we are the fightin'est men since Jenghiz Khan and are always selected to go in ahead of the Rangers. Others have not disabused their gals of similar ideas."

Further efforts were undertaken to alleviate fears of D-Day's lackluster weather. The Associated Press shared a report stating the "sun broke through heavy clouds at times in the Dover strait area this first day of the Allied invasion of Western Europe. . . . The wind had blown fairly hard during the night but lost some of its strength after dawn. A moderate sea was running." Those aboard landing craft that morning had a decidedly divergent assessment of the Channel's smoothness.[212]

The most indelible sermon of affirmation was heralded by the supreme commander himself. Summoning the spirit of the Gettysburg Address, Dwight Eisenhower crafted a concise, meaningful declaration of purpose—a 236-word rallying cry encouraging the pursuit of a moralistic ideal. The prose was promptly embraced as American Scripture, extolling the virtues of free society by denouncing oppression. Through thousands of leaflets and a sobering yet uplifting radio broadcast, Eisenhower shared a vision for a world many of his men would never see. The exceptionally confident call to arms appeared on the front page of almost every newspaper in the United States—poetically showcasing the unanimity of defending the freedom of man via the freedom of the press.

Appealing to the soldiers, sailors, and airmen of his vast command, Eisenhower invoked religious connotations, calling their months-long mission a "Great Crusade." The eyes of the world were upon them as were the "hopes and prayers of liberty-loving people everywhere." The arduous task of liberating the downtrodden from tyranny would be painful and costly. Yet, as the noose stiffened around the Axis domain, Eisenhower recognized that the tide had turned. The Allied coalition forged by determination was soon to rebound from the stark tragedies of Dunkirk and beyond. "The free men of the world are marching together to victory," Ike exclaimed. Nothing less than complete victory could be accepted. "Good Luck!" he concluded. "And let us all beseech the blessing of Almighty God upon this great and noble undertaking."[213]

"With these words," responded *Stars and Stripes*, "General Eisenhower in his order of the day to all troops put in motion the Allied Expeditionary Force fighting for the liberation of nations enslaved under the sign of the swastika." To remove the fascist stain from Europe's map, the infantryman would soon become accustomed to the "boom of mortars and the crack of machine guns in his ears." At sea, sailors would be "deafened by the full-throated roar of salvos of naval guns." Armed with immense power, these forces hoisted "the flags of free nations as a symbol of liberty." The noble crusade thus commenced.[214]

The toilsome weeks of endless training were complete. Practice maneuvers became memory. The mockery incited by Nazi propagandists faded. Prodding by politicians ceased. The real show was on. Amidst it all, Eisenhower appeared the calmest. Before and during the invasion, he approached the ranks with homespun wit and endearing empathy. At this grave hour, one correspondent recalled of Ike, "He greeted each

SUPREME HEADQUARTERS
ALLIED EXPEDITIONARY FORCE

Soldiers, Sailors and Airmen of the Allied Expeditionary Force!

You are about to embark upon the Great Crusade, toward which we have striven these many months. The eyes of the world are upon you. The hopes and prayers of liberty-loving people everywhere march with you. In company with our brave Allies and brothers-in-arms on other Fronts, you will bring about the destruction of the German war machine, the elimination of Nazi tyranny over the oppressed peoples of Europe, and security for ourselves in a free world.

Your task will not be an easy one. Your enemy is well trained, well equipped and battle-hardened. He will fight savagely.

But this is the year 1944! Much has happened since the Nazi triumphs of 1940-41. The United Nations have inflicted upon the Germans great defeats, in open battle, man-to-man. Our air offensive has seriously reduced their strength in the air and their capacity to wage war on the ground. Our Home Fronts have given us an overwhelming superiority in weapons and munitions of war, and placed at our disposal great reserves of trained fighting men. The tide has turned! The free men of the world are marching together to Victory!

I have full confidence in your courage, devotion to duty and skill in battle. We will accept nothing less than full Victory!

Good Luck! And let us all beseech the blessing of Almighty God upon this great and noble undertaking.

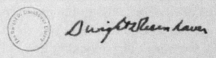

"With these words," observed *Stars and Stripes* of Ike's D-Day proclamation, "General Eisenhower in his order of the day to all troops put in motion the Allied Expeditionary Force fighting for the liberation of nations enslaved under the sign of the swastika." The concise declaration of purpose appeared on the front pages of most American newspapers that day. (9)

of us with a handshake and a friendly, lopsided grin." Eisenhower's sto-ical, military forbearance earned him respect. His fatherly compassion won him love.[215]

Eisenhower likewise sought to imbue his French allies with commit-ment to the cause. "This landing is but the opening phase of the cam-paign in western Europe," he assured them. "Great battles lie ahead. I call upon all who love freedom to stand with us. Keep your faith staunch—our arms are resolute—together we shall achieve victory." French civilians were instructed to move thirty-five kilometers inland to avoid saturated bombing and shelling. Avoid main roads. Do not travel in groups. Carry only necessities if forced to evacuate, they were told. Emmanuel d'Astier, French National Liberation commissioner for the interior, ordered French patriots to "strike now with full force and all the resources at your disposal." They were to make every German feel as if he was in personal peril. Fear was a potent weapon.[216]

Within hours, Eisenhower convened a press conference in his com-mand tent. He interrupted himself to peer out the flap and enthusiasti-cally comment on a ray of sunshine projecting through the gray clouds. Reporter E. V. Roberts rigorously scribbled notes as the forum resumed. He paid special note of Eisenhower's cool self-possession. "The general sat comfortably, slouched behind his big battered desk," wrote Roberts. "On the desktop was a green telephone, a desk lamp and inkwell, and a packet of cigarettes. During the conference he occasionally leaned for-ward to tap with a finger for emphasis. He smoked constantly, some-times lighting one cigarette from another. Beyond that he made no movement. He did not appear to notice the express train roar of con-stant Allied air patrols overhead." At face value, Eisenhower main-tained complete control.[217]

Associated Press correspondent Paul Kern Lee could not help but be impressed. "History's greatest overseas invasion is led by a quiet, me-thodical American soldier whose professional creed of taking big risks for big stakes is here put to its ultimate test." Transcending his own assessment of Eisenhower's professional qualifications, Kern Lee thought himself an excellent judge of character and deemed that Ike simply had a good face. The general's "pale blue eyes, a few remaining strands of pale hair, and a crinkly grin" nurtured "an air of friendly competence." But Ike possessed a stout poker face as well. Unafraid to gamble, Eisenhower used his grandfatherly charm as a useful façade in the games of military strategy and political calculation. In this sense, his surname was an appropriate one. Kern Lee wrote, "A legacy from forbearers who fled from Germany to Switzerland to escape persecution in the 17th century, and who migrated to America about 1750, it was originally spelled *Eisenhauer*." The name meant "Iron Striker."[218]

Not all correspondents covered the invasion from the relative safety of a headquarters tent. Some two dozen writers and photographers from the Associated Press were embedded among Allied forces in the opening waves. Chief among them was Wes Gallagher, the AP's future general manager who submitted one of D-Day's first field articles. At his side was "Beachhead Don" Whitehead, so named for the number of invasions he survived, and Bede Irvin—an intrepid photographer who was as talented as he was boyish. Many of the reporters landed shortly after 9:30 that morning. The AP embraced a variety of means to relay messages back to London, including sporadic radio transmissions and problematic carrier pigeons that occasionally flew in the enemy's direction. Reporter Henry Jameson, whose shoulder was dislocated during shelling, loyally salvaged a crumpled mass of field reports during his hasty evacuation to a hospital ship. The articles appeared in print within two days.

Gallagher commented, "German opposition apparently was less effective than expected, although fierce in many respects, and the Germans said they were bringing reinforcements continuously up to the coast, where a battle for life or death is in progress." Dispatches from other sectors were few but echoed the significant trend of the day: the Allies were gaining a foothold on "the strongest fortified section of coast in the world."

The battle for information and public opinion was also well under way. German radio was already broadcasting news of the invasion before some London war correspondents were even roused from bed. The purposeful news delay was thereafter explained to flustered reporters: "It was made known that the supreme command felt it necessary to yield the initiative in the war of words to the Germans in order to retain the initiative on land and keep the German high command in the dark as long as possible," Gallagher explained. Meanwhile, Capt. Ludwig Sertorius of the German DNB tersely commented over the airwaves, "They are coming."[219]

According to the BBC, Nazi media offered their own interpretation of events, which naturally boasted of the Reich's prime coastal defenses. A Berlin noontime broadcast declared German combatants were "nowhere taken by surprise." In fact, their ample preparation allowed for the annihilation of parachute units and the capitulation of entire regiments. Furthermore, hits "were also scored on battleships and on landing craft" approaching the impregnable Atlantic wall.[220]

Despite calm announcements over national radio, German leadership had good reason to worry. Nervousness over the impending Soviet offensive in the East staggered to new heights with the opening of the Western Front. "In view of the new military situation," said Col. Ernst von Hammer, a German News Agency commentator, "the German high command is paying particular attention to the lower Dniester sector where a strong Soviet offensive army has taken action stations and where Soviet artillery and mortar fire is gaining in intensity." With the invasion in progress, "it is likely that the Soviet divisions which have been massed here over a matter of weeks will now go over to the offensive in order to force a decision."[221]

The vice tightened, and the Soviet Union rejoiced. Russia's *Stars and Stripes* equivalent, *Red Star*, declared, "The Atlantic Wall is being overcome. This day will remain memorable in history. One cannot overestimate the significance of this leap across the Channel, which is being carried by one of the greatest of contemporary strategists." Soviet journalist Ilya Ehrenburg added, "The heroes of Stalingrad and the Dnieper are proud of their allies." On June 7, President Roosevelt disclosed that the approximate date for Overlord was established at the Tehran Conference with Stalin's emphatic blessing. At his post-D-Day press conference, Roosevelt gently scolded politicians who were once demanding an immediate open to the Second Front. That extra time, the president argued, enabled Eisenhower to procure additional divisions and landing craft. "You don't just walk to Berlin," scolded Roosevelt, "and the sooner this country realizes that the better."[222]

FDR intensely charted invasion movements in the White House's private map room. A naval officer daily repositioned pins on the wall map indicating the location of every U. S. ship in the Atlantic and Pacific. "Ever since Mrs. Roosevelt, Sr. found her son at the age of 14 reading Admiral Mahan, Roosevelt himself has been a naval expert," observed the Associated Press. As FDR wheeled into the lair on June 7, he was likely to discover a flustered ensign at work. There was little room to be had for more pins around the Cherbourg Peninsula.[223]

While D-Day was heralded as the pinnacle of Allied collaboration, smaller dilemmas on the public relations front ensued as minor details were lost in translation. One British news agency misinterpreted a report filed by an American correspondent which read, "Groups of GIs were aboard tank landing crafts which took part in operations." Perceiving Yank lingo as a typographical error or abbreviation, the British press replaced "GIs" with "Girls." Eleanor Roosevelt would have been pleased.[224]

More widespread pandemonium emanated from a wholly unconfirmed but widely publicized dispatch from Ankara announcing invasion in southern Greece. Specifically, Turkish officials reported Allied landings on the Peloponnesus Peninsula. United Nations radio in Algiers subsequently overheard a Berlin broadcast stating that beaching was underway not on Peloponnesus, but Patras. Additional hypotheses floated through more than one enemy headquarters. The German high command, at Hitler's insistence, believed the amphibious operations in Normandy were a feint cloaking a main thrust aimed at Calais. Compounded by the fall of Rome, rumors of Allied advances in the East and the Mediterranean stirred a flood of German speculation.[225]

In a piece fittingly entitled "Broad Overviews," reporter Drew Middleton cabled a lengthy summation to the *New York Times* highlighting five salient points regarding the military situation as of midnight on D+1. Firstly, Allied troops miraculously overcame underwater obstacles and beach defenses, including mines that extended over 1,000 yards inland. Secondly, the largest airborne offensive ever launched successfully compromised German infrastructure beyond the shores and was engaged with a second echelon of Nazi defenses. By that time, most coastal batteries had been silenced by ground troops and 10,000 tons of shells lobbed by 640 naval vessels. Middleton deemed the bombardment so intense that the HMS *Tanatside* exhausted her entire ammunition stores by 8 a.m. Over 800 naval guns roared across a fifty-mile chain of ships. "The air vibrated," attested Don Whitehead. In the eight hours prior, some 7,500 sorties were flown by the AAF and RAF, facing little to no opposition from the once mighty Luftwaffe. Lastly, there was reasonable optimism at supreme headquarters even though there was little effort to disguise concerns over weather and possible German counteroffensives. The Allies were not yet in the clear.[226]

DeWitt Mackenzie could not have agreed more. "[W]e must remember that this is only the beginning," he warned. "We don't even know that this is intended as the major assault or that the main thrust won't come somewhere else. What we do know, and it's important, is this: The all-out German counter-attacks are still to come." A new waiting game was afoot. Would the Nazis strike in Normandy or keep one hand behind their backs in anticipation of a larger operation? If so, how long would they wait? "He isn't going to risk flinging an army at any invasion threat until he is sure that it is the main enemy landing—or at least one of them," Mackenzie observed. "If he rushed a big force to Normandy the first thing, and the Allies then aimed a lightning blow at another distant point, he would be in a welter of trouble." Whether a second offensive arrived or not, the Germans were kept off balance with conjecture and infighting among the generals . . . all to Eisenhower's gain.[227]

Amid the headquarters and newsroom map-pointing, *Stars and Stripes* reflected on the cunning preparation that made D-Day a reality—particularly the efforts of average Joes. Units trained eleven or more hours daily. One outfit's pre-D-Day itinerary included "thirty minutes of rigorous calisthenics, a lecture on how to abandon ship, a demonstration on inflating lifebelts, a briefing on the unit's invasion mission, issuance of French money, practice with rifle grenades, overhauling of all weapons and inspection of weapons, preparation of fuses for demolitions, a lecture on German weapons and tactics, and even more calisthenics." Under their damp pyramid tents, GIs learned to say, "Halt, put up your hands," in German, and "Which way is the Boche?" in French. If captured, they were reminded to furnish only their names, ranks, and serial numbers. Herded into marshalling yards like cattle, they were cut off from the outside world. "Aboard the troopships, on the sides of which were suspended smaller landing craft, there were no complaints, despite the fact that the men were packed in like sardines, eating and sleeping by the hundreds in the same room." They vomited relentlessly. Finally, in conveyor belt fashion, they were ushered toward the abyss of battle.[228]

For those who would endure the onslaught, letter writing became an immediate compulsion—a badge of honor to recognize survival. Eugene Wood of Storm Lake, Iowa wrote to his wife, "We landed D-Day. The first time we came in the Germans shot the ramps off our boat. So we pulled out and came in in small boats. I'm sure there was no element of surprise to this invasion. The German's really had some nice fortifications." Regardless, he sneered at Rommel's opinion that the beach could never be taken. "It *was* taken," he assured his wife. "All I have to say is that the Lord was really watching over me that day. The invasion wasn't as easy as the pencil-pushers said it would be. In some sections maybe it was easy but not ours. I was so scared that I looked like a tree blowing in the wind." Correspondence as such eventually flowed to regional periodicals like the *Albert City Appeal*, offering citizenry relatable, intimate context—the information they desired most.[229]

Homeward bound letters were therapeutic for sender and receiver alike. Sgt. Harold Kuehl of Valparaiso, Indiana wrote to his family one week following the invasion, "Somewhere in France. Came over on D-Day. It was really hot, and I don't mean from the sun. Am writing this beside my good old foxhole—you'd call them wells back home. If I'm ever sent back from here to my former location it will not be too soon for me." Most importantly, he concluded, "I'm ok. Don't worry." Pvt. Leon Frank Jackson of the 506th PIR expressed a similar sensation with a higher degree of ardor. "I am alive, well, and without a scratch," he enthused. "I killed three confirmed Germans and helped bring in a fourth. I got to France on D-1 before any other outfit, and my outfit beat the devil out of Hitler's first and best troops."[230]

Eisenhower was quietly relieved that his own son, John, was far from the fray. Despite being over 3,000 miles from the front, John made news on D-Day by pure coincidence. It was his graduation day from West Point. The slim, blond Eisenhower received his commission as a second lieutenant with 473 fellow graduates—all of whom received identical letters from Ike welcoming them into the Army. Wife Mamie Eisenhower also presented John with a sealed message from his father, who wished to attend but was preoccupied with more pressing matters. The Academy's June 6 alumni also included 2nd Lt. Henry Beukema, who two days later married Elizabeth Cannel Bradley, the only daughter of Omar Bradley—who was also absent. Beukema was the son of West Point instructor Herman Beukema, who graduated with Ike and Brad in 1915. Their lives intersected in serendipitous ways that first week of June 1944.[231]

The Bradley-Beukema matrimony appeared in the "News From Home" section of *Stars and Stripes*, which often highlighted quirky anecdotes and celebrity divorces. The sports section was the most traded among readers. However, *S&S* was never overwhelmed by tabloid sensationalism and hearsay. Humor and healthy distraction were rarely taboo, but the paper's mission was clear and upstanding: educate the boys of the world's happenings. Six days following the assault, *Stars and Stripes* released its "Liberation Issue," which was "designed to bring frontline soldiers up to date on what has happened since they shoved off across the Channel last week." From that moment forward, the paper mailed its regular edition to France on a daily basis. The gesture did not go unappreciated in the ranks.[232]

As to the newsmen themselves, covering the Normandy operation was both a fantasy and a horrid nightmare. Hal Boyle described the invasion as "one of those stories any reporter dreams of having once in a lifetime and wouldn't want two of if he lived a thousand years." Warcos existed in separate worlds, with each posing their own distinct challenges. Reporters in the field "just hand their copy to the nearest passenger pigeon or public relations officer and trust that in the fullness of time it will get back to civilization. Then they can relax and go back to watching battles, ducking bullets, and trying to find a laundry." In a sarcastic sense, that environment seemed comfortable "compared to the horrors of the three daily headquarters press conferences which break up in a mad scramble for telephones, during which nobody's life or limbs are safe." This "catch-as-catch can school of journalism" required correspondents to labor at a rate somewhere between "a greyhound and a lightning typist."

On this point, Boyle particularly admired Wes Gallagher, "the newsman's newsman." As one of the first reporters to arrive at the stately granite building of the British Ministry of Information on June 6, Gallagher relished the opportunity to break the story. Secluded in a high-ceilinged room, Gallagher and his fellow correspondents briefly previewed the communiqué confirming invasion. Nearby, radioman Edward Murrow pounded away with his signature cigarette hanging from his lip. "Newspaper and magazine correspondents have maybe two, maybe one deadline a day," he sluggishly declared. "We have one every fifteen minutes."

"Now, gentlemen, you have exactly 33 minutes to prepare your dispatches," an officer informed them. According to Boyle, "Gallagher bent over his small portable typewriter—which nobody else in England can operate—and it began to whirl like a lawnmower on a golf green." In that half hour Gallagher cranked out a compelling 1,300-word report.

"In exactly five seconds you will be free to file your dispatches," a calm British brigadier announced in a punctuated accent. "One, two, three, four. . . ."

Upon reaching "five" the doors swung open "and through it flashed a human torpedo in an olive blouse and pink trousers. That was Gallagher—on his way to a telephone."

The six-foot, 180-pound reporter bolted down the hallway shouting, "Gangway!"

"Flash! And It's Off! Flash!" he barked into a phone. Within seconds his dictation was clicking away on the AP's teletype machines for global distribution. The article appeared on the front pages of America by that afternoon.

Gallagher received many pats on the back for his stellar speed but, after twenty-four hours on the job, he hoofed to bed with an ungratified disposition.

"You know, I never had a single fight with the censor all day," he fumed as his eyebrows curled upward. "I must be slipping."[233]

War correspondents toiled tirelessly to cobble together stories of incredible scope and profound importance, often with bureaucracy and limited resources hindering their efforts. Scores donned helmets and lifebelts for the sake of personally unveiling D-Day to the world. Some would not return. However, most agreed their own plights paled in contrast to the daily terrors beleaguering common soldiers. In the coming days and weeks, tales of those fighting men would emerge in print as the heart and soul of the expedition to free a continent.

The Allied airmen who had long flown over Normandy were soon to receive a helping hand. In the twilight hours of June 5, elite vanguards of the forthcoming assaults prepared to lunge into the dark undergrowth and flooded swamps of occupied France. With these men, clad in scrim and smeared in black, came the hope of tomorrow.

CHAPTER 6

Day of Daze

The base was alive with the melodies of organized chaos. The metallic grind of sliding rifle bolts, the clangorous snaps of parachute harnesses, and the coarse rumbling of jeeps crisscrossing runways bespoke a concerted whirl of preparation. Warrant Officer Ernest L. Dilburn, who already assembled his jump kit, impatiently tapped his fingers on his netted, steel helmet. Practically lost amid the unwieldy jumble of tethered straps and overstuffed pouches, the twenty-seven-year-old pathfinder sat practically anchored to a concrete slab, bristling with agitated energy. He was ready to *go*.

His comrades of the 506th Parachute Infantry Regiment appeared nonchalant in their own chores, laughing and gossiping in nearby tents and hangars. Some caught a camp movie earlier that day. Others diligently absorbed final briefings and scrutinized sand tables. By evening, they began to methodically layer some 100 pounds of gear and chutes over their brawny frames. A glimmer of sunlight sprouted through the overcast. The rains had passed, although mud from the sodden pastures still speckled the men's heavily-shined Corcorans. In tens and twenties, the encumbered paratroopers wobbled to the planes that, within hours, they would leap from. The aura was not one of fear, but of restrained elation.

Before he boarded Plane #9, Dilburn used these final spare moments to write his mother in Dothan, Alabama. Employing his reserve parachute as a lap desk, he remarked, "We didn't go last night because of technicalities, but we have had the final word that we go in tonight. I am able to tell you this for the letter won't be mailed until after the whole world knows the news." Thrill radiated from the warrant officer's words. "Thousands upon thousands of American parachutists are landing tonight to clear the beaches for the seaborne troops to come in and believe me, we are going to do a good job of it. I have the pleasure to know that I will be with the first of the parachutists," he beamed. "No one seems to be worried, but tonight at 12:40, we will ring the bell that will be heard around the world."

Dilburn's mother, Stella, then stopped receiving letters from her son. Weeks later she obtained the dreaded news that Ernest was missing in action. She feared the worst. Months of uncertainty followed as the widowed mother pondered the whereabouts of her absent boy. Not until October was she notified of his fate. Less than twenty-four hours after Dilburn composed his exuberant letter, the trooper was captured and endured the rest of the war as a "guest of the Third Reich." Stella prayed for him every day until his release. She savored another two decades of life with her son, a grace deprived of so many mothers that summer.[234]

Among others dwelling in prayerful vigilance was Pfc. Charles V. "Jackie" Bray of Pittsburgh, whose invasion account was published thereafter in the *Post-Gazette*. On the eve of D-Day, he and his comrades waited in line to attend religious services, which were held in steady shifts. Catholic priests donned in green vestments chanted the Latin sacramental words of absolution and communion. "It seems everybody was at church some time that day."

Having atoned for his transgressions, Bray soon waddled to the C-47 whisking him to France. It was 8:15 p.m. His fellow passengers' hands and faces were lathered in black grease, "just like Halloween," they giggled. "Loaded down with an entrenching tool, gas mask, four hand grenades, 15 pounds of TNT, about 100 rounds of ammunition, a trench knife, our toilet articles, change of underwear, and medical supplies, we were ready." Bray's plane barreled down the runway at 10:30, circling the sky until accompanying planes joined the formation. "Soon we were on our way."

Once in flight, few spoke. The constant throb of the aircraft's two Pratt & Whitney engines overpowered most conversations. The overburdened paratroopers clumsily wiggled in their concaved metal benches while rolling the flint wheels of their Zippos, "lighting one right after the other." A frequent comment among passengers was, "What time is it? *Mmm, mmm*, not long now." With mounting nervousness fatiguing them, others simply slept, their helmeted heads bobbing back and forth in the turbulence.

Original caption: "See You in Berlin. Resolute faces of paratroopers just before they took off for the initial assault of D-Day. Paratrooper in foreground has just read Gen. Eisenhower's message of good luck and clasps his bazooka in determination. Note Eisenhower's D-Day order in hands of paratrooper [Bob Noody]." (10)

Beyond the French coastline, the otherwise tranquil glide was thunderously interrupted by German flak punching through the plane like a fist through paper. The paratroopers gritted their teeth and clenched their narrow pods with white-knuckled fists. "We knew we weren't going to last long in that but we still had about 10 minutes to go, and it really dragged," said Bray. All stood together for a final equipment check. "Our red light went on, then the green came. That was it! Out that door we dove in a hurry. They were trying to machine gun us on the way down." Red and green tracers whizzed toward Bray, their lambent heat pulsating the sky. He gripped his chute riser and hurriedly

pulled down, expediting his descent. Rapidly approaching the dim coun-
tryside, Bray unsheathed his trench knife, slashing his belts and cables.
He was halfway freed from his harness when he hit the ground at 1 a.m.
Here it was, he thought. France.

Immediately, "the Jerries were spraying the field with machine gun
fire." The farm pastures flickered with the orange bursts of German
MG-42s and the staccato pops of small arms. Oblivious to their location,
Bray and some thirty disoriented companions darted toward a nearby
tree line to assemble into their respective outfits. The organizational
task proved impossible as parachutists had literally scattered to the
wind. Instead, Bray and company formed into extemporized squads,
setting into the night to wreak havoc. "We didn't get any rest for the
first few nights at all, we kept going all the time."

The men refueled with liberated stockpiles of champagne, wine, and
cider—intoxicated by the lively compounds of alcohol and adrenalin.
They reeked of body odor and booze. Bray lugged a bottle in his reinforced jump trousers until a heavy leap into a ditch shattered it. The
lost patrol meandered through the deluged swamps, struggling to keep
their heads above water. Elsewhere, scores succumbed to drowning in
flooded fields and impassable marshes. The occasional enemy round
zipped past Bray's head, casting ripples in the slimy muck. Mosquitoes
and gnats harassed him with even greater consistency. For five days,
Bray and his compatriots waged their own style of guerilla war, "attacking where we could, and causing as much damage as we could," he attested. Bray's tale of mischance and spontaneity was not the exception
but the norm for his paratrooper brethren.[235]

Cpl. Philip H. Bucknell's ordeal with the 506th was no less chaotic.
"The trip across was easy, and the paratroopers took it easy," wrote the
Stars and Stripes staffer. "Most of the men in my plane slept until we
hit the French coast." No sleep was to be had, however, when yellow
and green tracers lit up the sky with a vengeance. The terrain below
soon resembled the sand table maps paratroopers memorized in England.

"This is it, fellers," said the battalion commander. "Let's go."

"They were shooting at us as we came down," Bucknell continued,
"and we had to slip our chutes violently to escape the fire. That acceler-
ates the speed of drop, and the impact of landing was too much for this

reporter, who received a broken leg. This kind of injury was fairly common throughout the drops." For nearly eight hours, Buck sat in a state of semi-isolation while the rattle of small arms emanated from surrounding woodlots. He penned his article before an Army doctor finally set his leg. He did not want morphine to muddle his words.[236]

The primary function of the American and British airborne actions—the largest in history up to that point—was to thwart any German rebuttals to the larger Allied landings on the coast, particularly Utah Beach. Some 13,000 men descended from the night sky as a prelude to the amphibious operations. They were spearheaded by pathfinders such as Ernest Dilburn, who signaled approaching aircraft and illuminated the drop zones. The disjointed nature of airborne landings, entwined with subsequent piecemeal assaults, dumbfounded wholly unsuspecting German garrisons. No drop zones were designated behind Omaha Beach due to the flat, unbroken terrain. Airborne commanders, Brig. Gen. James Gavin among them, cared not to have their men mowed down in open fields of fire. The quaint hamlets of the peninsula were soon ravaged by seesaw clashes over the country lanes interconnecting them. The crossroads village of Sainte-Mère-Église—located behind Utah—became perhaps the most contested of all as GIs endeavored to withstand relentless German counterattacks. Most alarmingly, if the beach missions failed, the airborne would be forsaken between the Germans and the sea as a sacrificial lamb. The paratroopers vowed this would not happen.[237]

Comprised of battle-hardened veterans and greenhorns alike, the paratroopers were the "toughest, wiriest men of war," surmised Howard Cowan. They "cascaded from faintly moonlit skies in an awesome operation" to strike "a single sledgehammer blow paving the way for the frontal assault forces." Armed with weapons both primitive and sophisticated, their descending wrath was to demoralize and destroy any and all German resistance. They carried knives in their boots, brass knuckles in their pockets, and five cent cricket toys to discretely signal comrades in the darkness. "The steel-helmeted, ankle-booted warriors wore a red, white, and blue American flag insignia on the sleeve and camouflaged green splotched battle dress," wrote Cowan. The paratroops relished their own menacing grit and the fear they instilled in enemies. To fully embrace their warrior ethos, some shaved their heads in Mohawk style and applied "war paint" to their freckled faces. While visiting the troops on June 5, Eisenhower had inquired what the paint consisted of. "Cocoa and cottonseed oil," was the reply. "It tastes good." According to the *Fitchburg Sentinel*, "The sweat of invasion is pleasantly flavored for some." Cowan doubted the paratroopers' steely resolve, physical agility, and slick marksmanship would fail them.[238]

Due to rigorous airborne training, comparatively few journalists ventured out on C-47s that night. Wright Bryan and William Walton notably deviated from this pattern. Bryan, an NBC correspondent and managing editor of the *Atlanta Journal*, offered commentary of his rocky ride on a plane named *Snooty*. When boarding, each paratrooper was "so heavily loaded," wrote Bryan, "that he had to be pushed from behind and pulled from above to get up the steps into the plane." Pacing up and down the aisle, Lt. Col. Robert Cole offered words of comfort. The plane's cabin grew grimly silent. Paratrooper Robert C. Hillman of Manchester, Connecticut found consolation in the fact that his chute was manufactured by the Pioneer Parachute Company. His mother worked at the plant and her inspection initials were on his chute. Hillman was not concerned with factory defects.

Bryan peered through the dome of the plane and found no fighter escorts. He hoped the Luftwaffe would not make a surprise appearance. Views of the countryside flittered through a thick bank of clouds—revealing ground so close that parachutes hardly seemed necessary. "The small fields look peaceful with their orderly hedgerows," he thought. The plane neared the drop zone, the red signal glimmered, and men hooked their clips to the static line in robotic uniformity. The light flashed green. "Before I had counted to 10 seconds . . . our passengers had left us." One soldier banged himself so forcibly against the door frame that he bounced back in a daze. Comrades heaved his limp body aside and vaulted from the aircraft. When the battered trooper awakened, the drop zone was far past and the plane was homeward bound. Fearing his companions would think him cowardly, the bruised GI was inconsolable.

Bryan returned to England, compiled his notes, wrote his story, submitted it to censors, recorded the report, and had NBC transmit it from London to New York. Bryan's commentary, delivered in his rich southern drawl, was the first eyewitness account of the invasion broadcasted on the radio. He concluded his fourteen-minute reflection with the stirring words, "The battle of Europe had begun."[239]

William Walton, a thirty-four-year-old Illinoisan, came of age in a newspaper family while his father published the *Jacksonville Journal-Courier*. An amateur painter and correspondent with *Time* magazine, he befriended Ernest Hemingway and Robert Capa only weeks before the jump. Intrigued by Walton's crash course in parachuting, the thrill-seeking duo was immediately drawn to the reporter's boldness. The sleepless writer put his audaciousness to the test. He cabled during the invasion's opening phases, "I plunged out of the plane door happy to be leaving a ship that was heading toward flak and more Germans. The jump was from such low altitude there was only a moment to look around in the moonlight after my chute opened. The fields looked so small."

The *Time* reporter helplessly landed in a pear tree, what he called "a rather good shock absorber." He dangled three feet above the ground, unable to extricate himself from the tree's snarled grip. Walton's parachute harness snaked around his neck, limiting his breathing and blocking access to a switchblade in his breast pocket. He flapped as a perfect target for snipers lingering in the darkness. "In a hoarse, frightened voice I kept whispering the password, hoping someone would hear and help," Walton wrote. "From a nearby hedge I heard voices. I hung still a moment, breathless."

"Flash."

"Thunder!"

Friends.

"Never has a Middle Western accent sounded better," he sighed. "I called a little louder. Quietly Sergeant Auge, a fellow I knew, crept out of the hedge, tugged at the branches and with his pigsticker cut my suspension cords. I dropped like an overripe pear." Within seconds, Walton wrestled himself from the web of accoutrements and, with typewriter in hand, lunged toward the nearest brush enclosure where a handful of misplaced paratroopers sought refuge. By morning, all realized their position was untenable. The only escape route was a vast swamp heading toward a railroad line.

Into the chest-deep quagmire they ventured, holding rifles (and a typewriter) above their heads. "When machine gun bullets started pinging around us the sweat began to trickle," Walton recalled. "Water filled our pockets and every ounce became a pound. A few men were killed in that crossing, but most of us got across to the railway. By then our last

117

ounce of energy seemed gone. But we went on two miles, panting and puffing up the track to dry land. Snipers were still taking a wham at us every now and then. Half our equipment was gone, but my typewriter was waterproofed, and I have it still." Subsisting off the land, the crippled squad had only three hours of sleep in three days. On June 9, a brief intermission in a blooming apple orchard allowed Walton to compose his first report. The orchard "would be lovely if you could ignore the shelling, the dirt, the burning fatigue," he concluded.[240]

Pvt. Lawrence R. Dilley, age twenty, also experienced the hard hand of war. D-Day was his twentieth jump. Clothed in a foul-smelling gas-impregnated jumpsuit, Dilley sported a Thompson submachine gun and an apron-like kit brimming with classified maps. "It was a nice moonlight night, and below us as our plane sped over the Normandy coastline, we could see countless bombers had dropped their loads," he wrote. "At precisely 12:37 it came my turn to jump—the blazing ruins of a house in Carentan were visible below as I tumbled out of the plane. Less than 20 seconds later I landed on French soil, unharnessed my chute, and put my Tommy Gun together." Standing within range of German artillery, his company quickly assembled.

By dawn they converged on their objective at Sainte-Marie-du-Mont, where Dilley fired his first shots in anger. A German officer scaled an old French tank as the enemy withdrew from the commune. Dilley sprayed a burst of Thompson rounds at the retreating armor. "I don't know if I made a hit because the tank rumbled out of town," the private confessed. Not long after, Dilley himself was wounded in the right leg and out of the fight. From Neuville-au-Plain to La Fière, pastures and streets echoed with the incessant rattling of gunfire. In the thick of it all was Pvt. Daniel Day, who quipped about "D. Day" actively participating in D-Day.[241]

Numerous invaders enjoyed a flair for the dramatic. Such was particularly the case of Capt. Frank Lillyman, a cigar-chomping twenty-nine-year-old paratrooper from Syracuse. Lillyman descended from an off-beat military lineage. His father was an old school soldier of fortune, having served in the Argentine navy, the Brazilian cavalry, the American Navy, and the U. S. Army. That same cavalier zeal was apparent in the son's actions. D-Day was Lillyman's 48th jump, although it was his first into combat. During every flight, the 140-pound officer lit a cigar sent by his wife. "It's just a pet superstition," he told Howard Cowan. "I swallowed the end of one once." The superstition served the captain well, for he survived the jumps and much more.

Contemplating the horrors of the battlefield, Lillyman later yearned for the pleasures of home. He once wrote to New York's Pennsylvania Hotel, "I desire a suite that will face east so the sun will wake me in the morning. I do not desire to know in advance what dishes will be served, but I do not want a dish repeated. If meals are served after dark in the suite, I would like tapers for table lighting. I desire a one way telephone—outgoing only." Returning from Europe in 1945, Lillyman appeared at the hotel's front desk with $500 and inquired if his wartime fantasy could be accommodated. He was told to stow his money away, invite his family, and be a "guest of the house." Upon his death from a stroke in 1971, the *New York Times* recognized Lillyman as the "First Paratrooper at Normandy."[242]

Other combatants entered the bitter contest in more subdued manners. *Stars and Stripes* reported the unusual case of Charles E. Schmelz, a twenty-year-old private from Pittsburgh who served in a 9th Air Force ground crew. Not wishing to miss the "Greatest Show on Earth," Schmelz stowed away on a Horsa glider and fell asleep in a rear compartment. Twenty minutes into the flight he rapped on the door and was let out by baffled troopers, who promptly fed him and offered airsickness pills. The glider landed within stone's throw of a German emplacement and Schmelz ultimately distinguished himself by crawling 300 muddy yards to retrieve rations. However, his path of glory led him only to the guardhouse. The private was arrested on AWOL charges and speedily extradited to England. Although his illicit adventure became legendary in the ranks, Schmelz was slapped with a summary court martial, a thirty-day restriction, a $20 fine (deducting nearly half a month's pay), and eight days in the stockade. The stowaway was not remorseful of his actions, however. He wrote his mother, "That was some deal for doing more in three days in France than I have done in two years in the states and England."[243]

There seemed no shortage of stowaways in the ETO. In Britain, reporter Howard Whitman stumbled across a forlorn batch of paratroopers itching to fight. On D-Day, flak struck one of their plane engines. The transport feebly sputtered toward England but did not last the entire journey. "Cussing their bad luck, the airborne fighters had to bail out over the Channel. RAF patrol craft picked them up." Whitman later discovered the soggy paratroopers on an English pier as the second and third assault waves loaded onto LCIs. They furtively began scaling the gangplank.

"Sorry, boys, but all loading of ships is scheduled in advance. I'm afraid we can't take you," a condoling officer explained.

"We won't take much room; we'll stand on deck all the way over," one paratrooper pleaded to no avail.[244]

Meanwhile, Pvt. George W. Banfi, a former metal worker from Follansbee, West Virginia, discovered a more sympathetic host; or rather, she discovered him. Shattering his leg when toppling in a ditch, Banfi clambered into a nearby meadow where a civilian family offered brandy, water, and aid to American casualties. Night soon fell and, amidst the chirping of crickets and bullfrogs, Banfi feared every snapping twig was broken by a predatory German. Instead, out of the brush emerged a young girl Banfi described as "in her teens and very pretty." She comforted the agonized paratrooper with gentle serenades, placing his head in her lap. The girl kept Banfi's weapon at her side. *Yank* magazine even told "how she grabbed his carbine and killed a Jerry who was crawling over the hedge." The private was retrieved and returned to England. His jumping days may have been over, but he was thankful for the young girl who saved his life.[245]

Guardian angels of the battlefield manifested in many forms, including what paratroopers perceived as the spiritual shield of chaplains. Over 12,000 priests, ministers, and rabbis served in the American military during World War II and several hundred witnessed the moral complexities and challenges of the Normandy invasion. Capt. Raymond S. "Chappie" Hall, the Army's first parachuting parson, hurdled mountains of red tape to participate in the operation. When a correspondent asked Hall about his motivation to earn jump wings, the captain replied, "It increases attendance at church, and the men can talk to me now." The proactive team-building philosophy earned him the endearing nickname of "Jumping Jesus."[246]

Hall lunged from the C-47 named *That's All, Brother*, one of the leading American planes of the invasion. In surviving the assault, Hall penned a letter to the rector of his former church in Massachusetts. His correspondence appeared in the *Fitchburg Sentinel* two weeks later, proclaiming, "Thought you might like to know that I'm still alive and kicking after going through hell for a week after D-Day. . . . I have been fired at a number of times in broad daylight in spite of my Red Cross brassard. Those of us who got through that first night were lucky and that's all there is to it." Not even the Lord could spare men here.[i]

The chaplain painfully witnessed his boys stagger into aid stations, bloodied and tattered beyond recognition. "It was almost more than I could stand, but I had to take it." He supported their broken limbs, injected morphine, adjusted splints while under fire, and assured those writhing in pain that God loved them. With a striking endnote, he confessed, "The casualties among the Germans were terrific. The whole business seems senseless to me, and I'll sure be glad when it's over."[247]

The business was far from over. Within days, the 101st Airborne converged on Carentan to unify the American beach zones and to bolster the front against enemy counterblows. Half a millennium after the Battle of Formigny, vast armies once more swirled around the historic French city. Pushing inland, United Press correspondent Henry Gorrell discovered Hall on Carentan's outskirts as the battle raged.

"It's hell down there," Hall warned. "I know, because I've been with those kids for several hours." The two men rested on their stomachs and watched U. S. artillery hammer a cluster of German pillboxes pinning the Yanks in ditches. Panting runners darted to and fro with coordinates for a binoculars-wielding colonel. The commander roared into the field telephone with his singsong, "Okay, fire. . . . On the way!"

Gorrell and Hall were transfixed as the "shells went over with a freight train rush," shrouding the pillboxes in choking dust and "flashes of vivid red flame."

"Thank God for that one," ironically whispered the parson. "That had to be placed just right, because otherwise it would have hit our kids lying out there in the gutters."

At that moment Lt. Jack A. Borchert of Denver rushed to the guns, offering a personal report in light of his radio being peppered. With his helmet dented by bullet ricochets and his uniform ripped, Borchert shared a gloomy sketch of the dire situation: "We were in the leading assault company," he gulped. "We crossed three of the four bridges and were making good progress. But then the Germans rallied, reoccupied

---

[i] The plane named *That's All, Brother* was rediscovered in a Wisconsin aircraft boneyard in 2015 and has been restored to flying condition by the Commemorative Air Force and Basler Turbo Conversions.

prepared positions, and began to counterattack with bayonets and grenades. I haven't seen many of my outfit since the last time they hit us."
Whether they were dead, captured, or lost, he knew not. Liaison officer
Lt. Robert Dixon was equally concerned. "They've pinned us down with
mortars and 88s in the narrowest front. I fought in water up to my hips
and then crawled to the forward command post. I mean I half-walked,
half-crawled because if I'd gotten down on my belly I'd have drowned.
Men were falling all around me. I don't know why I wasn't shot."

The maelstrom spared neither man nor beast. With his field glasses
Gorrell sighted the bloating carcasses of cows, mules, and horses intermingled with the khaki and gray-clad corpses. He witnessed a shepherd
dog bolt out of a house struck by artillery. The whimpering, disfigured
creature scampered madly in circles until it collapsed and died mercilessly in the dirt. Species of all manners shared a common fate as car-
rion. A miasma of death clung to the air.

The all-consuming universe of battle failed to damper the spirits of
many. Gorrell trekked to a makeshift hospital where he discovered
"men still able to joke after being pinned down for hours in the swamps."
A medic with a minor fragment wound in the back of his neck was
greeted with dismissive laughter. "Oh ho," cried his fellows, "here comes
another candidate for the Purple Heart." The candidate smiled bash-
fully and went about his grisly chores. A spiteful wounded German officer spurned a bowl of hot soup and babbled for wine instead. None was
to be had. "The wounded came in with teeth chattering, drenched to the
skin," Gorrell continued. "First aiders held cigarettes to their teeth
while their blood-soaked clothing was cut away from the wounds. For
some it was their last cigarette. They just puffed silently, shut their
eyes, and died before me." The correspondent departed the aid station,
wiped away a tear, and marched onward.[248]

Like most uniformed non-combatants, chaplains were not spared the
emotional grief and physical injuries of war. Incorporating diluted profanities, Chaplain Hall fumed to a friend in describing his own wounding. "I'm as mad as a March hare," he raged. "They finally got me after
I had been through hell without a scratch. Our outfit was miles away
from the enemy, but some sniper fired a few shots and then threw a
grenade at me. It landed a few feet away. The concussion was so bad I
thought I had lost my left cheek, but it only hit me in the eye." The

wound was painful and temporarily impaired his vision. Now Hall, too, became a candidate for the Purple Heart.

As the first chaplain to land in France, Hall exhibited pride in his feat. However, periodicals reported of another padre making the same assertion. "Our boys were up in arms [about the claim] and wrote the newspaper asking for an apology as this chaplain landed an hour *after* H-Hour and I landed six hours *before* H-Hour. I jumped in plane No. 1 in the whole invasion. I was the first and the boys knew it. I got a kick out of this attitude." Regardless of his celebrity, Hall no longer feared empty pews at his services. The men adored their "Fighting Parson." He spilt his blood alongside them.[249]

Chaplain George B. Wood of Austin, Minnesota made his invasion plunge at nearly the same moment as Hall. His thirteenth jump was "far rougher" than previous dives into Sicily and Italy. The Episcopalian lauded his fellow chaplains in the press, claiming that a dozen other "Holy Joes" parachuted into France on June 6. One of them was Capt. Matthew J. Connelly, a Roman Catholic priest from Denver who fractured his vertebra on landing. Despite his injury, Connelly remained in the field for a month, insisting only his rib was slightly sore. Capt. Ignatius Maternowski, a Franciscan father, arrived in Normandy with the 508th Parachute Infantry Regiment around 1:30. Organizing relief efforts for the wounded, Maternowski was killed by a sniper in the village of Picauville. He was thirty-two years of age. His tombstone in Massachusetts was dedicated with the biblical passage, "There is no greater love than to lay down one's life for one's friends."[250]

Nobody was safe. The citizens of San Benito, Texas recognized this startling fact upon reading of the untimely death of Brig. Gen. Donald F. Pratt. The general once resided in their border town prior to the World Wars and his demise dealt a troubling blow. As the assistant division commander of the 101st Airborne, Pratt boarded a Waco glider bound for France and assumed his position in a jeep fatefully anchored to the floor. Near Sainte-Marie-du-Mont his aircraft skidded on the slick pasture grass and turbulently collided with a row of formidable Poplars. The general's neck snapped from whiplash. Of all the Allied personnel lost on D-Day, Pratt ranked the highest. Americans read his obituary and worried, if a brigadier is not safe, who *is* safe?[251]

German officers were no less endangered on the battlefront; men such as Malcolm D. Brannen assured as much. The lieutenant was thirty-three-years-old—truly an old man by Army standards. A former barber near the University of New Hampshire, he applied for the paratroops "to get out of college boys' hair and into Hitler's." According to his chums, the balding, stocky, and bowlegged cosmetologist possessed wit as sharp as the razor he used on freshmen chins.

Brannen now toted a new weapon of choice—the M-1 Carbine. Clark Lee of the International New Service chronicled how the comedic hair trimmer-turned-warrior single-handedly played "a large part in disrupting enemy defenses." Dropped with the 82nd Airborne, Brannen tediously dangled from a tree while unidentifiable columns of troops marched on an adjacent roadway. Stray bullets whizzed past the lieutenant's head until he cut himself free and discovered four equally adrift GIs. The group cautiously slinked across littered pastures and, as dawn neared, rapped on the door of a French farmhouse for directions. Before any orientation could be gained, the paratroopers heard a choked rumble down the gravel road.

A growing cloud of dust caught the light of the moon. A sleek, gray Phaeton rapidly approached. As the open-top automobile neared, Brannen jumped in the middle of the lane with carbine raised and ordered the motorist to halt. The car instead accelerated and barreled toward the lieutenant. The paratroopers opened fire, peppering the luxury vehicle with a stinging volley. A German major in the backseat slumped over, his blood thickly pooling onto the leather interior. The car careened into the farmhouse and the corporal driver speedily crawled through an open cellar window.

Brannen guardedly tiptoed toward another enemy officer sprawled on the gravel. The German glanced up and yelled, "Don't kill! Don't kill!" in English. All the while, his gloved hand crept toward his holstered Luger.

With his own pistol already raised, Brannen yelped, "Stop! Stop!"

The German did not cease. Brannen pulled the trigger. The Nazi officer flopped on the ground like a rag doll.

Little could have Brannen immediately recognized the ramifications of his roadside duel. The dead man's collar was adorned with the distinctive red and gold tabs of a general. Inside the general's hat was the name Wilhelm Falley. The Generalleutnant, commander of the 91st Division overseeing key coastal defenses, was returning from ironically-timed war games near Rennes when he stumbled into Brannen's ambush.

"I shot," explained Brannen, "because I figured if he got that Luger it would be one or more of us killed before we killed him. It was the first time I had shot my .45."

With the general's driver in tow, the men dashed toward the sound of the guns emanating from Sainte-Mère-Église. "We kept alert and avoided enemy patrols" the lieutenant explained. "I was with an American private as we forced an opening through a hedgerow into a field. Suddenly I heard bullets ping. The kid beside me looked at me with the most awful look I've ever seen and said, 'Who shot me?'" Brannen yanked the private over a hedgerow. He was already dead—shot twice through the back.

Separated from his mates, Brannen "lived like a hunted animal" for five days. He crawled in and out of scummy ditches amid a grim game of cat and mouse. Hoping to finish off the cornered soldier, Germans vainly fired continuously into the undergrowth. Brannen eventually plodded into a patch "so thick that not even Br'er Rabbit would have entered, especially with a Nazi machine pistoler just across the wall." There, Brannen remained for two and a half days with no fresh water and only a box of K-rations.

"I should be dead," he confided to Clark Lee.

Brannen's salvation was announced with a point of clarification. He could faintly hear a GI explain to a comrade the sound difference between the trills of American and German machine guns.

"Now that gun is for us . . . and that gun is agin' us," the distant voiced declared.

Brannen was ecstatic. "I knew no German would say 'agin' so I shouted to them. I was so weak when I tried to stand that I fell flat on my face." But the lieutenant was spared.

Lee presented Brannen additional good news. The lieutenant's lost followers returned safely to American lines—along with Falley's valise and chauffeur.[252]

From an embattled command post, Combined Press correspondent Leonard Moseley reported his own sensational rescue, one he deemed fitting for a movie screenplay. Moseley plunged into the invasion at 1:02

a.m. "Jumping by parachute is an action whose emotional side has been described before," he reported. "And yet no one ever gets it—that tremendous roar of the slipstream and then the blissful peace of the soft night, once your chute develops." His tranquility was short lived, for he quickly recalled the soggy terrain below was chock-full of flooded fields, sharpened obstacles, and a foe with a track record.

Moseley twisted his neck back and forth in search of his rendezvous point—a wooded area neighboring a church. The winds whisked him eastward, away from his predetermined objective. "Faster and faster I twisted, and I had to wrestle with my straps to get myself straight. By that time I had come down in an orchard outside a farmhouse. And as I stood up with my harness off and wiped the sweat off my brown-painted face, I knew I was hopelessly lost."

Dare he go to the farmhouse for guidance? It did not matter. Before he could collect an answer, his smock loudly ripped in the brush and a thundering of machine guns responded in kind. Clusters of hand grenades were hurled at him. "What do you do in those circumstances, when you are not allowed to carry arms?" he thought. Crouching through tangles of barbed wire, Moseley bypassed the silhouetted figures but soon encountered two more armed men not forty-five feet away.

Germans.

Moseley made his peace and prepared for what seemed the inevitable. A sudden crash of small arms, however, offered a reprieve. The advancing enemy crumpled to the ground. "Into the field stealthily came five men to challenge me—and I was with our own paratroopers again."

For nearly two hours their patrol roamed until a flask-toting French boy guided the paratroopers around German positions and to the elusive rendezvous point. What might have happened to Moseley had his airborne rescuers not appeared was one of the great "ifs" of his personal history, he observed.[253]

With even greater flair, Tom Hoge flamboyantly described a notorious lot of paratroopers known as the "Filthy Thirteen." A demolition team of the 506th assigned to blow bridges spanning the Douve River, the section gained a colorful reputation even before setting foot in France. Defying traditional military convention at every turn, the men were described as "the orneriest, meanest group of paratroopers." Refusing to sleep in barracks or tents, they bragged of not bathing since Christmas.

They were a suicide squad with an arrogance few challenged. "At night they flung themselves on the ground in full battle dress, their beloved knives and machetes close to them. And they refused to wash. Not until after D-Day, they said."[ii]

Loading for the invasion, the members shaved their heads and daubed war paint on their faces—much to the delight of the press. In the darkness of D-Day, "their painted features had a savage glare." Plummeting into violence and uncertainty, the firebrands went about tasks of sabotage and subversion. "No one knows yet just what happened to the Filthy Thirteen," wrote Hoge on June 9. "But all agree on one thing. Pity the poor Nazi who encounters them."[254]

Written like an enthralling bedtime fable, the report offered servicemen mythical interpretations of an elite fighting force defined by a gung-ho, can-do philosophy. The outfit was depicted as an admirable gang of killers. Yet the piece failed to convey a holistic depiction of the unit. "We weren't murderers or anything," later recalled Filthy Thirteen veteran Jack Agnew. "[W]e just didn't do everything we were supposed to do in some ways and did a whole lot more than they wanted us to do in other ways. We were always in trouble."[255]

The men were hardly heartless killers, although war compelled them to commit painful acts. Jack Womer, a private with the Thirteen, commented, "The most difficult part about killing is living the rest of your life with the knowledge of lives you've taken." Nobody he knew enjoyed killing, but it was their job. "One part about killing that I could never get used to," he recalled, "was seeing the eyes of an enemy soldier just as I shot him. It bothered me to observe the pain, fear, and horror in a man's eyes immediately after being shot and about to die." Womer therefore preferred using the M-1 Garand against his enemy due to its powerful capacity. "[Then] I wouldn't be able to see the expression in his eyes."

A moment of compassion arrived for Womer when he found an adolescent German soldier wounded and wiggling in the mud. "I couldn't help but feel sorry for him." Womer carried the youth across the lines to an American aid station in a farmhouse. Some GIs were livid since the private's selfless deed could have drawn enemy fire. "They had a valid

---

[ii] The "Filthy Thirteen" were the inspiration for the classic 1967 movie *The Dirty Dozen*.

point," Womer said, later in life, "but I wasn't about to let that boy die."[256]

The disclosed fierceness and stagecraft of American paratroopers bedeviled their foes. Harry Garrett of the United Press witnessed the enemy's angst firsthand. Bearing knives and grenades, a small band of paratroopers wiped out nests of 88-mm guns following a fierce, two-hour scrap. Entrapped Germans in the surrounding pillboxes were hesitant to surrender; paratroopers did not take prisoners, they heard. The threat of explosives persuaded them to yield. The Yank conquerors moved swiftly alongside an impressive white horse, which they had purchased from a civilian for 500 francs. Around the steed's neck was a yellow recognition flag. "He's hauling our equipment," the paratroops explained. "We need all our strength for the next fight." Garrett did not doubt their claim.[257]

While GIs such as Jack Womer were jealous of the Germans' chic gray uniforms, the Krauts apparently envied the abundance of airborne equipment. "No other unit in the world is so well equipped as the American paratroops," said Gunter Weber of the German Overseas News Agency. *Stars and Stripes* claimed staff officers at Field Marshal Rundstedt's headquarters described airborne units as "luxury divisions," a phrase that undoubtedly brought smirks to paratrooper faces. Their tiny compasses, luminous discs, medical equipment, silk maps, chewing gum, quantities of morphine, and "instruments for the imitation of animal sounds at night" impressed Weber. Yet, none of it would prevent the encirclement and defeat of the Allies, he assured.[258]

Capt. William J. Adams, a glider co-pilot from Dormont, Pennsylvania, much preferred the role of captor over captive. Diving into a crater following the destruction of his motorless craft, he found himself in a precarious situation. Most of his passengers were eviscerated by flak and the captain was soon surrounded. "When the mortar fire died down for a bit, I lifted my head out of a hole and began reaching for my rifle when I heard a bolt click. That's when I looked around into their muzzles," he said. The Germans dragged Adams to a nearby household.

"Soon I found one who spoke a few words of English, and I advised him that mortar fire would blow up the entire building if they didn't surrender soon," continued Adams. An accompanying scatter of mortar rounds offered emphasis to the captain's admonition. The guards abruptly grew chummy with the co-pilot, presenting him bread, butter, and vodka. Thanks to the bilingual skills of a fellow prisoner, the detainees realized their captors were predominantly Czechs, Poles, and Russians "pressed into frontline service by their Nazi overlords." Furthermore, the small number of bona fide Germans present had grown weary of the conflict. The reluctant combatants had been told Americans would slit their throats if they attempted surrender. Adams assured the conscripts that fate would not befall them. Within minutes the draftees agreed to be the prisoners of their prisoners—although they remained fearful of their stern German officers. Adams encouraged the men to coax their superiors into submission or shoot them.

Surprisingly, one of the officers entered the room and declared in broken English, "Here is my gun. Will you please consider me your prisoner?" Adams happily obliged.

The captain and his motley crew herded 156 prisoners into American lines. "When our infantry came up, they found 37-mm cannon and machine guns emplaced all over the area," Adams said. "So it saved us a lot of casualties when that gang gave up." Adams was thus hailed as the "Sergeant York of Oratory."[259]

Near Utah Beach, Adams encountered pal Alexis Neel, a glider lieutenant from Little Rock. Fleeing his decimated landing area, Neel fell in with paratroopers pushing toward the coast. "I didn't see many French people, but there were plenty of Germans—dead ones," he observed. "The paratroopers had taken care of them. Most of them had their faces blown off. Those paratroopers had really taken things over. I saw one wearing German boots and riding around in a German halftrack." The lieutenant also spotted some 150 German prisoners being corralled into a staging area. Some of the inmates were only thirteen or fourteen years of age. More were in their forties and fifties. "They must not have had their best troops in there," Neel thought. The prime of Germany's military manpower was quickly evaporating. In cattle-like fashion, prisoners were tagged and herded into pens. Adams and Neel received warm meals and showers on a departing LST. They celebrated their survival by sleeping until three in the afternoon.[260]

Lackluster enemy troops along coastal areas did not diminish the potentials of death or dismemberment. Shaved trees and poles impaled descending gliders and aircraft at an alarming rate. Combatants drowned in low-lying meadows. Beyond the dreaded 88s and MG-42s,

the ghastly German S-Mine known as "Bouncing Betty" spewed erup-
tions of marble-sized shrapnel upward into unsuspecting soldiers.
Countless thousands of mines were delicately removed by Allied forces.
In *Yank*, Flight Officer Primo Ceravolo attested to a murderous projec-
tile new to Americans. "The snipers we met were using wooden bullets
in some cases. They are red bullets, just a shade larger than our .30
calibers," he said. "They make a nasty sound. They're hollow and they
splinter and spread after hitting. I saw one paratrooper who was hit in
the leg. You never saw a bullet hole like that in your life."[261]

Miraculously, airborne casualty rates were fewer than commanders
anticipated. Eisenhower drew a sigh of relief. Scattered but determined,
the parachutists prevailed. "Casualties among our boys were so light it
was almost unbelievable," admitted Col. Ralph "Baz" Bagby. "But there
sure are a lot of German dead." By June 10, Bagby sported a full chin
of whiskers and sunken, bloodshot eyes. A decorated World War I veteran and pioneer of aerial observation, the aged daredevil was physically drained. His fatigue did not dampen his optimism, however. "With
a lot less confusion than a training exercise," he suggested, "the paratroopers captured bridges, viaducts, enemy gun positions, pillboxes,
road junctions, and other military objectives speedily and with very little opposition." Where others saw disorganization, Bagby recognized
learning curves. Like the glider stowaway who yearned to participate
in the assault, Bagby was not supposed to be in France. The fifty-one-
year-old colonel who assisted planning the airborne operations had no
intention of being chained behind a desk when glory was to be had. The
officer preferred jumping into Normandy to "see how things were going." He went AWOL to conduct his illicit reconnaissance. Bagby was
promptly reprimanded and then decorated. Rank surely had its privileges.[262]

According to the *Waterloo Daily Courier*, the paratroopers achieved so
total a surprise that "GIs entered one enemy post and found the table
set for breakfast, sat down, and enjoyed a hearty German-prepared
meal, including fresh eggs and milk." After the prolonged egg and milk
shortage in England, liberation never tasted so good. The presence of
fresh dairy items prompted Lt. Charles B. Ellington of High Point,
North Carolina to share a pertinent invasion tale with a correspondent.
"Making our way back for evacuation," Ellington said, "I died three or
four times. We knew there was fighting all around us. Once in the dark

I saw what looked like a line of men advancing against us. I told the other fellows, 'This is it, boys,' but when the line got near enough to see, it turned out to be a herd of cows. Those damned cows will always go where they hear human voices."[263]

Those less fortunate were served bullets for breakfast. Five tattered paratroopers who survived an emergency jump near Cherbourg spent the next two weeks on the run. "We had just one minute after the emergency bell sounded to get out of the plane," one recalled. "The first night we hid in the fields and the French brought us bread, butter, and milk. We had several skirmishes and finally got too hot and we moved on." One desperate firefight after another ensued. "It was tough," said North Carolinian Lloyd P. Porum. "We had 15 miserable days. At one time we were in the center of a concentrated artillery barrage behind us and on both sides, and infantry in front. We sneaked out that night, so close we could have shook the Germans' hands." On June 21, *Stars and Stripes* correspondent Robert Reuben discovered the bearded, "dusty and grime-covered quintet north of Montebourg" and provided a lift in an armored car he "borrowed" from the enemy.[264]

GIs used fists and wits to survive. Reporter Arthur Goodwin learned of one particularly creative trick from 1st Lt. J. F. Noonan of Meriden, Connecticut. "About 100 of our paratroopers were cut off near a little town behind the German lines," noted Noonan. "They didn't have much ammo or food—but they used their heads and had plenty of guts. They made the Fritzes believe that there were 1,500 of them. They used the French to give this impression—by all going to mass on Sunday so the civilians could see them. The boys said they were only the Catholics in the regiment—that all the rest were Protestants or Jews." The company then progressed onward to dismantle two German pillboxes and link up with the rest of their outfit in Carentan.[265]

Despite the perilous hardships of their Normandy journeys, the paratroopers and glider men of the 82nd and 101st Airborne Divisions lessened the strife for their counterparts soon to strike the beaches. Louisiana colonel G. M. Jones, a troop carrier group operations officer and veteran of the Sicilian Campaign, summed up the situation as well as any GI could: "The operation was satisfactory beyond expectations. It was the best example of airborne tactics that I have seen." It was his sixth invasion. He hoped there need not be a seventh.[266]

Exactly two weeks after D-Day, over 1,000 weary paratroopers crowded into Carentan's only movie house, Le Jeanne d'Arc. The cobblestone streets outside were still cluttered with blackened debris while the defaced, stucco dwellings were pocked with the scars of battle. For over four years the theater, owned by the English-speaking March Mouchel-Cafosse, was strictly limited to German propaganda films. The only French residents permitted in the establishment during that time were the local girlfriends of occupiers. All features were furnished by the Wehrmacht. The theater equipment, confiscated by the Nazis from a Parisian cinema, was manufactured in America.

The days of Magda Schneider and Heinz Engelmann movies were past. Now, *Stars and Stripes* hosted a special screening of the new comedy *Andy Hardy's Blonde Trouble*, starring the recently-inducted Mickey Rooney. Mouchel-Cafosse enthusiastically greeted his guests, exclaiming it was "a pleasure, monsieurs" to host "the parachutes." The parachutes, several of whom had just been awarded medals on the town square, gleefully piled into the auditorium. Thick cigarette smoke and juvenile laughter quickly blanketed the space. Reporter Charles F. King could not help but enjoy the spectacle. The "show was split into two performances and the only complaint from the paratroopers was that those blonde twins Pvt. Rooney couldn't handle were on the screen and not in the audience."[267]

The men were boys again, even if only momentarily. They slapped each other on their backs. They made lewd catcalls about actress Lyn Wilde's seductive figure. For some of them, it was their last movie. But they laughed just the same. They chuckled like giddy schoolboys, even as the dull thump of artillery forbiddingly echoed in the distance. The town had its theater back.

CHAPTER 7

"Sea of Bedlam"

The salty, forty-three-year-old port master maintained a sharp eye on the crowded wharf. His bluish pipe smoke drifted into the invigorating ocean air, his weathered black rubber boots squeaking on the wet planks. The superintendent was a veteran of Dunkirk. His combativeness was gone but his love of the sea remained. In the foggy morning hours of June 6, 1944, the seaman ushered American soldiers onto Normandy-bound buckets. Some dock workers labored thirty continuous hours during the great armada's mobilization. Among the port master's wartime souvenirs were fifteen bullets from his old Lee-Enfield. The honorably discharged Tommy handed the brass to a Yank filing up a gangplank. "I couldn't use them at Dunkirk," he muttered. "There wasn't time. So take them back and get a few Nazis for me." The rounds were incompatible with U. S. weaponry, but no matter. The gesture was sincere.[268]

The psychological weight of the moment was immense. Small demonstrations of levity therefore did not surprise the editors of Pennsylvania's *Uniontown Morning Herald*. "With heroic, tragic stories of the invasion filling the news columns, it is good to have from the beachhead stage some incidents to lighten the stark drama," they wrote. The "appearance of Mickey Mouse on the D-Day screen, of course, is part of that humorous outlook on battle danger and circumstances which we hold in common with the British and which Germans still do not share—nor understand—any more than they did in the first world conflict."[269]

Arthur Hall, a forty-one-year-old North Country tugboat captain, initially thought himself the hapless prey of American wisecracking when his unarmed harbor tug, *Empire Folk,* was summoned to service. When *LCT 413*, laden with ammunition, stalled outside port, *Empire Folk* was called to the rescue. When Hall and his "harbor ragamuffin" chugged alongside the handicapped landing craft, they bellowed to the skipper, "We are going to take you back to port."

No, was the reply. "You are going to take us to France."

"I thought he was pulling my leg," Hall recalled to correspondent Tom Yarbrough. But in a matter of minutes, the LCT captain scaled down the side of his ship and imparted navigational details to the begrimed, eleven-man crew. "We didn't know the course through the mine-swept channel—and we didn't know it was an ammunition ship, either, until he came aboard," said Hall. "If we had, we would have given her a longer tow line," first mate Francis West caustically retorted. Hauling the impaired ship to the invasion zone, Hall's grimy little boat spent a distressing twenty minutes near the beaches before hauling home another craft damaged by underwater obstacles. In the course of its journey, the veteran tug crew counted more ships than it had ever seen before.[270]

The sheer size of the naval operations, code-named Neptune, bespoke the substantial investment of men and materiel on the part of Great Britain. A fleet of wooden warships and dummy vessels was anchored at British harbors as imaginative decoys. Roads leading to English ports were widened to support the unprecedented traffic flow. More than half of the armada's 6,000 vessels flew the Union Jack. With their many guests, the seagoing peoples of the United Kingdom had once again set sail. The enthused Winston Churchill desired to be among them. King George VI, however, artfully persuaded his prime minister to resist youthful instincts and remain in Britain. Rear Admiral Sir Philip Vian, from the deck of the flagship *Scylla*, proclaimed the magnificent procession of ships "a heartening sight."

An American admiral most eloquently summarized the mission: "What Philip of Spain failed to do, what Napoleon tried and failed to do, and what Hitler never had the courage to do, we are about to do—and with God's grace, we shall." The crew burst with cheers.[271]

The romanticized allure of the occasion may have been lost on many passengers while imposing waves walloped the hulls of their vessels. The dingy waters of the Channel gushed over the decks and saturated any who dared exit hatchways. In LCTs, invaders uneasily flocked together in their harnessed vehicles, munching on K rations and vainly attempting to keep warm. Beyond their view, the vast multitude of

Coast guardsmen aboard a Landing Craft Infantry (LCI) vessel join a Catholic chaplain for an invasion mass. Noticing growing attendance at religious services in the weeks prior, Chaplain Curtin Tierman believed, "expectations of taking part in the invasion have made ETO soldiers aware of the seriousness of war." (11)

ships rendezvoused at the congested Area Zebra, nicknamed Piccadilly Circus, a seaborne staging area of epic proportions. National navies were joined by the Coast Guard and Merchant Marine. Dozens of U. S. Marines waited on the deck of the USS *Texas* but were generally barred from participation for fear they would steal headlines from the Army. When the colossal flotilla at last emerged from the Channel mists, enemy spotters were dumbfounded. Upon sighting the formation, Hein Severloh, a German lance corporal awaiting breakfast, could only utter, "Holy smokes! Here they are!"[272]

The self-assured Martha Gellhorn of *Collier*'s witnessed the procession as a stowaway. Defying husband Ernest Hemingway and military convention, she secreted herself in a hospital ship lavatory until the boat was underway. She gulped when the Channel fog cleared. "People will be writing about this sight for a hundred years and whoever saw it will never forget it," she vowed. "First it seemed incredible as a feat of planning; if there were so many ships, what genius it required to get them here, what amazing and unimaginable genius." The captain shouted from the bridge to his undocumented passenger, "Look at it! By God, just look at it!"[273]

Ernie Pyle was no less awestruck. At first, he dreaded the voyage. Those aboard were not only fearful of U-boats, E-boats, mines, and possible air attacks, but especially of what awaited them at voyage's end. "But fortunately," he rationalized, "I was too sleepy to worry about it. When I awakened at dawn, we had both engines going and were back in the line again in the swept Channel. Moral: always be too sleepy to give a damn."[274]

Once awakened, Pyle peered out on the incredible formation spanning the horizon. Never before in human history could one watch so many vessels from one place, he surmised. "As far as you could see in every direction, the ocean was infested with ships. There must have been every type of oceangoing vessel in the world" he wrote. "I even thought I saw a paddle-wheel steamer in the distance, but that was probably an illusion." From the largest battleships to the smallest patrol boats, every manner of nautical transportation was present, uncountable in their sweeping strength. "The best way I can describe this vast armada and the frantic urgency of the traffic," Pyle continued, "is to suggest that you visualize New York Harbor on its busiest day of the year and then just enlarge that scene until it takes in all the ocean the human eye can reach."

The long-anticipated moment of wading ashore was near. Upon the crew's request, Pyle autographed a deck gun barrel. The jittery queues of seasick men slowly shrunk as thundering artillery shells whammed overhead. The occasional corpse floated face down in the water. The reporter vigilantly stood at the slippery rail, spotting the orange and white flashes of death on the skyline. Wisps of grotesque black smoke vented from the beaches, a scene eerily reminiscent of Krakatoa. At the water's edge, young men—near drowning—desperately hauled their waterlogged gear into a seemingly unceasing vortex of hell. Pyle shuddered at the morbid scene and temporarily sought sanctuary in a wardroom. There he played gin rummy with Lt. Chuck Conick as the ship jolted from gun concussions. The soundtrack of war was starkly contrasted with the placid Hawaiian melody of Bing Crosby's "Sweet Lei-lani" exuding from the loudspeaker. "But it wasn't like that ashore," Pyle winced. "No, it wasn't like that ashore."[275]

Surveying the range of ships from his C-47, T/Sgt. Theodore W. Mrencso of Santa Monica wrote home, "I'm glad we didn't have to go down in the Channel for we would surely have hit one of the countless numbers of ships and landing craft—there just wasn't room." Enclosed with a copy of Eisenhower's D-Day address, a letter by Capt. Herschel D. West exclaimed "that one could use all the adjectives such as colossal, magnificent, stupendous, marvelous, greatest, immense, and still not give any idea of the number of men and material being moved." Soldier Jack Lucore was likewise inspired. "It is beyond all powers of imagination for anyone to think they could picture the Yanks hitting the beach," he thought. "Out in the harbor off the coast were enough ships that one could have crossed the Channel without ever getting his feet wet. It was a sight not to be forgotten. . . . You can easily imagine all the anxiety and pressure that everyone was under at this time."[276]

Associated Press correspondent Henry B. Jameson gained a vantage point too close for comfort. The thirty-two-year-old Kansan observed the first fourteen hours of invasion from a flat-bottomed Rhino ferry that endured a gauntlet of fire from camouflaged coastal batteries. His boat meandered through a no man's land of partially-submerged landing craft. "Three times during the first eight hours of the invasion we pulled toward the beach, but each time were forced to pull back." One crew member fell dead during the third attempt. Jameson succumbed to injury as well. The reporter dislocated his shoulder and was slightly wounded in the leg, making him one of the first correspondent casualties in France. Luckier than some colleagues, he recalled years later, "I have revisited the bloody Omaha Beach area of Normandy several times, never without choking up, shedding a tear and kneeling at the grave of one of my fallen co-workers. I left a little of my own flesh and blood there, too."[277]

Interdependence proved a pivotal factor for endangered vessels. Minesweeper George McKellar of Bath, Maine attested to the operation's imperative joint efforts. "[W]e have wonderful coordination between the air force, fleet, and troops on the beach," he affirmed. "The air show has really been something to see. I pity anything that was living around the beachhead before the invasion." Aerial and naval bombardments may not have been as effective as hoped, but immediate impressions among Allied personnel expressed otherwise. Lewis Hawkins of the AP commented, "Warship guns fired an ear-trying prelude before the swarms of homely hybrid landing craft broke away. . . . This bombardment was a combined chorus from the cannon of several navies, but British warships spoke the loudest because there were more of them." On the *Augusta*, an impassive Omar Bradley lodged cotton balls in his ears to muffle the racket. The symphony of noise, combined with the expansive assemblage of ships, "would have caused the eyes of John Paul Jones to pop wide open."[278]

Cool and confident, the unassuming general Omar Bradley observes ship and troop movements on D+2. Of the fighting he viewed from afar, Bradley later stated, "Men dragged themselves shoreward, leaderless, and scattered." Shown from left to right aboard the USS *Augusta* are: Rear Admiral Alan Kirk, Bradley, Rear Admiral Arthur Struble (with binoculars raised), and Maj. Gen. Ralph Royce. (12)

Hawkins squinted through his field glasses. The USS *Arkansas* and French cruisers *Montcalm* and *Georges Leygues* darted ahead to brace "bold little destroyers." Naval officers, potentially running their ships aground, improvised and veered dangerously close to the shoreline to assist troops otherwise immobilized. In these dire circumstances, spontaneous partnerships between soldiers and sailors determined survival. "These first forces of foot soldiers were light and helped the tanks, which fired from shallow water to pin down the enemy beach defenses so demolition teams could blast out the obstacles. The landing craft streamed in steadily through rough waves tossed up by a westerly breeze," noted Hawkins. Tactical leapfrogging persisted throughout the day.

From the bridge of the USS *Henrico*, journalist Jack Foster bit his lip as he spotted doughboys inch their way up the long slope. "Wave after wave of the Americans came ashore, firing rifle and carbine," he nervously remarked. "Nazi spotters on the ridge directed mortar and 88-mm fire to the attackers. Battleships, cruisers, and destroyers moved slowly along the area crashing out salvos against the strong points." A U. S. destroyer swung in and blasted a pillbox into scattered bits of cement. "Barking army rifles killed off the enemy wherever he came into the open." A white house inhabited by snipers at the center of Omaha Beach was readily set ablaze. Two *Henrico* crewmates sighted a German marksman displacing in the open. "We cut him in half with our guns," they stated with little remorse.[279]

Inch by bloody inch, infantrymen, engineers, and seamen together swelled the advance. From afar, correspondent Robert Miller was indelibly moved by the drama. "Dawn revealed the most amazing sight ever seen in this or any other war," he wrote from a patrol boat. Ships dotted the seascape in all directions and planes skimmed the gray clouds. Yellow flashes leapt through the shrouds of black powder smoke. The volume belched a near-indescribable roar of cacophonous fury. The artillery "burst in a terrifying bulb of crimson flame against the German shore installations." The resilient Pearl Harbor survivor USS *Nevada* was among the ships raining down shrapnel, delivering thunderously vengeful blows.[280]

Salvaged from defeat at Pearl Harbor, the USS *Nevada* unleashed fiery retribution upon Normandy's coastal defenses along with hundreds of Allied vessels. The symphony of noise, combined with the expansive assemblage of ships, "would have caused the eyes of John Paul Jones to pop wide open," marveled one witness. (13)

Near Bernières-sur-Mer, Desmond Tighe of Reuters witnessed the ferocity from a British destroyer anchored 8,000 yards off the Canadian sector code-named Juno. Penning his observations in real time, he hinted of the escalating state of urgency. "It is now exactly 7:25 a.m. and through my glasses I can see the first wave of the assault troops touching down on the water's edge and fanning up the beach." Hurried cruisers steamed parallel to the coast, pouring down "withering broadsides." Coils of rank cordite smoke spiraled upward from the increasingly glutted beach. The skies remained overcast and the tide slowly rose. "Conditions are not ideal." Still, the Luftwaffe remained conspicuously absent. The lack of an enemy air force delighted the energetic Sir Bertram Ramsay, Commander-in-Chief of the Allied Naval Expedition-

ary Force. He declared his ships 100% successful in their convoy responsibilities and asserted, "We have won the first round. I can see no sign
that the enemy will be in a position to beat us in the second round."[281]

Navy corpsman Dick Borden was no less sanguine. "The morning of
the invasion we watched the pre-invasion bombardment from the deck
of the ship and wished luck to the 1st Division as it went over the sides.
I must admit things looked good from the ship." His mindset changed
drastically as he neared Omaha. "Jerry had his 88 mortars and machine
guns zeroed all along the beach and they worried us quite a bit," he
recalled. Borden and his doused medics toiled endlessly over the next
thirty-six hours to save lives. Sparing his family little of the horror, the
corpsman wrote, "there was Hell everywhere!"[282]

Ernest Hemingway experienced a slice of that hell. The plumpish *Collier's* daredevil had no intention of missing the greatest adventure of
the century. In the pale morning light, his landing craft sped toward
the Fox Green sector of Omaha Beach. Few remembered the date of the
Battle of Shiloh, he speculated, but generations would long remember
this day. The "36-foot coffin-shaped steel boats took solid green sheets
of water that fell on the helmeted heads of the troops packed shoulder
to shoulder in the stiff, awkward, uncomfortable, lonely companionship
of men going to a battle," Hemingway continued. Surrounding the seasick men sat crates of explosives cushioned by rubber life preservers
and bazooka rockets "encased in waterproof coverings that reminded
you of the transparent raincoats college girls wear."

The novelist's boat was commanded by Robert Anderson, a young lieutenant from Roanoke, Virginia, and Coxswain Frank Currier of Saugus,
Massachusetts. With great detail and unsurprising style, Hemingway
chronicled the seamen's sometimes heated exchanges while gravitating
toward shore.

"What's your course, coxswain?" Anderson shouted from the stern.

*"Two-twenty, sir," the coxswain answered. He was a thin-faced, freck-
led boy with his eyes fixed on the compass.*

*"Then steer two-twenty, damn it!" Anderson said. "Don't steer all over
the whole damn ocean!"*

The boat doggedly heaved up and down. Attempting to retain their
greasy, bountiful breakfasts, the overburdened passengers cupped their
palms over their mouths. Some turned and clenched the steel rim of the
craft in preparation for the inevitable flood of vomit. Others glanced at

the nearby USS *Texas* with passing expressions of encouragement. Its colossal 14-inch guns emitted yellowish-brown fireballs that projected ripples across the water. With "the smoke still rolling, the concussion and the report would hit us, jarring the men's helmets," reported Hemingway. "It struck your near ear like a punch with a heavy, dry glove." The writer kept his mouth ajar to lessen the trauma.

All the while, the heavily-armed soldiers resembled pike men from a Medieval tale—crusaders about to encounter "some strange and unbelievable monster." The 225-horsepower craft engine hummed in the background, its argent diesel fumes filling the air. With their knees quivering from the waves, cold, and fear, the men otherwise stood still— awaiting their fates. "They hated that 10-mile ride to the beach almost more than anything," concurred coast guardsman Herman Fulton, Jr. of Atlanta, who ferried 1st Infantry Division troops ashore.[283]

Combat artist Dwight Shepler dramatically captured the chaos of Omaha's Fox Green sector as the USS *Emmons* pounded away at coastal fortifications. Witnessing similar scenes, journalist Jack Foster wrote, "Wave after wave of the Americans came ashore, firing rifle and carbine. . . . Battleships, cruisers, and destroyers moved slowly along the area crashing out salvos against the strong points." (14)

Although the jolt of friendly artillery diminished with distance, the intensity of its shrieks dominated the heavens. The guns of the *Texas* and *Arkansas*, Hemingway continued, "sounded as though they were throwing whole railway trains across the sky. . . . They were no part of our world as we moved steadily over the gray, white-capped sea toward where, ahead of us, death was being issued in small, intimate, accurately administered packages."

Despite the bickering and disorientation, the writer praised the skill of his seafaring chauffeurs. "I wish I could write the full story of what it means to take a transport across through a mine-swept channel; the mathematical precision of maneuver; the infinite detail and chronometrical accuracy and split-second timing of everything from the time the anchor comes up until the boats are lowered and away into the roaring, sea-churning assembly circle from which they break off into the attack wave," he wrote. The inspiring story of teamwork was worthy of a book, not merely a magazine piece.

Hemingway braced himself for landing as the craft gained speed and zoomed onward. He propped himself high on the stern to gain better perspective. Hemingway dried his binoculars and glared toward the fiery shore engulfed in billowing black clouds. The greenery of the bluffs grew increasingly vibrant. Atop them were machine gun nests flickering with the zipping patterns of MG-42s. He saw two tanks aflame at the water's edge, bodies floating in and out with the waves, tinged in red.

The boat came under fire, the clatter of rounds ricocheting off the ramp and hull. "I ducked my head under the sharp cracking that was going overhead," he remembered. "Then I dropped into the well in the stern sheets where the gunner would have been if we had any guns. The machine gun fire was throwing water all around the boat, and an anti-tank shell tossed up a jet of water over us." Brimming with eighty pounds of cumbersome gear, the passengers had little flexibility for evasion.

"Get her the hell around and out of here, coxswain!" a crewmate screamed. "Get her out of here!" The boat pivoted; the machine guns temporarily ceased. Although the recurring snaps of rifle fire persisted, Hemingway cautiously peered from his burrow and watched the beach battle ensue. The sailors spotted a wounded man floating in the surf and hastily heaved him aboard. With each hoist, scrambled viscera oozed from his lower abdominal wound. This lone casualty portended a grim spectacle. Underwater obstructions jutted into the sky when the initial landings occurred at low tide. The attached contact mines "looked like large double pie plates fastened face to face," Hemingway wrote. "They were the ugly, neutral gray-yellow color that almost everything is in war."

The ramp descended with a clunky grind. The men rolled out, practically shoving one another aside. Hemingway spotted three agonizingly slow tanks tread up the beach. Disarrayed in an open field of fire, the armor was doomed. The Germans waited for the vehicles to inch closer before springing their fatal trap. "Then I saw a little fountain of water jut up, just over and beyond the lead tank. Then smoke broke out of the leading tank on the side away from us, and I saw two men dive out of the turret and land on their hands and knees on the stones of the beach." The battered tankers were so close to Hemingway that he could see their singed faces screaming with fear and pain. No others escaped the red hot, sand-bogged vehicles.

Loaded with rescued casualties, the boat guardedly drifted away from the mined poles. Reaching a destroyer, the crew elevated the wounded in a metal basket to the deck. Meanwhile, other warships "had run in almost to the beach and were blowing every pillbox out of the ground." The writer was morbidly impressed with their accuracy. The tableau reminded him of *Petrushka*, the ballet burlesque about violent puppets. Through his binoculars, Hemingway spotted a severed German arm fly skyward amid a shell burst—almost as if it was tied to a puppet master's string.[284]

While many correspondents lacked Hemingway's literary flair, their chronicles of personal heroics were no less dramatic. Naval reservist Tom Bernard of *Yank* encapsulated the D-Day epic via his experiences on the USS *Doyle*. For three days, Bernard viewed the grim saga from the deck of the 1,650-ton Gleaves-class destroyer. From minesweeping to shelling to landing support, the ship sailed through the thick of the fight. "By twenty minutes before H-Hour," wrote Bernard, "a great curtain of smoke completely hid the assault beaches. Only the rocket flashes broke through. Lines of tiny landing craft moved in towards the beach and disappeared under the smoke to our right. That was all we saw of H-Hour of D-Day." In the consequent moments, Bernard witnessed levels of carnage equal to those experienced by Hemingway.

With the naked eye, Bernard traced the trajectory of Allied shells. "First there would be a flash and then a puff of smoke which billowed into the sky," he observed. "Several tanks and landing craft were burning at the water's edge. Through glasses, I watched troops jump from their boats and started running up the beach." Germans garrisoned beyond the coast had been conducting pre-invasion defense exercises. Little could they have imagined how promptly their lessons would morph into hazardous on-the-job training. "When we reached the beach," said Bernard, "there were burning tanks and fallen dead littering the sands. Several hundred men and some vehicles had moved along to the left under the shelter of cliffs." The remaining landing craft withdrew to the relative safety of the sea.

Evacuation of the wounded became priority as Higgins boats seesawed back and forth to larger ships. Bernard learned the tale of two rescued pharmacist's mates whose LCI had been destroyed. The coast guardsmen—Charles F. Mudgett, age twenty-four, and Robert V. Miller, age eighteen—were soaked and weary. "I hope and pray we can stay on here," said Mudgett. Earlier that morning, their vessel received a merciless downpour of German mortar fire. Rounds landed on the bridge and conning tower, annihilating the ship's communications and wounding several of the crew. Shells punched holes amidships as if the craft was made of tinfoil. A hail of artillery burst at the waterline. Within moments, the vessel was practically a stranded whale. "We were hit seven times before we abandoned her," noted Miller. "Our mess cook had a leg blown off. A soldier took five pieces of shrapnel and I guess he'll lose an arm." Mudgett and Miller were the lucky ones.

The *Doyle*'s cannonade continued. On the bridge, Bernard overheard a distressed admiral barking into an inter-ship telephone to nearby vessels. The concealed coastal emplacements had to be wiped out if the GIs were to have a chance. *Now*, the officer demanded. For hours, naval gunners fired speculatively at the bluffs, praying their marksmanship had affect. "Not until the next morning," Bernard continued, "when information came through from night reconnaissance parties, were the batteries silenced by the ships." The likes of the battleship *Arkansas* lobbed rounds into the Normandy countryside for another week, with a German railway gun reportedly among its victims.

On the prowl with the *Emmons* and *Harding* for German batteries, the *Doyle* dodged 88-mm shells near her stern. The "nerve-wracking whine" buckled even the most resilient sailors and the crew yearned for some "sack duty" as night fell. They were bound for disappointment. German aircraft periodically skimmed through the fighter screen and a Messerschmitt Bf 110 dropped a 500-pound bomb only 125 yards away, violently jolting the bedraggled crew. Raiders intermittently swooped downward, rendering sleep impossible. When afforded a moment, the sailors improvised lifebelts as makeshift pillows and curled beneath gun turrets. The crew of the *Doyle* stood at general quarters for an exhausting sixty-four hours.[285]

Sgt. Herbert Squire of Galesburg, Illinois confronted similarly fatiguing challenges. The sergeant and his mechanics shared restless nights salvaging military vehicles swamped by the formidable surf. In less than two days, the amphibious grease monkeys resurrected four jeeps and a three-quarter ton truck. "I think I put it into the water halfway across the Channel," one mechanic chuckled of his jeep during de-embarkation. "It was not funny then, but I can laugh now. An officer and I drove the jeep down a ramp and just went out of sight. I thought at first that I had better start swimming back to England rather than try and get to the beach."[286]

Some veterans were less inclined to laughter. An infantryman struck by shrapnel lamented, "If that doggone lieutenant had let me go on ahead and shoot some Germans instead of ordering me to fix a half-sunk jeep, I wouldn't have been wounded. Now I can't fight anybody, and I got to ride in one of these boats again."[287]

Vehicles and men alike were fished from the murk. Many a reporter witnessed monumental rescue efforts to spare combatants watery graves. Carter Barber of the Combined Press chronicled the heroic undertakings of *Coast Guard Cutter 16*, an eighty-three-foot rescue boat nicknamed the "Homing Pigeon" by its crew. "It was about 5:30 when we saw the first assault boat catch a shell from the coastal defenses," said Lt. R. V. McPhail of Gastonia, North Carolina. *Cutter 16* instantly veered toward the plodding masses of oil-covered men. Manropes were hurled over the side and wounded given aid. "Survivors were in groups of ten or so, or by themselves, clinging to wreckage," stated sailor Wesley Sutin of Newberry, Michigan. "We had to maneuver through them.

It took us about two hours to pick up all the wounded, but we didn't leave a single swimming man."

"Most of the wounded were suffering from broken legs and ankles and scalp lacerations," remembered George Banks, a first aid man from Auburn, Nebraska. "My most successful case was a boy who had suffered bad internal hemorrhages, but who had been able to crawl below by himself. When a transport doctor looked at the kid, he pronounced him dead. But the kid has a lot of life in him yet, and we were able to revive him and get him aboard another hospital-equipped ship, where his chances of recovery will be good." After transferring her wounded, *Cutter 16* returned to the engagement and extricated imperiled passengers from a burning ammunition carrier. The little ship rescued at least 126 men.[288]

Not all were as fortunate. The *Pittsburgh Courier* claimed, "The most heroic incident involving a Negro on D-Day was that of an invalided man aboard a Navy tug which was disabled after striking a mine. Spurning attention during the rescue, the youth conceded, 'I can't live anyway,' and insisted that others who could be reclaimed for service be attended." The boy lost both legs and an arm. He succumbed one hour later.[289]

Realizing her spouse confronted similar vulnerabilities, Ruth Harvey of Glen Burnie, Maryland feared for her husband, John. The chief boatswain's mate was reported sunk but rescued in the English Channel. It was not true. "On D-Day," Chief Harvey later clarified, "our cutter saved fifteen unconscious sailors from a sinking ship. But somewhere, the story became twisted, and we coast guardsmen were reported as survivors. My wife, Ruth, wrote that I was announced safe somewhere in England, and wanted to know how come I was in the water. I'll have a lot of explaining to do someday." In either case, Mrs. Harvey was soothed.[290]

Fellow coast guardsman John Graham, age twenty-three, also contemplated prospects of survival. "When we started into the beach it looked bad. The Germans had crisscrossed the approaches with utility poles to which mines were tied," he wrote home. Graham's skipper, Lt. Gene R. Gislason, delicately steered the craft through the daunting maze. Graham was nauseated when the ramp lowered. Infantrymen were cut in two before they could exit the boat. "It was no joy ride for them," he recalled. "Many didn't make the shelter of the beach. The water just seemed to swallow them up as they went under." With the boat emptied, the craft reversed until Graham noticed a mined pole inches from scraping the rising ramp. Graham immediately yelled to comrade Matthew Cody on the winch, "Wind it like hell!"

"He turned that winch faster than I ever saw it go," Graham exclaimed. "I just held my breath as we slipped past." No sooner were they clear of the mine when a shell hit the craft and killed three crewmates. The steering was out of commission. Cody and Graham ran aft. "We had practiced for this possibility," the latter confessed, "so we knew just what to do." The former bolted to the rear compartment to control the steering apparatus. Graham remained on deck with a megaphone, relaying commands from the conning tower to Cody. Thanks to quick thinking and synergy, the ship was able to gradually withdraw.[291]

The USS *Corry* did not share the joys of such durability. One of the leading escort ships of the invasion, the *Corry* was a veteran of North Africa and assigned a support role for the Utah Beach landings. After losing her air cover, she was struck by fierce shore battery fire, her rudder jammed, and her keel cracked. The destroyer sank rapidly in the coastal shallows, her tattered forty-eight-star flag fluttering above the waterline. First Class Machinist Mate William Sheppard was forced to abandon his beloved ship and plunge into 50-degree water. "Some of us had been aboard the *Corry* for two and a half years," Sheppard mourned. "She seemed like home to us."

Five minutes before the scheduled landings, Sheppard's duties were interrupted by an ominous sound. "I was in the engine room," he later recollected to a hometown reporter. "There was a grinding noise. It felt like we had rammed something." The machinist climbed topside to view the damage and already his buddies were lowering lifeboats. "Abandon ship!" a voice howled from above as the whirling shrill of German artillery remained steady.

"When the big shells hit the water close to us it felt like a kick in the stomach. It sickened us," Sheppard remembered. "Screams pierced a sea of bedlam—screams of wounded men—screams that could not be drowned out by the incessant drone of planes overhead." Watery ripples cast by the incoming rounds beat five-foot waves upon the heads of the evacuating *Corry* shipmates. The men paddled furiously as bits of metal peppered the water's surface with miniature geysers.

148

Sheppard despaired. "My best friend, a fellow I had been with for more than three years, was hit and killed close by me. I couldn't raise a hand to help him. Even with life belts, it's a battle to keep your head out of a sea like that." Others attempted to escape the descending destroyer's powerful suction by swimming toward shore—even though few Allied troops had yet arrived there. Many failed to flee the ship's mighty absorption.

"We endured constant fire for more than an hour," the twenty-four-year-old seaman continued. "When we threw back our heads to escape the pounding waves, we could see the sky black with our planes. It was like something out of a dream. Behind us were the troop ships. The big guns on shore had become hot. We could mark the great arcs their bullets made across the sky in the early dawn. A sheet of tracer bullets aimed at our aircraft was a solid curtain between us and the shore." Two dozen of Sheppard's shipmates perished. The remaining members were gleaned from the ocean after several hellish hours. They quickly-devoured glasses of brandy and were presented dry uniforms, but the agony of the frigid Channel remained embedded within them.

"I was shaking so hard from cold, fright, and shock that I couldn't hold the glass to my lips. I didn't stop shaking for more than two hours." Suffering from a leg wound and hypothermia, Sheppard recuperated in England and Scotland before arriving home in Coshocton, Ohio on July 11—only three days before word of the *Corry*'s sinking was publicly disclosed. His thirty-day leave was his first-time home in over three years. During his peaceful respite, Sheppard recounted his days on a battleship, his sub-chasing adventures across the Atlantic, and his six journeys through the Arctic. He had long dreamt of plans for homecoming but changed his mind regarding one suddenly undesirable activity. "I won't under any circumstances go swimming," he conceded. "In fact, you won't find me in anything larger than a bathtub."[292]

Plunging into the freezing depths was no less traumatic for John Lawrence Patman of Cheyenne, Wyoming. Invasion day was one he could never forget, no matter how thoroughly he tried. Although it was the day he lost his left hand, his life was spared by an unlikely savior. The night prior, Patman partook in pensive conversation with shipmates. "We talked all about what we would probably see," he said, "how we would react under enemy fire, what the folks back home would think if they knew what we knew. It was lots of scuttlebutt-fodder for the first few hours and then the boys drifted off to quiet places on the ship to be by themselves. Some made out wills." The bluejackets tacitly pondered the approaching hours. There was little energy for jaunty back-slapping or patriotic hurrahing.

Beyond the deck, everything from mine sweepers to escorts passed like racehorses in the darkness. "Man, those babies mean as much to sailors' protection at sea as the air forces covering the Army means to the infantry," Patman realized. "It's a safe feeling to see those fast-cruising babies playing about when the danger zone is reached." The sailor considered the passing armada a most glorious sight. "As far as you could see were boats, large and small, every type you ever heard of and all speeds. The prettiest sight you ever saw is the wake of a ship glistening in the moonlight. It didn't seem like war just then, it was more like pictures of a regatta on Miami Bay." The music of echoing skippers calling back and forth drifted through the chilled air.

By morning, the sentimentalism faded. The wake of the battleship *Texas* all but capsized Patman's landing craft as it chugged into the melee. Still, "it was a secure feeling to know she and others of her class were going to pave the way for actual landing." Veering ever closer to the beach, each wave crashed over the craft's prow and drenched passengers. Patman could hardly see fifty yards around him. "You just cruised along with others and kept your ordered direction and position, come hell or high water." The crew soon gained better views of the busy battlewagons at work. "Each burst of fire looked like the end of time. The next instant the repercussion hit you and your ears almost burst with each explosion." An army lieutenant aboard offered distraction with a string of profanities and the admission he could not swim. "Can you guarantee me a safe landing?" he jokingly asked the crew. His foot soldiers responded with half-hearted chuckles. One invader's stowaway mascot, a dog of many breeds named Muffin, soothed the men's spirits.

They were within sight of the shore when a deafening explosion disintegrated the landing craft. Shards of metal and chunks of flesh studded the overcast sky. "Our boat went down in seconds," Patman recalled. "Dead bodies were floating about, and cries of pain were heard all around. I must have been blown fifty feet from my controls and was stunned. The cold water revived me, and I started to inflate my Mae West. But it was gone. Evidently the explosion blew my life jacket clear off my body." The tall gray waves enveloped Patman, choking him with mouthfuls of foul saltwater. He gasped for air. His throat stung, and his eyes burned red. No other survivors appeared within immediate reach. He thought this was his end.

Patman suddenly heard whimpers in the waves. It was Muffin. The sailor called out, "Here I am, boy. Here I am!" With relief, Patman later declared, "I'll be damned if Muffin didn't come swimming over."

The seaman reached for the hound, but he discovered his left fist was useless. The grotesquely blue hand was smashed beyond recognition, swollen and resembling a football. "I suddenly became scared and if I ever was jittery it was then," he remembered. The dog paddled in and licked the ailing sailor's face, restoring Patman's sense of hope and awareness. He clutched the cur's tail and permitted the dog to tow him. Muffin "acted like it was a game."

The coxswain faded in and out of consciousness, but his new pet remained resolute. The wounded man could not recall how long they were adrift—maybe two hours, perhaps ten minutes. Patman was out cold until he felt being pulled upward into a boat. An English chap declared, "Take it easy, Mack." Patman was rushed to surgery on a British destroyer. He awoke to discover a stump where his left hand once was, but he had little room for complaint. Muffin was rescued as well. Patman spotted him prancing around the deck, already accepted as a new crewmate. The sailor owed the mutt his life. Near Utah Beach, LCT seaman Vincent Roberto of Brooklyn reciprocated the favor by rescuing a lost puppy paddling in the Channel.

Recovering in sickbay, Patman befriended a Tommy, smoked cigarettes, and discussed the universal plights of mariners. The British chum announced he had a brother stationed in Dallas, Texas with the RAF. Perhaps Patman could look him up when returning to Wyoming? The American initially had no intention of traveling home. He hoped the Navy would permit him to stay if superiors could find "anything for a one-handed man to do." Instead he was released to Cheyenne—with a promise. Amidst Patman's journeys, a reporter cornered him at an Amarillo train station, where the sailor imparted his incredible story of survival. The seafarer was on his way to Dallas as a "favor for a Limey."

In parting, the amputee concluded, "Tell your readers that every man who went over on D-Day was a hero. There wasn't a single one, soldier or sailor, but who did his part to make the invasion a success. Each man, regardless of rank or station, is worthy of a novel on his bravery and action." Patman expressed a single regret. He did not reach France. He was within sight of its shores but failed in his gallant ambition. "What the hell can I tell my grandchildren?" he wondered.[293]

By contrast, United Press correspondent Robert Miller had no fear of anecdotal shortages. He opened one invasion report with a sobering prologue. "I was torpedoed in the English Channel. My ship died in a black, slimy pool of her own fuel and oil. She went down forty seconds after the torpedo thudded home. Those forty seconds are gravened deep within me."

General quarters sounded in the dead of night. The reporter scaled the bridge and saw star shells arch against the backdrop of the equally radiant moon. Gun flashes flickered in the darkness off the starboard bow while red tracers dashed the sky. With a belching roar, Miller's ship was struck by an E-boat attempting to cut supply lines. "It tore into the ship's entrails," he remembered. "The whole ship shivered and then leaped. I went reeling down the deck, grabbing for a hold. Then a blinding flash like a photographic magnesium flare. Seawater erupted all over the ship. I was temporarily blinded in filmy spray." Miller was surprised to find his eyeglasses still intact.

The ship's portentous slant indicated the vessel's imminent doom. A sailor hollered, "The life raft—cut it loose!" A shadowy figure squirmed across the deck, lugging a maimed leg as if it was heavy luggage. Oil oozed over the men's feet as they frantically slashed away at the raft cables. "Abruptly, it came loose, and I plunged with the others on to a maze of ropes and debris, tearing to free myself as the raft bobbed teasingly away—just out of reach." He escaped not a moment too soon, for the ship capsized and went down with a trail of boiling black bubbles following her. Survivors were matted in syrupy sludge. The heavy slicks burned eyes, throats, and wounds with excruciating severity. The greasy sailors desperately clung to the raft. Within minutes Miller "saw a sudden great black shape knifing through the sea." Despite the survivors' bawling, the adjacent Allied ship sailed on. Not long after, another approaching vessel noticed a castaway's signal lamp. Miller and over half of the crew were recovered from the waves.[294]

With so many men intermingled and misplaced in the Channel, subsequent bureaucratic confusion was inevitable. In the New Hampshire household of Orville Hutchins, grief turned to elation when the sailor—mistakenly reported missing—personally surprised his wife and six children at their summer home. The thirty-two-year-old seaman was not present for duty on June 6 as he was in a British hospital undergoing jaw surgery. The Navy, believing Hutchins was aboard his lost ship, thus reported him missing. He was previously unaware of the false notification and arrived home to jubilantly reveal "he was very much alive."

Marjorie Coffill of Chicago experienced similar fright upon learning her husband, David, was killed on his landing craft. Eleven days after the invasion, Marjorie received an official correction declaring Coxswain Coffill was not dead but wounded. The Coffill family thereafter arranged a welcome home social for the resurrected husband, who yearned only for "a chance to feel at home, rest, relax, and smoke a good cigar."[295]

Like their airborne counterparts, Navy personnel welcomed a lower-than-expected casualty rate. One senior American officer described naval losses as "unbelievably low." The Merchant Marine suffered few casualties for a change. The Germans nightly released mines by plane into the sea hoping to reverse the tide. Nonetheless, even German radio was impressed with Neptune's resounding success. Kurt Dittmar, the Official Military Commentator of the German Armed Forces, noted, "This is an enormous achievement of transport for our enemies."[296]

The significance of the day did not go unnoticed by those who overcame its hazards. Gordon Miller, a fireman first class and avid reader of *Stars and Stripes*, coolly celebrated the moment in a letter to his parents. "I guess D-Day will be one I'll never forget," he wrote. "We can say we were in the invasion of France, but that's about all. I even took a little walk on French soil, but I don't think I would want to be in the Army and keep going." Sailor James Peckham of California expressed similar sentiment. He survived D-Day "with only a few bumps," he reported. "I decided souvenir collecting wasn't very safe on those beaches so all I am bringing back is myself. Some of the fellows have midget tanks, German helmets, and shrapnel. All I wanted was a German flag, but it seems that every other sailor had the same idea." Being alive was a greater gift. It was Peckham's nineteenth birthday.[297]

The youthfulness of D-Day's combatants rang especially true in the case of Gerald W. Haddon, who became a front-page sensation before he was old enough to drive. The broad-shouldered Chicago teenager falsified his birth date when enlisting in the Coast Guard. He was only fifteen when he sailed to Normandy. A member of *LST 27*, Haddon endured intense fire from German 88s as his ship approached Omaha Beach. Members of the 29th Division's 175th Regiment, awaiting their shoreward push in trucks below deck, nervously tapped their toes on brake pedals as the massive bow slowly opened like a giant vault.

Carnage immediately ensued. A disembarking Army truck detonated a mine, gushing forth bursts of flame. Steam arose from the tide as sizzling metal violently plopped into the water. The biting odor of fuel and scalded tissue overpowered the senses. The soldiers attempted to pry themselves from the twisted steel as the inferno consumed their vehicle. Haddon manned a fire hose as crewmates rescued the blackened infantrymen from the wreckage. The survivors reeked of gasoline. The spreading fire compromised the safety of the entire ship. Sporadic enemy rounds clanked off the open bow as the flames were battled. The coast guardsmen hastily dragged the mauled survivors to the infirmary, their blood and soaked uniforms leaving unsettling traces on the metal decks. "We had a narrow escape on our third trip across," Haddon later informed reporters. "Another LST pushed past us and hit a mine, which split her in two."

Over the following month, Haddon's ship conducted over a dozen landings. Having studied German for three weeks in high school, the fifteen-year-old was even placed in charge of prisoners en route to England. After forty continuous days of transporting, Haddon failed to report to muster one morning. When admonished by superiors, the youth divulged his true age. He rationalized his service, claiming he recently encountered a German soldier who was even younger. Haddon's captain was sympathetic, but the boy earned a ticket stateside. The coast guardsman thereafter informed the press of his desires to complete high school and study law. He first aspired to re-enlist at age seventeen. "He'll be a good lawyer," admitted one comrade. "He certainly had us fooled."[298]

For the men of the liberty ship *Frank R. Stockton*, June 7 offered a welcomed interlude. The *London Herald* reported, "A loudspeaker set up on deck for diversion of the soldiers was blaring forth hot jazz and swing music; three soldiers were playing an accordion, guitar, and violin. Four six-week-old kittens scampered about the boat deck. A two-month-old mongrel pup, Liverpool Brownie, added barks to the clamor." The melodies of boogie-woogie were punctuated by the distant growl of shore batteries. Sailors and GIs aboard stripped to the waists and sunbathed, indicating scant notice of nearby violence. An engineer came topside for a breath of fresh air. "It's kind of lonesome" down there, he remarked.[299]

Both near and afar, analysts formed fresh opinions of the naval actions. On June 18, the *New York Times* noted, "On D-Day it could have been another Dieppe. On D plus 2 it looked like Anzio. It was not until D plus 3 that it looked like a conquest. . . . It was probably the longest general quarters in naval history. The men stayed at battle stations three, four, and five days. All they got was K-rations. No hot food, except coffee. And they slept beside their guns, too." Naval lieutenant John Mason Brown's assessment was more forthright. It was "a wonder we got in at all," he marveled. Fears of a "magnified Anzio" never materialized.[300]

DeWitt Mackenzie similarly wrote with cautious optimism on June 9: "We are at a difficult and dangerous stage of the invasion of the Cherbourg Peninsula." The assault was executed "in business-like fashion" but hounded by sporadic bursts of lackluster weather. "I am feeling swell and confident. But I think it's smart to look this invasion giant right in the eye." To attain broader success, the Allies needed to capture Cherbourg, one of the most extensive ports in the world. Mackenzie prayed for its early seizure. Americans would be "sitting pretty" if the seaside bastion was nabbed before month's end. Mack concluded with words of confidence, "These early days of the invasion are the ones on which Hitler is gambling to produce a fluke which may give him a negotiated peace instead of unconditional surrender. He knows that, barring some freak of fortune, he is already beaten."[301]

Although the June 29 capitulation of Cherbourg would be instrumental to Allied success, the long-term logistical feat of shuffling men and supplies ashore was also achieved with the stunning creativity of the operation code-named Mulberry. John Camsell of the International News Service commented in retrospect, "The Mulberry Harbor was one of the most ingenious ideas of the war. It was situated off the northern coast of France and consisted of a long line of vessels which were sunk to form an artificial harbor." Dilapidated ships were scuttled and received final hurrahs as breakwaters while 200-foot-long blocks of floating concrete known as Phoenixes were sunk to form imitation harbors off Omaha Beach and Arromanches. Lengthy piers and pontoons linked ships to shore. The Omaha harbor site was annihilated by a June storm that was the worst in four decades. The Arromanches harbor—known as the bridge to France—endured. All the while, the unsightly but dependable LSTs remained the domineering force in transportation.[302]

More lethal storms brewed beyond the coast, however. Reporter Hal Boyle mingled among a queue of GIs in the harbor as they prepared for "their combat debut in France." The young men expressed the universal fears and longings of those thrown into Normandy's cauldron.

T/Sgt. James M. Barnett of Jackson, Tennessee was described by his lieutenant as "the best damn sergeant in any division." A former grocery clerk, Barnett appraised the invasion with a glimmer of hope. "I believe the hardest part is over," he suggested. "Combat is no harder than getting ready for it and some of us have been getting ready for almost four years. We've got confidence in our outfit; it won't be long before this thing is over." Dale Stockton of Indiana agreed with his trusted sarge. "It'll be rough, but we can handle anything the Heinies can put in."

Sgt. Percy Minion, a printer from Lewiston, North Carolina, meanwhile offered consolation to those across the Atlantic. "I wish the people at home knew how well prepared for this we are physically and mentally," he informed Boyle. "They worry more than we do. Tell them for us, not to worry." Cheers of agreement resounded among Minion's comrades. "Yes; tell the folks back home we're all right!" they exclaimed.

Ignacio F. Garcia, a café worker from Edinburg, Texas, shared a naturally boyish desire. "I hope we win this war pretty damn soon. I miss those Texas girls," he deviously grinned. Twenty-four-year-old Albert Rinaldo, a beer coil refrigerator technician from New York, wished to enhance his trade skills in Europe. "I'm anxious to get to Germany to see if their beer is as good as they say it is." Pvt. Basil Proc of Fall River, Massachusetts had more vengeful convictions in mind. "I've got a score to settle for a buddy of mine," he confessed. "Also, I promised my wife I would bring her Hitler's left ear. I know where he usually hangs out." Boyle wished the passengers well as they sloshed toward the epic confrontation ahead.

Aboard the USS *Henrico*, eighteen-year-old coxswain Richard Andrews of Hughesville, Pennsylvania shared Boyle's admiration of the foot soldier. "Everything was quiet as we approached the shore," he remarked. "Most of the soldiers thought the beach would be a pushover. . . . My gunners cranked down the ramp. The infantry officer drew his pistol and waved his men after him. As the first group of men left the boat the machine guns opened up. They mowed the troops down. Still the men in the boat pressed forward, some of them shooting toward the pillboxes. They plunged into the surf, but the fire dropped them into the water."

Crewmember Jerry Dever of Tacoma, Washington was even more vocal in his praise. "None of them faltered," he said. "They followed their officers, shooting as they went. But the fire was too much for them. I saw only one man reach the shore." Dever was so incensed by the slaughter that he jumped from his landing craft and nudged seven wounded aboard before shoving off. That night, the bloodshot boatmen convened in their mess hall crowded by foot soldiers only the night before. The weary seamen raised their coffee mugs and declared, "Those guys had what it takes."[303]

Ira Wolfert, who had received a Pulitzer for his coverage in the Solomons, watched the Normandy combat while sailing along the coast in an LCT. For Wolfert, it was a typical thirty-hour beachhead day (his fourth) which felt like "an eighth day of the week, peculiar to our times." While German aircraft was noticeably absent, Wolfert claimed one came so close to the vessel that he could feel the Hun's heat. "It hit like a bundle of fists against my face."

By twilight, the ship was evacuating wounded. Resembling tea roses, reddish-brown clouds serenely unfurled on the horizon. The peaceful scene starkly contrasted the image of men bleeding on the deck. Explosions still echoed in the distance. "A large, sooty cloud of smoke sprang up from the beach as abruptly as if prodded. Our LCT began to tremble all over," wrote Wolfert. "There was debris in that cloud—big, black, torn chunks of it—and sitting on top of the cloud, poised delicately there for a moment many feet in the air, was the body of a truck, all intact. It was silhouetted so sharply in the twilight that I could make out the wheels of it. Then the blasting sound of the explosion came clapping like a huge hand against our ears."

Wolfert was repelled by the sight. He turned to a chiseled, German prisoner sporting polished, spurred boots. Two pieces of shrapnel poked out the Nazi officer's side, but he stood impassively puffing a cigarette at the railing. Opposite the officer, a German medic administered plasma to a battered American paratrooper. "I don't know why but this sight made me even sicker than the rather ludicrous spectacle of the

Nazi superman posing at the rail," Wolfert confessed. "It made the whole world seem even more insane and I turned with a feeling of running away."

The reporter instead initiated small talk with the enemy officer. The "28-year-old, curly haired, pink-cheeked blond from Breslau" had enjoyed leave in Paris only eight days earlier.

"How are the girls in Paris? Still beautiful?" asked Wolfert.

"Ah," said the German with a kiss to the air, "very beautiful." He shouted his memories over the explosions.[304]

The daring and multifaceted naval efforts undertaken by numerous nations and services on D-Day foretold the coming strife on the beaches and in the hedgerows. Through the barbarity and brotherhood of war's unspeakable discord, seemingly common servicemen rose to new heights of endurance, improvisation, and camaraderie. Cooperation emerged as both a science and an art during amphibious operations. Seamen recognized their efforts as only the first of many necessary deeds to emancipate Fortress Europe. Past the obstacles and mines cemented below the Channel's uncertain waters lay another desperate engagement, however. Success rested not merely in technological capacities but the willpower of men to survive and forge on. Little could match a fighter with fear in his stomach and fire in his heart, Hanson Baldwin once observed. In scattered and scared groups of five and ten, such men would write history's next chapter. "Man is still supreme in a mechanistic war," Baldwin concluded. It was he who won the glory and paid the price.[305]

A chaplain on a nearby vessel considered additional forces at play. He offered a final, perhaps unconventional, invasion blessing to the kneeling members of his unit. "God bless you and give 'em hell."[306]

CHAPTER 8

"Somebody's Got to Get Hurt"

The Brooklyn corporal's stomach churned. With each downward wham of the Higgins boat, twenty-five-year-old Johnny Lacognata grew increasingly nauseous. His quivering legs pushed against the craft's stowage rack. Feeling like an overburdened pack mule, he readjusted the heft of the assault vest digging into his slender shoulders. The time was nearly six in the morning. The coast must be near, he thought. His view was obstructed by the haze and rhythmic crash of waves. The passengers were soddened. Not even the showers of water could erase the pungent odor of their gas-impregnated herringbone twill uniforms. A jittery GI excessively clicked at his empty lighter in futile efforts to ignite soggy cigarettes. He flicked the butts overboard after each failed attempt. To diminish the aftertaste of vomit, others vigorously chewed spearmint gum. The men inhaled deeply, hoping the nippy air would alleviate their seasickness.

Lacognata and comrades would be among the first amphibious troops to set foot in occupied France. Despite the stormy trek toward Utah Beach, the lengthy journey from ship to shore eased the corporal's nervousness. His chilled paranoia of death and defeat heated into agitated rage. "We crossed the Channel in an assault transport and were put over-side in a Higgins boat for a ten-mile run to the beach," Lacognata told reporter Howard Whitman. "I was as scared as hell on the transport, but once we got into little landing craft and started chugging beachward I forgot all fear. As I saw the beach loom ahead, I was so damned mad I just wanted to get in there and fight like hell."

From Lacognata's vantage point, the naval bombardment preceding his arrival was executed with "magnificent" exactness. The shelling was so precisely timed that the final volleys struck only one minute prior to the landings. "The entire beach was still wreathed with smoke and bomb explosions when we charged ashore," he confirmed.

Plowing ahead, several boats were struck by underwater mines and capsized. Their human cargo was slung into the tide, the extreme weight of gear making the trek ashore a task of Herculean strength. For many, Operation Overlord could well have been code-named *Overload*. The boys plodded onto the sand, falling to their knees under the mountains of equipment. Lacognata soon joined his squad of engineers endeavoring to burst a route inland. "Our engineer team found the wall we were to demolish as easily as if we had rehearsed the whole show on this very beach," said the corporal. "It was wonderful to have the whole thing explained to us in advance and then find it exactly as they said it would be. We planted our charges and blasted hell out of the wall without losing a single one of our men." Anxious to flee the open landscape, men darted onto the beach's grassy edge with a rush of energetic haste.

Lacognata's invasion was over as soon as it began. "Then, 'zing'—a shell came over and exploded nearby," he recalled. "A hunk of shrapnel smacked my right hand and—well, I guess my part in the show was over. I was ordered back to the Higgins boat for evacuation." The impact fractured his wrist and he was denied the opportunity to advance past the seawall. The corporal was surprised by his first taste of combat. "I sure thought it would be tougher than that." Whitman claimed some assault troops did not encounter a single German during their first hour. The unhindered progress led to the relatively prompt destruction of a concrete barricade that otherwise would have impeded the path of American armor. The only apparent glimpse of the enemy was a lone Messerschmitt, which was instantaneously evicted by punctual American fighters.[307]

The comparative mercy of Utah Beach was due to a lucky error in navigation. Currents and smoke landed the initial waves a half-mile away from the intended destination and piloted invaders to a lesser-defended sector. U. S. troops arriving there suffered perhaps one-tenth the casualties of those on the more formidable Omaha Beach. Spearheading the charge was the arthritic, visually-unassuming Theodore Roosevelt, Jr. of the 4th Infantry Division. The unorthodox brigadier was the son of the twenty-sixth president and a political rival of cousin FDR. Disliked by Patton for his informal style and discounted by Bradley for his affable command attitude, Roosevelt was unceremoniously relieved from the 1st Infantry Division following his frontline forays in North Africa.

"General Teddy," much like his high-energy father, did not shy from a brawl. Appointed assistant division commander of the Ivy Men the winter prior to D-Day, the physically-ailing Roosevelt unapologetically campaigned to hit the beaches with his boys. Division commander Raymond "Tubby" Barton reluctantly acquiesced, doubting Roosevelt would survive the campaign. Henry Gorrell of the United Press captured the little general's indomitable spirit in one of his many invasion reflections. Roosevelt "hit the beaches 16 minutes after H-hour, wearing coveralls, his only weapon an army .45 pistol. Hobbling on his cane, he waved on his doughboys whom he led into the interior under fire from German 88-mm cannon, rockets, and concrete-emplaced machine guns." At fifty-six, Roosevelt was the oldest invader wading ashore. Only miles away, son Quentin slogged into battle as a captain with the Big Red One. The brigadier personally oversaw the placement of demolition charges. His colorful wisecracks eased his men's strain. "I found him in the thick of it," wrote Gorrell, "cheering on his men and loving the hot smell of battle."

Yet the reporter noticed something wrong with Roosevelt's thumb. "What's the matter with the general?" Gorrell inquired to aide Stevie Stevenson.

"The general's luck is still holding out," Stevenson replied. "It's just a scratch from a piece of shrapnel."

Seeking cover in a nearby dune, Roosevelt assessed the situation and quickly recognized his division was not in the correct location. Defying concerns about linking with subsequent waves, he famously declared, "We'll start the war from right here!" The general's cavalier attitude and hands-on generalship would ultimately lead to his demise. Having largely concealed his worsening chest pains, his body became a ticking time bomb. His heart ultimately gave out on July 12. Roosevelt was only days shy of a promotion to major general.[308]

Gorrell was no stranger to such men intoxicated by the thrills of the campaign. A reporter of the Spanish Civil War, a friend of Hemingway, and the recipient of an air medal for saving a bomber crewman, the mustached, middle-age Gorrell was accustomed to unhealthy environments. The correspondent ventured out that morning in an LCT with men "prepared to wade fields of bullet-riddled mud and slime after vaulting Adolf Hitler's steel and concrete defense wall." The men were playing for keeps.

Members of the 4th Infantry Division's 8th Regiment press inland following a prompt battle to secure Utah Beach. Although invaders at Omaha Beach suffered casualty rates ten times greater, grave dangers awaited the Fourth's Ivy Men beyond the seawall. (15)

"As I write this dispatch," Gorrell continued, "our boys are peering skyward at a low-flying formation of their own aircraft. It is being flown low so our troops will be able to identify our newly-marked planes when they zoom low over the beaches." Eisenhower's address was presented to the men and Gorrell watched their faces as an officer summarized their forthcoming challenges. "They were serious," Gorrell observed of their expressions. "Many of them chewed their gum a bit faster than usual, but I could detect no evidence of fear." The GIs responded to their CO's oration with lively applause. Within minutes, they were back to poker games on wool blankets and tapping toes to Jazz playing from the ship's loudspeaker—almost as if they were off to a Sunday school picnic.

Despite their tranquility, all invaders were conscious of the fact they might not return. "I may be going to die, but I know we're going to win," said M/Sgt. James Chrest, a fifty-year-old veteran who received the

Purple Heart and Silver Star for deeds at Cantigny in the First World War. A fellow GI surrendered a pack of cigarettes on a poker blanket, declaring, "These are on me, fellas. Don't be bashful as I may not be handing out many more." Gorrell was well-acquainted with such fatalism. "I know that I am smoking my cigarette just a bit faster than usual myself and that somehow it doesn't taste quite right," he added.

Perhaps never before were soldiers so enthused to embark on a task so grim. Cpl. Alphonse Pesci of Stapleton, New York exhibited pragmatic earnestness for the occasion. "After you practice for a thing so long you get sick of practicing," the father of two said. "We know what we got to do and we want to get the damned thing done. Maybe if we get the damned thing done we'll get home someday."

Resting leisurely on a cargo hatch, Sgt. John Connors of Chicago and Pvt. Herbert Campbell of Owensville, Ohio were of the same opinion. "Let's get it over and knock their teeth out. That's the way we feel, and you can tell them back home that our morale was never better—I mean that," Connors exclaimed. "That goes for me [too]," Campbell echoed.

Cpl. Norman Paltzer of the Bronx expressed similar concern for the home front. "From what I hear it's the people back home who have the worst jitters."

"I know it sounds incredibly calm," Gorrell assured readers. "But that's the way it was."

Minus their rigid "skunk suits" shellacked with anti-gas agent, the Americans were better equipped than they were at Anzio or Salerno. Gorrell strapped his gas mask bag on his chest and was quickly told to place it on his back instead. When the bullets started flying, one needed to sink as low to the ground as possible. "We have enough K-rations to last two or three days and that's all," said Gorrell, "but they fed us some good army chow at the embarkation point and the boys were grateful." However, the hearty breakfasts would not rest well in their stomachs.

"You've never seen such laden troops as those who embarked here," Gorrell added. "You could hardly see their faces beneath the welter of equipment. Some of the things they carried were field packs, side arms, rifles, machine guns, walkie talkies, field glasses, medical supplies, jackets stuffed with hand grenades, smoke bombs, heavy loads of ammunition, prepared dynamite charges, flame throwers, grenade launchers, bazookas, TNT charges on the ends of poles, and anti-gas equipment." Other items included tobacco, water purification tablets, a box of insecticide powder, one razor, three boxes each of D-rations and K-rations, four boxes of matches, seven sticks of chewing gum, twelve sea-sickness pills, and two puke bags. One soldier had mounted on his back a red and white sign painted with the warning, "Danger—Minefield." Another peculiarly toted a weathered guitar. War showcased a diverse wardrobe.[309]

Among the encumbered travelers was combat engineer Bill Fischer. "I left my ship early in the morning on D-Day and boarded a barge about 7 miles out and started in for the beach," the corporal recalled to his hometown newspaper. "Due to the rough currents we drifted about ½ a mile or so from our designated spot. Thank God for that! While we were coming in the German 88s were dropping all around our barge but through the grace of God we weren't hit, at least while I was aboard. I took off for the small dune line like a streak of lightning and didn't have time to look back."

Fischer evaded a flurry of machine gun fire raining from an emplacement some 300 feet beyond the dune. "That is where the Jerries were entrenched, and I really do mean entrenched." For two days the corporal played potshot in the twisting knolls and pastures immediately beyond the coast. Fischer lost all essentials but his weapon and ammunition. He and his lieutenant ventured through the wavy beach grass "to see what we could scare out." Tossing grenades and spraying Tommy Gun rounds at anything that moved, they killed or captured two dozen of the enemy. It was "not bad for a morning's work," Fischer professed.

Foretelling a constant GI peril, Fischer bitterly encountered the deadly obstinacy of German marksmen. "The snipers will snipe until they run out of ammunition," he complained, "then come out with their hands up and nothing happens to them. They just get taken prisoners and that's that!" When Fischer returned to the beach, elusive deadeyes "were firing like hell." A chance escape from death stirred Fischer's emotions, evoking both gratitude and shock. "I tell you, that made me stop and think, for those Germans could have plugged me in the back when we got their buddies." Over time, some Americans became less accommodating of snipers attempting surrender. Captured combatants found with ammunition in their pouches were handed over to MPs. Enemy prisoners apprehended with no bullets often received a fresh one to the head.

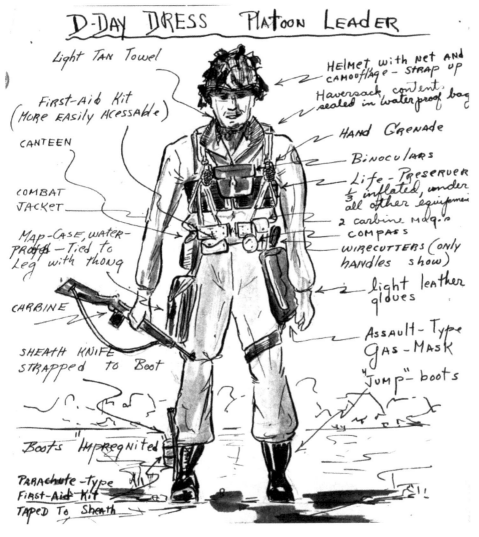

A soldier of the 29th Infantry Division sketched a lieutenant's invasion gear. "You've never seen such laden troops as those who embarked here," correspondent Henry Gorrell wrote from England. The weight of gear proved lethal for scores wading toward the beaches. (16)

African American troops stand over captured Germans enclosed in a barbed wire den on Utah Beach. In the background, the Sherman tank "Delphia" rolls past while *LCT 855* sits grounded in the sand. Silver barrage balloons hover in the distance. Of German prisoners Ernie Pyle remarked, "The expression on their faces was something forever unforgettable. In it was the final horrified acceptance of their doom." (17)

Having flushed out his share of snipers, Fischer sought respite in his newly-constructed home. "My foxhole is quite the modern thing," he boasted. "It's about 4 feet deep, 3 feet wide, and 7 feet long. It has dirt piled all around it with one layer of sand bags on top of that, then I have it covered with some three-inch boards and sand bags. It's water proofed with a shot down barrage balloon. Really, about the only thing it lacks is a built-in bathroom."[310]

Extemporized creature comforts were far from the mind of twenty-eight-year-old private Peter W. Boucovalis of the 4th Division. The former waiter from Essex, New Jersey endured some of the more immediate dangers posed on Utah. "Just before our boat hit the beach," he recalled, "I saw one of the landing barges hit a mine and rise high in the air, throwing the men into the seas." Dismembered chunks of comrades drifted by as the private's own craft jutted into the sinister labyrinth of obstacles.

Escaping the minefields, Boucovalis sprinted to the partial protection of the pocked seawall, where he experienced an uncanny state of aloneness. Panting with exhaustion, the private rested his helmeted head against the concrete and looked back upon the sweeping vista of destruction. Men rushing toward him fell like dolls dropped by careless children, their legs and arms contorting in all unnatural ways as they flopped headfirst into the sand. Boucovalis gasped for breath while awaiting the debarkation of more men. Welcomed support arrived via a fresh combat team. An American flamethrower cast fiery spurts at a nearby pillbox, prompting thirty-one shaken and partially-charred defenders to exit and relinquish their arms.[311]

Tom Treanor of the *Los Angeles Times* was surprised by the speed at which Americans conquered Utah Beach. "I stepped ashore on France, walking up a beach where men were moving casually about carrying equipment inshore. Up the coast a few hundred yards, German shells were pounding in regularly but in our area, it was peacefully busy."

"How did you make out?" Treanor asked one Ivy Man.

"It was reasonably soft," was the answer. "The Germans had some machine-gun posts and some high velocity guns on the palisades which made it a little hot at first. They waited until the landing craft dropped their ramps and then they opened up on them while the men were still inside. In a few cases we took heavy casualties, but then the navy went to work on the German guns and it wasn't long before they were quiet."[312]

Bill Stoneman of the *Chicago Daily News* was equally surprised when landing on Utah. "The more you think about our landing at the base of the Cherbourg Peninsula last Tuesday," he wrote, "the more mysterious the whole thing becomes." The opening stage of the invasion "has been a poor show on the part of the Germans, who presumably are fighting for their lives."[313]

Treanor was astonished by the lack of fortifications, which were little more than cattle wire. In every direction, he observed men scurrying about like advancing ants. Likewise, conversations with prisoners evoked stunning revelations. "There isn't much left of New York any more, is there?" questioned one captured German.

"What do you mean?" replied a puzzled GI.

The captive retorted, "Well, you know it's been bombed by the Luftwaffe."[314]

Military campaigns yield all manner of surprises. Weeks into the invasion, AP photographer Martin Lederhandler of Brooklyn unexpectedly rediscovered one of his own lost Utah Beach photographs. During the amphibious operations, he clipped film to a carrier pigeon, but the bird never reached the English news office. In fact, the pigeon was purportedly captured and Lederhandler's photo was thereafter published in a German military newspaper—a periodical the photographer subsequently unearthed among captured effects. The image caption claimed the barge shown was sunk by German artillery—a statement Lederhandler knew to be false.[315]

While processing prisoners, Peter Boucovalis pondered his recent travails. One does not have time to think in combat, he mused. "You hardly notice that shells are passing overhead and that waves of planes are flying overhead. In advancing you even get careless sometimes and your buddies have to warn you that your head or your tail is too high." Like Bill Fischer, the young man pressed his way down "many hard roads" in the ensuing days and confronted two Nazi snipers. "I killed the German soldier with my first shot and then sent six bullets into a French woman after becoming so enraged at her thinking she was engaging in sniper practices while attempting to aid the Germans." Boucovalis's suspicions of the local civilian populace compelled him to keep his rifle's safety off. By contrast, fellow 4th Division soldier William E. Jones sympathized with innocent non-combatants entrapped in the turmoil. "French people, of course, lived there. Us being there was as big a surprise as anything in the world to those people. They didn't really know how to take us, I guess."[316]

Few were more surprised than the defeated German defenders. Richard McMillan of the United Press strolled along the purportedly formidable Atlantic Wall when the smoke cleared. He thought it a sham. The elongated fortification "constitutes the biggest stuff of the whole war. I examined the so-called 'wall' with great care. It simply does not exist. It consisted of a few scattered pillboxes, some unfinished tank ditches, and little else. We could not have chosen a better point for our attack." Nearby prisoners confessed they had frantically tried to enhance their defenses, but the demanding labor proved too burdensome. Delayed fortifying cost the Germans dearly.

"You see," said McMillan, "they had staked all their cards on a landing over the short 21 mile stretch between Dover and Calais. We knew that to be their strongest link in the Atlantic Wall. So we took the longer route and caught the enemy napping." Within two days, Allied tanks widened the bulging advance and McMillan embarked on a thirty-mile tour of the frontlines. The vignettes of his expedition blended images of war and peace into a compelling invasion memory. Sudden freedom roused countless French citizens into exuberant hysteria. At the same time, the bloating and blackening corpses of Allied and German dead lay scattered and unburied along the many roads stemming from the beachhead. The occasional villager tended to makeshift burials.[317]

The exigencies of war brought forth the unexpected. This fact was not lost on the men of the 582nd Engineer Dump Truck Company, who literally paved the way off Utah Beach. A segregated African American outfit, such an engineer company was not classified as a combat unit in the eyes of the War Department. The 582nd valiantly proved otherwise. The crews not only demonstrated that heavy machinery units could fight and build simultaneously, but that stereotyped minorities had the willpower to excel under the pressures of battle. The 582nd preceded many of the seaborne infantry regiments with bridge equipment and explosives to be used by assault engineers. The company delivered the goods in the face of fierce small arms fire. Its powerful ten-tire dump trucks hauled away sea mines, sparing countless landing craft from a watery grave.

Stars and Stripes correspondent Allan Morrison heaved praise on the unit. His article described how 1st Sgt. Norman Day, a former Works Progress Administration athletic director from Illinois, utilized supervisory skills and physical prowess to coolly oversee beach traffic. Day's efficiency was recognized by a passing general and he was thus awarded the Silver Star. Later that week, Day rescued a colonel from a bomb blast near Sainte-Marie-du-Mont that left six others dead. Following hazardous beachhead duties, the 582nd was assigned to infantry supply transportation. Every man in the unit engaged in the guerilla-stop-and-go-style of combat that typified fighting in Normandy. Encounters with German regulars and the Boche seemed an hourly occurrence. Sgt. James L. Harris of Lexington, North Carolina even shot down a Luftwaffe plane attempting to strafe his dump truck (which was fortuitously mounted with a .50 caliber machine gun). Meanwhile, Sgt. William Goodwin of Abbeville, South Carolina summoned reinforcements in response to an ambush on paratroopers in a Norman village.

The tipper truck warriors proved indispensable. "Many a doughboy rode to war in a dump truck driven by a man from this unit," Morrison concluded. "Personnel transported to forward positions included men of the Fourth Infantry and the 82nd and 101st Airborne Divisions. They worked a military taxi service for fighting men running all the way to Cherbourg, entered many a town before it was officially captured, and assisted in the evacuation of many wounded and prisoners." Nobody could claim the 582nd was not comprised of genuine combat troops worthy of due recognition. Their deeds altered the views of many white service members. "These colored boys are good soldiers and do a good job with their trucks," wrote Lt. George Worth.[318]

There was little time for internal discrimination in the combat zone. Enemy fire did not distinguish between black and white. In a letter to his parents, S/Sgt. Leo "Bud" Laws of the 4th Division claimed, "them damn Germans don't care who the hell they hurt, everybody's alike to them so somebody's got to get hurt." The wounded sergeant added, "I was in the thick of it for three days and three nights before I was hit .... There are lots of things I would like to tell you only it would probably make you sick, so I won't say anything about it."[319]

Fellow infantrymen of the division's 22nd Regiment related to the sergeant's grief when approaching the heavily-armed, casemated Crisbecq battery near the village of Saint-Marcouf. The position's powerful 210-mm Kriegsmarine guns helped sink the USS *Corry* on D-Day and had the potential to unleash additional devastation. The men under Mississippi captain Thomas C. Shields advanced toward the position but were stunted by weltering artillery fire. Despite the offer of an observer to embark on the suicide mission, Shields grabbed a radio and sprinted onto a forward position to direct screening fire for his withdrawing troops. He sacrificed his own life so his men could escape the wrath.

"The captain was standing up urging us to hold the attack when a shell hit him, and he went down," said Sgt. Romeo Bourgoin of Waterville, Maine. "I got up to him and helped him to a hedgerow so he could hand over command to another officer. He was hit in several places and said he knew he was done for. Then the Germans charged and one of our men was killed. Capt. Shields ordered us to drop him and save our own lives. His last thoughts were for our safety."

Shields received a posthumous Distinguished Service Cross. The award was of little consolation to his mother, Mary. "D-Day came too soon," she later recalled. Mrs. Shields had earlier departed Mississippi to spend time with her daughter in New York City. While there she refused to read or listen to invasion reports. On July 3, however, a friend called her to share the dreadful news of the captain's demise. "Stunned, unbelieving, rebellious, I left the phone," Shields remembered. She exited her daughter's apartment in grief and aimlessly wandered the streets of New York until sunrise. Her boy was gone.[320]

Although the division suffered fewer losses on the beaches, the "Famous Fourth" withstood harrowing casualty rates in hedgerow country and beyond. By Independence Day, its soldiers had received hundreds of Purple Hearts, thirty-three Bronze Stars, and eleven Silver Stars. Among those recognized was Capt. Julian S. Ellenberg, a Protestant chaplain from Greenwood, South Carolina who was described as "a dynamo of good will." Making his way ashore only thirty minutes after the initial landings on Utah, the chaplain immediately administered spiritual and medical aid to those languishing. Crawling between the wounded, the padre granted blessings upon the maimed members of his flock. Offering unction, he placed his hands over the dying, uttering into their ears, "Of His great mercy, may He forgive you your sins, release you from suffering, and restore you to wholeness and strength." Carrying out his holy mission under intense fire and with slight shell fragment wounds, the chaplain moved grown men to tears.[321]

Sgt. William A. Moore of DuBois, Pennsylvania arrived in moderately safer conditions on June 7. In a V-Letter to his family he remarked, "Well, here we are on the road to Berlin, we landed on D-Day plus 1. We were out in the bay on D-Day and with the aid of glasses were able to observe the action. Our naval support was excellent, and the air umbrella was outstanding. On the eve of D-Day plus 1 our boats were subject to the Jerry night fighters, but they were given a hot reception, one would think they were in the midst of a 4th celebration. Shore batteries exchanged volleys with our Navy, and the tracers looked like streaks of lightning passing to and fro."

Moore's bumpy journey culminated with an unexpected reunion of hometown friends he idly discovered on the beach. The gathering "looked like a Legion convention of DuBois boys," he joked. Coincidentally, Moore also crossed paths with the venerated Ernie Pyle, who in his view, "didn't miss a trick" in his invasion reporting. In the following days, Moore grew enamored with the French citizenry, who threw flowers before their liberators and freely offered calvados. The sergeant concluded his family letter with a hearty "Bonjour!"[322]

Moore was not alone in savoring a chance encounter on the beachhead. A week after parachuting into France, 1st Lt. Don Driver, Jr. of El Paso hitchhiked a jeep ride to Utah Beach in search of his father, who the son knew to be a captain of a combat beach unit. In a command tent not far from the shoreline, the lieutenant detected his dad in a crowd of officers and hollered, "Hey, pop, come out of there." Foregoing formalities, the captain wryly replied, "Don't shoot." The father and son embraced in a moment of affection that neither expected on the battlefront. It was Father's Day. The reunion exemplified an editorial appearing in the *Lowell Sun* that same week: "D-Day also means Dad's Day. The head of a family somewhere in America is risking his life at the head of an invasion column every day somewhere in France, at Biak, on Saipan, and north of Anzio." In 1944, the national observance denoted the most pronounced separation of fathers from their children in American history.[323]

Peter Boucovalis, the infantryman who barely survived Utah Beach, evaded death once more and conveyed a tale even more astonishing. On the long and perilous road to Cherbourg, Boucovalis steadily marched in a drawn-out formation of men cautiously patrolling ten paces apart. With his rifle safety off, he budged at every crack of a twig. The private heard a whiz and was hit high in the shoulder, twirling him like a top and crashing him to the dirt. Additional shots were fired, and his platoon vanished into the surrounding brush. There was no pain at first, only surprise. Travelling diagonally from left to right, the round tunneled into his frame only inches from his spine. Then the pain came. Unable to move and panting for breath, Boucovalis lay in silent agony. He thought his "final moment had come." A comrade emerged from the greenery to render assistance, but he was shot in the groin and in both legs. The two shared the lane in anguish, squirming in the mud like pathetic road kill.

"We both lay there on the road for some time when some of our large armored tanks approached. I tried to pull myself out of the way, but I could hardly move," Boucovalis recollected. Although the time was near noon the tank drivers could not see the wounded men through their periscopes. The armor ominously inched closer. Boucovalis barely crawled a yard before one of the tanks rolled over his right arm. The twenty-eight-year-old let forth a chilling scream as each treaded wheel pounded his arm deeper into the ground. The tankers could not hear him over their engines. "Luckily for me the road was soft or I would have suffered the loss of the arm from it being completely crushed," Boucovalis recalled. Within moments medics arrived on the scene and treated the private and his would-be rescuer. Amazingly, his arm was spared.[324]

Although absurdly ineligible for combat pay, medics constantly evoked surprise in the hedgerows. Engineer medics Ed Janasik, Joe Fitzback, and Joe Nowicki were returning to the rear when three un-armed Germans suddenly appeared from the brush with hands raised. Armed only with knives, the medics dutifully marched the enemy to the nearest MP.

"What the hell do you mean by capturing enemy troops without the use of arms?" the policeman exclaimed. "What do you want to do, get shot? Where the hell are your arms?"

"We're medics, and not allowed to carry arms," Nowicki replied.

After brief contemplation the officer declared, "Well, don't do it again. You might get hurt."[325]

Despite their many successful endeavors, the men of the 4th Infantry Division thought themselves pariahs in Normandy press reports. "The hard-fighting soldiers of the Fourth Infantry were brassed off today," wrote Charles F. Kiley of *Stars and Stripes*. "After nine days and nights of bitter warfare without rest, from the Normandy beachhead to beyond Montebourg and on the road to Cherbourg, the boys of the Ivy Division heard that a lot of people were getting credit for the Allied advances in France. That is, almost everybody but the Fourth."

After receiving embittered letters from the division's ranks complain-ing of bias toward paratroopers, *S&S* offered a consolation prize to the

Ivy Men on June 20. "This is to let them know they were not entirely forgotten" the paper responded to the criticism. "The dead they left behind were not entirely forgotten. The dead they left behind—enemy dead as well as their own—told a vivid story of their tireless efforts. Now that Supreme Headquarters has announced the presence of the Fourth in Normandy the world outside France also will be hearing the story." Controversies regarding recognition in the press underscored the centrality of journalism in crafting the identities of fighting units. Perceptions of divisional or regimental character and fame were inextricably linked to the level of press coverage received.

Moreover, without mention of battlefield sacrifice in periodicals, combatants felt their efforts were taken for granted by superiors and readers alike. This factor, in turn, carried the potential of instigating challenges to morale and dampening military zeal. Every soldier yearned to read of a tale that resonated with his own experience. Depriving him of that honor not only posed dilemmas in maintaining resolve but also defied the democratic credo of an everyman story for every man. Throughout the war, *Stars and Stripes* constantly strove to highlight the valorous deeds of its readers. Many simply fell through the cracks. Subsequently, the newspaper occasionally beseeched forgiveness and offered compensation in print.[326]

There was little time for riflemen or reporters to catch their breath, however. The many actions on and around Utah Beach were no simple feats for their participants. They were among the most successful of D-Day. Several miles to the east, a confrontation of even greater proportions transpired on the sands near the picturesque villages of Vierville and Saint-Laurent. The futures of many hinged on the efforts of so few—all on a sliver of beach slightly longer than Coney Island. As one sergeant recalled, the power of prayer and the laws of self-preservation were set to the ultimate trial. For the liberators who endured the onslaught, the name of their landing zone would elicit vivid memories of pain and perseverance for decades hence. Omaha, bloody Omaha.[327]

As *Stars and Stripes* suggested, the losses of Utah Beach were still not completely obscured. Andy Rooney arrived on the landing grounds on June 10. He immediately spotted a Graves Registration Unit conducting its grim chores. A row of dead greeted him. "They were covered with olive-drab blankets, just their feet sticking out at the bottom. I remember their boots—all the same on such different boys," Rooney mourned. "Even if you didn't know anyone who died, the heart knows something the brain does not—and you weep."[328]

CHAPTER 9

"Hotter than Hell"

The stillness was unnerving. Both men and time seemed motionless, transfixed by uncertainty in this calm before the storm. "There was no bravado, no noticeable tension, and no visible elation." Clark Lee of the International News Service offered these ominous observations of men bearing toward Omaha Beach—the most forbidding of D-Day's landing sectors. "These were just a bunch of American youngsters who wanted to get their job over with as quickly as possible. They knew where they were going and why," Lee confirmed. Following months of uncompromising training and rehearsal, they were as prepared as they could be. Scores of them would not return. Others recognized they "would come back blind, limbless, and shocked." For many untried invaders, this was to be their first taste of battle. Some faithfully appraised the situation with inklings of certainty. "I feel the first step on the beach will be my first step home," one shavetail confessed. "For three years each step I have taken has been away from home. Now is the time to get started back."[329]

Omaha Beach was a towering, intimidating objective of cruel prospects. Located between the Douve estuary to the west and the rocky Port-en-Bessin to the east, the beach unveiled little sand at high tide. Tracts of innumerable landmines lurked beneath. Domineering cliffs hovered over the approach, posing considerable dangers to charging vehicles. Tucked within the steep ravines and embankments was a labyrinth of German trenches and concrete emplacements ideal for enemy cover and concealment. Artillery and heavy machine guns jutted from bulges in the rock, allowing for sweeping fields of crossfire. Securing this beachhead would be a central pillar of maintaining a continuous line of advance across a fifty-mile battlefront.

The clash at Omaha epitomized America's deadly wartime learning curve. The initial waves of untested GIs were led like lambs to the slaughter, tail spinning into chaotic breakdowns in communication, navigation, and chain of command. Nearly all that could go wrong did go wrong; yet total defeat was averted. Resilience withstood the chaos. As Col. George Taylor of the Big Red One harshly speculated, GIs were to be mercilessly thrown at the vaunted Atlantic Wall until it cracked. The culmination would stand as a triumph of the ages or devolve into an unmitigated disaster on the scale of Gallipoli. Every man involved guardedly weighed his odds.[330]

The doughty reporter Don Whitehead restlessly upheld his celebrated nickname of "Beachhead Don" that morning. Climbing down the knotted ropes of the USS *Samuel Chase* into a landing craft with the men of the 16th Regiment, he shuddered at what lay ahead. A "heavy burden of nerves" weighed on the shoulders of the huddled GIs in Whitehead's boat. The dispiriting silence was interrupted only by the sporadic roar of naval gunfire. Whitehead glanced over his shoulders. Every soldier was violently trembling. "I knew that everyone was scared," he wrote, "but not *that* scared." The AP correspondent suspected the men were quivering from the artillery concussions. "The air vibrated from the sound." The tremors created a sensation of some terrible force ripping a hole through the sky. Like massive cymbals, heaven and earth seemingly crashed together with jarring and unforgiving effect.[331]

The intense volume was not soon to diminish. Foamy Channel waters cascaded into the vessel, enhancing the anguish of the journey. From the wheel, the helmeted cluster of green heads resembled a dark cabbage patch after a heavy rain, a grim harvest. The craft hastened to the beach. Curtains of black smoke swirled beyond the sand. Whitehead's gut tightened. He worried not for himself; he had endured the punch of combat many times before. Whitehead despaired for the twenty-somethings to his left and right. He would be the last person to see many of them alive. The thought sickened him. The beach was now clearly in sight, its twisted assortment of Belgian Gates, Teller Mines, crisscrossed hedgehogs, and barbed wire standing as infernal lawn ornaments. Attempting to clear his mind, the reporter inhaled a deep breath of the crisp ocean air before the inevitable onslaught ensued.

A whistle screeched. The ramp clanked downward. Hell spewed forth.

"None who saw it can ever forget the horror of that day on Omaha Beach," Whitehead recalled. "None can forget the suffering, the sacrifice or the heroism of the soldiers and sailors who died or were maimed as they fought their way ashore with odds four to three against them." The incessant rattle of Hitler's Buzzsaws, the unnerving detonation of masked landmines, the gruff orders of sergeants, and the eruption of shells amongst the deadlocked masses orchestrated a veritable symphony of death—an ineffable wail of jarring madness. Men shouted over comrades as they tripped over the scorched corpses of others. They pointed and waved in all directions, attempting to rally survivors and scavenge for supplies lost in the crimsoned surf. Sand from inescapable bullet blasts temporarily blinded their eyes and coated their raspy throats. Both physically and emotionally, scores were consumed by the whirlpool of combat in this perfected state of perdition. All seemed lost before it even began.

"Wave after wave of troops hit the beach and then flung themselves into the gravel, which gave them little protection from the German fire," Whitehead continued. "They lay shoulder to shoulder as far as I could see in either direction. And each time a shell landed someone was killed or wounded." The troops piled on at an alarming rate, filling the bottle-neck and offering prime, amassed targets for enemy gunners. Red hot rounds whizzed past the invaders' heads. Men hugged the earth as they had never hugged their mothers. They unsheathed their entrenching tools and feverishly plowed into the sand, some scratching at the earth with bare fingers and bayonets. Those unable to find cover were eviscerated by raining fragments of gnarled shrapnel, splitting their chests, bellies, and skulls with ghastly ease. Others futilely clipped away at curls of dense barbed wire in the hope of inching up the scalded bluffs. Huddled in desperate ranks along the shingle and intermingled among the dead, the clamoring GIs awaited a miracle—or at least more men. [332]

Formidable 88-mm guns covered the approaches, reducing men to clumps of bloody pulp. The guns were shielded by reinforced concrete pillboxes four to six feet thick. At the bottom of the hill, Lt. Carl W. Oelze of Cleveland nabbed two German teenagers bewildered by the maelstrom. Assigned to one of the guns, they had dashed from the bunker's tunnel after a naval shell "ripped squarely through the gun port." The prisoners confessed to Oelze they had no desire to fight and were relieved the invasion had at last arrived. They hunkered alongside their captor as the heavy roar of fire persisted.

Notwithstanding the mounting casualties, infantrymen and engineers swarmed ashore in dramatic assembly line fashion. The battle was as much a fight against time as man. Rising tides narrowed the beach, diminishing cover and exacerbating the appalling traffic jam. "The troops were wet from wading through the surf and the bedding of most troops was lost in vehicles swamped on the beach," Whitehead observed. The panorama was a shambles of clogged wreckage. A fellow correspondent added that the soldiers were "immobilized by fear. Descending arcs of tracers were entering the water around them, and they could not bring themselves to move." In both time and space, they appeared permanently frozen.

A GI riding on the back of a nearby DUKW suddenly shrieked a haunting cry of pain and plummeted headfirst into the deep. Peter Kuffer, a medic from New York City, reentered the inhospitable waters and tediously dragged the wounded boy through fountains of exploding water and sand. Kuffer trudged to the shelter of a hedgehog where he administered treatment on the thigh wound. Incoming rounds ricocheted off the obstacles, evoking a constant din of deathly clanks and thuds. The cries of the injured were dampened as Whitehead's ears rang from the intense clangor. "Wounded men, drenched by cold water, lay in gravel, some with water washing over their legs, shivering and waiting for stretcher bearers to take them aboard returning small craft."

"Oh God, let me aboard a boat!" wept one youthful invader in semi-delirium. The misery was unyielding. "Shells burst on all sides of us, some so close they threw black water and dirt in showers." Man and machine were seemingly devoured by the ocean from which they sprang. The scant battle lines bent and flowed with the whisk of every debris-ridden wave. Seeking to break the stalemate, the mighty warships steered closer and closer to shore, belching fire the whole way. Armor-plated Caterpillar D7 bulldozers clambered up the sandy banks to gouge out crude roadways of escape. Men convulsed in anticipation of the outbreak. "We *gotta* get outta here!" they screamed. Meandering up the beach, attackers gripped the rims of their helmets, faces down, as if they were pushing into a forceful headwind.[333]

Life photographer Robert Capa waded in and out of the devilish obstacles. He plopped beside an exasperated combatant who morosely envisioned his "old mother sitting on the porch" with the soldier's insurance policy in hand. "It was very unpleasant there," Capa added, "and, having nothing else to do, I start[ed] shooting pictures." In doing so, he snapped the most iconic photographs of the invasion, images seared into

The Coast Guard's *LCI 93* ran afoul of underwater obstructions off Omaha Beach and was mercilessly riddled by German shells. The stranded vessel's fate was depicted in Navy combat artist Dwight Shepler's watercolor painting appropriately entitled "The Tough Beach." (18)

American consciousness. His blurry scenes of soggy, floundering GIs weighed down by gear became synonymous with the D-Day experience. Not long on the beach, Capa soon retreated to a landing craft. He recalled being coated in feathers—feathers from the jacket linings of men blown into oblivion. The correspondent rushed the photos back to England, where frantic colleagues developed the negatives late on June 8. When published, the stunning images had immediate effect. *Life* concluded that Capa's "pictures show how violent the battle was."[334]

British journalist Iris Carpenter re-imagined that havoc from the many soldier interviews she subsequently conducted. The invaders "took terrific punishment, as, feet slipping in the shifting sand, men stumbled through gray wave caps which raced over them to slap them down with their too-heavy equipment, toss them on the beach, suck them back, toss them on again among the nightmare of jumbled equipment, smashed boats, drowned and broken bodies." The landscape was

180

a cluttered heap of human and mechanical wreckage. "When, eventually, the first tanks debarked, the drivers cried and vomited as they had to drive over the bodies of their buddies."[335]

The beach turned red. Invaders forcefully elbowed each other in their desperate attempts to advance. Casualties became ensnared under the gruesome weight of their dead comrades. One infantryman writhed beneath the corpses, unable to free himself from the lifeless pile. Knots of scattered entrails denoted the prior locations of men who seemingly vanished into thin air. The gore of dearly departed friends clung to the hair and jackets of comrades nearby. Medic Bob Molinari, whose red-crossed helmet was sent flying by an enemy round, could not sit idle. "He crawled somehow—I don't know how—up through the crossfire," Army doctor Walter Sielski recalled. "He went better than a hundred yards to reach a man, slung him underneath to cover the wounded man's body, and then came through a hundred yards of the same fire."[336]

To the west, nineteen-year-old private William J. Mask of the 29th Division fared no better. Mask and company were greeted with inauspicious steel spiders mounted with high explosives protruding from the seaway. Each had the capacity to blow a landing craft sky high. As the boat delicately maneuvered the shoreline, its deck was consumed by an 88-mm shell. Survivors lunged over the side into twelve feet of water, many being pulled under never again to rise. "I lost my equipment and when I hit the shore, I had nothing to fight with," Mask wrote in Maryland's *Frederick News*. "The Germans had covered us with murderous machine gun crossfire and most of my company was casualties before they got ashore. I crawled fifty yards until I was hit." With his weapon at the bottom of the Channel and his thumb splintered by shrapnel, Mask helplessly curled in the sand for sixteen hours before he was evacuated.[337]

The wounded were ferried to English ports from whence they embarked only days or hours earlier. In the corner of one boat, reporter James McLincy noticed a wounded boy sobbing into his frail hands. McGlincy asked what was wrong. "For three years I've been training for this," cried the youth, "and what happens? As soon as I start off the boat, I get a hit in the eye. I didn't even get to fire a single shot at Germans."[338]

The weeping private managed better than Harold Baumgarten of the same division. Baumgarten, a New York City Jew and gifted baseball player, painted a sizable Star of David on his jacket as a gesture of defiance to his Aryan enemies. Within moments of landing, Baumgarten's friends were dead and the New Yorker was weaponless. A sudden blow felt as if a baseball bat had smashed his face. Chunks of shrapnel had torn away Baumgarten's cheek. The private's gory mouth was awash with blood, shattered bone, and fragments of splintered teeth; his left upper jaw completely gone. "My left cheek was actually flapping over my ear as my blood poured," he recalled. Baumgarten cleaned his disfigured face in the stinging saltwater of the rising Channel. He thought, *"When will I die?"*[339]

Amazingly, the tenacious nineteen-year-old withstood the pain. A 1945 newspaper article stated, "Before he was evacuated 36 hours later, he was wounded four times more. Shell fragments creased his skull, an S-mine shattered his knee, and machine gun bullets smashed the small bones of his right foot." Baumgarten underwent two dozen surgeries amid recovery and was discharged from military service the following February. A mere two days later, he enrolled at New York University to build upon his existing medical studies. Yearning to help others, Baumgarten aspired to be a physician. The college offered him free tuition and books even though his veteran benefits had not yet been processed. For the final three decades of his life, Dr. Baumgarten was an active champion of his generation. He spoke on behalf of those who could not speak for themselves. The memories of D-Day never left him.[340]

Baumgarten's assistant division commander, Norman "Dutch" Cota, attempted to rally the huddled masses. With a saturated cigar in mouth, the brigadier bellowed to a squad, "What outfit is this? Goddamn it, if you're Rangers get up and lead the way. . . . I know you won't let me down. . . . We've got to get these men off this goddamned beach." The soldiers heeded their general's demands and scavenged for Bangalore torpedoes to breach the seawall.[341]

Physical anguish became the prevalent pattern. Jack Foster of *Stars and Stripes* awaited the multitudes of wounded on a British wharf. Many suffered little more than exposure to the frigid waters, and most would soon find their way back to the front. Their experiences ranged from the humorous to the tragic, but the men were "in good spirits and anxious to get back to France." Awaiting recirculation at port, D-Day's first casualties imparted to Foster tales both mesmerizing and monstrous.

Naval Fireman 1st Class Robert Thompson of Jacksonville, Florida was among them. An 88-mm shell punched through the side of Thompson's LCM—compelling him and three crewmates to join the fight on foot. "We were carrying men of a mixed Army-Navy beach battalion who got ashore successfully," he recalled of the moments before sinking. The boat was entangled among the obstacles and floated within inches of mines, risking impalement. "Machine gun slugs were cutting all around us and an 88 battery was coming closer." The boat was hit and all abandoned ship before the craft erupted into a massive fireball. "Then the fun began," he sarcastically lamented. "We swam ashore and dug foxholes. The rising tide chased us from them. We burrowed under debris. For ten hours shells burst all around us."[342]

Thompson's testimony highlighted the inherent dangers of coastal mines—a peril known all too well to the men of the 146th Engineer Combat Battalion, whose thorny responsibility it was to obliterate the barriers. Each team was comprised of both Army and Navy crewmen. The engineers schemed to demolish wooden obstructions with 2.5-pound blocks of Composition C-2 plastic explosives. Steel hedgehogs would be detonated with fifteen-pound satchel charges. Pfc. Dewey Turner of Company C was well-acquainted with these tools of the trade.

Of his experiences, Turner later wrote home, "I have a little to tell. It's not a very good thing to talk about but here goes. . . . We were some of the first men to hit the French Coast and it was plenty hot. Machine gun bullets were as thick as bees. Our job was to clear the obstacles off the beach where the landing barges could get in. We did our job." He added, "All I can say is that the men that were in the first wave that made it had the Good Lord with them; it wasn't just good luck." In the ensuing weeks, Turner was understandably content living peaceably in the rear among French farmers and dairy cows.[343]

Those stranded on Omaha possessed an ardent desire to survive and propel the fight inland. Capt. John Clifford Hodges Lee, Jr. was especially prone to such vigor. A 1941 graduate of West Point and the son of a lieutenant general, Lee landed with 5th Corps engineers. Spearheading one of the first companies ashore, he charged the shingle only to be captured by Germans lurking in nearby dune grass. The captain was hauled behind the lines and left to the care of a single guard digging a foxhole. Lee sat vigilantly in the dirt with hands unbound, awaiting his opportunity to flee. The sentinel foolishly threw his shovel aside and Lee immediately pounced, seizing the tool and bashing his captor unconscious. Absconding with a Mauser, the officer anxiously retraced his steps but discovered the enemy was still between him and his own lines. All he could do was await liberation in an unoccupied trench. Luckily, advancing Yanks noticed the captain before any withdrawing Germans did.[344]

If endurance was a prevailing theme among D-Day survivors, so was fear. Norbert Norris of Iowa was a sergeant in the 97th Quartermaster Railhead Company, a unit assigned to the oversight of supply dumps, the evacuation of wounded, and the relief of truck drivers. Norris had little anticipation of combat, expecting to witness the invasion's opening chapter from the relative safety of a supply ship. His cross-Channel journey raised little suspicion of any alternative scenario. "We really enjoyed ourselves," he wrote. Norris and comrades were even treated to white bread and ice cream—the first they had since departing the States. The sergeant absorbed all the sensations described in so many invasion letters: "What a sight, the harbor had more ships and landing craft than one can imagine." Hardly could he have expected to enter the melee so soon. Quartermaster troops were the subject of friendly ridicule within the ranks, having a reputation as rear-echelon paper shufflers and crate pushers rarely in harm's way. On June 6, Norris was granted the opportunity to disprove that assumption.

"My boat team landed at H plus 200 minutes or about 3 ½ hours after the initial assault," he recalled. "The beach was a sight I'll never forget. When we landed the beach was under heavy fire. The German 88s are quite a weapon—you cannot hear them coming until it's too late and they were not sparing any shells that day. There was not a man who was not scared on D-Day and that definitely includes me." Troops gently flagged uncovered landmines with pocket handkerchiefs. Pinned on the beach, Norris felt as if every German gun was aimed at him. "I never realized I could get myself in such a little foxhole," he confessed. Lying in a nearby dugout, Pvt. John G. Bianchi of the same company peered skyward and pondered the irony of his predicament. "There were times when I would have given anything to be an infantryman, back with the reserves, safe from fire," he joked. Swelling in number, the mass of men exerted pressure like a reservoir soon to breach a dam.[345]

Coast guardsman Herman Fulton, Jr. was overcome with sympathy for anybody who dared step foot on the embattled beach. A former cabinet maker from Atlanta, Fulton transported GIs to the shores of North Africa, Sicily, and Salerno. Although accustomed to the chaos of amphibious operations, Fulton thought his newest mission particularly unnerving. "As we crashed through the minefields, we first thought the beach would be a pushover," he stated. "Not a shot was fired. The defenders had a deadly effective trick of holding fire until we lowered one ramp and the Yanks started to charge." A vulnerable stationary target, Fulton's boat abruptly came under "streams of machine gun bullets which brutally mowed down some soldiers as they struggled towards the beach through waist deep water."

Fulton helplessly watched disembarking passengers stumble into wholesale slaughter. "It was a pitiful sight, seeing men topple over in the water before us," he said. "The sound of this concentrated bullet barrage peppering the sides of our boat and watching the 88s roll overhead was the most terrifying experience we've ever had." Sprouts of water projected as high as Old Faithful. Wrecked landing craft resembled coffins drifting aimlessly at the water's edge. Burning tanks and heinously misshapen corpses littered the bitterly contested soil. The Atlantan reversed from the brawl, both entranced and repulsed by the dour spectacle.[346]

Reporting for *Stars and Stripes*, Lionel Shapiro was likewise spellbound by the unfolding tragedy. Shapiro encountered a battered company of assault engineers he described as "weary men, their eyes still bloodshot, their nerves frayed, and no wonder." The reporter likened their desperate task of removing mines to a zero hour suicide mission. "It was the toughest job we've ever had," one survivor claimed. "We had to work with water up to our necks, sometimes higher." And then snipers tallied their lethal toll. "They were nipping us off as I was working with two blokes on a tough bit of element, when suddenly I found myself working alone. My two pals just gurgled and disappeared underwater." Little else was said of the engineer's fallen comrades. The recent memory bore a grief too great.[347]

* * *

Beyond the excruciating loss of buddies, the sensory perceptions of combatants were overwhelmed. Donald Patrick, an engineer from Lowell, Massachusetts, felt as if he was living in some macabre cartoon, an animatedly grotesque distortion of reality. "Our feet seemed like leaden weights as we waded in from the barges only to be met with fire from all sides," he stated. "There were so many planes over us, and so much noise from the thousands of guns . . . that we hardly cared what happened." The unrelenting cycle of sights, sounds, and smells overpowered human faculties, instilling in some a sense of inescapable vulnerability.[348]

The fervor of helplessness shocked the well-traveled Bert Brandt. The photographer spent thirty ghastly minutes ashore before relocating to a cruiser sailing within rifle shot of the coast. Absorbing scenes of unparalleled butchery, he had seen enough. Racing through withering blasts of shot and shell, Brandt witnessed men climbing over stiff mounds of mortified buddies. Coated in sand and gummed with blood, the dead men appeared otherworldly, alien in nature. "It was hotter than hell over there," said Brandt. "I was at Anzio, but Anzio was nothing like this. . . . The whole thing was an unbelievable sight. Some boats were burning, and a pall of smoke hung over the beach. I saw some bodies of our soldiers who had been killed in the first landings floating on the water." Among the marooned, prior notions of confidence were faltering.

The landings demonstrated the widest possible range of behavior. While many were strangled by fear, others maintained encouraging poise. Reporter James McGlincy wandered the litter-strewn sands to discover Pvt. Charles Blackledge of Columbia, Mississippi perched incongruously amid a pyramid of Bangalores, bazookas, and explosives while paging a small pocket bible. Five minutes prior to his landing, the lad was asleep on the hood of a jeep. Here, thought McGlincy, was a man who felt shielded by his faith.[349]

Comfort was nonetheless a scarce commodity on Omaha. *Stars and Stripes* writer Arthur Goodwin recognized as much with a bittersweet article chronicling the 1st Infantry Division's 16th Regiment. Due to poor visibility, Company L landed a half hour late, only to discover capsized boats and infantrymen bogged in the mire. The squads frantically

186

charged up 600 feet of open beach, lunging into a cliff base for relative cover. Coarse sergeants hurriedly reorganized their breathless, cluttered outfits. The foot soldiers discarded their lifebelts and extraneous gear, lightening their loads for a climactic push. Dropped by the faceless enemy above, grenades tumbled from the bluff's edge. Destructive clouds of Trinitrotoluene pocked the earthen walls. A tumultuous exchange of explosive pineapples and Stielhandgranates rocked the embattled escarpment. A GI's hefty Browning Automatic Rifle rattled the ravine, silencing two pillboxes. Small mountains of expended, smoking brass lay at the foot of the ledge. A nearby sergeant blew gaps through the tangles of barbed wire while comrades delicately skirted adjacent minefields. Severed by the mounting power of close-at-hand machine guns, entire arms and shoulders disappeared in sprays of acrid red mist. Still, onward the men pushed to the crest.

Lt. Jimmie Monteith, an amiable college dropout from Virginia, was madly directing armor and troops. "Man, one thing is for sure," he confessed to a non-com. "This ain't our day." The words were tragically prophetic. The lieutenant advanced up the small ravine to organize his surrounded men against enemy reprisals. Goodwin remorsefully imparted what followed. "Lt. Montieth, who in a large measure was responsible for our effective defense, was killed while exposing himself to direct effective fire against the counterattacking forces." The redheaded officer was posthumously awarded the Medal of Honor ten months later. He rests under a gold star not far from the site of his untimely demise. "It's a new kind of country—and a new kind of war," observed Goodwin, yet all the cemeteries underscored the same tragedy.[350]

A subsequent press release issued by Omar Bradley singled out Montieth's regiment for its fierce mettle. "Men dragged themselves shoreward, leaderless, and scattered by loss of key personnel," noted the general. "Blocked from advancing by the minefields and pinned down by the annihilating fire, wave after wave piled up . . . until thousands of men lay huddled on the fire swept shore." Sheer willpower molded a "confused, hurt mass into a cohesive, determined fighting force." Privately, Bradley expressed guilt for exacting destruction upon the ennobled 1st Division. Its men had already sacrificed so much. However, the division was his most experienced. Dumping lesser troops into the inferno of Omaha Beach would have served nobody. "In the accomplishment of that mission," Bradley later noted, "there was little room for the niceties of justice." The Big Red One's distinguished combat record sentenced it to the gravest of dangers. Mercifully, their efforts were not in vain. The division rolled over Hitler's fabled Atlantic Wall and the broader campaign for France was on.[351]

In that most violent setting, the press corps lost one of its own. Thirty-year-old Peter M. Paris was a staff photographer for *Yank* and participated in several of the Big Red One's illustrious campaigns. A pulp magazine illustrator and graduate of Syracuse, he freelanced in New York and Europe prior to the war. Reflecting on his earlier days in France, the photographer yearned to see the City of Light once more. His celebratory return was not to be. Paris succumbed to enemy fire alongside his adopted brethren of the 1st Division. He became the second enlisted man on *Yank*'s staff to perish in the conflict.

The wholesale obliteration of their comrades left countless GIs with nothing but heated disdain for their enemy. "At first I was shy," confessed one soldier. "[Now] I'm out to kill every German I can get. The American soldier has to learn to hate; he has to learn to kill right away."[352]

There seemed little rhyme or reason as to who died and why. The random nature of death proved a morbid arithmetic. "Luck plays a great part in war," wrote John Moroso. "Watching it makes some men superstitious." Accordingly, veterans often adopted unusual quirks to deter misfortune. Moroso relayed the bizarre habit of Lt. Ralph F. Pullen of Shreveport, Louisiana—who sported his lucky invasion underwear on D-Day. "I carefully saved the same shirt I wore in the Sicilian invasion for this party," the lieutenant explained. "I still am wearing it and still am lucky. I was singed by machine gun bullets and knocked off my feet by the burst of an 88 shell but remain whole." The officer hoped to wear his thermal good luck charm down the streets of Berlin someday.[353]

Invasion charms, souvenirs, and mementos were as diverse as the men carrying them. Nonetheless, *Stars and Stripes* strongly encouraged troops to yield battlefield trophies (including *living* German prisoners) to G-2. An intelligence staffer imparted the significance of this request. "One of our boys broke into a German pillbox on the beach on D-Day," said the officer. "He picked up a map used by a forward observer of German artillery. It showed all the CPs on the beach. It showed church steeples and a big tower. It located every gun both on the beach and behind the beach." The map included the location of a divisional command post, which was promptly pounded by the Air Forces and Navy. "That document," he concluded, "paved the way to success on D-Day."[354]

Others grew indifferent to the allure of souvenirs. Passing a German prisoner stockade, engineer lieutenant Sam Haley noticed bundles of forsaken equipment and personal effects dotting the mud. His men scrounged for luxuries and oddities only to grow bored with their scavenging. "I've seen so many souvenirs I don't even pick them up anymore," the officer attested. "At first you want to pick up everything, but you don't have any place to carry it all." And then there were other unwanted discoveries. "Every once in a while, when we are looking for mines, we find another dead German and carry him out to the road where he can be picked up and buried," said Haley.[355]

Material goods were nonetheless on the lieutenant's mind. Pausing momentarily on a promontory overlooking the beach, Haley was overjoyed by the scene. "Ships were stretched as far as the eye could see. Men, trucks, and supplies were pouring ashore." Lt. Col. Juan Sedillo advanced perhaps the most unlikely military vehicle in the vast cavalcade—a brand new Packard. "It was my commanding officer's car and I was given the job of taking it off the ship," wrote the former Santa Fe lawyer. Sedillo was glad to keep his feet dry.

With the seemingly undaunted procession of supplies pouring forth, who needed captured contraband?[356]

Cpl. Mike Maslewski of New York City was one who never expected to capture much of anything, let alone prisoners. His weapon of choice seemed even more implausible: music. A welder with an ordnance maintenance company, Maslewski was repairing a wrecked anti-tank piece behind Omaha days after the landings. Taking his blow torch to the damaged gun, Maslewski soon realized he was being watched from nearby brush. With rifles raised in a menacing stance, four Germans warily entered the open. The technician nervously continued his tasks, supposing ignorant innocence was his best tactic for survival. He began humming an old Polish tune often sung to him by his mother. The Germans stared at the corporal with mystified expressions. To Maslewski's amazement, the enemy soldiers joined in the singing. They were conscripted Poles. The mechanic was in the clear. "Mike convinced them the place for a good Pole was on the American side of the line, shared his rations with them, talked them into helping him finish the job, and then brought them in as prisoners," stated one report. Maslewski may have been the only American to capture enemy combatants with a blow torch in hand.[357]

Among the myriads scouring the vicinity was also Don Whitehead, who had incredibly survived yet another amphibious undertaking. "Along the beach are still the khaki-clad bodies of boys who gave their lives in the United Nations bid to crush Germany's armed might. But there were not so many as I had expected to see, and I patrolled this strip from end to end," he remarked. On a more vocational topic, Whitehead was riled by the complete breakdown of the communication system intended for correspondents. A public relations officer requisitioned a jeep radio but was unable to locate the vehicle until June 7. An array of couriers was meant to transmit messages, but no couriers appeared. Whitehead dubiously handed his first story to a stretcher bearer heading for a control ship.

The reporter was further dismayed when he heard BBC radio reports chronicling the advances of British troops. Apparently, the Brits had little problem with their equipment. Robert Casey of the *Chicago Daily News* confronted similar challenges and joked his last message was "corked up in a bottle and tossed into the English Channel." Whitehead was unable to transmit updates for twenty-eight frustrating hours. His quibbles, however, were inconsequential compared to the strife of casualties he interviewed. Sgt. William McFadden of Olean, New York accurately sized up the collective demeanor. "I was damned glad to get on to the beach," he confessed, "and I'll be glad to get off."[358]

In a separate encounter, Whitehead struck a meaningful conversation with Capt. William Collins of Chicago, who was pinned down for hours but miraculously emerged unscathed. "Look," said the captain, "will you just say for me, 'Dear Marge, I am all right.' Will you?"

"I surely will," replied Whitehead.

Though surrounded by the pallor of death, many invaders never felt more alive.[359]

United Press correspondent Sandor Klein also shared spirited sentiments of endurance. "Sandy" was described by a fellow journalist as "a newsman's newsman, a legendary figure in the history of Idaho journalism. A five-foot seven-inch, cigar-chomping, violin-playing Hungarian Jew with a gravelly voice," Klein was keenly aware of the invasion's repercussions for untold millions. On D-Day, Klein encountered an

American sergeant staring out to sea from a ship's deck. Leaning against the railing and gazing blankly into the waters, the sarge uttered, "They can't stop us."

Yet many of them were stopped. Holbrook Bradley of the *Baltimore Sun* witnessed an unceasing procession of casualties flood onto Allied transports. "The wounded were handled skillfully despite the constant rise and fall of the ship. The men were swung over the sides by block and tackle, then carried below on litters," he observed. "Those first few hours on the beach must have been living hell. And we saw there had been no discrimination in the way men fell, for the two bars of captains were among the plain uniforms of the privates."[360]

The orchestra of battle faded from the shoreline as combat stemmed inland. Ernest Hemingway, having overcome his shaky voyage, tramped the marred sands of Omaha. Turning to the sea, he noticed bloated bodies bobbing with each gush of waves. Other fatalities rested inanimately as misshapen lumps caked by wet sand. The noxious odor of burning gasoline was inescapable. Lingering German marksmen unleashed sporadic bursts from veiled burrows. Bruised combatants, now almost oblivious to the random cracks of rifle fire, sluggishly filed up a nearby ridge. The earth itself seemed to quiver and wail beneath the pressure of unceasing caravans of vehicles. And with that, "we had taken the beach," Hemingway boasted.

But there was so much left to be said. "You could write for a week and not give everyone credit for what he did on a front of 1,135 yards," the novelist continued. "Real war is never like paper war, nor do accounts of it read much the way it looks. But . . . this is as near as I can come to it." Combat journalism posed trying limitations. Not even the most gifted artists could paint a canvas so large.[361]

Martha Gellhorn, although happily loosened from husband Ernest Hemingway's overbearingness, grew emotional aboard her hospital ship. "It will be hard to tell you of the wounded," she wrote, "there were so many of them. There was no time to talk; there was too much else to do." Piles of shredded clothes and boots accumulated on the decks. Nurses and orderlies toiled "like demons" while replacing plasma bottles and injecting needles. Beyond the fortitude of nurses, Gellhorn was amazed by the conversations she overheard.

"Give that boy a drink of water," one casualty asked of an orderly.

"Miss, see that Ranger over there, he's in bad shape, could you go to him?" begged another.

A junior lieutenant with a ghastly chest wound had eyes "full of horror and he did not speak." When he finally drifted into consciousness, he spotted a wounded German on the bed behind him.

"I'd kill him if I could move," the officer seethed.

Feet away, a seventeen-year-old French farmer wounded by a shell gained the affection of his bunkmates. The servicemen worried for the boy, who was now among strangers and separated from his family. One bandaged Yank asked the multilingual Gellhorn to serve as translator. He requested, "You tell that kid he's a better soldier than that Heinie in the bunk next to him."

Gellhorn eventually waded ashore in waist-high water on the Easy Red sector of Omaha Beach, stumbling on its melon-sized pebbles. Fluttering white tape nearby denoted unchecked minefields. "It was almost dark by now," she wrote, "and there was a terrible feeling of working against time. Everyone was violently busy on that crowded dangerous shore." She was the first female correspondent of the invasion to step on French soil.[362]

Iris Carpenter was not far behind. She had returned to England immediately following the initial assaults but greeted the many wounded as they returned to British piers. As was the case with Gellhorn, Carpenter was overcome by the scenes of despair. "Some of the men coming back aren't talking. They are carried off the ships on stretchers, bits of their clothing lying pathetically across their blanketed figures," she observed. "A few looked at the sky with unseeing eyes. Some are coming back who will never talk again. Their stories are finished."[363]

Like Whitehead, Ernie Pyle was tardy reporting the big show. Due to logistical challenges, Pyle did not arrive on the beach until the morning of June 7. The only occasional danger was a stray bullet or a "startling blast of a mine geysering brown sand into the air." Pyle discovered "a gigantic and pitiful litter of wreckage along miles of the shore line." Swamped tanks and capsized boats burned while little sad bits of personal items endlessly flecked the conquered shore. Blanketed corpses rested in neatly-arranged rows, their toes pointing skyward as though prepared for inspection. Several exposed wristwatches, unlike their departed owners, were still ticking. Uncollected bodies remained half-submerged in the sand.

With an M-1 Garand and '03 Springfield forming a makeshift cross beside his remains, an American youth lays lifeless in a pool of his own blood on Omaha Beach. "You've never seen a beach like it before," confessed a reporter. "Dead and wounded men were lying so thick you could hardly take a step." (19)

"Now that it is over," said Pyle, "it seems to me a pure miracle we ever took the beach at all. For some it was easy, but in this special sector where I now am our troops faced such odds that our getting ashore was like me whipping Joe Louis." With lyrical bluntness, Pyle spoke directly to readers so they could "forever be humbly grateful" of the tasks undertaken on their behalf. He vividly transported dedicated followers to the battlefront, encouraging them to imagine themselves amid the zigzag of landmines. Pyle illustrated the battlefield with descriptive ingenuity, presenting the forbidding nature of barbed wire and protruding iron. There, Germans huddled in cave-like dwellings like hunters await-ing prey, he warned. The words offered imagery as palpable as newsreel footage.

"Our first waves were on that beach for hours instead of a few minutes before they could begin working inland," Pyle continued. "Men were killed as they stepped out of the landing craft. An officer whom I know got a bullet right through the head just as the door of his landing craft was let down." Pyle's war was always personal. Of his previous inter-viewees, he was unable to keep track of how many had fallen. He could think of only one redeeming quality of their demise. The collective sac-rifice made possible the hope for final victory. "And so we took that beach and accomplished our landing," Pyle reported. "We did it with every advantage on the enemy's side and every disadvantage on ours. In the light of a couple of days' retrospection we sit and talk, and call it a miracle."[364]

The invasion's remarkable execution hardly tempered complaints from the ranks. GIs vocally engaged in Monday morning quarterbacking. Ac-cording to *Stars and Stripes*, many combatants thought it foolhardy to land at low tide. "We didn't do that in Sicily or anyplace else," bickered one infantryman. The weather was excessively rough, others claimed. Soldiers were equipped like pack mules and had the tendency of bunch-ing up on the battlefield. "A fellow wants to get with somebody else, and they get both of you," another moaned. "Some fellows who hadn't been in combat had been told to hit the beach, lie down as soon as they started firing. That's wrong."

According to survivors, inexperience pervaded the beachhead. "Our company lost half the men," a slightly wounded soldier noted. "They had a French .75 on a cliff. We were in LCVPs. They had zeroes on us. Every time a boat came up and grounded, they would let down the gate and they would hit it with that .75. We got about a hundred yards to a ditch and some of them new guys came along. They dropped to the ground and the Germans machine gunned almost all of them. We was hollering them to come ahead, but they couldn't hear us."

Mass confusion also precipitated cases of mistaken identity. Pvt. Al-lan Chinnock, a bespectacled sandy-haired farmer from Wisconsin, hit the shoreline near Vierville-sur-Mer at H-plus-60. Some Germans scur-ried like rabbits in the wake of the Allied advance, but others remained and fought like hell, he claimed. Chinnock scaled a dune, spotted a man straight ahead, and bellowed, "Hey, Bud, what outfit you from?" The figure answered with a machine pistol, his rounds whizzing past the American's ears. "I flopped on the ground and gave him a couple with my rifle, and he went down," said Chinnock. Recounting his close call with a grin, the private announced, "I didn't want to go up there any closer."[365]

By June 7, Sgt. Kenneth "Roy" Mickley of Gettysburg, Pennsylvania pushed beyond the seawall but was pinned down for another five hours before again advancing. Clearing mines and snipers, his squad endured a treacherous enemy crossfire—driving the GIs to seek shelter in a farmhouse. Just as Mickley sprinted through the gate, shrapnel tore through his right leg and left shoulder, knocking him to the ground with the force of a heavyweight. "I spotted a pig pen not far away, so we crawled into it and gave each other first aid," said the farm boy. "I guess the enemy figured we were done for, because they didn't direct any more fire in our direction. We were in the pen for several hours. Finally, our tanks moved up and drove out the Germans. Some of our first aid men then arrived and we were evacuated by trucks." Later relocated to a West Virginia military hospital, Mickley offered no complaints of his ordeal. After all, he was well accustomed to the aroma of pig shit.[366]

Recent battlefield experiences offered fresh perspectives of military life. Countless pre-invasion gripes among GIs were lodged against military police, "Satan's busy boys" who disrupted spirited parties and announced the suspension of weekend passes. Contrasting interpretations of Army cops were soon expressed. "When the foot sloggin' doughboys hit the shores of France, thousands who followed the first wave found MPs there ahead of them," claimed one paper. "The military police were directing traffic and aiding the wounded, for the beaches were busy— and unhealthy." MPs suffered some of the highest casualty proportions in the early assaults, the paper insisted. Lt. Charles M. Conover, a military policeman with the 1st Division, earned the Silver Star by directing beach traffic for three hours despite a serious shoulder wound. He herded vehicles and men across the landing grounds until the loss of blood collapsed him. "So next time you feel inclined to wise crack about the MPs," warned an Army article, "pause first and salute those courageous few who are taking everything Jerry can throw their way and who are in there doing a tough job without complaint."[367]

Members of the 29th Infantry Division were less content with their press coverage. Like their brethren in the 4th Division, the infantrymen believed the particulars of their gallant deeds were overshadowed by tales of encompassing strategy and paratrooper heroics. *Stars and Stripes* claimed "rules of censorship" were to blame for certain divisions not receiving their share of the glory. The 29th Division remained unconvinced and mailed strongly-worded letters of grievance to the newspaper. "Your overlooking the presence of the Blue and Gray in this battle sector was not overly appreciated," one GI complained. "Who in the hell lost all those fine boys we saw lying dead and wounded on the beach on D-Day? Who has fought through the toughest terrain and the worst hell of obstacles that any war-crazed nation could devise? Who has lost hundreds of men killed or maimed for life, and also has taken every objective given to them so far; fought and died for them without a murmur? It was the Blue and Gray of the 29th."

The grumbling did not cease. "The boys have missed meals; their clothes are torn, their nerves are shot from lack of sleep and rest, but there's not one word of complaint," an unnamed soldier argued. "They're a damn fine bunch of men doing the greatest job of any assault troops and we're damn proud of them. We appreciate what the other divisions are doing and we're proud of them; but we would like a little credit, too, and soon." *Stars and Stripes* offered a veiled apology, praising the 29th for its stamina and undying commitment. "Our frontline reporters are over there with you and you may be sure we're doing our damnedest to see that every brave one of you gets a break in the news," the paper assured. "Thanks for your letter."

Soldiers' cherished notions of the free press did not spare periodicals any scrutiny over a lack of well-rounded reporting. The 29th Division subscribed to GI cartoonist Bill Mauldin's conviction that "the infantry is the group in the army which gives more and gets less than anybody else."[368]

Unsurprisingly, anecdotes covering the Blue and Gray soon appeared in print. The Army newspaper described the exploits of an American private who shot a rifle grenade at three Germans riding a sidecar motorcycle. Stirred by the sudden enemy encounter, the enlisted man forgot to pull his grenade pin. Fired at exceedingly close range, the dormant grenade nonetheless ripped through the bodies of two riders. The motorcycle sped out of control and collided into a stonewall, killing the third passenger. The American riflemen casually walked to the adjacent tree and plucked the embedded grenade from the thick trunk. The private "put it back on his rifle and began hunting a new target." Finally featured in the headlines, readers of the 29th were undoubtedly pleased. [369]

Preempting further backlash, *Stars and Stripes* rededicated itself to reporting all realms of service. "While we are giving credit we might as well add a word about the Engineers," the paper added. Outlining efforts in blowing paths through minefields, building roads, and constructing bases, the periodical offered unsolicited praise of the American diggers. "For the Continental campaign they made millions of maps of French coastal areas that had gone unmapped since Napoleonic days," touted the newspaper. "But this is the kind of work expected of the Engineers; it is just part of their job. Like the 29th Division and all the rest, they are writing their chapter in the livid language of selfless deeds of which America can well be proud." Crisis averted. [370]

Few soldiers were more neglected in mainstream headlines than African American troops. Newspapers such as the *Chicago Defender* sought to rectify this injustice. Founded four decades prior, the *Defender* combated Jim Crow and was an ardent voice championing military integration. The European travels of correspondent Edward Toles chronicled the daring yet largely disregarded performance of minority troops. Fittingly, some of the first soldiers Toles encountered on the sands of France were African American balloon crews operating hydrogen-filled dirigibles as defensive weapons. The barrage balloons, often referred to as "silver sausages" by their handlers in the 320th Barrage Balloon Battalion, were inflatable buffers to safeguard landing areas from low-flying enemy aircraft. Thick cables spooled around portable reels kept both the balloons and incoming planes at bay.

"They're like kids," said South Carolinian Benjamin Brown of his balloons. "We get them up by 11:30 and put them to bed by five." Hoisting the inflated obstacles on June 6 was anything but child's play, however. Crews of four lugged the cumbersome balloons over rugged terrain while enduring blistering fire. The ballooners moved on undeterred. "We catch Nazi planes like fish in a net," said Lt. Cyril Spann of Chester, South Carolina. "We've been trained to recognize all types of planes. When friendly planes approach, we haul down our babies as fast as we send them up. We can't afford to miss out on any plane identification,"

Pvt. Morrisal Durham of Philadelphia elaborated. In a matter of seconds, the troops had the dexterity to unreel and release one of "their babies" 2,000 feet into the air. "If a Nazi bird nestles in my lines—he won't nestle nowhere's else," boasted Pvt. Cleveland Hayes of Okolona, Mississippi.

Toles observed Robert Hines of Norfolk, Virginia raise a balloon into the heavens when an abrupt wind dragged Hines through the sand. The private turned to Toles and laughed, "Don't think there's much danger of one of my babies carrying me up in the air. I've been bedding them since we came over and they kinda like me."

"But we never take any chances," Pvt. James Anderson of Philadelphia convinced the reporter. "We have more than one man handling them. And if they ever get away, you can bet your bottom dollar a German is blasted to hell on the other end!"

Astonishing many skeptics, the battalion superseded the expectations of numerous white officers. Even Eisenhower offered congratulations to the balloon unit for its D-Day heroics. "Your battalion landed in France on June 6 under artillery, machine gun, and rifle fire," lauded the general. "Despite the losses sustained the battalion carried out its mission with courage and determination. . . . This report is most gratifying to me." As president, Eisenhower later signed the first civil rights legislation since Reconstruction. A *New York Times* editorial incorporated even stronger language: "In courage, loyalty, and sacrifice there are no racial distinctions among Americans. That was the lesson a quarter century ago. It is being taught again."

By mid-July, nearly 10% of Yanks in France were African American—a proportion similar to the national average of those in uniform. They repeatedly defied racially-tinged assumptions of contemporaries and performed indispensable acts contributing to victory. They included a handsomely mustached twenty-one-year-old German-speaking medic with the 320th named Waverly "Woody" Woodson. After a shell painfully sliced through his rear and thigh, Woodson hobbled to cover where, for over a day, he performed makeshift surgeries on the wounded of Omaha Beach. The hard lines of intolerances faded in the maelstrom of combat. "At that time," Woodson later recalled, "they didn't care what color my skin was." The *Pittsburgh Courier* celebrated him as the ultimate D-Day hero. A superior nominated Woodson for the Medal of Honor but the presumable systemic racism within the War Department prevented such recognition. Not a single African American veteran of the Second World War received the honor until 1997.[371]

Reporter John W. Jarrell surveyed the carnage withstood by Woodson and company. In this ravaged environment, Jarrell was inexplicably drawn to the smoking detritus littering the beach—even more so than the exciting tales of barrage balloon men. The scattering of twisted metal and bodies left indelible marks on reporters who soaked in the monstrous vista. Similar to characterizations of World Trade Center wreckage following the 9/11 attacks, haunting details of the debris-strewn Omaha Beach became a recurring hallmark of D-Day reporting.[372]

Cpl. Victor M. Wingate of Frederick, Maryland offered heartfelt testimony in a letter published by his hometown newspaper. "American boys looked into merciless gun muzzles belching Nazi venom," he remembered. The shell-cratered landscape, mountains of abandoned equipment, and half-buried gear were poignantly corporeal affirmations of sacrifice. "Scattered among the machines of war," Wingate continued, "are many abandoned personal items that historians should not fail to recapture when they paint this picture for future Americans to view."[373]

Wingate channeled the emotional thoughts of Ernie Pyle, who was likewise entranced by this "horrible waste of war." With near-Shakespearian eloquence, Pyle underscored the campaign's haunting nature of destruction. Days after the landings, he strolled the historic coast, unable to mentally balance the seashore's natural beauty with its undignified human wreckage. Thousands of hand-sized jellyfish with four-leaf clover marks oozed among the litter; there was little indication of luck here, however. "Men were sleeping on the sand, some of them sleeping forever," Pyle observed of the wounded and deceased. "Men were floating in the water, but they didn't know they were in the water, for they were dead." The reporter kicked slowly through the sand, investigating the beach's infinite details of misery.

The vast landscape of ruins was incomprehensibly nightmarish. The war's terrific clutter was marked by scorched trucks and decapitated vessels. One craft was curiously floating upside down. The "vicious six-pronged iron snares" that snagged so many boats were still visible at low tide. Heaps of rusted rifles, smashed typewriters, discarded life-belts, and knotted spools of telephone wire remained as silent sentinels.

Original caption: "Scene on Omaha Beach on the afternoon of D-Day, 6 June 1944, showing casualties on the beach, a bogged-down Sherman tank, several wrecked trucks and German anti-landing obstructions. An LST is beached in the left distance and invasion shipping is off shore." (20)

"On the beach lay expended, sufficient men and mechanism for a small war. They were gone forever now," remarked Pyle. "And yet we could afford it." With an endless shuffle of reinforcements and supplies arriving from England, anything seemed dispensable.

The Indiana newsman was emotionally drawn to the "human litter" of D-Day. The sprinklings of gear and personal items never to be used again were expressive tokens of a generation's sacrifice. The untidy jumbles of sewing kits, cigarettes, bibles, rations, journals, toothbrushes, family photos, and cans of shoe polish comprised a "long thin line of personal anguish" representative of unfinished lives. Unused notebook pages intended for loved ones instead became soggy relics of unfulfilled dreams. An abandoned tennis racket rested "lonesomely on the sand, clamped in its rack, not a string broken." Trotting back and forth along columns of reinforcements, a stray dog pitifully barked for its absent master.

Pyle discovered a lifeless GI on the ground. The reporter first thought the lad was dead, but he was merely asleep. In the palm of the soldier's hand was a sizable, smooth stone. "I stood and looked at him a long time" recalled Pyle. "He seemed in his sleep to hold that rock lovingly, as though it were his last link with a vanishing world. I have no idea at all why he went to sleep with the rock in his hand, or what kept him from dropping it once he was asleep. It was just one of those little things without explanation that a person remembers for a long time."

Such were the evocative invasion memories Pyle carried with him the remainder of his days. Readers bore a similar weight of war. Pyle's deeply human perspectives imparted lucid accounts as seemingly vivid as reality itself. His ruminations transcended the archetypal demands of journalism by voicing the faith and fears of an entire people.[374]

In a blunter assessment, correspondent Jack Thompson confessed, "You've never seen a beach like it before. Dead and wounded men were lying so thick you could hardly take a step. One officer was killed only two feet away from me." The harshness of war could not always be conveyed poetically.[375]

Composing similar prose, Associated Press reporter Lewis Hawkins was engrossed by beachhead scenes greeting newcomers. "Shocking evidence of death and destruction still dominated these three miles of beach," he wrote on June 7. Gazing beyond the morose parade of death, there was reason for hope. Despite the choppy, polluted surf, supply convoys continued their slow but steady progression. From bulldozers to communication trucks, all the "vital paraphernalia of war" flowed freely.[376]

A swarm of inquisitive correspondents arrived with it all. The reunion of journalists kindled discussions of joy and misgiving. Scuttlebutt regarding friends possibly killed or wounded crippled Pyle with fear. "When I went ashore on the soil of France the first thing I wanted to do was hunt up the other correspondents I had said goodbye to a few days previously in England." Stumbling through an early morning fog, Pyle encountered a cadre of typewriter boys perched in a grassy knoll less than a mile beyond Omaha.

Stories were swapped and inquiries of colleagues were made. "Most of them were okay," Pyle remarked. "One had been killed, and one was supposed to have been lost on a sunken ship, but we didn't know who. One or two had been wounded. Three of our best friends had not been heard from at all, and it looked bad."

Correspondent Ivan Peterman perhaps best described the bustle of Normandy's shores in June 1944: "One of the world's busiest ports today has no harbor, lacks warehouses, customs officers, and immigration officials. It doesn't even have gangplanks or quarantine inspection. . . . For this is the fantastic beachhead of the Allies—the place where materials of war pour like a mechanical Niagara roaring uphill, streaming endlessly inland to mount the machine that will rid France of the Nazis." (21)

Although most correspondents safely rejoined their comrades, initial confusion and gossip addressed the innate risks of frontline reporting.[377]

Pyle was especially delighted to locate buddy Don Whitehead sleeping in a foxhole. "Get up, you lazy so-and-so," Pyle uttered with a friendly kick. Cocooned in a borrowed blanket with eyes still closed, Whitehead grinned upon hearing Pyle's familiar voice. He slept barefoot. His saturated boots and socks dried on nearby twigs. Rising from his deep slumber proved arduous for "Beachhead Don." The exhausted reporter had not rested since D-Day and took a sleeping tablet to ease his frayed nerves. Mustering the strength to rise out of his hole, Whitehead declared, "I don't know why I'm alive at all. It was really awful. For hours there on the beach the shells were so close they were throwing mud and rocks all over you. It was so bad that after a while you didn't care whether you got hit or not."

Considering the number of invasions Whitehead had survived, his stern account spoke volumes to Pyle. The continuous cycle of violence deeply unnerved Whitehead. "I think I have gone on one too many of these things—not because of what might happen to me personally, but I've lost my perspective," he admitted. "It's like dreaming the same nightmare over and over again, and when you try to write you feel that you have written it all before. You can't think of any new or different words to say it with."

Pyle later reflected, "I know only too well what he means. . . ."[378]

Certainly, correspondents were not immune to fatigue. George Hicks, the ever-calm radio reporter for the Blue Network (later to become ABC), was so overcome with tiredness that he fell into a heavy doze alongside a road jutting from Omaha. A graves registration truck slowly rumbled past and noticed the comatose Hicks lying parallel to a ditch. The soldiers dutifully scooped up the oblivious reporter in his blanket and hoisted him into the vehicle. Samuel Byrd, a North Carolina stage actor-turned-naval lieutenant, promptly halted the premature burial. Byrd later received the Bronze Star for his stouthearted evacuation of wounded from the beachhead. The sailor knew a dead body from a living one. "He slept through it all," marveled the lieutenant of Hicks. The reporter had good reason to be exhausted. The *New York World Telegram* called his recent D-Day broadcast from the deck of the USS *Ancon* "the greatest recording yet to come out of the war." Privately, Hicks felt inconsolable during his broadcast. The "white, agonizing faces" of men departing for shore stirred his soul. "It was horrible to see," he confessed. "My mouth tasted bad. I could hardly straighten up. I was sick and wanted to throw up but I was too tired. All I could think was 'My God, they're going in.'"[379]

Following his own spell of overdue shuteye, Whitehead was back in the field. Among his eventual assignments was a ceremony at which Eisenhower decorated careworn veterans of the Big Red One. The men stood in a haggard but proud formation outside a palatial chateau. Among the awardees was Lt. Carl W. Giles, Jr. of Gest, Kentucky, who completed his invasion mission after rescuing three subordinates from the water. Meanwhile, Pfc. Peter Cavaliere of Bristol, Rhode Island single-handedly killed eight oncoming Germans while defending a forward observation post. Each recipient boasted impressive credentials. "They had tried to clean the stains of battle from their clothing for the occasion," Whitehead noted of the weathered infantrymen, "but still their uniforms showed that they had just returned from the front, not far away."

None present at the ceremony were concerned with spit and polish—including Eisenhower—who pinned medals on the two-dozen raggedy, battle-tested GIs. The supreme commander offered the highest accolades. "I know your record from the day you landed in North Africa and through Sicily. I am beginning to think that your regiment is a sort of Praetorian guard which goes along with me and gives me luck. I know you want to go home, but I demanded if I came up here that you would have to come up with me. You've got what it takes to finish the job." Few, if any, in the ranks felt otherwise. Yet the war had changed them all.[380]

Col. John Seitz, a thirty-six-year-old West Pointer who commanded the Big Red One's 26th Regiment, felt uneasy about his newfound aloofness to the discord surrounding him. "I don't know if we have met the best Jerry has or not, but we certainly have taken everything put to us so far and we have plenty to give back," he wrote to wife Helen. "We are so intent on what we are doing that the horror of it doesn't get us. You find that you take with impassionate coldness the news that a man to whom you were talking a moment before has been blown to hell." The callous emotions of combat would only harden in the months to come.[381]

Also experiencing extreme emotional upheaval was Capt. Kenneth E. Richards. An officer in the 2nd Infantry Division artillery, he and his guns were dragged into the combat emanating from Omaha Beach. Roosted on a ridge several miles inland, his pieces bracketed distant enemy machine guns, flattening them with methodical precision. Richards was browsing a map with his battalion commander when he suddenly blacked out. "Then I woke up," he later recalled. "I'd been hit but I never did know what hit me. I didn't hear anything coming. I was vomiting blood, and I felt like the whole side of my face had been blown off. I wondered what had happened."

He could not stand up. His radio was a mangled jumble of smoking rubble. It started to downpour. "I didn't like the idea of lying there and bleeding to death in the rain," Richards confessed. "I thought of my five-month-old son at home in Oklahoma, Kenneth, Jr., whom I had never seen." Eventually, the mangled captain mustered all his strength and staggered 100 yards to the rear where he luckily discovered medics. From a stateside hospital bed Richards concluded, "The war over there—it's tough—even when you're not in combat, the people over here just don't realize what the fellows go through. It's not fun. You're always wet and cold."[382]

Over the following weeks, T/Sgt. Ed Privott of the 29th Division experienced similar disaffection. Standing atop a hillside in a chilled rain, he looked out upon the beach where forty-six days earlier he stepped foot in France for the first time. The Channel tides had washed away the blood, restoring the sandy white appearance. The din of combat was replaced with the placid wisps of incoming sea breezes and the soft beat of rain on his helmet. With resilient dune grasses concealing the recently inflicted scars, the land was already healing. Hospital ships quietly embarked on their voyages of mercy. Privott turned to a comrade and simply stated, "It's changed."

Time marched backward. The sergeant dug 104 foxholes during his first month and a half in Normandy. His feet were blistered. He lost weight. His hands were lashed and eyes hollowed. He was on his fourth lieutenant. After countless firefights in the imposing hedgerows, this was Privott's first reprieve from the lines. He attempted to make sense of everything he had seen and everything he had done. "My mind isn't as clear as it was," he admitted. "I can tell it isn't. It's the shells landing so close. You get a little that way after a while. You get a little like when you are starting to get drunk. I'll never get used to it. They tell you you'll get used to it up there, but I never will. You can't get used to climbing over a hedgerow into an open field when you know the Germans are behind the next row with machine guns, rifles . . . always automatic pistols. You can't get used to that."

Since D-Day, Privott had evolved into a reluctant killer, a merciless warrior born of combat's heated bitterness. He recalled the four wicked hours he endured on Omaha Beach and seeing his friend, Stack, be struck down. Contemplating the recent past, the sergeant recognized

June 6 as the seminal apogee of his life. "I never wanted to kill anybody," he claimed. "I never hated the Germans, or anybody, but when I saw Stack get it—well—there are 13 dead Germans for him, I know."

"Funny," Privott continued. "You have to kill the young Germans. They won't run and they won't give up. They just fight until you kill them, mostly. The older ones run or give up. We wonder how we are doing with the way this thing was planned. We wonder if we're doing OK or are we behind schedule. I don't think they planned on all these hedgerows."

A former wheat field atop the bluff was now sprinkled with white wooden crosses and stars. Some of the markers denoted the final resting places of men Privott desperately tried to keep alive but ultimately could not. He trudged to a nearby command tent and paged through a dog-eared leather book with "Hotel Register" embossed on its cover. It was the burial directory.

Privott asked the graves registration clerks the whereabouts of a lost man from his platoon. A private ushered him down a long row of graves and pointed with one hand at a single marker. Privott knelt and examined the dog tag nailed to the cross. He stared silently at the grave for several minutes, seemingly lost in a pool of emotions and memories. Nobody spoke as the rain drizzled from the gray sky. After a long moment of meditation, Privott arose and brought his large, square hand upward in a crisp salute. He stood almost as a statue, biding a final farewell to one of his brothers. The sergeant turned away and meandered through the maze of crosses, beginning the long trek back to the front. He would soon carry on the fight begun those remarkable forty-six days prior. The long road to Paris and Berlin lay ahead.[383]

PART III: THE MESSAGE

I know that I'll wander with a cry:
"O beautiful men, O men I loved,
O whither are you gone, my company?"

– Herbert Read

CHAPTER 10

Fearful Jubilation

Fourteen-year-old Paul Pritchard did not expect to become a front-page sensation. Two months prior to the invasion, the Wichita boy entered a contest speculating the invasion's date. When he in fact predicted the correct date, newsmen flocked to his home to inquire about his methodology. With unassailable teenage logic, he declared, "We've been hearing about D-Day. D is the fourth letter of the alphabet. I multiplied four by two . . . because this is World War II . . . and got eight. Then I subtracted two which gives you six. That made it the sixth day of the sixth month."

When informed the invasion was originally scheduled for June 5 but delayed because of poor weather, Pritchard shrugged. "Anyway, it came on June 6, didn't it?"[384]

Beyond initial outpourings of spiritual expression, the Normandy invasion triggered emotional responses somber and celebratory, paranoid and patriotic. Many simply did not know how to react other than to absorb the swift flow of vague information. Before citizens could reinvest themselves in wartime causes, scores halted in deep meditation. Humbling acts of introspection emerged even in the most unlikely of places. An unnamed inmate at the historic Iowa State Penitentiary offered moving memories of June 6 to the *Fort Madison Evening Democrat*. His day began like any other; prisoners trooped from their cell houses into the massive dining hall for a breakfast of cornflakes, fruit, and coffee. As the assembling commenced, a voice from London reverberated over the static of the prison speakers. The men clustered under the PA system with silent anticipation. Thoughts immediately swept to the fates of brothers, cousins, and uncles who were participating in the military action far beyond the penitentiary's ornate stone walls.

At 10:45 that morning, the bustle of the prison machine shops grinded to a halt. Inmates who no longer had names convened under the compound's flagpole for a stirring rendition of the national anthem. The flag violently flapped above the windswept field. "As the last faint strains echoed among the hills back of the gray walls, there were, here and there, on leathery cheeks glistening teardrops that no amount of winking could have kept back," wrote the prisoner. "Maybe they, all of them, had forgotten once what good citizenship meant, but they knew now."

While watching the intramural baseball game that afternoon, the men further discussed the invasion's possible outcomes. One skeptic muttered, "That invasion don't mean nothin' to us guys."

"Perhaps not," the anonymous inmate admitted, "but we rather think it does. For these are men in our midst whose hearts lie thousands of measured miles away, across the trackless watery wastes that lap on the shores of stricken France. It is not so that we are forgotten. How can we be when in our population live men whose sons will die that freedom might live?"

The prisoner concluded, "History will record the date as the beginning of the end for the brutal political philosophy that has brought death and destruction to millions."[385]

Eloquent reactions to the invasion were displayed in every state. Few domestic journalists offered more articulate summations of wartime America than Al McIntosh. The reporter's talents could have propelled him into the pantheon of newspaper fame, but McIntosh opted to run the humble *Rock County Star-Herald* in Luverne, Minnesota. Throughout the war, his expressive accounts of 1940s life were representative of the nation as a whole.

McIntosh's D-Day began shortly after 3 a.m. when his living room telephone rang. He expected the sheriff on the other end, probably informing the reporter of a local car accident. "Instead it was Mrs. Lloyd Long, playing the feminine counterpart role of Paul Revere, saying 'Get up, Al, and listen to the radio, the invasion has started.'" McIntosh could hardly believe the moment had at last arrived. He and his wife sat breathlessly beside the radio for an hour. They soon returned to bed and a sleepless, early morning.

"What Rock County boys are landing on French soil tonight?" they thought.

"Please Lord, may this not be another Dieppe."

Thus, D-Day arrived in Minnesota quietly. "There were no whistles, no sirens. People got up and automatically turned on their radios to get the biggest news in all the world's military history," wrote McIntosh. "There were no demonstrations—not much was said." In the over-crowded coffee shops and drugstores, newspaper extras "were grabbed up like hotcakes and eagerly scanned." Customers sat in a sedated mood. A mother at the counter pushed aside coffee offered to her. "I just want to listen to the radio," she kindly whispered to the waiter.

"Her boy, by all the odds, was *there*. One didn't have to be psychic to know what was in her mind—or her heart. The prayer that she was uttering right then as she listened to the announcer was multiplied a thousand times and more in Rock County countless times during the day." McIntosh likewise encouraged his readers to appraise the invasion with serious reverence. "This is no time for any premature rejoicing or cockiness because the coming weeks are going to bring grim news. This struggle is far from over—it has only started. . . ."[386]

In Brownsville, Texas, a hardware store owner appeared shoeless at the *Herald*'s office at 4:30 a.m. The businessman heard the newspaper staff heading to work at the ungodly hour and correctly surmised that the invasion was in progress. Waving a wad of cash at the front counter he asked for the first copy of the paper and shouted, "I'll buy every man on the *Herald* staff a drink!" Press foreman Chico Alvarez obliged him and handed over a copy. The store owner, who had one son in the Pacific and another in England, shoved $17 in Alvarez's pocket before darting into the darkness. Another customer entered and confessed, "I'm very upset about the invasion. I have a son who is probably there today."

"Where is your boy stationed?" a solicitous staffer inquired.

"In Australia."

One Burlington, Iowa café proprietor was equally despondent. "I just can't work today," he mumbled. The owner served a hearty breakfast to a gaggle of local reporters and then closed his establishment for the day. It was at 2:32 that morning that the nearby *Burlington Hawk Eye Gazette* "wires crackled and radios hummed with the dynamic news." The paper reported of a peculiar omen shared by several residents. "Many had spent restless nights. They did not know why, but they couldn't sleep. Some got up in desperation and turned on radios for entertainment only to learn of the invasion." Within hours, the periodical released its advanced edition. "It was a pleasant surprise to be able to have the invasion news in the paper so early," declared one content subscriber. [387]

From Minnesota to Massachusetts, hometown editors scrambled to offer their readership continuous updates. Adele Glazer of the *Lowell Sun* imparted a particularly chaotic recounting of her own invasion activities. "D-Day (D for dreaded) finally came, and I entered the holy of holies—the Editorial Room. What would you expect to see there?" She was not surprised to find "editors talking on a dozen phones at once, liquor bottles everywhere, wads of frustrated stories crumpled up on the floor, reporters yelling 'COPY,' everyone rushing around, overflowing spittoons, noise, confusion—in short, bedlam." Similar clamor unfolded in the busy offices of the *Griffin Evening News*, which inadvertently set three pages of the invasion edition upside down. Not wishing to delay the paper's release, the editor simply yelled, "Keep 'em rolling!"[388]

The runner of the *Liberty Vindicator* embraced D-Day with greater restraint. "Back in the late twenties as a youthful reporter," he said, "I longed to climb to such a peak in my profession that I would one day be privileged to write of momentous events, the world my audience, to write of murder and fire and flood and changing governments." Like Al McIntosh, however, he grew comfortable with small town existence. His ambitions grew "cheerfully muted" over the years. June 6 nonetheless provided him the rare opportunity to report an earth-shattering event of monumental scope. His entry into a diner revealed amateur tacticians pouring over newspaper maps and swapping notes. "There was no trace of hysteria, no display of cheap human vanity," he observed. "I found no Republicans, no Democrats. No Protestants, no Catholics, no Jews. Only Americans. And all of them were, in their individual ways, looking to an Omnipotent Hand for D-Day, guidance of our leaders and our boys."[389]

Mrs. James Brakebill of Alva, Oklahoma would have readily welcomed a D-Day so placid. News of the invasion arrived at an especially inopportune time for the housewife, considering her home was on fire at that same moment. When "she asked the telephone operator to ring the fire department—quick—the operator thought she was merely another citizen wanting to flash the word to have the fire sirens blown for the invasion signal." Luckily, Brakebill persisted and her residence was spared with minimal damage. Emergency or not, the shrill of sirens was heard in thousands of towns. In St. Joseph, Michigan, police cars slowly traversed the streets to assure all were awake and fully aware of the day's events.[390]

It was half past midnight in New York City when first word of the invasion streamed across the electric news tickers of Times Square. Thousands of passersby craned their heads upward in startled fascination. "As they read," observed the *New York Times*, "a young sailor and his girl, holding hands, clenched them a bit tighter. American and Allied men in uniform received admiring glances from womenfolk as if the adulation felt for the invasion forces was being transferred to their brothers-in-arms here." Elderly couples sat in silence before the statue of Father Duffy, the revered chaplain of the Great War's Fighting 69th Regiment. Showings of the popular movie *Going My Way* played to empty houses. One theater manager empathized, "Everybody has someone in this and they are listening to the radio and getting bulletins. Who wants to see a picture show at a time like this?" A WAC recruiting officer stood guard at her 46th Street booth. Urging female enlistment, she declared, "When it is over you will have the right to stand on the curb and say, 'I pitched in.' It is a woman's war as well as a man's."[391]

For many readers and listeners, speculations of the invasion's location were wildly off base. An inexplicable pastime of Chicago restaurant patrons was to draw potential invasion routes on table linens featuring a faintly embossed world map. The employees of the Linen Supply Association of America, who laundered the soiled covers, ultimately observed how poorly the tablecloth strategists performed in their estimations. "Only about one in 20 tablecloth defacers picked the Seine Bay area," the United Press noted, "and about 10 out of every 11 picked the Bordeaux sector in the Bay of Biscay for the main assault. The so-called strategists picked nearly every spot from Norway to the Hellenic Peninsula with the Marseille-Toulon area in Southern France as one of the favorites."[392]

In Baltimore, the beverage options of hearty customers became temporarily limited. Beer and liquor distributors previously agreed to shut down "for the rest of the license day whatever time the invasion is announced as a period of prayer for our men overseas." In other communities such as Amesbury, Massachusetts, business owners agreed to do the same. Celebrating D-Day with booze was deemed a graceless means of commemoration.[393]

As their countrymen stormed Juno Beach nearly 3,500 miles away, these Canadian airmen experienced D-Day in the lively atmosphere of New York City's Times Square. Thousands congregated under the electronic news crawlers, transfixed by the latest updates. The front page of the airman's paper partially states, "Invasion Begins!" (22)

A more sobering beverage was the choice of the day. The operator of Maryville, Missouri's White Owl Café announced to guests, "It's D-Day: Coffee's on the house." All the customers "partook of the caffeine toast to the success of the forces attempting to liberate the downtrodden of Europe." Among the clients was Aage Jorgenson, a World War I veteran and immigrant whose native Denmark had been under Nazi occupation since April 1940. His eighty-year-old mother and two sisters lived under fascist rule near Copenhagen. The same week as D-Day, Jorgenson received a letter from his entrapped family via the International Red Cross. The grandmother had seven grandsons from multiple countries waging war against the Axis. Jorgenson prayed the invasion would set into motion a chain of events that would ultimately free his loved ones. Such were the deeply personal stories shared at lunch counters all across the nation.[394]

Those most dramatically touched by the announcement were the parents and spouses of invasion participants. Home front concerns, in turn, troubled those overseas. Don Whitehead succinctly summed up this agitation. "More than anything else, the men who came safely through the bloody beach battle in our sector on D-Day want their sweethearts, wives, and parents to know they are all right," he wrote. "As usual, a soldier is generally more worried about not worrying the people at home than about himself." When Capt. Max Zera was stranded on the beachhead, he spotted Whitehead and smirked, "Mama's going to be awfully worried about me. She knows now that my outfit came in with the first waves. Just let her know that I am well and was not hurt." Likewise, Cpl. J. B. Johnston of Port Arthur, Texas peered up from his foxhole and chuckled, "Tell 'em at home I'm having a happy birthday."[395]

Lt. Col. Mark J. Alexander of the 101st Airborne wrote to his parents on June 14, "I am very well, although dead on my feet. We had to fight like hell for the first four days to hold our own and have since been attacking from the west and north. In the process of fighting we have of course lost many good men, among them a battalion commander and his executive officer." The colonel did not mince words. "War is indeed a nightmare of hell and more do I realize that these men of ours are the most courageous in the world. They will never back up, no matter what the odds. German prisoners tell us that our paratroopers are the fiercest and most determined fighters they have ever seen."[396]

Meanwhile, journalist-turned-officer Roy Craft wrote with a greater jauntiness. "Never in the history of warfare," he noted, "has a campaign been opened with more fanfare, whoop-de-do and breathless public interest than that which greeted news of the Normandy invasion. The cheers and prayers which went with us into France were sincere and wonderful and are not to be taken in jest." With keen historical foresight, he encouraged soldiers and sweethearts to preserve their D-Day correspondence. "They are full of love and rash promises. Brother, hang on to your copy." The letters might be useful someday, he added. "We repeat, save those Articles of Liberation, those martial Magna Cartas. Then next time your wife climbs down your throat for burning a hole in the rug, just look her in the eye and say, 'Honey, that ain't what you wrote on D-Day!'"[397]

Family members expressed difficulty in recognizing what lay past the invasion. Reporter James Thrasher commented, "To some, D-Day seemed an end itself, a sort of final examination before the diploma—the exaltation—of certain victory. To others it was a day of bristling defenses, secret devices, and other nameless terrors." Individuals around the world had so long awaited the opening of the Second Front that they had little concept of what could follow. Eleanor Roosevelt offered clarification on this point, remarking that D-Day was "the day which has been hanging like a sword over our heads, but in itself isn't very important." As her husband's celebrated D-Day prayer alluded, the struggle was by no means over. The first lady, who herself had four sons in the service, reflected, "This type of war is costly—people must go through anxiety, suffering, loss. The cost of liberation to many of these countries will be great at the moment of liberation. . . . This is not a happy day." Thrasher added on June 12, "Now that those hurdles are past, we can appreciate Mrs. Roosevelt's comments." The harsh realities became all the more apparent.[398]

Mamie Eisenhower, who was a guest at West Point's luxurious Thayer Hotel in anticipation of her son's graduation, was surprisingly caught off guard by the invasion's arrival. A *New York Post* reporter revealed the news to her in a predawn phone call. "The invasion? What about the invasion?" she groggily asked.

"Well, it's started," replied the reporter.

In stark contrast to battlefront photography, newspaper art heralded D-Day with celebratory fervor. Resurrecting the old U. S. battle cry of the First World War, the *Washington Evening Star*'s James Berryman depicted an American proudly declaring, "Lafayette, We Are Here . . . Again!" An equally determined Brit and Canadian join him. (23)

"Please forgive me," she begged. "Did you say the invasion has
started? I'm still asleep, you know. . . . But why hasn't somebody told
me?" Mrs. Eisenhower (who often preferred remaining in bed until
noon) overcame her early morning daze and quickly turned exuberant.
"Why, that's wonderful! I'm so excited. . . . If I were at home, I would
have heard all that."[399]

A more composed Mrs. Eisenhower stated after graduation, "We know that our men are attacking our enemies. We know that they will be victorious. But we also know they will have many trying hours ahead, hours in which we shall find it difficult not to be restless and unnerved." Maintaining confidence was the tonic to the nation's many woes.[400]

Word of D-Day prompted members of the press to chase down anybody with the last name of Eisenhower. The Supreme Allied Commander's eighty-two-year-old mother, Ida, was too ill to receive visitors in her Abilene homestead. A devout pacifist who believed war was "rather wicked," she "didn't like it" when Dwight chose a military career. The general's engineer brother, Earl, presented no such qualms. "Ike's luck will keep pace with his ability," the brother supposed.[401]

Comically, numerous figureheads in Washington were taken aback when informed of D-Day. Washington correspondent Drew Pearson observed War Department officials "laughing behind their hands at the fact that military intelligence, supposed to know all about everything going on behind enemy lines and inside our own lines, chose D-Day to move their offices" at the Pentagon. Generals, politicians, and reporters calling for updates were left empty-handed. "Sorry," said the operator, "but the telephones are all torn out. G-2 is moving." All was confusion as detached telephones, furniture, and cabinets bearing vital records were log-jammed in the Pentagon's many circuitous hallways. "[M]ilitary intelligence . . . didn't know when the big day we were to cross the English Channel was scheduled."

Even Secretary of War Henry Stimson admitted being out of the loop. "I was just about as surprised as anyone else when I heard a news correspondent telling how he had just returned from an airplane trip from France where parachutists were dropped." Secretary of State Cordell Hull, meanwhile, was noticeably absent from the national stage—having sought a healthful reprieve at a Hershey, Pennsylvania resort. Few comparable historical events "truly represented the cause of liberty and mankind," he told prying newsmen. Other than the helmeted guards around its fenced perimeter, the White House appeared dark and rather lifeless. Inside, the president could only comment how "splendidly" all was transpiring. The White House Scottie dog, Fala, scurried between the legs of 200 inquisitive reporters.[402]

The greatest frustration of all was directed at the Office of War Information, whose apparent uselessness had become a gradual, "creeping paralysis." Newspaper Enterprise Association columnist Peter Edson (whose later investigations compelled Richard Nixon to deliver his famous "Checkers Speech") was unrelenting in his journalistic derision of OWI director Elmer Davis. The information coordinator "held a press conference on D-Day morning, but like a lot of other civilian officials in Washington, he didn't have anything important to say," claimed Edson. The Office had been assigned the task of "propagandizing Europe and psychologically softening up Germany for the kill" but had yet to deliver despite its substantial fiscal appropriations. On June 6, the organization could not have emerged more ineffectual. At the OWI and elsewhere, "Bigwigs who try to say something appropriate somehow sound and look silly."[403]

Within the halls of Congress, D-Day postponed a session of the House Foreign Affairs Committee—an entity that facilitated portions of the invasion. The delegate from Alaska concluded, "there's no use in our meeting, with the boys landing on the beaches of Europe." The incendiary scapegoat proceedings against Rear Admiral Husband Kimmel and Lt. Gen. Walter Short for their supposed transgressions at Pearl Harbor two and a half years prior were also temporarily halted. The sudden invasion malaise fostered a capital even duller and less productive than usual. All other manners of legislation and public policy seemed utterly inconsequential. "Who cares about Sewell Avery of Montgomery Ward and his little fight with the government over a labor union?" Edson wondered.[404]

Washington's laudatory speeches dragged on. Skeptical reporters somehow doubted the sincerity of the many political orations. "The men who regularly cover congress, looking down on the spectacle from the press galleries, may have been a little on the cynical side. Cynicism is the nature of an occupational disease for them, but I'm inclined to accept the judgment of these knowing veterans," remarked Marquis Childs.

"They look kind of solemn down there today, don't they?" observed one journalist of the politicians below.

"Yeah, that'll last until tomorrow," scoffed a colleague.

"You mean it'll last until they bring up that Kimmel-Short court-martial business in about half an hour."

With ears glued to radios, few would care about governmental bureau-cracy in the ensuing weeks. The political drama of the day was none-theless revealing to reporters. "One thing that D-Day did was to throw into sudden, sharp relief the particular kind of partisan politics that has been afoot here," remarked Childs. "As though seen in the harsh light of landing flares, the figures of those who cripple our home front war controls were abruptly revealed. They had a stealthy, skulking look."[405]

However brief, solidarity was the word of the hour. Army chief of staff George Marshall toiled restlessly at the War Department all day, leav-ing only temporarily to the Soviet embassy to be awarded the Order of Suvorov—one of Russia's highest military honors. The Soviets had com-pelling reason to celebrate. "The catastrophe of fascist Germany is drawing nearer. What Hitler and his criminal clique have dreaded most has happened. Germany is forced to carry on the war on two fronts," Ambassador Andrei Gromyko declared. "There is no doubt that the com-bined blows of the powerful Allied coalition will insure a speedy and complete victory over the enemy."[406]

Drew Pearson described the grand Beaux-Arts Russian embassy on Washington's 16th Street NW (formerly owned by the Pullman Car fam-ily dynasty) as usually "not very convivial." The place was occupied by emotionless diplomats and attaches consumed by the calamities of their bedeviled country. Only on the anniversary of the Bolshevik Revolution were the grandiose, gold-leafed halls opened to the general public. Ex-ceedingly few Americans had insider perspective of embassy happen-ings. Betty Carter, a Washington wife of a U. S. Army captain, taught language lessons to Russian officers at the residence and received a wel-come on June 6 she would not soon forget. "Arriving inside the embassy on D-Day, Mrs. Carter found it impossible to give her usual round of English lessons" wrote Pearson. "A dozen Russians—officers and civil-ians—crowded around her, congratulating her, telling her what a great country they were in."

"I was the first American citizen they had seen that day," explained Carter. "They had been waiting for this invasion for three long years and they couldn't restrain themselves."[407]

Reaction was less defined at the Berghof, Hitler's posh alpine retreat in Bavaria, where the ruler of Germany exhibited severe D-Day mood swings. Told not to disturb the fuehrer, Hitler's staff did not dare awake

219

their leader despite morning news of invasion. When the fuehrer arose to breakfast, he screeched, "Is this the invasion or isn't it?" After an injection of Eukodal, Hitler's spirits lifted. Convinced that the incursion into Normandy was a ruse, Hitler remained seemingly aloof and unconcerned with developments in France. He was, however, delighted to learn that Joseph Goebbels had given up smoking. Later, Hitler quixotically boasted, "The news couldn't be better. . . . Now we have them where we can destroy them." Rommel knew better.[408]

Both physically and psychologically, the Third Reich began to crumble. According to one Iowa newspaper, "Allied strategy did not unfold in its entirety on D-Day. The Allies can launch new offensives in so many places that Hitler is like a man who wants to fight with his back to the wall but can't find a wall." While Americans trudged across Western Europe, the Reds sought to recapture Minsk and evict all Germans from the Soviet Union. Outlined at Tehran, Operation Bagration would eclipse Overlord in scope, with two million Russian troops tightening the vice from the east. The campaign began June 22 and resulted in the annihilation of seventeen German divisions. All the while, Hitler's distrust in his generals prevented strategic initiative—paranoia that only intensified after the unsuccessful July 20 plot to assassinate the fuehrer. The end game was set. D-Day, though miniscule in contrast to costlier Soviet offensives, was nonetheless publicly heralded by Russians as a magnificent military triumph. "The history of war does not know of any such undertaking," said Stalin of D-Day, "so broad in conception, so grandiose in scale, and so masterly in execution."[409]

Coincidentally, Vice President Henry Wallace was abroad in the Soviet Union and passing through the Siberian city of Irkutsk when he received word of Overlord. According to the Russian news agency Tass, "Wallace received the news with emotion, considering the offensive of the Allies as having tremendous significance not only for the conduct of the war but for future humanity. He saw it as bright proof of the solidarity and determination of the Allies." The perpetually neglected vice president (soon to be dumped by his party for the more moderate Harry Truman) later complained of his exiled international travels, "I didn't receive any news on the political front—none whatsoever." Soldiers on the front lines were arguably better apprised of war news than the man second in line to the presidency.[410]

Elsewhere in international reaction, London residents were more concerned than jubilant. Britons were distressed not only for their own sons but also the homesick Americans they had welcomed into their communities. Correspondent Judy Barden recognized that Englanders already missed their Yank guests. "Londoners no longer recognize London," she observed. "Since most of the Yanks have gone to France, the city is deserted. There are taxis and seats at the movie houses and theaters. English gals are looking a bit lost, too."

"What will it be like when the Americans go home to America and give us back London?" the Brits asked. They now had the answer, and most did not care for it at all. An exception was the elders of the Lincolnshire market town of Grantham, who had previously bickered about the lewd Yanks chasing their young ladies up the brick sidewalks. Now, it was "the girls who have the complaint," wrote Barden.

One pub owner likewise complained of his downturn in business. The neighborhood, once lively with distinctive American laughter and horseplay, was now as quiet as a morgue. "We haven't had one glass broken," he muttered. "Every time the Yanks broke a glass, I made them put money in the prisoner of war box. I emptied it on D-Day." He decided to donate the £10 to the American Red Cross instead. "After all, it was the American boys who gave it." Some 400 miles to the south, the Yanks were now giving much more than spare change to the war effort.[411]

At another pub, one curvaceous barmaid cried, "Thank goodness, now we're beginning to get it over with." In the view of AP reporter Barbara Wace, this mindset epitomized Britain's reaction. "The news brought back to London some of the comradeship and friendliness which was expressed on all sides when the British capital was undergoing the Blitz." Londoners suddenly felt so depreciated by the departure of the young men that one anxious wife even declared, "I almost wish they'd bomb us too in London. It would make me feel better."

Outside the 500-year-old church of St. Dunstan's in Stepney, an aged verger surveyed the heavy damage inflicted by German incendiaries. Despite the devastation to his beloved place of worship, the caretaker's heart was filled with quiet, reticent joy. "I'm glad it started," he remarked from the chalky scaffolds supporting the roof, "though you can't help thinking of them who won't come back." However, he interpreted the invasion launching at the mouth of the Seine River as a good omen. "That's where Henry V landed for Agincourt you know."[412]

A reserved but sentimental joke highlighting the prim nature of British humor circled through the bars and streets. "I understand," muttered one Briton to another, "that an Englishman is actually able to get a taxi in Piccadilly now."

One bus conductress observed how her passengers seemed kinder than ever. Somehow, they had previously taken for granted the warmheartedness Americans instilled in them. For better and for worse, for reasons peculiar and poignant, Londoners realized their wartime city would never be the same.[413]

For the few Americans left behind in the city, life advanced at a slower pace. Yes, the reduced male to female ratio improved the odds for romantic encounters, but those old priorities now seemed trite. Largely gone were the "Piccadilly Commandoes" so humorously described by Andy Rooney. Red Cross centers were duller with half-filled halls. White-capped military policemen who previously spent nights breaking up boisterous bar brawls stood as silent sentinels outside Allied office buildings. "Christ, I wish I was over there with them," snarled one.

A portly British bobby strolling through the hazy streets compared the mood to that of September 3, 1939—the day Great Britain entered the war. "We waited and worried a long time then before we knew for certain whether we had to fight," he said. "We've waited a long time for the invasion. Now it's here, I think everybody will be calmer than ever before. It's the waiting and worrying that gets you down." Not far away, Big Ben unknowingly ticked ever closer toward V-E Day and peace. At Westminster Abbey's Tomb of the Unknown Warrior, residents knelt in prayer. "In the queer hush," wrote Mollie Panter-Downes, "one could sense the strain of a city trying to project itself across the intervening orchards and cornfields, across the strip of water, to the men already beginning to die in the French orchards and cornfields."[414]

In every American military installation and outpost at home and overseas, GI Joes, Flyboys, Swabbies, and Leathernecks pondered how the assault would affect their war—if at all. At the University of Wisconsin naval station in Madison (where it snowed the morning of June 6), 1,500 trainees eagerly listened to invasion broadcasts following reveille. For perhaps the first time in the institution's short history, there were no late hammocks, sad sacks, or sleepy sailors attempting to steal a few extra winks.

"All the radios were turned on full blast after Ensign Sanders called us," said Yeoman Second Class Louis Berman of New York City. "We were pretty excited. I thought about all the boys I know who might be in it."

"The first thing I thought about was my brother," related Bryant Burke of Portland, Oregon. "He's over there with the army."

"It's a swell deal," asserted radio trainee Gerald Beistle, "Only I'm not there." Many would be soon enough. [415]

Dog-faced American infantrymen on Italy's scarred Anzio beachhead received one of the best D-Day proclamations of all. Their announcer was none other than Hollywood glamour goddess Marlene Dietrich, the famous German actress and Nazi hater who was on a ten-week performing tour in the Mediterranean. Preparing for an afternoon show on June 6, she heard the invasion news and immediately rushed to the stage where a massive military audience awaited. The boys "went wild and whistled like mad," she fondly recalled. Despite her atypical olive drab wardrobe and recent bout of pneumonia, Dietrich delivered one of her most electrifying performances during the war. The enthusiasm was irresistible. [416]

A less extravagant declaration occurred on a naval vessel transporting Marines through the Mariana and Palau Islands in the South Pacific. Capt. John T. Popham of Brooklyn heard the warning buzz of the ship's speakers followed by a crackled voice matter-of-factly stating, "Now hear this. The invasion of France has started. That is all."

Officers casually playing games of chess, bridge, and pinochle in the ward room grew deadly silent. Only the hum of the ship's churning engines and the faint splash of waves against the hull could be heard. The Marines folded their arms and stared blankly at the piped ceiling— wondering what was unfolding on the other side of the world. An officer reading in the corner placed his open book on his khaki lap and blessed himself. One of the men blurted, "Thank God!"

On the deck and in the cramped corridors, battle-tested veterans of Guadalcanal and Bougainville restlessly smoked cigarettes and sipped coffee.

"I've got two brothers with the infantry," said one of the Marines.

"My kid brother is there," said another. "He's a machine gunner." Although separated by 7,000 miles, siblings traversing the Pacific invariably felt the same emotions as their kin in France.

Word of the battle for Normandy consumed all conversation. The sailors and Marines read and reread Eisenhower's and Roosevelt's addresses. There was talk of being home by Christmas; every war is supposed to be over by Christmas. They celebrated with chocolate bars and chewing gum from the Post Exchange. Beneath the merriment was a grim, twisting anxiety that deprived many of their sleep. Their fears were not for their brothers in Europe alone, but for themselves. The men were sailing toward their own D-Day. Saipan.[417]

CHAPTER 11

"Peace Tomorrow"

Martha Gellhorn was furious. While the days and weeks following D-Day demonstrated the best of American character, they also revealed an unsavory underbelly. Female reporters attached to the ETO continuously confronted inequity and doubt casted by male counterparts. Many of the nineteen women reporters accredited to SHAEF were experienced combat correspondents. Yet, their fortitude did not prevent the Army limiting the journalists' access. Gellhorn condemned this prejudiced paternalism in a fiery letter to a colonel on June 24. "As you know," she fumed, "General Eisenhower stated that men and women correspondents would be treated alike and would be afforded equal opportunities to fulfill their assignments." All too often Gellhorn sensed "that women correspondents were an irritating nuisance who, very tiresomely, kept asking to be allowed to do their jobs." None of them would be in their positions if they were not proficient in their work, she persisted.

The condescending manner in which female reporters were treated was as preposterous as it was degrading. Gellhorn and colleagues pledged thoroughness to their readers. "I do not feel that there is any need to beg for the right to serve as eyes for millions of people in America who are desperately in need of seeing, but cannot see for themselves," Gellhorn concluded. Her own daringness lent uncompromised credence to her demands for inclusion. SHAEF directives ordering that "women correspondents were to go no further forward than women's services go" proved impossible for public relations officers to regulate.[418]

As Gellhorn's passion attested, reporters and service members collectively embraced D-Day as a foundation for societal progress. The invasion instilled devout purpose and compelled citizens to seek higher meaning from the war. D-Day served as the national compass pointing to inevitable victory and prospects of peace. At this critical hour, Americans reinvested themselves in the war effort and sought to perfect their world in Overlord's wake. Citizens were both inspired and distressed by what this future might entail. Inevitably, the nation's newspapers emerged as the sounding board for dramatic currents of change—cultural shifts that would ripple through the ensuing decades.

The evolutions of American life were no more evident than in wartime factories. A supervisor at Kingston, Tennessee's Holston Ordnance Works voiced a recurring D-Day theme among war laborers on June 6. "Those of us whose lot is has been to furnish the materials of warfare to American and Allied troops can really be proud." The previous day, a lofty article by aircraft worker Ann Pendleton appeared in Oklahoma's *Ardmore Daily Ardmoreite*. Chronicling the "real-life adventures of a society girl who goes to work in a war plant," Pendleton's column, entitled "Hit the Rivet, Sister," inspired untold readers. Toiling in a Kerry Kraft factory, Pendleton mastered the "alarming little machine" known as the rivet gun, deciphered complex blueprints, and oversaw the construction of new fighter planes. "[M]y fellow-workers now," she proclaimed, "are no longer girls but fellers, for I am at last out of Bench and on the Lines. . . . At last I am a riveter."[419]

The stirring account evokes all the pride and color of J. Howard Miller's iconic "We Can Do It!" poster produced for Westinghouse. Pendleton's works, syndicated throughout the nation, signified a growing surge of energy among women rising through patriotic fervor. Nonetheless, the actions of the OWI sought to conform home front ideals solely to the survival of the nation "rather than advancement of any individual or group of individuals," writes Professor Maureen Honey. The *Magazine War Guide* issued by the Bureau of Campaigns fortified the notion that women's role in the workplace was only a temporary exigency of war. While the percentage of females in industrial jobs skyrocketed during the conflict, that segment of workers still remained proportionately small. Similar to the plights of Gellhorn's colleagues and African American combatants, female plant workers' quests for agency and autonomy were not a priority of military planners. For both civil liberties and civil rights, however, D-Day was a spark igniting lively public debate regarding definitions of equality.[420]

The main priority of domestic activity was to secure the continuous flow of goods from the assembly lines to the battle lines. To forge his

"Arsenal of Democracy," Franklin Roosevelt partnered with corporate chairmen whose scorn he previously relished. American business was radically re-invented in the process. Desiring to be recognized as legitimate participants in the conflict, factory workers looked to the federal government and media to vindicate rights earned on factory floors.[421]

The dockyards of Britain were filled to the brim with crates postmarked Detroit, Philadelphia, San Francisco, Pittsburgh, Mobile, and Hershey. These pieces of home were integral components of forays into foreign lands. The *New York Times* calculated, "When Joe wades ashore on the Continent, about eight tons of supplies of various sorts must go with him and fifty or sixty pounds more must get to him every day." The operation made the largest private enterprise in the States resemble "a corner newsstand." In Pennsylvania, the state's War Manpower Commission deemed that 400 *billion* board feet "must be met or surpassed to provide D-Day needs." The timber was utilized for the manufacturing of crates in which weapons, ammunition, clothing, and food would be transported. "Every time a soldier leaves for overseas, it takes 300 feet of lumber to box and crate his initial supplies," said one official, and then "50 feet a month is required to keep him supplied." Over 10,000 workers were summoned for timbering in Pennsylvania alone.[422]

DeWitt Mackenzie wrote of the inherent dangers of these logistical challenges. "This represents one of the most trying and dangerous moments of the war and for our home front, which not only provides Uncle Sam's fighting forces but equips them with all the sinews of war. It's trying because of the terrible strain of waiting for D-Day." A potential deficit in aviation fuel was no small factor of Mackenzie's anxieties. "Here are involved not only the production and the various operations necessary to land it on the fighting fronts, but conservation of gas by the home front," he wrote. "The black-market operator in gasoline is a traitor to his country" because the heavies over Germany were flying roundtrips of nearly 2,000 miles. If 1,500 bombers each flew 1,500 miles on a single mission, the planes collectively consumed 8.25 million gallons of gas. For one day.

Nothing short of an "Amazonian flow of gasoline" could sustain the thousands of bombers tearing into Europe. "And it can be said that all the oil and gasoline which our home front has given up to rationing in the war effort has been absorbed by our fighting forces. That shows how necessary conservation has been. It would be a sad day if we ran short of gasoline on the fighting fronts," he lamented. "Any slowing up means unnecessary protraction of the conflict. It means additional bloodshed and suffering."[423]

Concerns over "slowing up" did not always resonate with American workers. The growing influence of labor unions spurred thousands of work stoppages—including several immediately prior to D-Day. Over thirteen million man-days were lost to labor disputes in 1943. Beyond demands for better pay and conditions, complaints of gender and racial discrimination were rampant. Industrial employees stood under a constant microscope of public scrutiny. Their efforts and grievances were contrasted to the marble image of fighting men overseas. Many citizens perceived strikers as unpatriotic, spoiled dissidents when, in reality, workers wished to reap the benefits of a rapidly-changing world. Most service members did not make the correlation. Nor did those in the military pay mind to industrialists who profited exponentially from wartime production.[424]

The *Athens Sunday Messenger* of Ohio reported of sailors who had gone without liberty for more than a year. The mariners sarcastically offered to "buy off" strikes if their paltry income would keep "money hungry" protestors at bay. The battle-tested seamen forwarded cash to the War Department to distribute to "needy" strikers of an Ohio Wright air plant who demonstrated that wage increases were apparently more important than the lives of service members. The veterans caustically offered monthly contributions to "save the war workers from starvation." A dismissive postscript noted, "If the Wright strike is over, just choose another. There are always plenty at hand."

The sailors' letter was viewed as "one of the most effective indictments of war strikes that has come from the men of fighting fronts." The *Messenger* added a thinly-veiled condemnation of the strikers by praising those "men who want to come home to see the ones they love, to see their sons and daughters they have never seen, and their wives and parents whose memories live with them day and night. At the fronts, they are close to their foreign enemies. Their enemies at home they cannot reach." The deeds stood in contrast to the coddled strikers' attempts to earn money "dishonestly." There seemed little room for dissension in wartime.

Labor unions could no longer appear subversive. One union boss informed colleagues, "public opinion has become inflamed against us and on the outcome of this crisis depends our survival in the postwar period." The number of strikes slackened in 1944, equating to 8.7 million man-days lost. Six battleships and over 14,000 B-24s could have been constructed within that unused time. One day into the invasion, CIO president Philip Murray declared complete loyalty to America's fighting men and that no "violation of our no-strike pledge can be tolerated by the consciences of our members." A leader of the Michigan Labor Board attributed the spring's outpouring of strikes to "D-Day jitters." The "slightest incident will touch off a wave of labor disputes," he insisted. [425]

In response to such declarations, one enraged Air Forces wife wrote to the *Chicago Tribune*, "Are we becoming completely mercenary? Our boys need tools and weapons, blood plasma and life-saving serums. . . . Do you strikers care more for a few dollars than you do about your men in service? Your answer will be in your actions."[426]

Harsh critiques did not halt picketing. Thirty major strikes continued on D-Day, although the number of revolts shrunk to seven by week's end. "When these first shocks of the invasion have passed," speculated Peter Edson, "it is expected that strikes will again increase in numbers. It may happen any day, brought on by nothing more tangible than tiredness, irritation, nervous tension—manifestations of home front psychoneuroses." Over 1,000 steel workers campaigning for reduced hours at Pittsburgh's C. G. Hussey plant were shamed back to work when federal conciliation representatives warned, "You can't back up the boys by striking." According to plant officials across the nation, strikes were most rampant when production was highest. Other revolts erupted at Birmingham, Alabama coal mines, the Botany Mills in New Jersey, and Illinois metal foundries. [427]

Overwhelming invasion needs triggered numerous labor uprisings— but not all of them. At Cincinnati's Wright Aeronautical Corporation plant, 450 strikers held the factory idle. The standoff was a protest against seven African Americans promoted to operate the cylinder shop. Animus was apparent from the outset, as the black workers were led into the shops under armed guard for protection. Chaos ensued at what became known as the "D-Day Strike." As many as 15,000 plant employees were absent that week. The not-so-diplomatic Air Forces colonel George Strong faintly threatened the stewards, declaring that if the workers were in Germany, they all "would be shot." If they did not cease "this monkey business" they would regret it as long as they lived. The

229

Cincinnati Post agreed, stating, "You Wright workers, what will you say to the fathers and mothers of those men who fall in France?"[428]

Columnist Harry S. McAplin of the *Chicago Defender* openly mocked the hypocrisy of the Wright plant strikers. In a scathing editorial, he paraphrased their insensitive battle cry: "To hell with D-Day. To hell with beating Hitler and his racial supremacy theories," the strikers might as well have claimed. "We've got a racial supremacy of our own to maintain by keeping Negroes in their places, even if they do want to help win the war. So, while the Allies strike against occupied France, we'll strike against the Negroes." Following additional threats and banter, the strike ceased after four tumultuous days. In many communities, citizens cast aside differences on D-Day in the name of national solidarity. In other locales, racism still trumped patriotism. There were "Hitler Lovers everywhere," complained one Georgia newspaper.[429]

A similar incident later unfolded in Philadelphia. Some 6,000 white transit operators walked from their positions due to the hiring of eight black motormen. Dr. John P. Turner, a highly-skilled African American surgeon, noted, "this is a sad commentary on the supposed democracy born right here in Philadelphia. It will not be solved until the hearts of the people are right—and the hearts of the people here are not right." He proclaimed, "Our Negroes have died on battlefields. How do you suppose a Negro mother feels when she has lost a son and now finds her second son deprived of a decent means of earning a living—the things her dead boy fought for."[430]

Whether prompted by heavy work hours or long-simmering racial tension, labor unrest was ever on the mind of J. Edgar Hoover. The FBI director feared the discord was triggered by anarchists, socialists, or full-blooded Nazis. On June 5, the *Edwardsville Intelligencer* of Illinois featured a Hoover press release in which the director announced, "there is the pro-Nazi enemy, the deliberate saboteur operating without direct orders from abroad but suffering from a perverted sense of patriotism." On the other hand, there were also "equally dangerous" individuals "from the ranks of disgruntled employees, practical jokers, thrill-seekers, mischievous youths, egotistical crackpots, and careless citizens." Wartime strikes were tantamount to treason in Hoover's eyes.

Worried intelligence officers expressed concerns to Hoover "of a concerted wave of sabotage when D-Day comes." The director replied, "If the American worker continues to remain alert, I do not think we need fear any greater wave than the one which we have met and beaten back." Hoover's calm, public reassurance was emblematic of his successful public relations initiatives to convince "loyal" Americans how much they needed the Bureau to safeguard their interests.[431]

The FBI announced to the press, "The method of operation of the typical enemy agent is to frequent tap rooms, hotels, restaurants, and other places where the public, especially soldiers, congregate. Here he will mingle with the crowd, buy drinks when it is his turn, and play the role of good fellow out for an evening's fun." German spy Ernest Lehmitz, who worked as a barkeep and air raid warden on Staten Island, operated in this manner until his arrest one year prior to D-Day. "Be careful to whom you talk, and even more careful as to what you say," the Bureau warned.[432]

The spy games crisscrossed the Atlantic—with newspapers playing a distinct role in D-Day duplicity. As Tsar Nicholas I purportedly stated during the Crimean War, "We have no need of spies. . . . We have *The Times*." Periodicals served as prime outlets for siphoning military information. This was especially true of local newspapers which highlighted personal details regarding marriages, graduations, transfers, and promotions. As British intelligence officer Jock Haswell wrote, "Newspapers can be a useful and apparently undirected and independent confirmatory source, but, like every source of information, they can be exploited for deception."[433]

The broad spectrum of pre-invasion paranoia was even uncovered in the crossword puzzle section of London's *The Daily Telegraph and Morning Post*. A British intelligence officer keen on the word sport shockingly noticed several invasion code words scattered throughout multiple puzzles over several days: Utah, Omaha, Overlord, Neptune, Mulberry. Were Nazi agents relaying signals via the *Telegraph*'s crosswords? The two schoolmasters who created the puzzles, Leonard Dawes and Neville Jones, were promptly interrogated. Allied investigators discovered the two scholarly gents often prepared the word games six months in advance. They had been doing so for twenty years. The two bewildered educators were thus released. The beach code names were generally not disclosed by the press until after the invasion.[434]

Beyond saboteur and spy threats, domestic quandaries such as the Soldier Voting Act stirred furious debate. Five months after D-Day, service members would vote for a president in wartime—a first since the

Civil War. The topic embraced a key issue of American exceptionalism: ensuring the survival and growth of the democratic experiment. The process soon became a political football and a contest over free speech. Polls indicated that seven out of ten service members intended to vote for Roosevelt in November. As a result, Republicans sought to muddle military voting measures while Democrats sought to expedite a bill. An imperfect voting act eventually passed but an amendment pushed by Republican senator Robert A. Taft (son of the late president) initiated widespread censorship on soldier reading materials. Taft feared Democrats would indoctrinate soldiers with party propaganda. The *Tipton Tribune* of Indiana derided the provision, saying, "The Taft amendment raises the question whether American soldiers are children or adults. If they are adults, the Taft amendment ought to be amended." The editor of *The Infantry Journal* interpreted the law as a petty campaign "to bar any and every scrap of printed material which might be favorable to the Roosevelt administration." Partisan letters to the editors of military newspapers were likewise curbed.[435]

As the national controversy unraveled in the weeks bookending D-Day, the *Bakersfield Californian* confirmed the difficulties of maintaining transparency in wartime. "By statute, popular demand, and constitutional law, free speech and freedom of the press may be assured, but actually it is a constant battle of the press to maintain its freedom for the benefit of its millions of readers throughout the world." Taft's strategy to limit the dissemination of information ran counter to the ideals American readers held sacred. The amendment was scrapped that summer and GIs read as they wished.[436]

Politicos had bigger fish to fry. Only six days after the invasion, the Treasury Department initiated the Fifth War Loan Drive, a military fundraiser seeking $16 billion in war bond and stamp sales. Treasury Secretary Henry Morgenthau's office predicted two possible scenarios if the invasion coincided with the preplanned bond tour: "If our troops achieved brilliantly in the early stages, bond buying would lag because of the feeling that it is all over but the shouting. Should they meet stiff opposition on the beachheads, the reverse would probably stimulate sales." In this unusual calculation of wartime financing, winning was losing and losing was winning. Luckily, the bond drive surpassed its goal by over $4 billion. An exhibition of captured Axis aircraft at the

Washington Monument alone raised $3.4 million. D-Day unarguably bolstered Americans' confidence to invest.[437]

Citizens donated not only funds but the very blood from their veins. Reporter Ed Stennett wrote, "News of the American landings in France almost swamped some of the blood donor centers. Volunteers shot up 700 percent before nightfall." At a Philadelphia blood bank, a queue formed around the block before the sun rose on June 6. A Washington center witnessed a 1,000 percent increase in blood donations within three days. Similar reports arose from Dallas, Denver, and St. Louis.

A different pattern emerged in San Antonio. "The blood bank," reported the city's newspaper, "with extra volunteer workers on hand, was ready. But San Antonians—many of them at least—were not. And this is to San Antonio's shame. No, blood bank officials reported, there was no rush on D-Day, or the next, or the next." In addition, fifty scheduled appointments failed to show. One resident who kept her appointment was Doyle Virginia Cockrell, a Gold Star Mother who sent three sons to war. One died in a plane crash. In tribute to her son, she enlisted in the WACs at age forty-eight. "For her, D-Day meant that she would make another visit to the blood bank," wrote the *San Antonio Light*. "She had been there before but had been waiting until the doctor pronounced her strong enough to go again." She insisted, "Don't make a fuss over me."[438]

On an international stage, individuals and organizations contributed to the invasion in their own unique ways. The American Red Cross pled for donations to cover the $3 cost of mailing one pint of blood. "With the gigantic Allied offensive . . . the need of blood plasma will be intensified by a hundredfold," the charity claimed. The Red Cross oversaw the preparation of nearly one billion surgical dressings in 1943. Volunteers, employees, and nurses were also urgently required. "What the women who are not helping probably have overlooked is the impending invasion of Western Europe, where the Allies are liable to suffer casualties that will make all that has gone before appear insignificant," remarked one Ohio paper that March. The murderous campaign then in progress south of Rome was indicative of violent confrontations on the horizon. "Not many undefended beachheads are likely to be discovered on the coast of France and the Low Countries, or even Denmark and Norway."[439]

Additionally, the Red Cross was instrumental in maintaining the physical and psychological health of invasion forces. Innumerable service members wrote home applauding the philanthropic work of the institution created by Clara Barton sixty-three years prior. Capt. Clyde Thomas offered nothing but adulation of the "five excellent American girls" who operated his local Red Cross Center in England. Recreation rooms, a library, a letter-writing station, and a kitchen serving decidedly non-army food offered a relaxing means of escape from the rigors and monotony of military life.[440]

In the factory, at the blood bank, or at the recruiting office, American women committed themselves fully to build upon D-Day's achievements. Even young ladies of immense privilege were obliged to contribute. Thirty-one-year-old Doris Duke Cromwell, daughter of tobacco tycoon James Buchanan Duke, inherited $100 million upon her father's death. Known as "the world's richest girl," she accepted her first job at the United Seamen's Service for $1 per year. Cromwell informed reporters, "If you are going to live, you have to be part of life. I could not live with myself if I did not do something real." Likewise, recruitment escalated at enlisting centers across the country. Many recruits falsely surmised the war would be over before they deployed overseas.[441]

Additionally, the Normandy invasion provided a final, grand moment of introspective oratory for the dwindling ranks of America's deadliest conflict. Aged Civil War veterans could not help but draw parallels between D-Day and the iconic battles of their youths. Newspapers actively sought their seemingly divine commentary. Former drummer boy John C. Adams of Indiana was none too impressed by GI Joes, thinking them somewhat wimpish. "They don't have to eat hardtack, the girls dance with them, and they are being rehabilitated," he complained to a reporter. "These GIs had it sort of easy that way."[442]

In a sad twist of fate, the psychological tolls of D-Day may have killed one inconsolable Civil War veteran. Ringgold W. Carman, who enlisted in the 124th Pennsylvania Infantry at age sixteen, descended into "a depressed state of mind caused by the news of D-Day from the battlefields in France," reported the *New York Times*. Now 100 years old, he followed war news with great interest and chronicled the advances of armies on a large wall map in his Queens, New York home. When hearing of D-Day on the radio, he immediately telephoned his daughter and despondently said, "I saw 24,000 dead on the field at Antietam. This is going to be worse." Over the following week he "slumped into a stupor from which he did not rally." Carman passed away on June 16 as one of the last Civil War veterans of New York City. The thought of Americans experiencing carnage similar to what he endured was too much to bear.[443]

Anxieties of armed conflict long resonated with the ancient warrior. The *Brooklyn Daily Eagle* reported of Carman's angst as early as June 1940. "The troubling belief that America is at the crossroads," observed the *Eagle*, "that the future of our country for the next century or two is poised in the scales of warfare which younger men are experiencing for the first time in their lives is a familiar state of mind to the Civil War veteran." Nonetheless, Carman believed that "In union there is strength." These words still rang true in 1944.[444]

Former Confederates also shared thoughts of D-Day. The ninety-eight-year-old Julius F. Howell, formerly of the 24th Virginia Cavalry, appeared in the U. S. House of Representatives on June 8, "resplendent in a Confederate gray dress uniform, to plead for national unity in the fight against the Axis." The congressmen courteously obliged the veteran, dispensing with rules prohibiting non-members from speaking. The irony of an ex-Confederate calling for the liberation of oppressed peoples was realized by few in the audience—with the possible exception of Congressman William Dawson. As the lone African American member of the House, Dawson used D-Day's political capital to invoke equality. "American boys, black and white, are in the vanguard. Many will die," he remarked. "If by their death the Freedoms are brought to Mankind everywhere, they, indeed, shall not have died in vain. Our hopes and prayers are with them." Dawson highlighted the contradiction that white and black soldiers were permitted to die together but not live together.[445]

While D-Day reached a "frightening crescendo" in Europe, the forces of American greed and racial supremacy wielded substantial power, loudly counterpointing the invasion's moral directive. Eleanor Roosevelt, who was far more progressive on race than her husband, highlighted these domestic dangers at the NAACP's convention in Baltimore on May 22. In praising minority service members, she exclaimed, "We have learned that is it not the color of your skin, your religion, or your race which makes you more able to do certain things better than other people."[446]

The likes of Mississippi senator Theodore Bilbo interpreted such rhetoric as an uncompromising left-wing conspiracy to undermine the nation's racial traditions. He revealed his Jim Crow sensibilities in a heated June letter to the federal government's Fair Employment Practice Committee—an entity established to prevent discriminatory wartime hiring practices. The "Negrophistical scheme of the Roosevelts and CIO is to cram Negro equality down the throats of the good white people of America," he complained. "With due deference to you, I think you are acting as secretary of a movement that is rendering a real and lasting disservice in a white man's country. You ought to be ashamed of yourself." Bilbo unknowingly mailed his hate-filled letter to Anna Hedgeman, the young woman of color who rose as a vocal leader of the FEPC. [447]

Despite press reports of unfathomable bigotry, Michigan's *Benton Harbor News Palladium* celebrated what seemed the death knell of America's most established terrorist organization—the Ku Klux Klan. The KKK, which once boasted five million members and held toxic strangleholds on state governments, appeared to fade from prominence. Only days after the invasion, Klan leadership announced the league of fanatics would "meet and reincarnate" when the pressures of war subsided. "Probably Adolf Hitler never heard of the Ku Klux Klan, but the Klan and Hitler's Nazi party were blood relations," wrote the *Palladium*. "America, after fighting a second war for freedom and democracy, can't afford another Ku Klux Klan." Sadly, as the Klansmen promised, the hate group reincarnated—just as it has done after every major American conflict since Reconstruction. [448]

Racism often persisted in more subtle attacks on black citizenry. In the invasion's aftermath, however, protests against institutional intolerance grew more livid. When the Chicago Bar Association prohibited four qualified African American lawyers from membership, D-Day served as a rallying cry for justice. In unrelenting terms, the *Pittsburgh Courier* grumbled, "The day of the Invasion, Deliverance, and Liberation dawned on Chicago concurrently and concomitantly. With the announcement of the undemocratic fascist-tainted action of the Chicago Bar Association, American men of color landed on the shores of France and marched into the mouth of hell and into the jaws of death." Meanwhile, the bar association embraced the mentality of, "You may conquer

Europe, but here, in Chicago, you shall not pass." Activists were compelled to action. "D-Day will not be our Doomsday in Chicago," they promised. The following year, Earl Dickerson became the first black member of the association.[449]

In Atlanta, meanwhile, writer Frank Marshall Davis proposed a "Home Front D-Day" to foster greater empathy and brotherhood among the races. After all, it was racial and domestic strife that fueled the ascendancy of Hitler and Hirohito, he warned. The nation's inner struggles could only be combated with brotherly love and interracial harmony. "The police departments should get special attention," said Davis. "Their attitude can often foment or halt a riot. They cannot show favoritism and expect peace. You know what happened in Detroit, how most of the Negro victims were slain by cops. Police officers with the right kind of attitude would have nipped this clash in its infancy." A symbolic home front "D-Day" could only be achieved via "intelligent cooperation between the races."[450]

For Chanie Durnham, a sixty-five-year-old black Chicagoan, D-Day represented "Diploma-Day." Like many stateside senior citizens, Durnham opted to expand her knowledge and better contribute to the war effort. She graduated at the Wendell Phillips Evening High School on the night of June 6. During the Great Migration, she and her family fled Mississippi so her children could attain proper educations; now it was her turn. In the view of the grandmother-turned-valedictorian, notions of service and self-empowerment were paramount to success. Speaking for twelve adult graduates, Durnham declared, "The women who sit at home and worry and gossip are lost. By qualifying ourselves to act less at random in making the world a better place to live in, we can give valuable aid to our boys who come home physically, mentally, or spiritually handicapped." With a slight glimmer in her eyes, she added, "I offer my classmates and myself as an example of the fact that it is never too late to learn."[451]

W. D. Armentrout, vice president of Colorado State College, too realized the power of higher learning in "D-Days" to come. "It is Demobilization Day when millions of men and women in service, industry, and other work now geared to war, are demobilized for days of peace," he stated. "This second D-Day will bring problems that demand quick and sure answers in a great many fields, but especially in education."

African American periodicals such as the esteemed *Pittsburgh Courier* served as the vanguard for civil rights advocacy during and after World War II. Boasting a national circulation of 200,000, the paper believed that D-Day served as a foundation for societal progress. Here, *Courier* correspondent Ted Stanford interviews 1st Sgt. Morris O. Harris of the 784th Tank Battalion on March 28, 1945. (24)

Regardless of age, race, or circumstance, D-Day served as a fitting moment to commemorate the accomplishments of determined individuals.[452]

This revelation was no more apparent than on the battlefront. "In almost every section there are colored soldiers working side by side with their white comrades. The friendship that has sprung up between them is remarkable and may well lead to a new order of things to come," reported the *Atlanta Daily World*.

The camaraderie did not ensure open-mindedness in all realms of the military establishment. Black GI Leo Jason was sentenced to fifteen years imprisonment for disobeying the orders of a white officer who continuously harassed him. The *Pittsburgh Courier* argued it was time for America to prioritize and cease waging war on the black man. "On the Normandy beachhead on D-Day, whom did the white soldier from Georgia or Florida fear the more, the armed Negro beside him, or the German, who is white like himself?" The war in Europe was being fought against other white men even more pronounced in racist ideology. Yet, African American service members were barred from lunch counters and passenger cars while Nazi prisoners were granted first class treatment. "Even England," the *Courier* concluded, "mother of the color-line, has abolished Jim Crow in her army."[453]

The claim was no exaggeration. After two years of convivial interaction, many of the British public relinquished its prior, racially-tinged misgivings about African American troops. Rev. J. P. Giles of Nuneaton, England noted after D-Day, "The impression our Negro guests made on a certain Midland town, at any rate, was one of natural and profound culture. Their courtesy, their politeness, their manly bearing and, above all, their unfailing cheerfulness and good humor, quickly endeared them to inhabitants. . . . We were sorry when they left us." This sentiment was underscored when Elizabeth, Queen of the United Kingdom, visited recuperating African American troops at a British hospital. Second Lt. James A. Bowman, a twenty-five-year-old engineer hailing from Fisk University, was shocked to discover royalty standing matronly at his bedside. "All of you are so very brave and we are so proud that you are fighting for us," proclaimed the queen. Little wonder Hitler referred to her as the "most dangerous woman in Europe."[454]

Hitler yet posed additional dangers. The ascending liberation of France brought forth even greater pressures upon the persecuted Jews of Europe. Time was scarce for salvation. "Since the invasion of France, the Germans have intensified their anti-Semitic propaganda," observed the *New York Times*. On June 6, Brussels radio reported Nazi promises to accelerate obliteration of the Jews in the face of Allied advances. The regime "would wipe out every Jew on whom they could lay their hands." To validate their atrocities, Nazi leaders announced their Hebrew prey as animalistic "belligerents" unworthy of rights. Franklin Roosevelt warned Congress on June 12 of the time sensitive nature of the crisis. "[K]nowing they have lost the war, the Nazis are determined to complete their program of mass extermination," the president warned. "The fury of their mean desire to wipe out the Jewish race in Europe continues." While FDR's War Refugee Board claimed to have saved 200,000 Jews from war-ravaged Europe, far more could have been spared had it not been for the anti-Semitic tendencies of Roosevelt's own State Department. Among the beleaguered Europeans denied refugee status in America was Anne Frank and her family.[455]

D-Day's boundless potentials nevertheless presented an opportunity to rescue untold millions, argued columnist Anne O'Hare McCormick. "Hopeless or not, humanity has to assert itself for its own sake. The worst thing the Germans could do is to dehumanize other people and silence the voices that protest against cruelty and injustice," she stated. If the Nazis muted moral outrage on a global scale they could stifle the spirit of mankind. "Hopeless or not, the world has to cry out against the awful fate that threatens the Jews. . . . And it is not hopeless."[456]

There was, in fact, still hope—including for fifty-one immigrants in Newport, Rhode Island who swore oaths of citizenship on D-Day. For the new citizens, June 6 would denote a moment of rebirth. The ceremony "should be full of meaning for all of us. Even while the invasion was in progress, we had right before our eyes an example of the things that our boys are fighting and dying for—our adoption as brothers those from other lands," observed the *Newport Mercury and Weekly Press*. The splendid "machinery of Democracy was at work."[457]

Less than 200 miles away, Federal Judge John C. Knox instilled comparable civic virtue in 600 men and women who became citizens in New York City. D-Day, Knox said, "could be interpreted as a symbol of Deliverance Day, the day that promises deliverance for the suffering peoples of Europe."

Prayerful citizens depart New York's West 23rd Street Emunath Israel synagogue on June 6. American Jews, many of whom had family members in Europe, were especially mindful of D-Day's ramifications for the oppressed peoples of conquered lands. Regardless of religious denomination, countless houses of worship were open around the clock when the invasion commenced. (25)

Several of the immigrants standing before him had escaped Hitler's wrath. "Many of you," the judge continued, "have relatives and friends still over there, people trodden to earth under oppressors who are foolish enough to pride themselves on supposed invincibility. This is the beginning of sunrise for them." New citizenship offered privileges as well as responsibilities; all needed to invest in the war and contribute to society. "And let no one bring foreign hatred based on bigotry and prejudice to these shores or tolerate them," he advised.[458]

The invasion demonstrated the vital nature of a free and independent press in preserving national principles. Dwight Eisenhower—privately fatigued but publicly confident—embodied the democratic credo with candor and congeniality. "I've been informed by the newspapers that an operation is impending," he chuckled to 450 reporters. The Supreme Allied Commander summoned populist spirit regarding his public relations outlook. "I believe that the old saying—public opinion wins wars—is true," he admitted. "Our countries fight best when our people are best informed. You will be allowed to report everything possible, consistent, of course, with military security. I will never tell you anything false." His was a task of controlling reporters without alienating them. As he informed Churchill, his goal was "to discover the best means of keeping the press securely in the dark, while at the same time not appearing to treat them as complete outsiders." On a personal note he added, "I should feel disturbed if I thought that I or my public relations staff were held as anything but friends of the press."[459]

Spotting light at tunnel's end, the global correspondent community hoisted Normandy as a rallying cry for transparency and shared dialogue. One Swedish newspaper commented after the invasion that every "obstacle to communication between peoples is a threat to international peace. . . . For ten years the atmosphere in Europe has been poisoned by official propaganda of lies and hatred. This would have been impossible had the news services been independent." The freedom of the press needed to be the concern of all nations. John S. Knight, president of the American Society of Newspaper Editors, likewise contended that the root "causes of war would be exposed and discouraged by daily publication of news free from influence or self-interest." Military censorship under the guise of security was no excuse for political blackouts in the name of expediency.

A colorful mixture of speeches, prayer, song, and Western Union telegram updates comprised a massive D-Day rally in Madison Square. Mayor Fiorello La Guardia demanded that New Yorkers support "the great and valiant struggle for the liberation of the world from tyranny." Signs proclaiming, "Back the Attack!" are sprinkled throughout the crowd. (26)

"At war's end," he concluded, "we believe that a free and honest press in every country would contribute greatly toward lessening the chance of future wars and also increase the probability of a firm and enduring peace."[460]

Similarly, Ralph McGill of the *Atlanta Constitution* demanded a removal of "unnecessary restrictions on the freedom to gather and transmit news throughout the world." News could be freely disseminated only if safeguards preventing widespread falsification were established. "The most powerful thing in the world," said McGill, "is truth." These were words to live by—and perhaps die for.[461]

Declaring invasion day as "the most critical day of our generation," an IBM advertisement in Ohio's *Zanesville Times Recorder* lauded American news agencies. "We are deeply indebted to the press, radio, and newsreels which, since the beginning of the invasion, have kept us fully informed as to the movements of the Allied forces," exclaimed the ad. D-Day marked the most substantial collection and dissemination of information in history. Not mentioned was the corporation's previous technological collaboration with the Third Reich that enabled Germany to collect data pertaining to European Jews. Even so, D-Day emphatically compelled IBM to "more fully understand the depth of our obligation as individuals and organizations in backing up our armed forces."[462]

Like the Fourth of July and the Seventh of December, the Sixth of June entered the pantheon of American holy days. The invasion became a moment of destiny on which the fate of free civilization hinged. Citizens celebrated its near-religious implications with vigor. Physically, emotionally, and financially, Americans collectively contributed to the cracking of the Atlantic Wall. The pages of the *Fitchburg Sentinel* extolled the righteousness of national society with a crucial reminder. D-Day became reality thanks to the newfound loyalties of immigrants willing to serve, the schoolboy who worked long evening hours on the farm during his father's absence, and the daughter who overcame the challenges of polio to travel to high school. All of these manners of citizens "taught others how the human spirit can conquer insurmountable obstacles."[463]

"To know what one is fighting for is as much a part of a soldier's equipment as his weapons," noted Lt. Gen. John C. H. Lee, Deputy Theater Commander. In eloquent terms, Lee summarized the anti-authoritarian doctrine echoed in so many newspapers. "We fight for the right to lock our house doors and be sure that no bully with official sanctions will break the lock. We fight for schools built on a foundation of books— not bayonets." The ability of the editor to write what he pleases, the wish of the radio announcer to voice his opinions, the choice to read books and papers regardless of politics, the desire to listen to music notwithstanding the composer's race—these were among America's reasons for fighting a war that would claim 418,500 of its citizens. "These rights, these privileges, these traditions are precious enough to die for," concluded Lee. "They are not easily won."[464]

Americans were not oblivious to their own shortcomings. Yet 1944 offered hopes of magnanimity. "Whatever our domestic differences, we can try to give them teamwork as good as they are giving each other," opined South Dakota's *Evening Huronite* on June 13. "We can try to match their spirit and discipline and courage in the job that matters most. There is still much to be done at the beginning of the end."[465]

Newspapers offered a vision of a world not as it was but as it could be. With views of promise also emerged words of caution. "Someday the world must recognize that economic friction leads directly to war," penned David Lawrence of U. S. News. Reason and empathy crumbled in the wake of fascism's avarice and division, leading to the "intense economic nationalism" that empowered Hitler's empire. "Man has not learned to live in peace because man has not learned to live under any law of compensation except that which is figured in terms of money and material things." Not until man recognized life as a finite resource could he strive toward an enduring peace. The ambitions of human existence needed to transcend the pursuit of self-interest. D-Day could steer the chase for that sweeping dream.[466]

Such was the hope of Capt. Fred A. Bigelow, who had different cause to celebrate on June 6. His newborn, Barbara Arleen, entered life in Chicago at 6 a.m. that morning—the sixth baby born in the city on D-Day. For Barbara Arleen's sake, her father prayed for a world never again to be consumed by the fires of war.[467]

The lofty themes of peace resonated in the minds of American GIs as they endured the squalor of the French battlefront. Pooling soldierly emotions, *Stars and Stripes* sponsored an essay contest entitled "Why We Fight." T/5 Jack J. Zurofsky of Brooklyn received a $100 war bond for his winning entry, part of which read:

I fight because it is my fight.

I fight because my eyes are unafraid to look into other eyes; because they have seen happiness and because they have seen suffering; because they are curious and searching; because they are free.

I fight because I believe in progress—not reaction, be-cause—despite our faults, there is hope in our manner of life, because if we lose there is no hope.

I fight because only by fighting today will there be peace tomorrow. [468]

A great crusade indeed.

JARED FREDERICK

EPILOGUE

A Distant Shore

Normandy's bucolic pastures and dense hedgerows were silent. The countryside's many apple trees added splashes of seasonal color to the drab landscape of war. The chirps of the Goldcrest rang from the vibrant branches. French vacationers jubilantly returned to their beaches with lunch baskets and calvados in hand. No longer threatened by enemies lurking in the brush, Lt. Stanley R. Seltzer paced the French orchards with a carefree grace not felt since England. The trials of the beachhead seemed far behind the young engineer who now contemplated the future. "Will our sons sit here in newer uniforms with more destructive weapons in years to come?" he wondered. The avoidance of future calamity would require vigilance and literacy, he thought. Most importantly, America's children must recognize the harsh price paid on their behalf. "Here today in fields bent with the blast of shells and still carry the odor of decay of the dead," wrote Seltzer, "we have become educated to the responsibility that is ours to the world of tomorrow." The nation need not deploy a third generation to the trenches of Europe.[469]

Few tangibles of war are more evocative than the dead it produces. Medic John Worthman, among countless others, was long haunted by the experience. "The dead and dying," he wrote, "behind all the hedgerows was an appalling sight. So was the aroma. The smells became worse, the sights of mutilation and death more terrible, but strangely, we began to live with them and accept them." For some, this numbness produced longstanding psychological anguish. Thirty-five years before Post-Traumatic Stress Disorder became a clinical term, many on the home front realized their once-innocent boys would return as changed men. "They are giving their all—their futures, their hopes, their dreams, their lives," wrote Ruth Taylor in her religious column of Alabama's *Cullman Banner*. "Those who come back will not be the same

247

for they will have passed through the refiner's fire. They will have become so accustomed to death, that it will be hard for them to face life. They will have laid their youth as sacrifice upon the altar." Many bore these invisible scars of battle for decades to follow.[470]

Accompanying perceptions of war casualties stirred vivid emotions. The white crosses and stars dotting the greenery of Colleville-sur-Mer and elsewhere helplessly water the eyes of even those born long after the war. "France will always be part of America because of the dead that lie in French soil—soil hallowed anew by the bodies of those who were or should have been their sons," observed the *Philadelphia Tribune*. Yanks waged two world wars to prove it.[471]

Although the press often shielded readers from the horrid imagery of mangled bodies, it could do little to spare them from the staggering human costs. Perpetual mourning became a staple of American wartime culture as death notices appeared in papers and gold stars were solemnly hung from parlor windows. Beyond drawing meaning from the premature demise of their youth, citizens sought to honor the fallen in ways both humble and grandiose. Rekindling Lincolnian rhetoric to assuage heartache with purpose, the aggrieved symbolically resurrected their dead sons and husbands as the exemplars of democratic virtue. The combatants may have been physically dead, but their demise fostered determination amongst the living in earnest terms. *Let them not have died in vain.*

Throughout 1944, war correspondent Hal Boyle searched for a young sailor named John Norbert Murphy. The seaman's sister was married to Boyle's older brother. Kin thus encouraged the roving reporter to seek out Murphy. In early July, Boyle found him . . . in Plot B, Row Five, Grave 84 of the Normandy cemetery. "Into the mound of earth was a stake to which was wired his identifying dog tag," Boyle lamented. Also visible was "a withered Normandy rose left there by French peasants who have put a flower over each of the 2,000 American graves in the cemetery." A witness told Boyle the boy had been instantly killed by an enemy flak gun. An abandoned 88-mm stood several hundred yards away with its barrel raised skyward. Boyle wondered if it was the gun that claimed Murphy's promising life.

"We were badly mauled that day," Murphy's commander remarked. His naval beach battalion was embroiled in a struggle so fierce that it essentially became a "backstop" for slowly-advancing infantrymen. In retrospect, another comrade of Murphy noted, "I saw him just before he came ashore here. He wasn't worried. He never talked much except about his girl, Dolly, back in Kansas City, and his dad." They were just the words Boyle hoped to hear. Rarely were family members offered such stirring testimony of a loved one's final moments. Parents and spouses were all too often left to speculate. No measure of consolation could replace the void of the Murphy family, but Boyle at least offered a degree of closure—a comfort many families were sorrowfully denied.[472]

Laying the war dead to eternal rest was a poignant process of logistics. Less than a week after D-Day, Howard Cowan witnessed the first mass burial of invasion victims in England's Brookwood American Cemetery. "Rows of flag-covered caskets of brown, polished wood lay at the bottom of mass graves opened by a steel-jawed steam shovel," he observed. "As a double column of officers and enlisted men led by five chaplains approached in a slow march, the English operator of the steam shovel stood silently in his cab, his hand clutching his cap, his black hair blowing in the wind." The brisk ceremony denoted the "increased tempo" of combat along the French coast.

Cowan bummed a jeep ride to the burial ground with Capt. Sumner Johnson, a 9th Air Force chaplain. The drive was a quiet one; neither of the men expected the morning to be pleasant. Walking into Brookwood, Cowan gasped. Here already rested several hundred American dead from the Great War. An ornate, white stone chapel with opulent pillars and gold trim guarded over them. The phrase "With God Is Their Reward" was carved in the sanctuary. Surrounding pine trees scented the chilled English breeze. Walls of perfectly sculpted rhododendrons secluded the garden of headstones. The cemetery "must be one of the most beautiful in the world," Cowan thought.

The lone civilian mourner present was a young British woman, "eyes red and puffy from weeping, stood in the road a few feet away, and chewed nervously at a wrinkled handkerchief." She was attending the funeral of her husband, an American P-38 pilot. Four planes from the husband's squadron flew over in echelon, with one ceremoniously disappearing into the sky. "We stood at attention and saluted while a firing squad set the hills echoing with three volleys," Cowan continued. "Swelling and then fading as the wind rose and died came the answering taps from the far side of the hill, where the flag stood at half-mast before the white chapel with its ivy-clad columns." By summer's end, the cemetery would be full.[473]

Ironically, one of the more fortunate outfits on D-Day was a Graves Registration unit—an entity tasked with cataloging and burying American dead. "We were just lucky—we didn't have a single casualty," said Pvt. James F. White, a former railroader from Kentucky who spent twelve hours stranded on the beachhead. "I was glad I was six feet one and a half inches tall when we slid into water up to our shoulders and started wading ashore carrying our carbines," confessed White. "But when we hit that beach, I would have been glad to have been a midget."

"We saw men all around us being killed," added platoon leader Lt. Robert E. Berry, a career undertaker whose first military mission was to recover the dead of Pearl Harbor.

By D+3, the burial party interred 457 men who perished on Omaha Beach. Sometimes the crew converted the incomplete graves into foxholes to evade ongoing enemy fire. When the barrages subsided, Graves Registration placed the corpses in tidy rows in a former minefield. "Then we started processing the bodies—that is, identifying them fully and removing personal effects for shipment home," White continued. "We do everything possible to check the dead man's identity—even list the laundry marks in his clothing if there is any doubt about who he is." The ghastly number of dead quickly overwhelmed the small unit of eighteen—so much so that the men had engineers excavate a long, four-foot deep burial trench with a bulldozer. As the remains were placed in the pit, one dog tag remained on each body and another was nailed to a stake.

"It is a hard, tough job to collect and bury dead properly—one nobody wants and which we didn't ask for. But somebody had to do it and we were assigned to it," White told Boyle. No matter how thoroughly uniforms were scrubbed, the odor of death constantly clung to the grave diggers.[474]

The scene was pitifully gut-wrenching—teenagers and twenty-somethings stretched lifelessly on their backs with puddles of personal belongings scattered beside them. The smell was overpowering. GIs kept their side arms at ready to scatter animal scavengers. Time and again correspondents were drawn to the macabre tableau. Standing over these mounds of fresh dirt, one could gain a sense of what the invasion truly was. "They lie here mutely," observed the Associated Press, "waiting while troops dig long trenches for temporary mass burial. Nearby, also awaiting burial are the bodies of 10 Germans and two Britons. Negro troops digging these common graves labor silently with an occasional awed glance at the stiff forms under the white covers that had been thrown over them." Unlike Brookwood, the cemetery was neither aesthetically beautiful nor manicured. Its tragic beauty was instead found in its many unwritten stories of "men who will not fight again."[475]

The cemetery was officially established on July 11, 1944. The battle-tested ranks of the 29th Infantry Division stood with bowed heads under gray skies as Maj. Gen. Charles Gerhardt, division commander, offered elegiac praise. "The men that lie here I have seen personally on many occasions on the battlefield," he remarked. "They are comrades in arms in this division and we do honor to their supreme sacrifice for liberty today."

Following a sobering twenty-one-gun salute and an emotional rendition of the "Star-Spangled Banner," Gerhardt shouted, "Now let these brave dead hear the battle cry of the division!"

"Let's go!" the formation cried in unison.

The cemetery gravel crunched under the pivot of the men's tattered boots. The band played on. The soldiers of the "Blue and the Gray" Division marched off, slogging ever-closer to Brest, the Elbe, and home.[476]

The Yanks were not alone in their efforts to grant liberators fitting memorials. One elderly French couple buried sixteen American paratroopers, constructed white crosses, and tenderly decorated the humble plots with flowers and pink ribbons. Such gestures did not go unnoticed. Despite infrequent reports that the French were unappreciative and lazy, United Press reporter Richard McMillan thought quite the contrary. "Without exception I have found them grateful for liberation," he wrote. "This has been a spontaneous expression on the part of a people, many of whom could look around and see nothing but ruin. Homes, shops, farms, livestock—everything they held dear, even their relatives and friends—might have been crushed under the heel of war, but they still thanked us for bringing that which they did not dwell with before—freedom."[477]

On the opposite side of the Atlantic, additional emotional trials developed in every American town. Beginning around the Fourth of July, thousands of parents and wives received the dreadful onslaught of

Western Union telegrams. The concise but distressing notes often began with the bone-chilling phrase, "The Secretary of War desires me to express his deep regret. . . ." Few scenes on the home front were more frightful than a bicycled messenger boy pedaling up one's sidewalk. In most instances, summaries of harrowing telegram messages appeared in hometown newspapers the next day. The following announcement from the *Times* in Salisbury, Maryland exemplifies the many newspaper notices of that bittersweet summer:

> *"Salisburians Die in France, One On D-Day"*
> Salisbury Times - *July 7, 1944*
> *Two Salisburians fighting with the 29th Division in France have been killed in action and six others from this city and Wicomico County have been wounded in the European, Mediterranean, and Pacific war zones.*
> *Killed in France were:*
> *Staff Sgt. Ernest Lawrence Esham and Pfc. Johnnie C. Long. . . . Sgt. Esham, 35, member of Company I for 18 years, landed on the Normandy Peninsula on D-Day. Long served in Company B of the 29th Division and met death during the first few hours of the invasion. He was brother of City Police Officer Carl H. Esham.*
> *Pfc. Long, father of a 16-month-old son he has never seen, was killed on June 12 while fighting with Company I. His mother is Arra Davis, 206 Arch St.*
> *In the last letter his mother received from Sgt. Esham, dated 3 days before the invasion began, he wrote:*
> *"If I don't come back take care of Billy, but I am coming back." Billy is Sgt. Esham's 15-year-old son, Charles William Esham, Wicomico High School student.*
> *Before the time Company I was formalized, Sgt. Esham and his brother Carl, city motorcycle patrolman, were the two oldest ranking sergeants in the company.*
> *Pfc. Long, who was 23 years-old on June 2, ten days before he was killed, was the husband of Helen Taylor Long, now living with her parents in Bloxom. Their 16-month-old son, John Jr., never saw his father.*[478]

The residents of Lowell, Massachusetts read a similarly compelling namesake tragedy exactly one month after their community's air raid siren heralded the invasion. The parents of twenty-six-year-old 1st Lt. John J. Shaughnessy received a telegram on July 6 indicating that their son was among the dead. A veteran of North Africa and recipient of the Purple Heart, Shaughnessy was cut down by enemy fire while wading ashore with the Big Red One. John J. O'Donnell, the uncle for which Shaughnessy was named, was killed on a naval destroyer in 1918. For several families, history had the terrible tendency of repeating itself.[479]

The wife of thirty-four-year-old Pfc. Herbert Bachant received ambiguous news that was no less discomforting. Muriel Bachant of the Bronx was delivered a telegram revealing her husband was missing in action in France. The wife prayed he was captured "because I just couldn't believe anything else," she admitted. "I hope the Americans will get him back from the Germans as we advance, and then I hope they'll send him home."

Three months prior to D-Day, the twenty-two-year-old Mrs. Bachant gave birth to three girls. Sporting pink sun suits, the blue-eyed triplets crawled in the playpen of their three-room apartment when their tormented mother poured her heart out to a *New York Times* writer. Immediately before the invasion, Herbert wrote home, "I understand I have quite a family. I'm glad they're so big and strong. Nothing will give me greater pleasure than to see my little girls grow up. I'm praying that I may soon see you and the family."

Herbert Raymond Bachant was killed in action on August 1, 1944 near Rennes while serving with the 4th Armored Division. A widely-publicized photo of the three daughters he never met was incorporated into a hugely successful war bond drive dedicated in the father's honor. The triplets—Janet, Karen, and Nancy—traveled to France in 2014 to mark the seventieth anniversary of their father's demise and the liberation he symbolized. "This will close the circle," said Nancy.[480]

In other instances, war reporters were compelled to write of the passing of friends. By late July, the *Chicago Tribune*'s Robert Cromie ventured daily into the cratered ruins of the French countryside where dead men and artillery were arranged in a "foolish ménage." An officer informed Cromie that a correspondent had been killed in a friendly fire incident earlier that afternoon. The reporter cautiously inched toward the front in search of his colleague. Who would it be? He gingerly stepped over dead GIs with blown off limbs and gaping holes punched through their mangled bodies. Cromie then spotted a war photographer's patch amidst the jumble of bloodied uniforms. It was Bede Irvin. The fallen Associated Press cameraman had a note sticking out of his boot indicating identification.

Irvin was snapping photos when a misplaced bomb from an American B-26 Marauder fell nearby. Lt. Gen. Lewis H. Brereton of the 9th Air Force commented of the photographer's passing, "Mr. Irvin's death, which I understand is the first casualty among American civilian war correspondents in the present campaign, can but serve to exemplify the role that he and his colleagues have played and will play in this war. He was an unarmed observer who, heedless of personal danger, flew with us, lived with us, and worked with us that through the medium of his profession he might bring home to all of us the truths of war." Sadly, Irvin would not be the last to fall.[481]

Before war's end, avid newspaper readers suffered a jarring blow when a general's April 18, 1945 press release indicated, "I regret to report that War Correspondent Ernie Pyle, who made such a great contribution to the morale of our foot soldier, was killed in the battle of Ie Shima today." Shot right under the rim of his helmet by a Japanese sniper, Pyle ascended to saintly status in death. Normandy was only one of many invasions he witnessed in his vibrant career, but ultimately, he witnessed one too many. Pyle was forty-four. "I was so impressed with Pyle's coolness, calmness and his deep interest in enlisted men. They have lost their best friend," lamented a fellow reporter. At the site of his death, grief-stricken infantrymen erected a simple whitewashed sign which said all that needed to be said:

AT THIS SPOT
The 77th Infantry Division
Lost a Buddy
ERNIE PYLE
18 April 1945

The humble epitaph was all Pyle could have asked for. "People found it hard to believe that he was gone," mourned Howard Handelman of the INS. "His death saddened the nation."[482]

By D-Day+365, the war in Europe was over and Japan was panting its final breaths. Sgt. Dewitt Gilpin of *Yank* magazine pondered the dramatic change of scenery at Omaha Beach. "Only the sun and the wind now rake the long beaches of Normandy, and kids with toy shovels play in the sands where a year ago great armies came by sea. From scarred pillboxes, silent coastal guns point aimlessly down the beaches that on June 6, 1944, were covered with dead Americans." The pocked emplacements and rusted hulls offshore remained, but the French had their country back—mostly. Beyond Omaha were "fields and apple trees, lush and inviting." Yet nobody dared enter them. Nearby signs still warned, "Achtung! Minen!"[483]

Don Whitehead also revisited the battlegrounds in June 1945. In the American cemetery he encountered a French family who had received a letter from the mother of James Simonian of New York. The mother requested that a letter to her dead son be read over his grave. Teary eyed, a girl named Hélène Chapelle translated aloud, "My dearest and unfortunate son, on June 16, 1944, like a lamb you died and left me alone without hope. Day and night I weep and grieve and miss you and still you are gone." Mrs. Simonian, too, was a casualty of Normandy.[484]

In the ensuing years, writers and journalists revisited D-Day as the story of the age. An American Valhalla, Normandy evolved as a cultural and commercial Mecca for veterans and their Baby Boomer children. While observing D-Day's 1954 anniversary, former 2nd Ranger Battalion commander James Earl Rudder returned to the heights of Pointe du Hoc he had scaled a decade prior to dismantle enemy guns. Now employed by an aviation company, he had grown heavier and exchanged his olive drabs for a gray overcoat and fedora. Alongside the aging colonel was his fourteen-year old son, Bud, and *Collier*'s gifted writer W. C. Heinz. In wonderful detail, Heinz presented a multigenerational tale of mature introspection juxtaposed with childlike curiosity.

"Hey, Daddy!" the son shouted as they explored the base of the Pointe. "Come here."

The adventuresome boy had joyously discovered a rusted metal hook jutting between the rocks and tall grasses.

"A grapnel," Rudder declared with an outstretched hand. "One of the grapnels." The six-pronged hook, roughly the size of a small anchor, shot Ranger rope up the cliff on that misty June morning in 1944.

"This is amazing," the colonel marveled. "After ten years you can walk back here and find one of the grapnels on the ground."

"Can we take it home?" inquired the son, dressed in a red sweater and blue jeans.

"Certainty we'll take it home," Rudder replied, "This must be the last of those grapnels."

He gazed up in wonderment. "Will you tell me how we did this?" he asked Heinz. "Anybody would be a fool to try this. It was crazy then, and it's crazy now."[485]

Another decade later, Dwight Eisenhower still pondered that same mesmerizing question. His admired generalship propelled him to the presidency—a scenario unlikely to have occurred had Overlord failed. Unlike most moviegoers, he held the 1962 D-Day blockbuster *The Longest Day* in contempt. Now in his golden years, the old general roamed Normandy's beaches and burial grounds with Walter Cronkite's CBS News crew in anticipation of the invasion's twentieth anniversary. From Southwick House to a jeep excursion on Normandy's beaches, the two icons of the Cold War era traced the invasion's many steps. The interviews powerfully culminated in the American cemetery. As the ancient commander-in-chief gazed out upon the 9,388 tombstones, he confessed, "I devoutly hope that we will never again have to see such scenes as these. I think and hope and pray that humanity will learn more than we had learned up to that time. But these people gave us a chance, and they bought time for us, so that we can do better than we have before." In Eisenhower's view, the strategy of peace should not be a dream but a promise.[486]

Omar Bradley returned to Normandy as well. The general spent three days at Omaha, roaming the beach and burial grounds. The battle seemed so long ago. "It was hard to believe that so many lives, and so much effort, and such bravery on the part of so many had gone into gaining a five-mile sliver of land." He reflected on the campaign's costs every day. "That chilly morning off the coast of Normandy left with me many memories that the intervening 20 years have not dimmed," he admitted in a *Stars and Stripes* retrospective.[487]

By 1964, the makings of the Vietnam War were in progress; yet not even that controversial conflict would dampen the enduring allure of D-Day in American consciousness.

Even so, the nature of reporting war had changed in those two decades. Wartime readers at home in the 1940s were largely oblivious to
the daily trials and tribulations of military life. Correspondents, generally erring on the side of optimism for the benefit of national morale,
guardedly withheld many terrors they witnessed. In 1977, writer John
Steinbeck let the cat out of the bag. "We were all part of the war effort,"
he confessed of newsmen. "We went along with it, and not only that, we
abetted it. . . . I don't mean that the correspondents were liars. . . . It is
in the things not mentioned that the untruth lies." Their chronicles of
the war largely omitted unsavory tales of the incompetents, cowards,
racists, looters, and rapists who comprised small portions of the Allied
armies. By the 1970s, such secrets of military life could no longer be
brushed under the rug in an age of television.

Patriotic censorship during World War II was a key factor in determining what Americans of the time read in their newspapers. "The foolish reporter who broke the rules would not be printed at home," Steinbeck continued, "and in addition would be put out of the theater by the
command." Nonetheless, reporters embodied the ideal of truth even
when the system strove to prevent it. Correspondents' heated (and often
unsuccessful) feuds with censors indicated their intentions to convey an
accurate picture to the masses. Though often hindered, their efforts
were far from meaningless.[488]

In June 1981, a handful of D-Day correspondents convened at Ohio
University for a reunion. By that point, half of World War II's reporters
had passed away. Jack Thompson, formerly of the *Chicago Tribune*, interpreted the gathering as a last hurrah. With a scotch and water in
hand, he thoughtfully told Douglas Kneeland of the *New York Times*,
"War, I'm sorry to say, is a very exhilarating experience. Everything
else is a little bit duller. The war experience binds together those who
have experienced it in a way that's not possible in any other kind of
experience."

Thompson had no regrets. He was honored to have been on Omaha
Beach and grateful to have survived. "German shell fire was landing
everywhere. I was petrified with fear and holding my typewriter in front
of my face," he admitted. "I was there when Col. George Taylor said:
'Gentlemen, we are being killed on this beach. Let us move inland and
be killed.' In about two hours we were inland. I don't know whether it
was his speech, but those are the kind of things history is made of and

I was there to hear it and write it." Thompson gladly would have endured it all again.[489]

Half a century after the fact, Normandy veterans continued to honor their fallen brothers while also maintaining a spirited zest for life. On the fiftieth anniversary, forty-one silver-haired paratrooper veterans once again plummeted from Normandy's skies. The weathered warriors, average age seventy-two, stole the show from active duty paratroopers before a crowd of 30,000 adoring spectators. On this jump, the parachutists were greeted with roses and champagne rather than bullets and flak. Veteran Richard Tedesky of the Bronx (who described himself as "135 pounds of pulsating fury") nearly struck a cow on his descent. Regardless, this mission was easier than the original—even with his "arthritis and everyone wanting autographs." Meanwhile, the adventures of Earl Draper proved nearly as lethal as his actual D-Day experiences. He became tangled in his chords and his emergency chute opened automatically at 1,000 feet. The close call would have "made my father proud," Draper boasted.

Adventurer and stuntman Rene Dussaq, age eighty-three, was a former Office of Strategic Services operative who landed ahead of the invasion to partner with the French resistance. During the 1994 jump, the suave daredevil went missing for several hours and some assumed the worst. Fears were alleviated when he was later discovered in a nearby town signing autographs after winds swept him miles off course. He became perhaps the last of all Normandy mis-drops. In an equally cavalier mood, seventy-two-year-old Ed Manley shouted to a *Washington Post* reporter, "I've got two dates in Paris and one in Le Havre!"[490]

The pains and joys of the Normandy invasion continue to resonate, especially among the descendants of veterans. The astounding cultural impacts of *Saving Private Ryan* and *Band of Brothers* raised awareness and appreciation of World War II history not exhibited since the early 1960s. Veterans opened up to an eager public anxious to hear firsthand stories "of the last great invasion of the last great war." For some, it was too late. Granddaughters and grandsons who already lost their paps were left picking up pieces of family puzzles. First Sgt. John Samuel Colvin died the same year *Saving Private Ryan* brought cinema patrons to tears. Eleven years later, Colvin's grandson and *Newsweek* writer

Steve Tuttle sojourned to France hoping to trace portions of his grandfather's dangerous odyssey. Instead, he discovered obnoxious tourists in Speedos and gift shops rife with trivial knickknacks. The power of place did not resonate.

Not until Tuttle discovered a rich blackberry patch up a winding pathway stretching inland did his emotions let loose. "I picked a handful, and when I ate the first one my eyes welled up," he said. "I was reminded of how I used to climb up into the hills with my grandfather back home in rural Virginia and how we'd fill up white plastic milk jugs with blackberries and then rush them home so my grandmother could make us a drop-biscuit cobbler." Between bites of pie and gulps of fresh milk, the two casually discussed baseball and fishing. This was the stuff dreams were made of. Perhaps these are the memories survivors would prefer us to remember. "He made it home, unlike so many of his friends, and he got the chance to have grandchildren and a long, full life," Tuttle concluded. "That's what he'd been fighting for all along."[491]

Few sites in the United States evoke the seismic consequences of D-Day more than Bedford, Virginia. Nestled in the picturesque Blue Ridge Mountains, the community of 3,200 was like many small towns; everybody knew their neighbors, Main Street was the hub of life, the local newspaper was a civic compass. Bedford's commonness vanished in a heartbeat when townspeople learned of the deaths of twenty-two of their sons in Normandy—reportedly the highest per capita invasion loss of any town in the nation. The *Bedford Bulletin* offered what consolation it could, stating that the boys died for a "justice toward which mankind has been struggling since the dawn of time." The community thereafter became something of a lifeless shell. "People didn't feel like going out and doing things for a good while," reflected resident Marie Powers. No dances. No picnics. No laughing. For years, the town was shrouded by a cloak of grief too painful to endure. "It was such a sad time. It was terrible," said Powers. "But people loved one another, and people supported each other." Much of that melancholy was released in 2001 when Bedford become home of the impressive National D-Day Memorial.[492]

Even so, some Bedforders understandably cannot erase the anguish of the summer of '44. Lucille Hoback Boggess lost two of her brothers—Bedford and Raymond—on D-Day. They were one of thirty-three known pairs of brothers to participate in the invasion. Seventy years later, Boggess recalled the moment that forever changed her life.

Dedicated on the 57th anniversary of the Normandy invasion, the National D-Day Memorial in scenic Bedford, Virginia pays tribute to "the great crusade." Bedford lost twenty-two of its sons in the campaign. For many, the monument provided much-needed closure after decades of grief. (27)

"It was the middle of July before the telegrams started coming in," she told local reporters. A telegram regarding Bedford, who was engaged to a local girl, arrived on a Sunday. Notice of Raymond's death appeared the next day. "Getting one telegram was bad, but then getting a second, it was just more than my mother could handle," noted the sister who turned fifteen on June 8, 1944. Bedford rests in the American cemetery but his brother remains missing to this day. His bible was discovered by a GI on D+1 and was mailed to the Hobacks. Of her lost siblings, Boggess concluded, "My mother used to say, they left home together, and stayed together all through the service, they died together."493

The Hoback brothers were not the only siblings to share a common fate in Normandy. Henry and Louie Pieper were nineteen-year-old twins from Esmond, South Dakota who both served as radiomen second class on *LST 523*. Their ship collided with an underwater mine off Utah Beach two weeks after D-Day—killing them and 115 crewmates. Louie's body was recovered but Henry's remains were unidentified until 2017. After seventy-four years, the twins were reunited in burial at the Normandy American Cemetery. "They are finally together again, side by side, where they should be," announced their niece at the graveside service. [494]

Many families and survivors long sought to erase the psychological burdens of 1944. Leo "Boot" Scheer, a former Navy corpsman, witnessed unspeakable horrors as he attempted to save the lives of battered men on the beaches. He felt immeasurable guilt for having survived and for being unable to rescue more. "I was down . . . depressed, sad, just totally screwed up," Scheer told the *Washington Post* in 2014. "You think you're dead or going to die. And then you find out you're not. It's an emotional damned thing." He wrestled with those emotions until he finally concluded a guardian angel shielded him from the hail of shrapnel. Scheer subsequently traveled to Normandy twice and even flew on an Honor Flight to the National WWII Memorial in search of closure.

The old sailor shook the hands of grateful passersby and readily answered their inquiries.

"Was he on D-Day?" a tourist asked a guide. The reply was in the affirmative.

"Oh, my gosh," the visitor replied. "I can't imagine." [495]

Beyond lingering as a moving memory, World War II also serves as a potent warning. Dispirited by the perceived selfishness of Baby Boomers, modern political isolationism, and the dangers of nationalism, RAF veteran Harry Leslie Smith expressed concern in 2018 for the future of humanity. "It's why with the little time I have remaining on this earth," he announced, "I plan to journey to the refugee hot spots of the world and use my voice to end this crisis and teach people that xenophobia only leads to repression and war. On my 95th birthday, I will toast my longevity with sherry and declare that my last stand as a human being was to not go gently into the good night." Moral resolve hardly has to diminish with age. [496]

Fellow Briton Harold Bradley turned twenty-one the day he came ashore Sword Beach. The veteran minced few words in a seventieth anniversary interview for CNN: "It would be a dream to say stop wars but at least reduce them, because at the end of a war what have you got? No one's won anything. Millions dead and you still have the same problem." All the more reason to remember history, retorted S/Sgt. Jacques

Jones, who placed a wreath in the American cemetery that same day. "I don't want them to be forgotten," he said of his long-buried buddies. It is too early to forget. [497]

Dismissal of the past is unlikely in the small Normandy town of Les Ventes. At age twenty-one, 1st Lt. Billie Harris of the 355th Fighter Squadron was killed in a plane crash outside the town. Locals laid him to rest with the honors of war. By 1946, Harris was reinterred in the American cemetery overlooking Omaha. Widow Peggy Harris of Vernon, Texas coped with her husband's death for the next six decades. Her love remained steadfast; she never remarried. Peggy visited her husband's white headstone for the first time in 2006. She waited "All of my life," for this moment, she confessed.

Upon her arrival in Les Ventes, she noticed that a main village road was named after Billie. The townspeople filed in procession on that road every year to honor the pilot who symbolized their liberation. They placed flowers on his white cross and kept his memory vividly alive. Perhaps assuming Lt. Harris had no family, the residents embraced him as part of *their* family.

Standing in the woods where her husband met his fate, Peggy was overwhelmed. "How can I not be grateful and hold these people very dear?" she told CBS News.

Guy Surleau, the only living witness to the crash, regretted he could not have done more to save the American flyer.

Peggy assured Guy. "I like to think that he was still conscious enough to know that a friend stood by him," she muttered with tears gushing down her rose cheeks.

The people of Les Ventes are reminded of the Normandy invasion every time they walk their streets. Their lasting appreciation requires little explanation beyond the village sign marked *Place Billie D. Harris – Aviateur Américain, 1922-1944.*

"We don't forget," said the mayor of Les Ventes. [498]

How can we?

JARED FREDERICK

ACKNOWLEDGEMENTS

Dwight Eisenhower once admitted, "I could never face a body of officers without emphasizing one word—teamwork." Although my tasks proved far less consequential than his, I certainly related to the sentiment as I penned this book. Gratitude is due to a number of individuals who committed considerable time and effort to make *Dispatches of D-Day* a reality.

I wish to thank the talented historians who reviewed the manuscript and wrote advance testimonials for the project. They include Larry Alexander, Rick Beyer, Marcus Brotherton, Dr. Peter Caddick-Adams, R. C. George, Dr. Christian Keller, Martin Morgan, Dr. Craig Symonds, and Bob Welch—each of whom have contributed their own noteworthy studies to the vast scholarly canons of the Normandy invasion and military history. I stand on their shoulders. Likewise, my good friends and fellow reenactors Ryan Brown, Michael Carper, Thomas Frezza, and John Heiser frequently provided insights on issues ranging from period politics to GI life.

I express my deepest gratitude to my family who, as always, has wholeheartedly supported my various endeavors to better understand and convey the importance of history.

Finally, I owe immense credit to my agent and publisher, Greg Johnson, of WordServe Literary. Greg exhibited confidence in me from the outset and has been invaluable at every stage of the book's evolution. I embrace the opportunity to work with him again.

All those mentioned above made this a stronger book—and I sincerely thank them.

263

BIBLIOGRAPHY

Newspapers and Magazines

Abilene Reporter News – Texas
Ada Evening News – Oklahoma
Albert City Appeal – Iowa
Albert Lea Evening Tribune –
  Minnesota
Alton Evening Telegraph – Illinois
Altoona Mirror – Pennsylvania
Amarillo Daily News – Texas
Amarillo Globe – Texas
Anniston Star – Alabama
Argus-Leader – South Dakota
Atchison Daily Globe – Kansas
Athens Messenger – Ohio
Atlanta Daily World – Georgia
Austin Daily Texan – Texas
Austin Summer Texan – Texas
Bakersfield Californian – California
Bath Independent – Maine
Beatrice Daily Sun – Nebraska
Beckley Raleigh Register –
  West Virginia
Bedford Gazette – Pennsylvania
Benton Harbor News Palladium –
  Michigan
Biddeford Daily Journal – Maine
Big Spring Daily Herald – Texas
Bonham Daily Favorite – Texas
Bowie News – Texas
Bradford Era – Pennsylvania
Brownsville Herald – Texas
Burlington Hawk Eye Gazette – Iowa
Canyon News – Texas
Carthage Panola Watchman – Texas
Cedar Rapids Gazette – Iowa
Centralia Evening Sentinel – Illinois
Charleroi Mail – Pennsylvania
Charleston Gazette – West Virginia
Chicago Defender – Illinois
Chicago South End Reporter – Illinois
Chicago Tribune – Illinois
Circleville Herald – Ohio
Clearfield Progress – Pennsylvania

Collier's Weekly – New York
Comanche Chief – Texas
Coshocton Tribune – Ohio
Council Bluffs Iowa Nonpareil – Iowa
Cullman Banner – Alabama
Cumberland News – Maryland
Daily Herald Suburban Chicago –
  Illinois
Daily Kennebec Journal – Maine
Daily Spectrum – Utah
Delta Democrat Times – Mississippi
Denton Record Chronicle – Texas
Dothan Eagle – Alabama
DuBois Daily Express – Pennsylvania
East Liverpool Review – Ohio
Edwardsville Intelligencer – Illinois
Eugene Guard – Oregon
Evening Independent – Ohio
Findlay Republican Courier – Ohio
Fitchburg Sentinel – Massachusetts
Fort Madison Evening Democrat –
  Iowa
Frederick News – Maryland
Fredericksburg Standard – Texas
Galveston Daily News – Texas
Gettysburg Star and Sentinel –
  Pennsylvania
Gettysburg Times – Pennsylvania
Golfdom – Ohio
Greeley Daily Tribune – Colorado
Hamilton Daily News Journal – Ohio
Hanover Evening Sun – Pennsylvania
Hattiesburg American – Mississippi
Healdsburg Tribune – California
High Point Enterprise –
  North Carolina
Hull Daily Mail – Yorkshire
Huntingdon Daily News –
  Pennsylvania
Hutchinson News Herald – Kansas
Independent – London

Indiana Evening Gazette –
 Pennsylvania
Jefferson City News and Tribune –
 Missouri
Joplin News Herald – Missouri
Kannapolis Daily Independent –
 North Carolina
Kingsport News – Tennessee
Kingsville Record – Texas
Laredo Times – Texas
Lawrence Daily Journal World –
 Kansas
Lebanon Daily News – Pennsylvania
Liberty Vindicator – Texas
Life – New York
Lima News – Ohio
Lincoln Nebraska State Journal –
 Nebraska
London Daily Express – London
Long Beach Independent – California
Los Angeles Times – California
Lowell Sun – Massachusetts
Lubbock Morning Avalanche – Texas
Mabank Banner – Texas
Madison State Journal – Wisconsin
Marion Star – Ohio
Maryville Daily Forum – Missouri
McKean County Democrat –
 Pennsylvania
Miami Daily News Record – Oklahoma
Moberly Monitor Index – Missouri
Moorhead Daily News – Minnesota
Nevada State Journal – Nevada
New Castle News – Pennsylvania
Newport Mercury – Rhode Island
New York Daily News – New York
New York Times – New York
New York World Telegram – New York
Nippon Times – Tokyo, Japan
North Adams Transcript –
 Massachusetts
Oakland Tribune – California
Ogden Standard Examiner – Utah
Ottumwa Daily Courier – Iowa
Philadelphia Inquirer – Pennsylvania
Piqua Daily Call – Ohio

Pittsburgh Courier – Pennsylvania
Pittsburgh Post-Gazette –
 Pennsylvania
Pittsfield Berkshire County Eagle –
 Massachusetts
Port Arthur News – Texas
Portsmouth Herald – New Hampshire
Raleigh Register – West Virginia
Rapids Daily Tribune – Wisconsin
Ruthven Free Press – Iowa
Salt Lake Tribune – Utah
San Antonio Light – Texas
San Diego Union-Tribune – California
Sandusky Register Star News – Ohio
San Mateo Times – California
Santa Fe New Mexican – New Mexico
Sikeston Herald – Missouri
Somerset Daily American –
 Pennsylvania
Southtown Economist – Illinois
St. Joseph Herald Press – Michigan
St. Louis Post-Dispatch – Missouri
Stars and Stripes – London
Sweetwater Nolan County News –
 Texas
Syracuse Herald Journal – New York
Taylor Daily Press – Texas
Thomasville Times Enterprise –
 Georgia
Time – New York
Tipton Tribune – Indiana
Troy Record – New York
Tucson Daily Citizen – Arizona
Uniontown Morning Herald –
 Pennsylvania
USA Today – Washington, D. C.
Valley Morning Star – Texas
Valparaiso Vidette Messenger –
 Indiana
Vashon-Maury Island Beachcomber –
 Washington
Victoria Advocate – Texas
Warren Times Mirror – Pennsylvania
Washington Evening Journal – Iowa
Washington Post – Washington, D. C.
Waterloo Daily Courier – Iowa

Wellsboro Gazette – Pennsylvania
Whitewright Sun – Texas
Wichita Daily Times – Texas
Wilson Daily Times – North Carolina

Yank – London
Youngstown Vindicator – Ohio
Zanesville Signal – Ohio

Books

Alkebulan, Paul. *The African American Press in World War II: Toward Victory at Home and Abroad.* Lanham, MD: Lexington Books, 2014.

Astor, Gerald. *June 6, 1944: The Voices of D-Day.* New York: St. Martin's Press, 1994.

Atkinson, Rick. *The Guns at Last Light: The War in Western Europe, 1944-1945.* New York: Henry Holt, 2013.

Baer, Alfred E., Jr. *D-For-Dog: The Story of a Ranger Company.* Self-published, 1946.

Balkoski, Joseph. *Omaha Beach: D-Day, June 6, 1944.* Mechanicsburg, PA: Stackpole Books, 2004.

_____. *Utah Beach: The Amphibious Landing and Airborne Operations on D-Day.* Mechanicsburg, PA: Stackpole Books, 2006.

Bando, Mark. *Avenging Eagles: Forbidden Tales of the 101st Airborne Division in World War 2.* Mark Brando Publishing, 2006.

Barbier, Mary. *D-Day Deception: Operation Fortitude and the Normandy Invasion.* Mechanicsburg, PA: Stackpole, 2009.

Baumgarten, Harold. *D-Day Survivor: An Autobiography.* Gretna, LA: Pelican Publishing, 2006.

Beevor, Antony. *D-Day: The Battle for Normandy.* New York: Penguin Books, 2009.

Bennett, G. H. *Destination Normandy: Three American Regiments on D-Day.* Westport, CT: Praeger Security International, 2007.

Berthon, Simon. *Allies at War: The Bitter Rivalry Among Churchill, Roosevelt, and De Gaulle.* New York: Carroll & Graf Publishers, 2001.

Bradley, Holbrook. *War Correspondent: From D-Day to the Elbe.* Lincoln, NE: iUniverse, 2007.

Brée, Germaine, and George Bernauer. *Defeat and Beyond: An Anthology of French Wartime Writing, 1940-1945.* New York: Pantheon, 1970.

Caldwell Sorel, Nancy. *The Women Who Wrote the War.* New York: Arcade Publishing, 1999.

Campbell, Doon. *Magic Mistress: A 30 Year Affair with Reuters.* London: Tagman Press, 2000.

Carafano, James Jay. *After D-Day: Operation Cobra and the Normandy Breakout.* Mechanicsburg, PA: Stackpole Books, 2000.

Carse, Robert. *Dunkirk 1940: A History.* Englewood Cliffs, NJ: Prentice-Hall, 1970.

Casey, Steven. *The War Beat, Europe: The American Media at War Against Nazi Germany.* New York: Oxford University Press, 2017.

Collier, Richard. *Fighting Words: The Correspondents of World War II.* New York: St. Martin's Press, 1989.

Collins, W. L. George. *Into Fields of Fire: The Story of the 438th Troop Carrier Group During World War II.* Bloomington, IN: Xlibris Corporation, 2004.

Cousins, Jenny. *Somewhere in England: American Airmen in the Second World War.* London: The Imperial War Museum, 2015.

Cronkite, Walter. *A Reporter's Life.* New York: Alfred Knopf, 1996.

Cronkite, Walter IV, and Maurice Isserman. *Cronkite's War: His World War II Letters Home.* Washington, D. C.: National Geographic Society, 2013.

Culver, John C., and John Hyde. *American Dreamer: The Life and Times of Henry A. Wallace.* New York: W. W. Norton, 2001.

DePastino, Todd. *Bill Mauldin: A Life Up Front.* New York: W. W. Norton, 2008.

D'Este, Carlo. *Eisenhower: A Soldier's Life.* London: Cassell Military, 2004.

Dorsett, Lyle W. *Serving God and Country: U.S. Military Chaplains in World War II.* New York: Penguin, 2013.

Engel, Jeffrey A. *The Four Freedoms: Franklin D. Roosevelt and the Evolution of an American Idea.* Oxford: Oxford University Press, 2016.

Fussell, Paul. *Wartime: Understanding and Behavior in the Second World War.* New York: Oxford University Press, 1990.

Gay, Timothy. *Assignment to Hell: The War Against Nazi Germany with Correspondents Walter Cronkite, Andy Rooney, A. J. Liebling, Homer Bigart, and Hal Boyle.* New York: NAL Caliber, 2012.

Gellhorn, Martha. *The Face of War.* New York: Atlantic Monthly Press, 1988.

Gildea, Robert. *Fighters in the Shadows: A New History of the French Resistance.* London: Faber & Faber, 2015.

Graves, John. *Leadership Paradigms in Chaplaincy.* Irvine, CA: Universal-Publishers, 2007.

Grint, Keith. *Leadership, Management, and Command: Rethinking D-Day.* New York: Palgrave Macmillan, 2008.

Hambucken, Denis. *American Soldier of World War II – D-Day – A Visual Reference.* Woodstock, VT: The Countryman Press, 2013.

Hansen, Randall. *Fire and Fury: The Allied Bombing of Germany, 1942-1945.* New York: NAL Caliber, 2009.

Haskew, Michael E. *The Airborne in World War II: An Illustrated History of America's Paratroopers in Action.* New York: St. Martin's Press, 2017.

Hastings, Max. *Overlord: D-Day and the Battle for Normandy.* New York: Simon & Schuster, 1984.

Haswell, Jock. *D-Day: Intelligence and Deception.* New York: The *New York Times*, 1979.

Hervieux, Linda. *Forgotten: The Untold Story of D-Day's Black Heroes, at Home and at War.* New York: Harper Collins, 2015.

Honey, Maureen. *Creating Rosie the Riveter: Class, Gender, and Propaganda During World War II.* Amherst: University of Massachusetts, 1984.

Irwin, Will. *Abundance of Valor: Resistance, Survival, and Liberation: 1944-45.* New York: Ballantine Books, 2010.

Jones, Benjamin F. *Eisenhower's Guerrillas: The Jedburghs, the Maquis, and the Liberation of France.* Oxford: Oxford University Press, 2016.

Jordan, Robert Smith. *A Newsman Remembered: Ralph Burdette Jordan and His Times 1896-1953.* Bloomington, IN: iUniverse, 2011.

Kaufmann, J. E. and H. W. Kaufmann. *The American GI in Europe in World War II: The March to D-Day*. Mechanicsburg, PA: Stackpole Books, 2009.

Keegan, John. *Six Armies in Normandy: From D-Day to the Liberation of Paris*. New York: Penguin Books, 1994.

Kennedy, David M. *The American People in WWII: Freedom from Fear*. Oxford: Oxford University Press, 2004.

Kennedy, Paul M. *Engineers of Victory: The Problem Solvers Who Turned the Tide in the Second World War*. New York: Random House, 2013.

Kershaw, Alex. *The Bedford Boys: One American Town's Ultimate D-Day Sacrifice*. Cambridge, MA: Da Capo Press, 2003.

Kingseed, Cole C. *Conversations with Dick Winters: Life Lessons from the Commander of the Band of Brothers*. New York: Berkley Caliber, 2014.

Kloeber, Leonard. *Victory Principles: Leadership Lessons from D-Day*. New York: Morgan James Publishing, 2009.

Kluger, Steve. *Yank: World War II from the Guys Who Brought You Victory*. New York: St. Martin's Press, 1991.

Kruse, Kevin Michael, and Stephen G. N. Tuck. *Fog of War: The Second World War and the Civil Rights Movement*. New York: Oxford University Press, 2012.

Leff, Laura. *Buried by the Times: The Holocaust and America's Most Important Newspaper*. Cambridge: Cambridge University Press, 2005.

Lewis, Jon E. *Voices from D-Day: Eyewitness Accounts from the Battle for Normandy*. New York: MJF Books, 2014.

Library of America. *Reporting World War II: American Journalism 1938-1946*. New York: Literary Classics of the United States, Inc., 2001.

Manning, Molly Guptill. *When Books Went to War: The Stories That Helped Us Win World War II*. Waterville, ME: Thorndike, 2015.

Matzen, Robert. *Mission: Jimmy Stewart and the Fight for Europe*. Pittsburgh: GoodKnight Books, 2016.

Mayo, Jonathan. *D-Day: Minute by Minute*. New York: Simon & Schuster, 2014.

McIntosh, Al. *Selected Chaff: The Wartime Columns of Al McIntosh, 1941-1945*. Minneapolis, MN: Zenith Press, 2007.

McManus, John C. *The Americans at D-Day: The American Experience at the Normandy Invasion*. New York: Forge, 2005.

_____. *The Dead and Those about to Die: D-Day: The Big Red One at Omaha Beach*. New York: NAL Caliber, 2014.

Miller, Donald L. *D-Days in the Pacific*. New York: Simon & Schuster, 2005.

_____. *Masters of the Air: The Bomber Boys Who Fought the Air War Against Nazi Germany*. New York: Simon & Schuster, 2007.

Miller, Robert Earnest. *World War II Cincinnati: From the Front Lines to the Home Front*. Charleston, SC: The History Press, 2014.

Monahan, Evelyn, and Rosemary Neidel Greenlee. *And If I Perish: Frontline U. S. Army Nurses in World War II*. New York: Anchor, 2004.

Moore, Christopher Paul. *Fighting for America: Black Soldiers – The Unsung Heroes of World War II*. New York: Random House, 2007.

Moorehead, Carolina. *Selected Letters of Martha Gellhorn*. New York: Henry Holt and Company, 2007.

Morgan, Martin K. A. *The Americans on D-Day*. Minneapolis: Zenith Press, 2014.

Mort, Terry. *Hemingway at War: Ernest Hemingway's Adventures as a World War II Correspondent*. New York: Pegasus Books, 2016.

O'Donnell, Patrick K. *Dog Company: The Boys of Pointe du Hoc – The Rangers Who Accomplished D-Day's Toughest Mission and Led the Way Across Europe*. Boston: Da Capo, 2013.

Ohler, Norman. *Blitzed: Drugs in the Third Reich*. Boston: Mariner Books, 2018.

Olson, Lynn. *Last Hope Island: Britain, Occupied Europe, and the Brotherhood That Helped Turn the Tide of War*. New York: Random House, 2017.

Penrose, Jane (ed.). *The D-Day Companion: Leading Historians Explore History's Greatest Amphibious Assault*. Oxford: Osprey Publishing, 2004.

Pike, Francis. *Hirohito's War: The Pacific War, 1941-1945*. London: Bloomsbury, 2015.

Prados, John. *Normandy Crucible: The Decisive Battle that Shaped World War II in Europe*. New York: Dutton Caliber, 2012.

Pulwers, Jack E. *The Press of Battle: The GI Reporter and the American People*. Raleigh, NC: Ivy House Publishing Group, 2003.

Pyle, Ernest. *Brave Men*. New York: Grosset & Dunlop, 1945.

_____. *Ernie Pyle in England*. New York: R. M. McBride, 1941.

_____, and David Nichols. *Ernie's War: The Best of Ernie Pyle's World War II Dispatches*. New York: Simon & Schuster, 1987.

Rees, Laurence. *WWII Behind Closed Doors - Stalin, the Nazis and the West*. New York: Pantheon, 2008.

Roberts, Geoffrey. *Stalin's Wars from World War to Cold War, 1939-1953*. New Haven, Connecticut: Yale University Press, 2008.

Rommel, Erwin, Basil Henry Liddell Hart, and Paul Findlay. *The Rommel Papers*. New York: Da Capo, 2003.

Rooney, Andy. *My War*. New York: Public Affairs Books, 2000.

Ross, John. *The Forecast for D-Day: And the Weathermen behind Ike's Greatest Gamble*, Guilford, CT: Lyons Press, 2014.

Ryan, Cornelius. *The Longest Day: June 6, 1944*. New York: Simon & Schuster, 1959.

Sebba, Anne. *Les Parisiennes: How the Women of Paris Lived, Loved, and Died Under Nazi Occupation*. New York: St. Martin's Press, 2016.

Shapiro, Robert Moses (ed.). *Why Didn't the Press Shout? American & International Journalism During the Holocaust*. Jersey City: Yeshiva University Press and KTAV Publishing, 2003.

Sizer, Mona D. *The Glory Guys: The Story of the U.S. Army Rangers*. Lanham, MD: Taylor Trade Publications, 2009.

Smith, Howard K. *Last Train from Berlin:* London: Phoenix Press, 2000.

Sparrow, James T. *Warfare State: World War II Americans and the Age of Big Government*. New York: Oxford University Press, 2011.

Stafford, David. *Ten Days to D-Day: Countdown to the Liberation of Europe*. London: Little, Brown and Company, 2003.

Sterne, Joseph R. L. *Combat Correspondents: The* Baltimore Sun *in World War II*. Baltimore: The Maryland Historical Society, 2009.

Sweeney, Michael S. *Secrets of Victory: The Office of Censorship and the American Press and Radio in World War II*. Chapel Hill: University of North Carolina, 2001.

Symonds, Craig L. *Neptune: The Allied Invasion of Europe and the D-Day Landings*. New York: Oxford University Press, 2014.

Thomas, Evan. *Ike's Bluff: President Eisenhower's Secret Battle to Save the World*. New York: Little, Brown and Company, 2012.

Tobin, James. *Ernie Pyle's War: America's Eyewitness to World War II*. New York: Free Press, 2006.

Tolischus, Otto David. *They Wanted War*. New York: Reynal & Hitchcock, 1940.

Van Der Vat, Dan. *D-Day: The Greatest Invasion – A People's History*. New York: Bloomsbury, 2003.

War and Navy Departments. *A Short Guide to Great Britain*. Washington, D. C., 1943.

Whidden, Guy C., Julia Ann Whidden, and K. Bradley Whidden. *Between the Lines and Beyond: Letters of a 101st Airborne Paratrooper*. Self-published, 2009.

Whitehead, Don, and John B. Romeiser (ed.). *Beachhead Don: Reporting the War from the European Theater, 1942-1945*. New York: Fordham University Press, 2004.

Winik, Jay. *1944: FDR and the Year That Changed History*. New York: Simon & Schuster, 2015.

Womer, Jack, and Stephen C. DeVito. *Fighting with the Filthy Thirteen: The World War II Story of Jack Womer – Ranger and Paratrooper*. Havertown, PA: Casemate Publishers, 2012.

Websites

1st Battalion, 22nd Infantry, 4th Infantry Division: www.1-22infantry.org

591st (Antrim) Parachute Squadron, Royal Engineers: www.591-antrim-parachute.info

ABC News: www.abcnews.go.com

Ancestry – Newspapers & Publications: www.ancestry.com

Boise Guardian: www.boiseguardian.com

British Broadcasting Corporation (BBC): www.bbc.com

Catholic News Service: www.catholicnews.com

CBS News: www.cbsnews.com

CNN: www.cnn.com

D-Day Overlord – D-Day and Battle of Normandy Encyclopedia: www.dday-overlord.com

The Independent: www.independent.co.uk

Kansas Press Association: www.kspress.com

King's College of London War Memorials: www.kingscollections.org/warmemorials

Library of Congress Prints & Photographs Online Catalog: www.loc.gov/pictures

Los Angeles Times: www.latimes.com

National Archives and Records Administration: www.archives.gov

Naval History and Heritage Command: www.history.navy.mil

Newspaper Heroes on the Air: www.jheroes.com

Newsweek: www.newsweek.com
Operation Overlord – Landings and Battle of Normandy: www.6juin1944.com
The Peabody Awards: www.peabodyawards.com
Penn State University Libraries: www.libraries.psu.edu
       Chicago Defender, 1910-1975
       Chicago Tribune Historical (1849-1990)
       Japan Times Archives
       Newspaper Archive – Genealogy & Family History Records
       Pittsburgh Courier, 1911-2002
       Pittsburgh Post-Gazette, 1786-2003
       ProQuest Historical Newspapers: *New York Times*
Reuters: www.reuters.com
San Diego Tribune: www.sandiegotribune.com
Syracuse University Libraries: www.library.syr.edu
USA Today: www.usatoday.com
U. S. Army Quartermaster Museum: www.qmmuseum.lee.army.mil
Vashon-Maury Island Beachcomber: www.vashonbeachcomber.com
Washington Post: www.washingtonpost.com
WSET ABC 13: www.wset.com

Photo Credits

(1) Photo by Milton J. Pike, Library of Congress, LC-USZ62-61128.
(2) U. S. Army Signal Corps Photograph, National Archives, 111-SC-192100.
(3) National Archives, 44171526.
(4) U. S. Army Signal Corps Photo, National Archives, 111-C-1247.
(5) U. S. Army Signal Corps Photo, National Archives, 111-C-1258.
(6) U. S. Army Photograph, Library of Congress, LC-USZ62-25600.
(7) National Archives, Dwight D. Eisenhower Presidential Library, 186470.
(8) Victor A. Lundy Archive, Library of Congress, LOT 14007-3, no. 08.
(9) National Archives, Dwight D. Eisenhower Presidential Library, 186473.
(10) National Archives, 342-FH-51766AC.
(11) U. S. Coast Guard Photograph, National Archives, 26-G-2407.
(12) Official U. S. Navy Photograph, National Archives, 80-G-252940.
(13) Official U. S. Navy Photograph, National Archives, 80-G-252412.
(14) U.S. Navy Art Collection, Washington, D.C., KN-570.
(15) U. S. Army Signal Corps Photo, National Archives, SC 190062.
(16) National Archives, 18558249.
(17) U. S. Army Signal Corps Photo, National Archives, SC 320897.
(18) U.S. Navy Art Collection, Washington, D.C., KN-17825.
(19) U. S. Coast Guard Photograph, National Archives, 26-G-2397.
(20) Official U. S. Navy Photograph, National Archives, 80-G-45714.
(21) U. S. Coast Guard Photograph, National Archives, 26-G-2517.
(22) Office of War Information Collection, Library of Congress, LC-USW3- 054023-C.
(23) James T. Berryman Cartoons Collection, National Archives, 5743133.
(24) National Archives, 208-AA-32P-14.

(25) Office of War Information Collection, Library of Congress, LC-USW3-054043-C.
(26) Office of War Information Collection, Library of Congress, LC-USW3-054047-C-A.
(27) Photo by Carol M. Highsmith, Library of Congress, LC-DIG-highsm-04050.

ENDNOTES

Prologue: Dependence

[1] Horace Busby, "D-Day Has Passed – But Waiting Goes On," *Austin Daily Texan*, June 7, 1944, p. 1. Busby later became an adviser and speechwriter in the Lyndon Johnson Administration.
[2] Baer, 30. Alfred Baer, a member of the 2nd Ranger Battalion's D Company, offers a concise yet lively account of the Pointe du Hoc assault in this rare album compiled for his fellow veterans of the unit.
[3] Sweeney, 5, 9, 77; Leff, 239-240.
[4] "How Newspapers Told D-Day Story," *Ottumwa Daily Courier*, July 26, 1944, p. 15.
[5] "A Fateful Spring," *Stars and Stripes*, March 30, 1944, p. 2; Pulwers, 421-422.
[6] Ibid.
[7] Kluger, 179.
[8] DePastino, 106.
[9] Hanson W. Baldwin, "Advantages Balanced in Invasion Battles," *New York Times*, June 4, 1944, p. E5.
[10] "A Stake in the Future," *Stars and Stripes*, April 8, 1944, p. 2.
[11] Kluger, 163-164.
[12] Tolischus, 97-101.
[13] Sweeney, 3. Italics added by author.
[14] "Famous European Woman Journalist Talks On Freedom," *Uniontown Morning Herald*, April 17, 1944, p. 5.
[15] "World Free Press," *Denton Record Chronicle*, June 3, 1944, p. 6.
[16] "Freedom of the Press," *Abilene Reporter News*, March 12, 1944, p. 2.
[17] Engel (ed.) and Linda Eads, 40.
[18] "Await D-Day," *Evening Independent*, April 10, 1944, p. 2.
[19] Don Whitehead, "Foot Slogger Carries Ball in Big Push," *Stars and Stripes,* May 19, 1944, p. 1.
[20] Pierre J. Huss, "Invasion D-Day Will Bare The 'Secret Weapon' Help Score K. O.," *Lowell Sun*, March 17, 1944, p. 58.
[21] "Family Hero," *Lebanon Daily News*, March 1, 1944, p. 1.
[22] Fussell, 145.
[23] Pyle, *Ernie Pyle in England*, 1.
[24] Pyle, *Brave Men*, 470.

Chapter 1: Of Beer and Bombs

[25] "Ten-Shun!" *Troy Record*, March 1, 1944, p. 17.
[26] *A Short Guide to Great Britain*, 8.
[27] Allan M. Morrison, "Britain Goes About Its Business Calmly, Come Hell or Invasion," *Stars and Stripes*, May 16, 1944, p. 2.
[28] "Brothers Meet in English Camp," *Fredericksburg Standard*, April 12, 1944, p. 4; "Carroll Bros. – 2 Meet in England," *DuBois Daily Express*, April 10, 1944, p. 7.
[29] "To Give Wedding Gown," *Daily Kennebec Journal*, January 21, 1944, p. 8; "Weds Miss Leigh Mallory," *Stars and Stripes,* May 21, 1944, p. 2.
[30] "Welcome Mat laid Out For Stork Passengers," *Salt Lake Tribune*, March 5, 1944, p. 39.
[31] "Letter from English Girl," *Circleville Herald*, March 7, 1944, p. 5.

[32] "Our Neighbors," *Kingsville Record*, April 12, 1944, p. 7; "Ensign Billie Neel Writes Interesting Letter from England," *Comanche Chief*, May 19, 1944, p. 20.

[33] 1st Sgt. J. W. Collins, "1st Sergeant's Call," *Wichita Daily Times*, May 21, 1944, p. 21.

[34] Arthur W. White, "GIs Sleep on Floors, Chairs in London," *Stars and Stripes*, March 13, 1944, p. 1; "Hash Marks," *Stars and Stripes*, April 4, 1944, p. 2; "Private Breger," *Stars and Stripes*, March 27, 1944, p. 7.

[35] "With the Yanks," *Laredo Times*, May 11, 1944, p. 7.

[36] Collier, 138-141; Bennett, 37.

[37] Tobin, back cover.

[38] Pyle, *Brave Men*, 214.

[39] "With the Yanks," *Laredo Times*, May 11, 1944, p. 7.

[40] "Pyle, GI Joe of Correspondents, Honored for His Soldier Stories," *Stars and Stripes*, May 3, 1944, p. 1; James M. Long, "Big News Staff Attached to Invasion Headquarters Set to Cover Great Story," The Associated Press.

[41] "Drought Proves Blow to Britain," *North Adams Transcript*, April 3, 1944, p. 1; "Meat Consumption in '43 Highest in 36 Years," *East Liverpool Review*, April 8, 1944, p. 5.

[42] "Better Victory Gardens," *Circleville Herald*, May 22, 1944, p. 4.

[43] "Paper Salvage Drive Gets More Householders' Aid," *New York Times*, April 20, 1944, p. 21.

[44] "They Packed For D-Day," *Oakland Tribune*, July 4, 1944, p. 18.

[45] "Dick Whiting Writes of Tour Through London," *Bedford Gazette*, March 17, 1944, p. 1.

[46] Gay, 249.

[47] "Venereal Disease in Army Down to New Low in '43," *Stars and Stripes*, March 24, 1944, p. 4.

[48] "London Paper Says Cab Tours Fleece Yanks," *Stars and Stripes*, April 3, 1944, p. 3; "Victor Palousek Arrives Overseas," *Taylor Daily Press*, March 8, 1944, p. 3.

[49] Cronkite, *A Reporter's Life*, 93. Italics added by the author for emphasis.

[50] "Hash Marks," *Stars and Stripes*, April 8, 1944, p. 2.

[51] James B. Reston, "Anglo-U. S. Unity Getting Its Real Test Right Here," *Stars and Stripes*, March 4, 1944, p. 2.

[52] "Hash Marks," *Stars and Stripes*, March 8, 1944, p. 2.

[53] Mort, 70-75; Gellhorn's quote affirming her desire to report the war was highlighted in the BBC online article "The women reporters determined to cover World War Two" by Lyse Doucet, published on June 5, 2014. www.bbc.com.

[54] "Yanks Aid Rescuers, Firemen As Nazis Renew London Raids," *Stars and Stripes*, March 16, 1944, p. 1; "Cpl. Tom Wilcox Vividly Describes Blitzed London, 'Cosmopolitan Center of Europe's Freedom,'" *Wellsboro Gazette*, April 27, 1944, p. 1-2.

[55] "This Is The Army," *Stars and Stripes*, March 30, 1944, p. 2.

[56] Richard Wilbur, "U. S. Lends A Hand," *Stars and Stripes*, March 30, 1944, p. 5.

[57] Eleanor Roosevelt, "Mrs. Roosevelt Appreciates Hospitality of British People," *Youngstown Vindicator*, November 18, 1942, p. 18.

[58] G. K. Hodenfield, "Orphans' Fund Passes Its Original 50,000 Pound Goal," *Stars and Stripes*, March 20, 1944, p. 3.

[59] "Hash Marks," *Stars and Stripes*, June 15, 1944, p. 2.

[60] Kruse and Tuck, 154-155.

[61] Bennett, 43.

[62] Cousins, 71; "Smash Color Lines in French Drive," *Atlanta Daily World*, August 8, 1944, p. 1.

[63] Kruse and Tuck, 154-155; Shapiro and Hollander, 47.

[64] "This Is The Army," *Stars and Stripes*, April 6, 1944, p. 2.

[65] Alkebulan, 47; "Double V Creed," *Pittsburgh Courier*, April 11, 1942, p. 1.

[66] Richard Wilbur, "Yanks Learn About Tommy's Army," *Stars and Stripes*, May 5, 1944, p. 1.

[67] "Cpl. Tom Wilcox Vividly Describes Blitzed London, 'Cosmopolitan Center of Europe's Freedom,'" *Wellsboro Gazette*, April 27, 1944, p. 1-2.

[68] Eleanor Dempsey, "Harlingen Sergeant Writes Interesting Letter on Expressions Used in England," *Valley Morning Star*, April 20, 1944, p. 8; Stafford, 121; *A Short Guide to Great Britain*, 13-14.

[69] "This Is The Army," *Stars and Stripes*, May 12, 1944, p. 2.

[70] "With the Men in Uniform," *Whitewright Sun*, May 18, 1944, p. 1.

[71] Wade Werner, "Nazis Trying to Bolster Morale on Home Front Picture Britain and United States as Hysterical Over Invasion Outcome," *Thomasville Times Enterprise*, May 12, 1944, p. 1; Wade Werner, "Nazi Expand Army Training in Universities, Program is Effort to Bolster Morale of Younger Men Among Troops," *Lima News*, March 1, 1944, p. 7.

[72] "Hitler on the Master Race," *Stars and Stripes*, May 18, 1944, p. 5.

Chapter 2: "A Mechanical Niagara"

[73] "Invasion Already On, Arnold Says, Citing Giant Air Attacks," *Stars and Stripes*, March 30, 1944, p. 1.

[74] "DeWitt Mackenzie Papers: An Inventory of His Papers at the Syracuse University Archives." Syracuse University, www.library.syr.edu; "German Fighters Return to Skies," *Wichita Daily Times*, May 1, 1944, p. 5.

[75] DeWitt Mackenzie, "German Fighters Return to Skies," *Wichita Daily Times*, May 1, 1944, p. 5.

[76] "Repair Job Cut from 6 Hours to 1 Min.," *Stars and Stripes*, May 1, 1944, p. 3; Hansen, 187-188.

[77] "Builds Lunch Wagon," *Altoona Mirror*, March 22, 1944, p. 6.

[78] Allan M. Morrison, "Bakers Will Be in There Pitching for the Invasion," *Stars and Stripes*, March 20, 1944, p. 6.

[79] "Sea-Heaves? (Gulp!) Try Dry Bread or Gum, Chum," *Stars and Stripes*, May 25, 1944, p. 3.

[80] Ralph Harwood, "'Bullets Don't Hurt,' Wounded Say," *Stars and Stripes*, June 1, 1944, p. 5.

[81] Collier, 152.

[82] Ernie Pyle, "With U. S. Troops on Italian Front," *Laredo Times*, March 20, 1944, p. 11; Symonds, 166.

[83] "This Is The Army," *Stars and Stripes*, March 23, 1944, p. 2.

[84] G. K. Hodenfield, "The Army Where the GI Is a Gob," *Stars and Stripes*, May 1, 1944, p. 6.

[85] Allan M. Morrison, "Port Men Truly Sweat Out Invasion," *Stars and Stripes*, May 20, 1944, p. 2.

[86] Symonds, 130, 185.

[87] "Victory Ideas," *Piqua Daily Call*, April 13, 1944, p. 2.

[88] John A. Moroso III, "Great Armada Set For Allied Invasion," *North Adams Transcript*, June 2, 1944, p. 2.

[89] "Glider Crate Houses Three Soldiers," *Troy Record*, April 14, 1944, p. 29.

[90] "Scientists Tested Invasion Beaches," *Philadelphia Inquirer*, June 11, 1944, p. 3.

[91] "Soil Scientists Set Stage for D-Day," *Golfdom*, April 1945, p. 43.

[92] "Hash Marks," *Stars and Stripes*, June 16, 1944, p. 2.

[93] "Corp. George McConnell Sorts Mail in England," *North Adams Transcript*, April 20, 1944, p. 3.

[94] Manning, xiv-xv.

[95] "This Is The Army," *Stars and Stripes*, April 11, 1944, p. 2; Manning, Ibid.

[96] "Gunner's Body Hangs from Bomb Bay," *Wichita Daily Times*, March 9, 1944, p. 7.

[97] Neal Estes, "Finis Colborn Killed in Action," *Carthage Panola Watchman*, March 23, 1944, p. 1.

[98] "Offers Eye to Soldier," *Indiana Evening Gazette*, March 22, 1944, p. 1.

[99] "Paradise Lost Is Where Hell is, Graduate Decides," *Austin Summer Texan*, May 11, 1944, p. 1.

[100] "Warns Invaders of the Luftwaffe," *Stars and Stripes*, May 23, 1944, p. 4.

[101] Ernie Pyle, "Doolittle Meets Doolittle," *Healdsburg Tribune, Enterprise and Scimitar*, Number 38, June 23, 1944, p. 2.

[102] "*Memphis Belle* Back – On Film," *Stars and Stripes*, May 13, 1944, p. 1.

Chapter 3: Scuttlebutt

[103] "Just Around the Corner," *Daily Herald Suburban Chicago*, June 16, 1944, p. 4; "'D' is For Invasion," *Abilene Reporter News*, May 4, 1944, p. 1.

[104] "D-Day Need Keep You Guessing No Longer," *Wichita Daily Times*, May 28, 1944, p. 1.

[105] "Hears About D-Day," *Piqua Daily Call*, May 11, 1944, p. 1.

[106] "Southwest's Top Mosquito Hunter in San Antonio," *San Antonio Light*, May 19, 1944, p. 25; "You're Telling Me!" *Circleville Herald*, May 13, 1944, p. 4; "Calendar," *Bonham Daily Favorite*, June 5, 1944, p. 12.

[107] "Tech Graduation," *Lubbock Morning Avalanche*, May 16, 1944, p. 12; "WAC Anniversary," *Daily Kennebec Journal*, May 15, 1944, p. 6.

[108] "D-Day Comes for Boy Hero," *Altoona Mirror*, May 23, 1944, p. 13.

[109] "Spiritual D-Day Noted," *New York Times*, May 29, 1944, p. 19.

[110] "Flooded Towns Evacuated As More Rain Forecast," *Ogden Standard Examiner*, April 25, 1944, p. 1.

[111] "London to Give Tip on Invasion," *Coshocton Tribune*, May 6, 1944, p. 1.

[112] "U. S. General Demoted for Hinting D-Day," *Centralia Evening Sentinel*, June 7, 1944, p. 4.

[113] "Needless Warning," *Lowell Sun*, May 19, 1944, p. 6.

[114] "False Report of Invasion Turns U. S. Into Bedlam," *Stars and Stripes*, June 4, 1944, p. 1; "Newspaper Editors Cheer Girl Who Flashed Error," *Biddeford Daily Journal*, June 6, 1944, p. 1.

[115] Stafford, 233.

[116] "Ernie Goes to England Again," *Amarillo Globe*, May 5, 1944, p. 10.

[117] Walter Lippman, "Visiting some Troops," *Amarillo Globe*, May 5, 1944, p. 10.

[118] John A. Moroso III, "D-Day Rehearsal Held in England," *North Adams Transcript*, May 5, 1944, p. 8.

[119] "29 U. S. Soldiers Killed By Accidental ETO Blast," *Eugene Guard*, March 22, 1944, p. 1.

[120] "Germans Claim Attack on Allied Invasion Fleet," *Bradford Era*, April 29, 1944, p. 1.

[121] Atkinson, 16-17, 63, 191; "Adm. Don Moon, Task Force Commander Off Normandy, Suicide from Battle Fatigue," *Greeley Daily Tribune*, August 8, 1944, p. 1.

[122] "Experienced Men Used in Attacks," *Troy Record*, April 24, 1944, p. 12.

[123] Hanson W. Baldwin, "Weather Delays Allied Air Drive: Continuation of Effort to Ground the Luftwaffe Now Awaits Long Period of Clear Skies for Pre-Invasion Campaign," *New York Times*, April 7, 1944, p. 5; Pyle, *Brave Men*, 230; McManus, *The Dead and Those About to Die*, 36-37.

[124] McManus, *The Dead and Those About to Die*, 36-37; *Amarillo Daily News*, May 9, 1944, p. 4; 1st Sgt. J. W. Collins, "1st Sergeant's Call," *Wichita Daily Times*, May 7, 1944, p. 5.

[125] Carse, 80; Ross, 1; Atkinson, 31.

[126] "Weather Ideal for Invasion in Western Europe," *Ogden Standard Examiner*, May 9, 1944, p. 1; "Weather Good for Invasion, Officials Say," *Port Arthur News*, May 11, 1944, p. 23.

[127] "Bad Weather Keeps Planes Off Europe," *Somerset Daily American*, May 18, 1944, p. 1.

[128] Frederick Graham, "Weather Affects Destiny of D-Day," *New York Times*, May 23, 1944, p. 5; DeWitt Mackenzie, "Weather May Change Invasion Date," *Uniontown Morning Herald*, May 5, 1944, p. 4.

[129] Bascom N. Timmons, "Weatherman Selects the Day," *Amarillo Daily News*, June 26, 1944, p. 4; "Don Pedro and The Weather," *Brownsville Herald*, May 25, 1944, p. 1.

[130] Bascom N. Timmons, "Weatherman Selects the Day," *Amarillo Daily News*, June 26, 1944, p. 4; Ross, 2-3.

[131] Waldemar Kaempffert, "Meteorology Had an Important Part to Play in Planning Invasion of the Continent," *New York Times*, June 11, 1944, p. E9; Edward V. Roberts, "Weather More Problem Than Allied Enemies," *Tucson Daily Citizen*, July 10, 1944, p. 4.

[132] "Slashing of Train Travel Boosts Invasion Tenseness," *Lima News*, May 23, 1944, p. 1, 4.

[133] Howard Kingsbury Smith, "London Tensely Awaits D-Day," *San Antonio Light*, May 31, 1944, p. 1. Also refer to Smith's memoir, *Last Train From Berlin: An Eye-Witness Account of Germany at War.* Sixteen years after D-Day, Smith moderated the first televised presidential debate.

[134] Barbara Wace, "British Housekeepers Will be Anxious for GIs on D-Day," *Abilene Reporter News*, June 4, 1944, p. 27.

[135] Tom Wolf, "German Jitters Prove Potency of Allies' Factual Propaganda," *Wichita Daily Times*, May 4, 1944, p. 5; DeWitt Mackenzie, "Nazis' Nerves in Sorry State Over Invasion," *Gettysburg Times*, May 30, 1944, p. 2; DeWitt Mackenzie, "Big Allied Drive Seen as Part In Great Invasion Move But Does Not Mean D-Day has Arrived, German Controlled Paris Radio Thinks," *Thomasville Times Enterprise*, May 12, 1944, p. 1, 7.

[136] Gayle Talbot, "See Invasion Tactics," *Uniontown Morning Herald*, March 1, 1944, p. 14; Roberts, 221.

[137] Hanson W. Baldwin, "Where Will We Strike the Enemy?" *New York Times*, May 3, 1944, p. 6.

[138] "Stalin Tells FDR Hitler Defeat Near," *Findlay Republican Courier*, March 1, 1944, p. 1; "Invasion of Europe to Come from Two Directions – Molotov," *Taylor Daily Press*, May 11, 1944, p. 1; "Red Star Predicts Invasion Success," *San Antonio Light*, May 11, 1944 p. 2.

[139] "Second Front Delay Asked by Woman Congressman," *Stars and Stripes*, March 20, 1944, p. 2.

[140] Grayson Jordan, "Gilespian Gives Impression On War," *Fredericksburg Standard*, March 1, 1944, p. 8.

[141] C. V. R. Thompson, "Invasion Talk on All U. S. Lips As Tense Nation Waits Its Start," *London Daily Express*, March 2, 1944.

[142] Lewis, 32.

[143] Atkinson, 31.

[144] DeWitt Mackenzie, "Allied Forces 'Tug at Leash,' Prime for D-Day," *Lima News*, June 3, 1944, p. 3.

[145] Collier, 150.

Chapter 4: "Invasionitis"

[146] Brée and Bernauer, 161.

[147] Sebba, 77.

[148] Brée and Bernauer, 213.

[149] "France on the Eve," *New York Times*, April 22, 1944, p. 12.

[150] Gay, 260; Jones, 5.

[151] "U.S. Radios A Promise Of Freedom," *Stars and Stripes*, May 1, 1944, p. 1; Irwin, 157.

[152] Gildea, 242.

[153] Wes Gallagher, "Legal Framework for Invasion of Europe Waits Okay," *Sandusky Register Star News*, March 2, 1944, p. 1.

[154] Beevor, 16-20.

[155] Stafford, 167.

[156] Berthon, 302-303.

[157] Gene Currivan, "Civil Rule Forces Ready For D-Day," *New York Times*, May 12, 1944, p. 3.

[158] DeWitt Mackenzie, "The War Today," *Hanover Evening Sun*, April 20, 1944, p. 8.

[159] Jordan, 56.

[160] Ralph B. Jordan, "Report France Plans To Start Aid On D-Day," *New Castle News*, May 17, 1944, p. 2; "They Await D-Day Too," *San Antonio Light*, May 15, 1944, p. 1.

[161] "Underground Makes Plans For Hitler on D-Day, Reports United Press Agent," *Taylor Daily Press*, May 14, 1944, p. 4; Lee E. Cooper, "Pain of Leaflets Will Aid Invasion," *New York Times*, May 16, 1944, p. 5.

[162] "French Ordered to Stand By for D-Day," *Abilene Reporter News*, May 24, 1944, p. 14; "ABSIE Starts Instructions to Undergrounds," *Stars and Stripes*, May 22, 1944, p. 2.

[163] Olson, *Last Hope Island*, 304; Harold Denny, "Eisenhower Asks New Invasion Data," *New York Times*, May 25, 1944, p. 5.

[164] Ralph Heinzen, "French Underground is Ready: Mobilized Power Awaits D-Day," *Amarillo Daily News*, June 5, 1944, p. 4.

[165] Taylor Henry, "French Units Await D-Day," *Amarillo Globe*, April 17, 1944, p. 1.

[166] E. C. Daniel, "Marin, At 73, Fled France In Disguise," *New York Times*, April 30, 1944, p. 8; "So They Say," *Piqua Daily Call*, June 1, 1944, p. 12.

[167] Symonds, 153, 198; Kenneth L. Dixon, "Speculation on D-Day Runs Riot," *Somerset Daily American*, May 29, 1944, p. 6.

[168] McManus, *The Americans at D-Day*, 32.

[169] "Invasion News Sent Direct From London," *Altoona Mirror*, May 16, 1944, p. 1; Nieson Himmel, "Virgil Pinkley; Mirror Publisher, UP Chief," *Los Angeles Times*, December 27, 1992. www.latimes.com.

[170] Virgil Pinkley, "Invasion News Sent Direct From London," *Altoona Mirror*, May 16, 1944, p. 1; "Cutter Defies Heavy French Guns To Open Path into Harbor at Oran," *Youngstown Vindicator*, November 18, 1942, p. 19; "First Purple Heart for Working Reporter." *Newspaper Heroes on the Air*, June 22, 2013. www.jheroes.com.

[171] Cronkite, *Cronkite's War*, 166, 143.

[172] Cronkite, *A Reporter's Life*, 95.

[173] Cronkite, *Cronkite's War*, 187, 144.

[174] Whitehead and Romeiser, 119-120.

[175] McManus, *Those Dead and Those About to Die*, 179; Casey, 236; Grint, 98.

[176] John Hall, "Secret Is Kept Until D-Day By U. S. Soldiers," *Ogden Standard Examiner*, June 29, 1944, p. 3.

[177] McManus, *Those Dead and Those About to Die*, 65.

[178] DeWitt Mackenzie, "Today's War Comment," *Abilene Reporter News*, June 5, 1944, p. 12.

[179] "On This Day: 1944: Celebrations as Rome is liberated," BBC Online Archive. www.bbc.com; Collier, 157.

[180] DeWitt Mackenzie, "Hitler Rages While Rome Falls," *Hutchinson News Herald*, June 5, 1944, p. 6; "Allies planned four years for continental invasion," *Lincoln Nebraska State Journal*, June 5, 1944, p. 11.

[181] Daniel J. O'Connor, "Evening Verse (For your Scrapbook)," *Sandusky Register Star News*, June 5, 1944, p. 7.

[182] Collier, 154.

[183] Ryan, 6; Raymond Daniell, "SHAEF: Eisenhower's Thinking Machine," *New York Times*, July 30, 1944, p. SM9; Stafford, 71, 173.

[184] Doyle Rice, "D-Day: The Most Important Weather Forecast in History." *USA Today*, June 6, 2014, www.usatoday.com.

[185] Mayo, 19-24, Thomas, 24.

[186] Lewis, 39; "Used Cartridge Shells Make Invasion Coins," *Philadelphia Inquirer*, June 12, 1944, p. 10.

[187] "Invasionitis Grips Britain," *Marion Star*, June 5, 1944, p. 6.

[188] Beevor, 26-27.

[189] Stafford, 269.

[190] Kloeber, 223.

[191] Lewis, 38-39.

[192] Don Whitehead, "Tunis Fell to Allies Year Ago," *Wichita Daily Times*, May 7, 1944, p. 4.

[193] Anne O'Hare McCormick, "Abroad On an April Morning in the Year 1944," *New York Times*, April 26, 1944, p. 18; Stafford, 258.

[194] Casey, 218; Olson, *Citizens of London*, 321; Collier, 155; Thomas, 7; "Ike Directs From Camp on Hillside," *San Antonio Light*, June 6, 1944, p. 12; "Telek, Eisenhower's Scottie, Gets Out of 6 Month Quarantine," *Chicago Tribune*, July 21, 1944.

[195] D'Este, 530; James P. O'Neill, "From Rome, Where GIs Couldn't Believe the News," *Yank*, June 30, 1944, p. 9.

[196] Collier, 157.

[197] "Mt. Union Holds Memorial Service," *Huntingdon Daily News*, May 31, 1944, p. 9.

Chapter 5: "Well, This Is It"

[198] "Secret Is Kept Until D-Day By U. S. Soldiers," *Ogden Standard Examiner*, June 29, 1944, p. 3.

[199] "Men O' War," *Raleigh Register*, March 24, 1944, p. 4; "Pt. Pleasant Social Notes," *Athens Messenger*, November 2, 1944, p. 6; "Success is Certain," *Athens Messenger*, June 7, 1944, p. 4.

[200] Hanson W. Baldwin, "News Men Thrill To Real Briefing," *New York Times*, June 7, 1944, p. 7; Atkinson, 30.

[201] Grint, 98.

[202] Caldwell Sorel, 224-226.

[203] "2,500,000 Words Cabled Since Start of Invasion," *New York Times*, June 11, 1944, p. 34; "Strawberry Shortcake," *Ogden Standard Examiner*, June 8, 1944, p. 4.

[204] Robert L. Moora, "How *Stripes* Covered the Big Story," *Stars and Stripes*, June 6, 1964, p. 21.

[205] "Yanks Were Grim, Set When Boats Pulled Out," *Stars and Stripes*, June 7, 1944, p. 3.

[206] Cpl. Victor M. Wingate, "Channel Crossing," *Frederick News*, July 20, 1944, p. 8.

[207] Ernie Pyle, "How Correspondents Felt on D-Day," *Mabank Banner*, June 28, 1944, p. 6; Casey, 226.

[208] Sandor S. Klein, "They Can't Stop Us! Says Walking Arsenal," *Madison Wisconsin State Journal*, June 6, 1944, p. 9. The account describing Klein was written by colleague Ralph Nichols and published on www.boiseguardian.com.

[209] "Moro Army Officer Writes D-Day Letter," *Alton Evening Telegraph*, June 20, 1944, p. 12.

[210] "Opposition Less Than Expected; Troops 10 Mi. In," *Stars and Stripes*, June 7, 1944, p. 1.

[211] James Long, "Yank Troops Slash Nazi Cherbourg Lines," *Philadelphia Inquirer*, June 10, 1944, p. 2.

[212] "Second Front Sidelights," *Stars and Stripes*, June 8, 1944, p. 2; "Something to Remember!" *Stars and Stripes*, July 6, 1944, p. 2; "Sun, Clouds Alternate Over Dover," *Benton Harbor News Palladium*, June 6, 1944, p. 1.

[213] "Order of the Day," *Benton Harbor News Palladium*, June 6, 1944, p. 5.

[214] "The Great Crusade," *Stars and Stripes*, June 7, 1944, p. 2.

[215] "This Is It," *Stars and Stripes*, June 7, 1944, p. 2.

[216] A. I. Goldberg, "Grand Assault to Crush Nazi War Machine," *Benton Harbor News Palladium*, June 6, 1944, p. 1; "Eisenhower Tells French To Flee Coastal Region," *Benton Harbor News Palladium*, June 6, 1944, p. 1; "Strike Now, French Told by Algiers Commissioner," *Stars and Stripes*, June 8, 1944, p. 1.

[217] E. V. Roberts, "Gen. Ike, Calm and Confident, Jokes With Troops at Takeoff," *Stars and Stripes*, June 7, 1944, p. 2.

[218] Paul Kern Lee, "Supreme Commander of Allied Invasion Forces Shows Great Ability As Leader," *Benton Harbor News Palladium*, June 6, 1944, p. 2. Italics added by author for emphasis.

[219] Wes Gallagher, "AP WAS THERE, 1944: Allies win footholds in France," *San Diego Union-Tribune*, June 5, 2014, www.sandiegouniontribune.com.

[220] "BBC On This Day - 1944: D-Day Marks Start of Europe Invasion." *BBC News*, June 6, 1944, www.news.bbc.co.uk.

[221] "Nazis Fear Blow From East Next," *Stars and Stripes*, June 7, 1944, p. 1.

[222] "Across the Channel," *Stars and Stripes*, June 8, 1944, p. 2; "Tehran Set Landing Time With Stalin's OK, Says FDR," *Stars and Stripes*, June 7, 1944, p. 1; Stafford, 305.

[223] "President Follows Progress of Invasion on Own Huge Map, *Alton Evening Telegraph*, June 12, 1944, p. 4.

[224] "Second Front Sidelights," *Stars and Stripes*, June 8, 1944, p. 2.

[225] "Turks Claim Allied Landings in Greece," *Centralia Evening Sentinel*, June 7, 1944, p. 9.

[226] Drew Middleton, "Broad Overviews," *New York Times*, June 7, 1944; Atkinson, 57.

[227] DeWitt Mackenzie, "West Wall Broken at One of Strong Points," *Centralia Evening Sentinel*, June 7, 1944, p. 1.

[228] "Behind D-Day, Long Preparation," *Stars and Stripes*, June 2, 1944, p. 7.

[229] "News Of Our Men and Women In Uniform," *Albert City Appeal*, July 6, 1944, p. 1.

[230] "The Home Front," *Valparaiso Vidette Messenger*, July 6, 1944, p. 7; "Mission Youth Among First To Land in France on D-Day," *Valley Morning Star*, July 11, 1944, p. 10.

[231] "Bradley's Daughter Weds," *Stars and Stripes*, June 12, 1944, p. 7.

[232] "Gen. Eisenhower's Son, 473 Others Get West Point Diplomas," *Centralia Evening Sentinel*, June 7, 1944, p. 8.

[232] "Bradley's Daughter Weds," *Stars and Stripes*, June 12, 1944, p. 7; "This 'Liberation Issue' Goes to Yanks Across," *Stars and Stripes*, June, 12, 1944, p. 1.

[233] Hal Boyle, "Once Is Enough For A Dream Story Of All Newspapermen, *Frederick News*, June 8, 1944, p. 7; Casey, 231.

Chapter 6: Day of Daze

[234] "Dilburn Writes Home On Eve of Invasion," *Dothan Eagle*, July 14, 1944, p. 8; "Prisoner," *Dothan Eagle*, October 5, 1944, p. 6.

[235] "Elliott Paratrooper Writes to Mother of D-Day Landing, Battle Wounds," *Pittsburgh Post-Gazette*, July 20, 1944, p. 1, Section 2.

[236] Philip H. Bucknell, "How Outmanned Yanks Held Nazis," *Stars and Stripes*, June 14, 1944, p. 4.

[237] Astor, 127-129.

[238] Howard Cowan, "Paratroopers Are First To Land Behind Foe Lines," *Benton Harbor News Palladium*, June 6, 1944, p. 11; "What is D-Day," *Fitchburg Sentinel*, June 8, 1944, p. 6.

[239] "NBC Man Aboard Plane With Paratroopers," *Benton Harbor News Palladium*, June 6, 1944, p. 9. Wright Bryan's entire broadcast is available for listening on the website SoundCloud, published on June 5, 2014.

[240] William Walton, "World Battlefronts: Parachute Landing in Normandy, *Time* Magazine, June 19, 1944.

[241] "Janesville Paratrooper Wins Purple Heart Medal in Normandy," *Waterloo Daily Courier*, July 24, 1944, p. 10; "Hash Marks," *Stars and Stripes*, August 3, 1944, p. 2.

[242] Howard Cowan, "140 Lb. Captain First in France," *San Antonio Light*, June 8, 1944, p. 4; "Frank Lillyman Is Dead at 55; First Paratrooper at Normandy," *New York Times*, March 8, 1971.

[243] "Stowaway on a U. S. Glider Learns Paths of Glory Lead but to the Brig," *Stars and Stripes*, June 16, 1944, p. 4; "Invasion Stowaway Defends Act," *Pittsburgh Post-Gazette*, July 22, 1944, p. 2.

[244] Howard Whitman, "Yanks Worry, Too; but Over Folks at Home," *Chicago Tribune*, June 9, 1944, p. 1.

[245] "Pretty French Girl Saves Wounded Yank From Nazis On D-Day," *Chicago Tribune*, July 2, 1944, p. 1; *Yank*, Vol. 3. No 27: March 2, 1945.

[246] Graves, 46.

[247] "Paraparson Says Normandy Invasion 'Hell For A Week,'" *Fitchburg Sentinel*, July 13, 1944, p. 1.

[248] Henry T. Gorrell, "He Landed on D-Day: Lowell Parachuting Chaplain At Battle for Carentan," *Lowell Sun*, June 13, 1944, p. 1.

[249] "Capt. Hall Tells Story Of Wound, D-Day Landing," *Fitchburg Sentinel*, July 19, 1944, p. 1. Italics added for emphasis.

[250] "Chaplains Jump With Chutists Into Normandy," *Chicago Tribune*, July 28, 1944, p. 3; "Franciscan, only priest killed in D-Day invasion, recalled for heroism," *Catholic News Service*, June 6, 2014, www.catholicnews.com.

[251] "San Benito Pioneer Killed in Invasion," *Valley Morning Star*, July 11, 1944, p. 10.

[252] "Yank Kills Nazi General With .45," *San Antonio Light*, June 19, 1944, p. 2.

[253] Leonard Moseley, "Lost After Landing, Writer Saved By Pals' Bullets in 'Movie Rescue,'" *Stars and Stripes*, June, 9, 1944, p. 2.

[254] Tom Hoge, "Filthy 13 Squad Rivaled by None In Leaping Party," *Stars and Stripes*, June 9, 1944, p. 4.

[255] Haskew, 97.

[256] Womer and DeVito, 170-174.

[257] Harry Garrett, "Yanks KO Gun Nests With Knives, Grenades," *Stars and Stripes*, June 12, 1944, p. 3.

[258] "U. S. Chutists' Kit Amazes Germans," *Stars and Stripes*, June 27, 1944, p. 4.

[259] "The Sgt. York of Oratory: Yank Talks 156 Captors Into Giving Up," *Stars and Stripes*, June 10, 1944, p. 1.

[260] Lt. Alexis Neel, "U. S. Glider Pilot's Story of Landing," *Stars and Stripes*, June 10, 1944, p. 2.

[261] Sgt. Saul Levitt, "Airborne Action," *Yank*, August 18, 1944, p. 6.

[262] "Parachutist Back, Says Losses Low, Mission a Success," *Stars and Stripes*, June, 10, 1944, p. 4; "AWOL Colonel to Be Decorated," *Waterloo Daily Courier*, June 11, 1944, p. 6.

[263] "Glider Troops Land on Roof of Nazi Area Headquarters," *Waterloo Daily Courier*, June 9, 1944, p. 1.

[264] Robert Reuben, "Bearded Yanks Come Home After 15 Days Behind Nazi Lines," *Stars and Stripes*, June 22, 1944, p. 1. The paratroopers in question were corporals Bennie C. Arbaugh of St. Albans, West Virginia and August Famalaro of New Orleans. Also included were privates George

Dougherty of Whitmore Lake, Michigan; Lloyd P. Porum of Hickory, North Carolina, and James Carlson of Decatur, Illinois.

265 Arthur Goodwin, "GIs Attend Mass; Foe Baffled," *Stars and Stripes*, June 22, 1944, p. 3.

266 "Invasion No. 6 for Many 9th Troop Carrier Pilots," *Stars and Stripes*, June 8, 1944, p. 4.

267 "Movies Come to Yanks in France," *Stars and Stripes*, June 23, 1944, p. 2.

Chapter 7: "Sea of Bedlam"

268 "This is the Army," *Stars and Stripes*, July 6, 1944, p. 2.

269 "Hash Marks," *Stars and Stripes*, June 21, 1944, p. 2; "Attack Password: 'Mickey Mouse,'" *Philadelphia Inquirer*, June 8, 1944, p. 3; "Password from Hollywood," *Uniontown Morning Herald*, June 19, 1944, p. 4.

270 Tom Yarbrough, "Tiny unarmed tug tows LCT clear across channel to invasion beaches," *Lincoln Nebraska State Journal*, June 10, 1944, p. 1.

271 Lewis Hawkins, "Eyewitness Story Of Invasion," *Benton Harbor News Palladium*, June 7, 1944, p. 1.

272 Symonds, 243-251,

273 Gellhorn, *The Face of War*, 110, 120.

274 Ernie Pyle, "Ernie Tells of Historic Voyage," *Abilene Reporter News*, June 15, 1944, p. 4.

275 Pyle, *Brave Men*, 381-383.

276 "'Grand Show,' Says Air Crew Chief Of French Invasion," *Chicago South End Reporter*, July 26, 1944, p. 3; "Letter Written on D-Day," *Hillsboro Press Gazette*, June 23, 1944, p. 2; "Tells Of D-Day Dangers," *Dubois Daily Express*, July 24, 1944, p. 1, 8.

277 Henry B. Jameson, "Aboard Admiral Hall's Flagship," *St. Louis Post-Dispatch*, June, 9, 1944, p. 5; Dave Bergmeier, "Jameson, Henry B." *Kansas Press Association*, www.kspress.com.

278 "Bath Boy Writes From Service On Invasion Front," *Bath Independent*, July 6, 1944, p. 6; Lewis Hawkins, "American Navy Has Big Part in Landing Troops," *Benton Harbor News Palladium*, June 6, 1944, p. 1.

279 Jack Foster, "Riflemen, Navy Teamed to Win in Beach Duel," *Stars and Stripes*, June 8, 1944, p. 1, 4.

280 Robert Miller, "Nazis Off Guard, Discovered Assault Too Late to Stop It," *Stars and Stripes*, June 7, 1944, p. 3.

281 Desmond Tighe, "Awesome Sight as Fleet Bombards," *Stars and Stripes*, June 7, 1944, p. 1; "Carry Out Great Convoy Job With Only Few Losses," *Centralia Evening Sentinel*, June 7, 1944, p. 1.

282 "Goldsboro Boy Writes of Invasion," *Wilson Daily Times*, July 20, 1944, p. 8.

283 "Atlantan Serves On Ship With Europe Invaders," *Atlanta Daily World*, July 9, 1944, p. 1.

284 Ernest Hemingway, "Voyage to Victory," *Collier's* Magazine, July 22, 1944.

285 Tom Bernard, "64 Hours of Battle," *Yank*, June 18, 1944, p. 4-8.

286 "4 Jeeps Fished From Channel By Illinoisan," *Chicago Tribune*, June 15, 1944, p. 2.

287 Jack Foster, "Riflemen, Navy Teamed to Win in Beach Duel," *Stars and Stripes*, June 8, 1944, p. 1, 4.

288 "Cutter Rescues At Least 126 in Assault Drama," *Stars and Stripes*, June, 10, 1944, p. 4.

289 Randy Dixon, "Port Battalions Set Record On Beachheads," *Pittsburgh Courier*, June 24, 1944, p. 5.

290 "John P. Harvey Is Still Aboard Coast Guard Boat," *Cumberland News*, July 7, 1944, p. 7.

[291] "Keeler Residents Read Of Son's D-Day Survival," *Benton Harbor News Palladium*, July 27, 1944, p. 18. This article originally appeared in the *Chicago Sunday Tribune* on July 24, 1944 and was also broadcast on WGN radio.

[292] Charlotte Parrish, "Wounded Navy Man Tells How His Ship Was Sunk On D-Day," *Coshocton Tribune*, July 21, 1944, p. 1.

[293] "D-Day Sailor Believes Cur Dog Named Muffin Saved Him From Death in Icy Channel Water," *Amarillo Globe*, July 26, 1944, 5, 12; Jack Foster, "Channel Survivors Eagerly Wait Chance to Get Back Over," *Stars and Stripes*, June, 10, 1944, p. 4. The author was unable to locate additional records on Lawrence Patman. The *Amarillo Globe* possibly altered his name in its original reporting.

[294] Robert Miller, "UP Writer Dunked in Channel When E-Boat Torpedoes His Ship," *Stars and Stripes*, June 16, 1944, p. 2.

[295] "Sailor Missing On D-Day, Turns Up at N. E. Home," *Biddeford Daily Journal*, July 11, 1944, p. 1; "Reported Slain, Sailor Returns For Rest, Cigar," *Chicago Tribune*, August 2, 1944, p. 10.

[296] Richard Wilbur, "Naval Losses In the Channel Are Very Low," *Stars and Stripes*, June 26, 1944, p. 2.

[297] "Miller in Invasion," *Kannapolis Daily Independent*, July 7, 1944, p. 3; "Landing On D-Day Birthday Present For Martinez Man," *Oakland Tribune*, July 16, 1944, p. 13.

[298] "Chicagoan, 15, on 13 Trips to Invasion Beach," *Chicago Tribune*, August 13, 1944, p. 1. Supplemental information on *LST 27*'s D-Day experience was found in the account of shipmate Anthony Leone at www.6juin1944.com.

[299] "News Of Our Men and Women In Uniform," *Clearfield Progress*, July 15, 1944, p. 5. (Originally printed in the *London Herald*.)

[300] "Invasion Described As Almost A Dieppe," *New York Times*, June 18, 1944, p. 3.

[301] DeWitt Mackenzie, "Invasion Forces Need Good Port Most of All," *Centralia Evening Sentinel*, June 9, 1944, p. 1.

[302] John Camsell, "British Coast Guardsman Suing His Government," *High Point Enterprise*, September 28, 1947, p. 8B; Symonds, 318-328; Penrose, 133-135, 143.

[303] Jack Foster, "Infantry Wins Foothold With Terrific Attack," *Stars and Stripes*, June, 9, 1944, p. 2.

[304] Ira Wolfert, "Invasion channel man-made inferno," *Lincoln Nebraska State Journal*, June 12, 1944, p. 1.

[305] Miller, *D-Days in the Pacific*, front matter.

[306] "Hash Marks," *Stars and Stripes*, June 10, 1944, p. 2.

Chapter 8: "Somebody's Got To Get Hurt"

[307] Howard Whitman, "Unopposed, Shock Troops Blast Nazi Block 'Exactly as Briefed,'" *Stars and Stripes*, June 8, 1944, p. 7.

[308] Henry T. Gorrell, "Ted Roosevelt, Jr. Dies: Was in D-Day Spearhead," *Cedar Rapids Gazette*, July 14, 1944, p. 1-2.

[309] Henry T. Gorrell, "Allied Invaders Know Game Is For Keeps," *Fort Madison Evening Democrat*, June 6, 1944, p. 8.

[310] "A GI Tells His Story," *Jefferson City News and Tribune*, July 16, 1944, p. 10.

[311] "Former Saco Man Writes Of D-Day Thrills," *Biddeford Daily Journal*, July 26, 1944, p. 8.

[312] Bennett, 96.

[313] Casey, 235.

[314] Beevor, 121-122.

[315] "This is The Army," *Stars and Stripes*, August 19, 1944, p. 2.

316 "Former Saco Man Writes Of D-Day Thrills," *Biddeford Daily Journal*, July 26, 1944, p. 8; Beevor, 120-121.

317 Richard McMillan, "Freedom Sends French Town Wild," *Stars and Stripes*, June, 9, 1944, p. 1, 4.

318 Allan M. Morrison, "Dump Truckers Unload on Nazis," *Stars and Stripes*, July 18, 1944, p. 2; Moore, 176.

319 "Staff Sgt. Laws Says 'Somebody's Got To Get Hurt,'" *Cumberland News*, July 4, 1944, p. 14.

320 "Officer Saves His Unit, But Dies Doing So," *Stars and Stripes*, August 9, 1944, p. 2; The account of Mary Shields and her son's death is detailed on his biographical page at www.1-22infantry.org.

321 Charles F. Kiley, "11 Silver Stars Awarded Men of 4th Infantry," *Stars and Stripes*, July 6, 1944, p. 8.

322 "DuBois Battery Is Participating In Invasion of France," *Dubois Daily Express*, July 4, 1944, p. 1.

323 "Shout of 'Hey, Pop' Reunited a Father, Son on Beachhead," *Stars and Stripes*, June 21, 1944, p. 4; John F. Kenney, "The Lookout," *Lowell Sun*, June 19, 1944, p. 37.

324 "Former Saco Man Writes Of D-Day Thrills," *Biddeford Daily Journal*, July 26, 1944, p. 8.

325 "This is the Army," *Stars and Stripes*, August 2, 1944, p. 2.

326 Charles F. Kiley, "How the Fourth Infantry Fought Through to Reach Paratroops," *Stars and Stripes*, June 20, 1944, p. 4.

327 McManus, *Those Dead and Those About to Die*, 96. Paraphrase of a quote by Sgt. Harrison Marble.

328 Gay, 25.

Chapter 9: "Hotter than Hell"

329 Clark Lee, "No Bravado In Yankees' Shining Hour," *Cedar Rapids Gazette*, June 6, 1944, p. 1.

330 Van Der Vat, 86; Balkoski, *Omaha Beach*, 6, 344.

331 Balkoski, *Omaha Beach*, 83.

332 Whitehead and Romeiser, x.

333 Don Whitehead, "Gallantry and Skill on Beaches," *Moberly Monitor Index*, June 9, 1944, p. 1; Grint, 389.

334 Casey, 240.

335 Caldwell Sorel, 227.

336 Bud Hutton, "S&S Reporter Tells of Medics' Heroism On Bloody Beaches," *Stars and Stripes*, June 12, 1944, p. 2.

337 "Shell From 88-MM. Gun Hit Landing Craft with Pvt. Mask," *Frederick News*, July 11, 1944, p. 1.

338 James McGlincy, "French Beaches Really Hot Spots," *Moorhead Daily News*, June 7, 1944, p. 1.

339 Baumgarten, 70.

340 Sgt. Bill Davidson, "GIs returning to college find it difficult to adjust selves to changed circumstances of school environment," *Lincoln Nebraska State Journal*, July 8, 1945, p. 8-C.

341 Atkinson, 73.

342 Jack Foster, "Channel Survivors Eagerly Wait Chance to Get Back Over," *Stars and Stripes*, June, 10, 1944, p. 4.

343 "Dewey Turner Sends Full Details on D-Day Experience," *Canyon News*, July 6, 1944, p. 4; Balkoski, *Omaha Beach*, 145.

344 "Nazis Seize Son Of Ike's Aide, But He Flees," *Chicago Tribune*, June 10, 1944, p. 2.

345 "Sgt. Norris Writes Account of D-Day," *Washington Evening Journal*, July 1, 1944, p. 1; Kaufmann, 29; The account of Pvt. John Bianchi is featured on the website of Fort Lee's U. S. Army Quartermaster Museum website at www.qmmuseum.lee.army.mil; "Army Photo Chief Tells of Irresistible Assault," *Stars and Stripes*, June 12, 1944, p. 5.

346 "Atlantan Serves On Ship With Europe Invaders," *Atlanta Daily World*, July 9, 1944, p. 1.

347 Lionel Shapiro, "Suicide Mission: Assault Engineers Went In First, Cleared Out Defenses Under Fire," *Stars and Stripes*, June 10, 1944, p. 2.

348 Donald Patrick, "Graphic Letters From Lowell Men Describe D-Day Landings," *Lowell Sun*, July 18, 1944, p. 3.

349 James McGlincy, "French Beaches Really Hot Spots," *Moorhead Daily News*, June 7, 1944, p. 1.

350 Arthur Goodwin, "One Day of Battle – The Story of Company L ," *Stars and Stripes*, June 29, 1944, p. 6; McManus, *The Dead and Those About to Die*, 235-236.

351 "New York's 16th Cited in France," *New York Times*, July 23, 1944, p. 4; McManus, *The Dead and Those About to Die*, 21.

352 "Photographer For Yank Killed," *Stars and Stripes*, August 2, 1944, p. 1. The first enlisted *Yank* correspondent killed was Sgt. John Bushemi, who met his end earlier in 1944 on Eniwetok in the South Pacific; Arthur Goodwin, "Dead Men Can't Talk," *Stars and Stripes*, July 6, 1944, p. 3.

353 John A. Moroso III, "Gertrude Lawrence Toured Invasion-Ready Sectors," *Portsmouth Herald*, June 20, 1944, p. 3.

354 Arthur Goodwin, "Wanted: Live Kraut," *Stars and Stripes*, July 27, 1944, p. 3.

355 "Find Luxuries in France," *Jefferson City News and Tribune*, July 16, 1944, p. 10.

356 "Invades Normandy In New Packard," *Santa Fe New Mexican*, July 19, 1944, p. 8.

357 "Mike's Torch Song," *Stars and Stripes*, July 27, 1944, p. 6.

358 Don Whitehead, "Gallantry and Skill on Beaches," *Moberly Monitor Index*, June 9, 1944, p. 1; Casey, 243.

359 Don Whitehead, "Yank on Beachhead Tells 'Dear Marge' In Chicago He's Safe," *Chicago Tribune*, June 15, 1944, p. 6.

360 Sterne, 83-85.

361 Ernest Hemingway, "Voyage to Victory," *Collier's Weekly*, July 22, 1944.

362 Gellhorn, *The Face of War*, 110-115.

363 Caldwell Sorel, 232.

364 Ernie Pyle, "Even to Land Was a Miracle: Sprawling Bodies Tell Mute Story of Death in the Murderous Fire," *Kingsport News*, June 12, 1944, p. 1.

365 "Fighting Men Relate Their Stories," *Stars and Stripes*, July 4, 1944, p. 2.

366 "Pig Pen Used As Refuge by Wounded Men," *Altoona Mirror*, July 28, 1944, p. 4.

367 "Valorous MPs," *Stars and Stripes*, June 22, 1944, p. 2.

368 "The Fighting 29th," *Stars and Stripes*, June 29, 1944, p. 2.

369 "Unexploded Grenade Kills Three Germans," *Stars and Stripes*, July 11, 1944, p. 4.

370 "Soldier Engineers," *Stars and Stripes*, June 29, 1944, p. 2.

371 Edward Toles, "Crack Troops Catch Nazis In Barrage Balloon Net," *Chicago Defender*, July 15, 1944, p. 3; "The Negro As A Soldier," *New York Times*, August 6, 1944, p. E8; Hervieux, 213, 241-242.

372 John W. Jarrell, "Establishment of Normandy Beachhead Ranked With St. Mihiel, Cheateau Thierry, Salerno," *Port Arthur News*, June 11, 1944, p. 16.

373 Cpl. Victor M. Wingate, "Channel Crossing," *Frederick News*, July 20, 1944, p. 8.

[374] Ernie Pyle, "Wreckage Litters Beach But It Was Expendable," *Ruthven Free Press*, July 5, 1944, p. 3; Ernie Pyle, "The Horrible Waste of War," *Daily Spectrum*, June 8, 2014, p. C3 (republished from Pyle's original June 1944 account).

[375] "Pyle Tells of Writers In Invasion," *Joplin News Herald*, June 19, 1944, p. 7.

[376] Lewis Hawkins, "Death Litters French Beach," *Oakland Tribune*, June 9, 1944, p. 2.

[377] Ernie Pyle, "How Ernie's Fellow Correspondents Fared," *Ruthven Free Press*, July 5, 1944, p. 3.

[378] "Pyle Tells of Writers In Invasion," *Joplin News Herald*, June 19, 1944, p. 7.

[379] John A. Moroso III, "Gertrude Lawrence Toured Invasion-Ready Sectors," *Portsmouth Herald*, June 20, 1944, p. 3. Byrd later incorporated his D-Day experiences into the novel *Hurry Home to My Heart*. Hicks's D-Day report was added to the Library of Congress's National Recording Registry in 2013. The *New York World Telegram* quote is highlighted in Matt Shedd's June 6, 2014 article entitled "Remembering D-Day through the Peabody Archives" at www.peabodyawards.com; Casey, 229.

[380] Don Whitehead, "1st Division Men Win Decorations For D-Day Deeds," *Charleston Gazette*, July 5, 1944, p. 3.

[381] "Deluge of Letters Reveals Col. Seitz In D-Day Spearhead," *Chicago Tribune*, July 6, 1944, p. 2.

[382] "Veteran Tells Invasion Story," *Miami Daily News Record*, July 30, 1944, p. 1.

[383] "Time Marches Back for a Veteran," *Stars and Stripes*, July 25, 1944, p. 1.

Chapter 10: Fearful Jubilation

[384] "Hit D-Day on Nose," *Atchison Daily Globe*, June 6, 1944, p. 5.

[385] An Inmate, "Prison Inmates Join in Observance of D-Day," *Fort Madison Evening Democrat*, June 7, 1944, p. 2.

[386] McIntosh, 153-154.

[387] "Prayers of All Go With Army of Liberation," *Burlington Hawk Eye Gazette*, June 6, 1944, p. 3; "D-Day Here, Burlington Keenly Alert," *Burlington Hawk Eye Gazette*, June 6, 1944, p. 3.

[388] Adele C. Glazer, "Samascoopies," *Lowell Sun*, July 5, 1944, p. 9; "Inverted Crusade," *Stars and Stripes*, June 12, 1944, p. 7.

[389] "County Welcomes D-Day With Tears and Prayers," *Liberty Vindicator*, June 8, 1944, p. 1.

[390] "D-Day Mixup," *Waterloo Daily Courier*, July 6, 1944, p. 13; "St. Joe Takes News Calmly," *St. Joseph Herald Press*, June 6, 1944, p. 2.

[391] "Times Square Crowds Make It 'See-Day,'" *New York Times*, June 7, 1944, p. 10.

[392] "U. S. Café Strategists Miss on Invasion, Laundrymen Find," *Oakland Tribune*, June 20, 1944, p. 3.

[393] "Baltimore Bans Liquor on D-Day," *Pittsfield Berkshire Evening Eagle*, May 23, 1944, p. 5.

[394] "D-Day Is Taken In Stride Here," *Maryville Daily Forum*, June 6, 1944, p. 1.

[395] Don Whitehead, "Yanks Anxious To Allay Fear," *Charleston Daily Mail*, June 15, 1944, p. 9.

[396] "Alexander Sends Beachhead Letter," *Lawrence Daily Journal World*, June 29, 1944, p. 2.

[397] "Something to Remember!" *Stars and Stripes*, July 6, 1944, p. 2.

[398] James Thrasher, "A Column of Comment," *Ada Evening News*, June 12, 1944, p. 4; "Wives of D Chiefs Voice Fortitude," *New York Times*, June 7, 1944, p. 8; James Thrasher, "Topics of the Day," *Altoona Mirror*, June 12, 1944, p. 8.

[399] "Mrs. Ike Excited at Invasion Start," *San Antonio Light*, June 6, 1944, p. 12.

[400] "Wives of D Chiefs Voice Fortitude," *New York Times*, June 7, 1944, p. 8.

[401] "Mrs. Eisenhower too ill to receive interviewers," *Lincoln Nebraska State Journal*, June 7, 1944, p. 3; D'Este, 58; "Hopes luck matches ability," *Lincoln Nebraska State Journal*, June 7, 1944, p. 3.

[402] Drew Pearson, "The Washington Merry-Go-Round," *Nevada State Journal*, June 15, 1944, p. 4; "Stimson Surprised By Invasion News," *Kingsport News*, June 7, 1944, p. 1; "D-Day Finds Mood of Work and Prayer in State's Observance," *Gazette and Bulletin*, June 7, 1944, p. 12; "War Dept. Keeps All Night Vigil," *Benton Harbor News Palladium*, June 6, 1944, p. 13.

[403] Peter Edson, "OWI – May It Rest in Peace," *Daily Globe*, June 16, 1944, p. 4.

[404] "America Takes Invasion Calmly," *Council Bluffs Iowa Nonpareil*, June 6, 1944, p. 10; Peter Edson, "D-Day Was Dull in Capital," *Ada Evening News*, June 12, 1944, p. 4.

[405] Marquis Childs, "Capitol Hill United for Short Time on D-Day," *Council Bluffs Iowa Nonpareil*, June 8, 1944, p. 4.

[406] "Stimson Surprised By Invasion News," *Kingsport News*, June 7, 1944, p. 1; "War Dept. Keeps All Night Vigil," *Benton Harbor News Palladium*, June 6, 1944, p. 13; "Hull Calls Fight All-Time Pivotal," *New York Times*, June 7, 1944, p. 9.

[407] Drew Pearson, "D-Day For Russians," *Anniston Star*, July 9, 1944, p. 4.

[408] Ohler, 151-152; Penrose, 261.

[409] "Hitler Wants to Fight With His Back to the Wall but He Can't Find a Wall," Waterloo *Daily Courier*, June 8, 1944, p. 4; Rees, 264; "Global War," *Stars and Stripes*, June 16, 1944, p. 2.

[410] "Wallace Learned of Invasion From Reds," *Centralia Evening Sentinel*, June 9, 1944, p. 1; Culver and Hyde, 331.

[411] Judy Barden, "Londoners Sadly Miss Yanks Now," *Lincoln Nebraska State Journal*, June 22, 1944, p. 5.

[412] Barbara Wace, "London Reaction," *Lowell Sun*, June 6, 1944, p. 13.

[413] "Here-There," *Portsmouth Herald*, June 19, 1944, p. 4.

[414] Arthur W. White, "London Calm But Tense at D-Day News," *Stars and Stripes*, June 7, 1944, p. 4; Stafford, 304.

[415] "D-Day News Forces Sleep's End as U. W. Navy Groups Chatter," *Madison Wisconsin State Journal*, June 6, 1944, p. 3.

[416] "Gave Invasion News," *New York Times*, June 22, 1944, p. 23.

[417] "Pacific Veterans Heard of D-Day On Way to Saipan," *Wisconsin Rapids Daily Tribune*, June 20, 1944, p. 2.

Chapter 11: "Peace Tomorrow"

[418] Moorehead, 166-167; Pulwers, 119.

[419] Ellen Crawford, "Plant Heads Find Employees Serious About War Effort," *Kingsport News*, June 7, 1944, p. 10; Ann Pendleton, "Hit the Rivet Sister," *Ardmore Daily Ardmoreite*, June 5, 1944, p. 4.

[420] Honey, 55.

[421] Sparrow, 161.

[422] Harold Denny, "Vast supply Machine Is Geared For Invasion," *New York Times*, March 12, 1944, p. E5.

[423] DeWitt MacKenzie, "Gas for Bombers Must Be Saved on Home Front," *Athens Sunday Messenger*, April 30, 1944, p. 4.

[424] Herman, 247; Sparrow, 161.

[425] "Reaction at Front," *Athens Sunday Messenger*, April 26, 1944, p. 3; Herman, 246-247; "Solemn Nation Greeted News With Prayers," *Stars and Stripes*, June 12, 1944, p. 2; "Hull Calls Fight

All-Time Pivotal," *New York Times*, June 7, 1944, p. 9; "2ⁿᵈ Big Plant Closed By Foreman's Strike," *Philadelphia Inquirer*, May 17, 1944, p. 8.

[426] "The Man Who Wouldn't Strike," *Chicago Tribune*, June 10, 1944, p. 10.

[427] Peter Edson, "Washington Column," *Edwardsville Intelligencer*, June 15, 1944, p. 4; "Scattered U. S. Strikes Mark D-Day," *Long Beach Independent*, June 7, 1944, p. 2.

[428] "Wright Plant Idle in Strike Amid Invasion," *Greeley Daily Tribune*, June 7, 1944, p. 1; "Back Home," *Cincinnati Enquirer*, June 5, 1944, p. 53; Miller, *WWII Cincinnati* [Digital version], Chapter 5.

[429] Harry S. McAplin, "Un-Covering Washington," *Chicago Defender*, June 17, 1944, p. 3; Frank Marshall Davis, "Passing Parade: Watch Home Front D-Day," *Atlanta Daily World*, June 4, 1944, p. 4.

[430] W. A. Fowlkes, Jr., "Sad Commentary," *Atlanta Daily World*, August 6, 1944, p. 4.

[431] "Hoover Reveals Saboteurs' Ways," *Edwardsville Intelligencer*, June 5, 1944, p. 1.

[432] "Untitled," *Clearfield Progress*, May 8, 1944, p. 4.

[433] Haswell, 118.

[434] Haswell, 157.

[435] "Are Soldiers Adults?" *Tipton Tribune*, August 15, 1944, p. 2; Jay Franklin, "We, the People," *Hamilton Daily News Journal*, August 23, 1944, p. 4; Pulwers, 431.

[436] "Political Censorship," *Bakersfield Californian*, May 20, 1944, p. 12; "Soldier Vote Bill," *Mckean County Democrat*, April 6, 1944, p. 2; Manning, 134-150.

[437] Ray Tucker, "The National Whirligig," *Bradford Era*, May 29, 1944, p. 4; "5ᵗʰ Loan Drive Tops the Goal," *Stars and Stripes*, July 10, 1944, p. 3.

[438] Ed Stennett, "Washington in Wartime," *Bakersfield Californian*, July 5, 1944, p. 12; "D-Day Blood Gifts High in Midwest," *San Antonio Light*, June 11, 1944, p. 20; "D-Day Fails To Arouse S. A. Blood Donors," *San Antonio Light*, June 11, 1944, p. 1.

[439] "Seek Funds to Cover Plasma Delivery Cost," *Lowell Sun*, April 11, 1944, p. 41; Sam A. Simmons, "Mason Women Urged to Take part in War Effort," *Athens Messenger*, March 2, 1944, p. 11.

[440] "Clyde Thomas Writes From England About Good Work Of Red Cross," *Big Spring Daily Herald*, April 5, 1944, p. 5.

[441] "World's Richest Girl Takes Her First Job – at $1 a Year," *Stars and Stripes*, August 5, 1944, p. 1.

[442] "Civil War Vet Says GIs Have It Soft," *The Times* (Munster, Indiana), August 28, 1946, p. 1.

[443] "100 Mourn Carman, G.A.R. Centenarian," *New York Times*, June 19, 1944, p. 19.

[444] "Vet, 96, "See Times Like Civil War Days," *Brooklyn Daily Eagle*, June 30, 1944, p. 6.

[445] "Confederate Uniform in House," *Stars and Stripes*, June 9, 1944, p. 4; Harry McAplin, "Invasion Day Finds Colored Fighters In The Vanguard," *Philadelphia Tribune*, June 10, 1944, p. 1.

[446] W. A. Fowlkes, Jr., "D-Day Comes," *Atlanta Daily World*, June 11, 1944, p. 4.

[447] "Bilbo Fights Race Equality on D-Day," *Chicago Defender*, June 17, 1944, p. 2.

[448] "A Ghost From Another Post-War Day," *Benton Harbor News Palladium*, June 16, 1944, p. 2.

[449] Joseph D. Bibb, "Old Chicago," *Pittsburgh Courier*, June 17, 1944, p. 7; "Atty. Dickerson Admitted to Chicago Bar Association," *Pittsburgh Courier*, November 17, 1945, p. 1.

[450] Frank Marshall Davis, "Passing Parade: Watch Home Front D-Day," *Atlanta Daily World*, June 4, 1944, p. 4.

[451] "Grandmother Graduates From Phillips On D-Day," *Chicago Defender*, June 17, 1944, p. 14.

[452] "Another D-Day To Come, Says Armentrout," *Greeley Daily Tribune*, June 19, 1944, p. 1.

[453] "Smash Color Lines in French Drive," *Atlanta Daily World*, August 8, 1944, p. 1; J. A. Jones, "Rogers Says: Treatment of Negroes In Armed Services Is Unjust and Illogical," *Pittsburgh Courier*, July 8, 1944, p. 7.

[454] Randy Dixon, "British Okay Conduct Of Race Troops," *Pittsburgh Courier*, July 8, 1944, p. 9; "Queen Elizabeth Cheers Ex-Fisk Grid Leader," *Philadelphia Tribune*, August 12, 1944, p. 13.

[455] "Hungary Deports Jews, Eden Says," *New York Times*, July 6, 1944, p. 6; "Nazis Still Determined To Wipe Out Jews – FDR," *Stars and Stripes*, June 13, 1944, p. 1.

[456] Anne O'Hare McCormick, "Victims of the Last Fury of the Nazis," *New York Times*, July 15, 1944, p. 12.

[457] "Naturalization," *Newport Mercury and Weekly News*, June 16, 1944, p. 4.

[458] "D-Day Seen As Symbol," *New York Times*, June 7, 1944, p. 12.

[459] "General Ike Pledges Truth in War News," *Waterloo Daily Courier*, June 9, 1944, p. 1; Casey, 219.

[460] "Freedom of Press Vital, Says Swedish Newspaper," *New York Times*, July 27, 1944, p. 2; "Asks World pact on Press Freedom," *New York Times*, June 24, 1944, p. 11.

[461] "Editors Stress Free Press Plank," *New York Times*, July 19, 1944, p. 17.

[462] "Gratitude," *Zanesville Times Recorder*, June 8, 1944, p. 9.

[463] "What is D-Day," *Fitchburg Sentinel*, June 8, 1944, p. 6.

[464] "Why We Fight," *Stars and Stripes*, June 30, 1944, p. 2.

[465] "The Beginning of the End," *Evening Huronite*, June 13, 1944, p. 4.

[466] David Lawrence, "Must Serve Higher Cause Than Greed," *Albert Lea Evening Tribune*, June 19, 1944, p. 5.

[467] "Hash Marks," *Stars and Stripes*, July 20, 1944, p. 2.

[468] "Why We Fight," *Stars and Stripes*, July 13, 1944, p. 6.

Epilogue: A Distant Shore

[469] Lt. Stanley R. Seltzer, "Profit of War," *Stars and Stripes*, August 26, 1944, p. 2.

[470] McManus, *The Deadly Brotherhood*, 87; Ruth Taylor, "The Altar of Sacrifice," *Cullman Banner*, July 20, 1944, p. 3.

[471] "Just A Moment . . . ," *Philadelphia Tribune*, July 22, 1944, p. 5.

[472] Hal Boyle, "War Reporter Finds Kin – In D-Day Grave," *Brownsville Herald*, July 12, 1944, p. 1.

[473] Howard Cowan, "First Yank Dead Rest in British Soil," *Argus-Leader*, June 11, 1944, p. 1.

[474] Hal Boyle, "Undertakers Luckiest On D-Day – Didn't Lose A Man," *Salisbury Times*, July 20, 1944, p. 3.

[475] "Yank Soldiers Who Paid With Lives Buried in France," *Greenville Delta Democrat Times*, June 13, 1944, p. 2.

[476] "29th Division Men Dedicate Cemetery For Fallen Comrades," *Salisbury Times*, July 24, 1944, p. 1.

[477] "French Couple Buries Yanks," *Fitchburg Sentinel*, June 16, 1944, p. 12; Richard D. McMillan, "French Grateful For Their Freedom," *New York Times*, June 29, 1944, p. 5.

[478] "Salisburians Die in France, One On D-Day," *Salisbury Times*, July 7, 1944, p. 1.

[479] "Gives Life to Country as Namesake Did," *Lowell Sun*, July 6, 1944, p. 1, 9.

[480] "Young Mother of Triplets Hopes 'Missing' Means That Husband Is Prisoner in France," *New York Times*, August 23, 1944, p. 12.; Susan Riemer, "Daughter finds closure in family's war story," *Vashon-Maury Island Beachcomber*, July 16, 2014, www.vashonbeachcomber.com.

[481] Robert Cromie, "Tells Of Yanks' Attack Across Norman Fields," *Chicago Tribune*, July 27, 1944, p. 5.

[482] "Ernie Pyle Is Killed on Ie Island; Foe Fired When All Seemed Safe," *New York Times*, April 19, 1945, p. 1; Pulwers, 123.

[483] Sgt. Dewitt Gilpin, "D-Day +365," *Yank*, July 6, 1945, p. 3-5.

[484] Whitehead, 365.

[485] W. C. Heinz, "I Took My Son To Omaha Beach," *Collier's*, June 11, 1954, p. 22-28.

[486] "Eisenhower Recalls the Ordeal Of D-Day Assault 20 Years Ago," *New York Times*, June 6, 1964, p. 1, 6.

[487] Omar N. Bradley, "Command Decisions," *Stars and Stripes*, June 6, 1964, p. 19.

[488] Fussell, 285-286.

[489] Douglas Kneeland, "Reporters Mark D-Day Plus 37 Years," *New York Times*, June 8, 1981, p. A12.

[490] Ken Ringle, "A Leap Back Into History and Hearts," *Washington Post*, June 6, 1994, www.washingtonpost.com; Julian Nundy, "50th Anniversary of D-Day," *The Independent*, June 5, 1994, www.independent.co.uk.

[491] Steve Tuttle, "D-Day: Retracing Grandfather's Steps at Normandy," *Newsweek*, October 15, 2009, www.newsweek.com.

[492] Kershaw, 205, 208.

[493] Angela Hatcher, "Woman Recalls Losing Two Brothers on D-Day," ABC 13 – WSET, May 30, 2014, www.wset.com.

[494] Mark D. Carlson and Virginia Mayo, "Twin brothers reunited 74 years after WWII death at Normandy," ABC News, June 20, 2018, www.abcnews.go.com.

[495] Michael E. Ruane, "Seventy years later, a D-Day veteran believes a guardian angel shielded him from death," *Washington Post*, June 5, 2014, www.washingtonpost.com.

[496] Harry Leslie Smith, "Brexit threatens everything I fought for in the Second World War. On my 95th birthday, this is what I need people to know," *Independent*, February 24, 2018, www.independent.co.uk.

[497] Jim Bitterman, Erin McLaughlin and Bryony Jones, "D-Day veteran: I don't want them to be forgotten," CNN, June 5, 2014, www.cnn.com.

[498] Steven Hartman, "They don't forget: Normandy still honors American WWII pilot's sacrifice," CBS News, June 7, 2012, www.cbsnews.com.

ABOUT THE AUTHOR

Jared Frederick has a lifelong passion for American History. His many books include *Images of Modern America: Gettysburg National Military Park* and various historical books for young adults.

Prior to his career in academia, Frederick served as a park ranger at Gettysburg National Military Park and Harpers Ferry National Historical Park. Following the Battle of Gettysburg sesquicentennial in 2013, Jared received the park's Incentive Award for his contributions during the commemoration.

Jared has long been involved in the world of Public History, including historical interpretation and development at numerous sites. He has completed projects in conjunction with the Smithsonian Institution, Pennsylvania Civil War 150, and a multitude of state and national organizations. As an active reenactor, he believes the past can be taught in spheres beyond the traditional classroom.

Having served as a commentator on the American Battlefield Trust's *Civil War in Four* series, Frederick has also appeared on C-SPAN, PBS, the Pennsylvania Cable Network, National Park Service productions, and various online documentaries. In 2019, he acted as a guest host on Turner Classic Movies for the channel's 25th anniversary.

Frederick currently serves as an Instructor of History at Penn State Altoona, where he specializes in various realms of American History and civic engagement.

Jared is available to present a broad range of historical lectures and presentations. Visit www.jaredfrederick.com to learn more.